ALWALEED

ALWALEED

BUSINESSMAN BILLIONAIRE PRINCE

RIZ KHAN

HarperCollins*Publishers*

My thanks to Prince Alwaleed's private and family photographer, Mohammed Al Jandal, for providing pictures from His Highness's many high-powered meetings across the globe. He always has his work cut out for him!

Also, a big thanks to Karim Ramzi, a professional photographer I have been friends with for some years now. His style and quality of work is evident in the cover photograph of the Prince—capturing the intriguing character of Alwaleed: businessman, billionaire, prince.

HarperCollins*Publishers*
77–85 Fulham Palace Road,
Hammersmith, London W6 8JB
www.harpercollins.co.uk

Published by HarperCollins*Publishers* 2005
1

ISBN-13   978-0-00-721513-3
ISBN-10   0-00-721513-4

Designed by Jeffery Pennington

Printed and bound in Great Britain by
Clays Ltd, St Ives plc

I write this book with thanks to the long list of people in Saudi Arabia and Beirut who welcomed me so warmly into their homes and spoke so openly with me.... But above all I dedicate this work to Zahra, my mother, who knows the true meaning of the word sacrifice ... and my wife, Gihan, who has shown me the value of true love and loyalty.

CONTENTS

FOREWORD
by President Jimmy Carter

A successful businessman, caring philanthropist, and strong civil rights supporter, Prince Alwaleed has done much to relieve poverty and enhance women's rights, education, and health care. He also has been instrumental in the Carter Center's efforts to strengthen relationships between the United States and the Arab and Islamic worlds. Rosalynn and I are grateful for his partnership in our mission of waging peace, fighting disease, and building hope around the world.

INTRODUCTION

Everyone dreams of winning the lottery.

It's easy to make plans with millions of dollars. It's probably quite easy to *spend* millions without too much thought.

But what would you do with *$21.5 billion*?

Doesn't life become a little more complicated?

That's the estimated worth of the subject of this book as I begin writing it.

A year after I first sat face-to-face with His Royal Highness Prince Alwaleed Bin Talal Bin Abdulaziz Alsaud, the value of his investments rose by $3.8 billion according to *Forbes* magazine, which tracks the rich and famous. That's around $10.4 million per day, nearly $434,000 per hour—or a little more than $120 every second. (By the *Forbes* 2005 list he was up to $23.7 billion.)

In 2004, *Forbes* listed him as the fourth-richest man in the world. That year the magazine listed a total of 587 billionaires, nearly half of them—277—in the USA. Only one Arab was in the top thirty. Guess who!

A few years earlier, *Forbes* had described Prince Alwaleed as "the second most influential businessman in the world behind Bill Gates."

A number of books have been published about the likes of Gates, Warren Buffet, and Paul Allen—all among the top five richest on the planet. These usually outline the story of their companies or suggest business models on how the average person might try to emulate such massive financial success. Others on the list are low-key or reclusive characters, and their lives are more the subject of guesswork than established facts and figures.

Alwaleed was in the latter category until he hit the financial press in the early 1990s, when he became the largest shareholder in Citicorp—now Citigroup—but his complete story has not been made public until now. I had to interview a number of key people to piece together the details of how it all happened.

Incidentally, in connection with this authorized biography, Prince Alwaleed has expressly authorized certain Citigroup officials including, among others, his private banker, Mike Jensen, to be interviewed and quoted with respect to the Prince's banking, investment, and other activities.

When I first met the Prince in October 2002, I didn't know what to make of him. That's actually the reaction most people have. He's fast-paced, incredibly organized, and a unique mix of Middle East and West. In the Arab world, Prince Alwaleed's image is larger than life. Globally, it's his deals that are larger than life. Almost everything you touch or see in the world is something in which he has a stake. Finance, hotels, media, technology, retail goods, agriculture, foods—the list is endless.

So how did this man become so wealthy?

More important, why is he so driven to succeed?

What makes Prince Alwaleed a little different from most of those on the list is that his money is not from one, original, world-winning product, such as Bill Gates's Microsoft, or Larry Ellison's Oracle, or the Walton family's Wal-Mart stores.

What makes him even more different is that he's an Arab—with no oil money—who has made his fortune in the same way as respected American investment guru Warren Buffett, by doing business in the Western way, and winning on Wall Street.

The Prince has strategically built up his diverse portfolio of investments and, judging by the long-term results, is clearly the most successful investor outside America.

From what I witnessed, he is, arguably, the hardest-working billionaire on the planet.

What really makes him stand out is his character.

He's Muslim, Arab, and Royal.

Any one of those is enough to make him the target of incredible speculation, admiration, jealousy, and curiosity.

Whether you like it or not, Prince Alwaleed has made his mark globally. His business successes are on a massive scale. Each one would, in itself, be a deal of a lifetime for an ordinary businessman, providing enough income for a wonderfully wealthy retirement.

His failures are few, though sometimes high profile, but represent such a tiny proportion of his overall wealth that he can comfortably disregard them.

Prince Alwaleed's huge diversity of investments have caused him to hit the headlines across the world for short periods at various times.

In the United States, he made his mark on Wall Street with a very significant move, by saving an ailing Citibank in 1991, and he made his mark in the public eye globally when he flew to New York after the September 11, 2001, attacks and offered $10 million to Mayor Rudolph Giuliani for the Twin Towers Fund, which was rejected following comments in a press release issued at the same time by the Prince.

In the overall big picture of his life, it was not really that significant an event, but it received so much media attention that it was somewhat blown out of proportion. I know that, ironically, it is the reason so many people in the West began to recognize his name, which is why I started the book with a recount of what happened, trying to give a broad perspective on the subject. I think, however, you'll find the rest of Prince Alwaleed's story far more intriguing and interesting.

To many Britons he's known as the "Canary Wharf" man, for his huge investment and bailout of Europe's biggest real estate venture in the heart of London's docklands.

To Italians, he's the man who teamed up with their leader, Silvio Berlusconi, in a big media deal, while in Korea, he was the Middle Eastern investor putting money into their economy when it was desperately needed.

To the French, he's the "Euro Disney" man, for financially

propping up the theme park just outside Paris—a deal that has yet to make any money for the Prince—and he gained fame in the country for buying and renovating the George V Hotel in the heart of France's capital, turning it into the world's best hotel.

In Lebanon, he is the enigmatic Saudi Royal with a strong Lebanese heritage (his grandfather was the country's first independent prime minister), who stirs up the political scene with controversial comments in the media. He is also well known as a heavy investor in that nation.

And to Saudis he is by far the country's top businessman and most visible nongovernmental Royal.

He is simply—"Alwaleed."

My original interest in doing a written feature and television interview with him evolved very rapidly into an authorized biography and up-close-and-personal documentary. I had heard a lot of the gossip and rumors. Everything from him working as a CIA operative, to money-laundering the resources of other wealthy people, to being a one-hit wonder with the Citibank deal that put him into the list of global billionaire businessmen.

After some thought, the Prince agreed to give me unprecedented access to his life and the people around him. It was the opportunity to look inside his world firsthand, to see him operate as a businessman, listening to the whispered strategies in high-level meetings, to open the doors to his palace and board his massive yacht, and to meet people who knew him before he had built his remarkable business empire. It was an assignment the journalist in me could not refuse.

The time I spent with him also inspired the title for the book. I realized that his name, Alwaleed, an honorific derivative from his given name of Waleed, had become something of a brand. When the name "Alwaleed" is mentioned to most Arabs, they will automatically assume it is Prince Alwaleed Bin Talal.

Furthermore, I soon witnessed how focused he is as a business-man, and how central his work is to his life. The fact that he is a billionaire came from his business deals, and his Royal status is also incidental to everything else that is business focused about him. Hence the sequence of "businessman," "billionaire," and then "Prince" in the title of the book.

It was actually very tough keeping up with him for more than a year as he jetted around the planet—often a couple of countries per day—but I got to see the real Prince at work and play, and it didn't take me long to realize that his story is unique and original.

I was surprised by many of the things I discovered about Prince Alwaleed. His incredibly sharp mind is tempered by frustration that others can't keep up with him. His outgoing, sociable nature strains against the inevitable loneliness of those who have to concentrate on protecting their fortune from opportunists. His fastidious micromanaging of his business is offset by his relaxed, warm, and close relationship with his son and daughter.

Arabs have long suffered stereotyping, whether as religious fanatics and terrorists, or as unsophisticated people with little education, carrying wallets bulging with oil money. Many wealthy Arabs did themselves a huge disservice during their oil boom of the 1970s, when they flooded expensive boutiques in the heart of London, Paris, Geneva, and New York willing to pay hugely over-inflated prices for customized goods of poor taste. That, unfortunately, is an image that has taken time to erode, and it is one that the Arab world still struggles against, despite a new generation of highly educated and traveled people in the Middle East, willing to embrace and certainly accept Western lifestyles and tastes.

A lot needs to change in the Kingdom of Saudi Arabia. Even its own people are aware of that and are starting to embrace reform. Prince Alwaleed has been championing that reform more and more vocally. From denying any interest in politics right up until the end of 2003, the Prince is now more candid about his possible role as a social and economic reformer, and perhaps as a bridge between the Middle East and West.

Relations between the Arab and Western worlds are extremely strained. Islam is viewed with suspicion, particularly in the United States of America. The United States is regarded as a bully in much of the Arab world, especially in light of the military action there, sanctioned by the hard-line conservative administration of President George W. Bush.

The resulting communication breakdown has only served to raise tensions, destroy the quality of life for almost everyone, and dented the global economy.

As the biggest single foreign investor in the U.S. economy, Prince Alwaleed has not only influence but also a vested interest in closing the gap that separates two important parts of the world. Over the past year or so, I have witnessed a change in his direction. His business drive is stronger than ever—and I write about the roots of that in the pages of this book—but he is now also starting to mature as a political player and philanthropist.

Why would you want to know about Prince Alwaleed?

Well, something of a mystique surrounds those who never have to look at a price tag—even when it stretches into the millions of dollars. There is even a romantic air about the jet set life—but few get to see the machinery that builds it and fuels it . . . and it is never as simple as it seems.

We live in a suspicious world, where different cultures and religions have grown further apart and more wary of one another.

Beyond Prince Alwaleed's wealth there is, as I mentioned, a very unique and original person, whose identity straddles the mellow traditional culture of the Arab world with desert tents, camels, and sun-beaten Bedouins carrying old rifles . . . and the fast-paced, hungry, pin-striped world of Wall Street with limousines and bespoke financiers carrying gold pens to sign big deals.

How does he do it?

You're about to find out.

CHAPTER 1

Hitting the Headlines

I speak, first of all, as a Saudi citizen, then as a businessman, and then as a member of the Saudi Royal family.

— Prince Alwaleed Bin Talal

Ask any American over fifty if they remember when John F. Kennedy was shot, and they'll tell you in detail exactly where they were and what they were doing.

Ask almost anyone in the world where they were on September 11, 2001, and you will get a breathless recount of how they heard about, or actually watched television pictures of, the passenger jets crashing into the Twin Towers of the World Trade Center in New York.

Around four o'clock in the afternoon Prince Alwaleed Bin Talal Bin Abdulaziz Al Saud was rapidly punching the buttons on his phone at his palatial home in Riyadh, calling his director of communications, Amjed Shacker. The Prince, a nephew of Saudi Arabia's King Fahd, is a news junkie, and it's rare to find him anywhere without at least one television screen in front of him. When the U.S.-based Cable News Network, CNN, reported airliners crashing into the World Trade Center towers, the Prince prayed that this was not a terrorist act, but an accident. Even though he was so familiar with the years of trouble in the Middle East, he could not imagine the horror those people in New York were going through at that moment. He was glued to the screen, stunned that something like this could happen in a city he knew so well—a city where he had so many friends.

He realized very quickly that he had to do something, and with a sinking feeling in his stomach at how America was going to change, he started planning his next steps—in particular how he should respond.

First, he needed to cancel an appearance inaugurating the new, high-end shopping center he had just built in the heart of the Saudi Arabian capital. It was obvious to him that it would not be appropriate to be celebrating anything at such a terrible time. Then, being the single biggest foreign investor in the United States, he needed to be realistic and assess the impact of this potential act of terrorism on his relationship with Wall Street.

Shacker remembers very clearly getting the urgent call from Prince Alwaleed at home, and switching on his television. Just as the Prince's executive director of domestic investments, Talal Al Maiman, was being conferenced in to the call, all three, clutching their phones, found themselves witnessing the second passenger jet striking the other World Trade Center tower.

Shacker recalls the Prince exclaiming, "Did you see what happened?! What a shocking thing. This is terrible!"

Even now, the Prince goes wide-eyed and speaks quickly when he remembers that afternoon. "At that time, everybody was just looking at this horrendous attack, and my first reaction was, 'who?' Who did this attack? My first thought was that it was most probably Bin Laden," he says, explaining that he, as a Saudi, was familiar with the threat the Al Qaeda leader posed on the global stage.

He knew that even after the dust had cleared there were potentially disastrous consequences for both his country and his own personal and business relationships in the short term and the long term: "Unfortunately. I was thinking of the aftermath. What was going to happen? For such a terrorist attack to take place in the middle of New York . . . I immediately began to think of the implications between America and Saudi Arabia."

Shacker says it stunned everyone: "We were shocked. Complete disbelief, horror and shock. I mean when something like this happens, your brain freezes for a second because there's so much disbelief. I mean, you cannot analyze it but, quickly, you try to regain composure and think my God, this actually happened. These images are reality."

On the phone to the Prince, Shacker could hear his reactions, too: "He was completely stunned, but realized quickly that this was going to have a major impact on how the U.S. handles its foreign policy. He knew he would have to make some sort of statement, being the most visible Saudi to the American business community."

Sure enough, possibilities were already ticking in the Prince's head.

Alwaleed does a lot of his deep thinking while spending weekends at his camp in the desert. Most Wednesday evenings—the Saudi weekend being Thursday and Friday—Alwaleed heads out to a specially prepared area, about an hour from the center of Riyadh, where he can get close to nature and think through business and personal matters away from the noise of the city.

Looking back, Shacker describes what happened sometime after the attacks: "We were sitting in the desert with the Prince, at his camp, and he said 'I must go to the U.S. and offer my condolences personally, because we cannot just sit here.' I don't think the Prince was prompted to go by the fact that, by then, it had been revealed that Saudis had hijacked the plane and terrorized America. I think he would have gone there regardless of who had done it because he wanted to show solidarity and sympathy, and to offer his condolences to the Americans. He truly believed that was needed."

A few days later, when New York City's mayor, Rudolph Giuliani, launched the Twin Towers Fund for the victims and families of the attacks, Alwaleed saw the ideal vehicle for his gesture.

Through his close friend, the chairman of Citigroup, Sanford "Sandy" Weill, Alwaleed was put in direct contact with the mayor. The Prince recalls: "I have many friends in New York. Most of the companies I invest in have bases in New York, and I studied in New York, at Syracuse University. I have very close links with many people in that community. So I approached Mr. Giuliani's office and told them of our wish to give a contribution to the fund."

The Prince was then invited by Giuliani to attend a memorial being held one month after the attacks at Ground Zero, on October 11, at 9 A.M.

"I wanted to show the American people that they had a friend in the Middle East, especially in Saudi Arabia," explains the Prince, adding, "There is a lot of blame when it comes to Arabs and Muslims. Even before it was known who was behind this terrible act, it was assumed that Muslim extremists were responsible. In fact, the same happened when the bomb went off in Oklahoma. Muslims and Arabs were blamed, but then people found out that it was a white, Christian American. I wanted to make sure the American people knew they had sympathy and understanding in the Arab world. There are such a small number of extremists, but they create a negative image for the whole region and Muslim world."

GROUND ZERO

The Prince rapidly gathered his travel team and made arrangements to fly to New York on his private jet, for just a short visit. The plan was to arrive the day before, to see Rudolph Giuliani before the mayor went to attend a Ground Zero memorial service on the morning of October 11. The Prince would then fly straight back to Saudi Arabia. Twenty-six hours of travel, with only half a day on the ground.

In some ways, the trip was ill-fated from the start.

Robert El Hage, the Prince's travel manager, found himself struggling to ensure a smooth passage for the Royal party through U.S. Immigration and Customs upon their arrival in America. Normally, with everything arranged beforehand, it is a very straightforward VIP experience for the Prince and his team at any airport. They land, limousines are waiting at the tarmac, Robert and his team handle the passport and Customs clearance, and the group is rapidly whisked off to its destination. Alwaleed prides himself on the efficiency of his travel staff, but things had changed in the United States following September 11.

Robert recalls: "At the last minute, there was somebody who messed the whole thing up, and I was stuck with persuading the Customs and Immigration to let His Royal Highness pass through as a VIP and Royal family member. To some extent, I managed, but, still, the damage was done, and His Royal Highness was not happy."

The unusual delay entering the country was a result of the heightened security and visible tension at airports in the United States in the immediate aftermath of the attacks. In fact, the government had stopped all flights for a brief period after 9/11. Despite so much prior planning and clearly alerting the authorities, the procedure ended up being far from smooth. It was certainly not the warmest reception for someone carrying a $10 million check for the Twin Towers Fund.

"We went for that purpose only. To show our alliance with the people of New York, and to give condolences to the people of New York through their representative, Mr. Giuliani," stresses Alwaleed, emphasizing that he had told key people at home of his intent.

"This came with the full approval and authority of the Saudi government. It's very important I tell you that the Saudi government did know that I was going there and giving a contribution, and it was blessed by the Saudi authorities."

What the Prince didn't know, as explained by Giuliani in his book *Leadership*, was that the Prince's request also went to the highest authorities in the United States.

> *We consulted with the White House and State Department about whether we should take the Prince there. We were advised that we should, because he was generally friendly to the United States, someone who had an open mind. The hope was that the site might have an effect on him and make him more favorably disposed to the actions we were going to take against Bin Laden and Afghanistan.*

After clearing the airport, the Prince and his entourage went straight to the prestigious Plaza Hotel, overlooking Central Park in Manhattan. They had an overnight stay at the building, which was partly owned by the Prince at the time, before being escorted to Ground Zero the next morning.

At 8 A.M., on October 11, one of the mayor's aides came to collect the Royal party and took them to the site of the smoking rubble in downtown Manhattan, where they would meet Giuliani, to present him the $10 million donation. The famous New York mayor was recognized internationally for his leadership skills, and his dramatic improvement of living conditions in the Big Apple. Crime had fallen by almost two-thirds under him, and his tough tactics and "zero tolerance" for crime had earned him a high degree of respect.

Alwaleed and his team were taken aback at the scale of the damage. The smoke was still rising from the debris and ashes: "I really felt just saddened, upset, and concerned about this horrendous act. There were 3,000 innocent lives—Muslims, Christians, Jews—who were dead and buried. So I really thought that with my small contribution, I could at least begin bridging the gap that inevitably would take place between Saudi Arabia and the United States, and more generally between the West and East—and even more dangerously between Christianity and Islam."

The Prince remembers the somber but relatively friendly

greeting by Giuliani at Ground Zero: "He welcomed me, and was very nice, very humble. He explained to me what took place, and what they were doing right now. He also explained to me the purpose of the fund, and I told him that I was on his side. He was very appreciative and thanked me. We stayed with him maybe twenty minutes, and then left."

Rudolph Giuliani's take on the meeting and the tour of Ground Zero was a little different, as he recalled it in *Leadership*:

> *When the Prince arrived, he was wearing an opulent gold robe and headdress along with seven or eight aides in black robes. He gave me a cashier's check for $10 million, for the Twin Towers Fund. Looking at the site from the small podium, the Prince was saying the right things. . . .*
>
> *He discussed how badly he felt and how he wanted to help the victims. . . .*
>
> *But something wasn't quite right. There was a smirk to his face, which seemed to carry over to his entourage. He was the only visitor who was unmoved by what he saw.*

This view was offered in retrospect by the mayor when he wrote his book, and it could be perceived that he was being extremely unfair in such an assessment. The Prince was surprised at what the mayor wrote, stating that he and key members of his entourage had worn official Saudi national dress as a sign of respect—that nothing "opulent" had been chosen. Additionally, from the interaction filmed at that meeting between the two men, it was clear that the Prince was not smirking, but seriously concerned at what he was witnessing.

Alwaleed's communications chief, Amjed Shacker, was traveling with the Royal group: "I briefed the Prince on the short meeting we'd have with Mayor Giuliani, and what to expect as far as media coverage."

The Prince thought it would be wise to answer many of the questions about the visit that might be raised by the media, by making a statement through a press release. Once put out to the media, most of Alwaleed's team thought little about it. Then, just as they were about to set off back to Riyadh, the blow came.

A line in the release about U.S.–Middle East policy was considered unacceptable by Giuliani's people. A statement came from the mayor's office that the money would not be accepted. The press release described the September 11 attacks as a "tremendous crime," but added a comment that upset the mayor:

> *I believe the government of the United States of America should re-examine its policies in the Middle East and adopt a more balanced stance to the Palestinian cause.**

Giuliani said that his first reaction was to give the money back. He wrote:

> *Making the case that the attacks on the Trade Center were justified, or even understandable, was not a point of view I could accept.*

The Prince retorts that there was certainly no justification intended, and he stands by his action to issue the press release. He says he felt that he should be totally honest with the people of the United States and remind them that terrible acts of terrorism are a result of the ill-feelings many people in the Middle East have toward the United States due to its policy of support for Israel, while ignoring the plight of the Palestinian people. The view that the United States allows Israel to use full military force against the Palestinians fuels anger and frustration that cannot be expressed freely, and it is channeled into terrorist activity by young people who are easily recruited as they have no sense of hope.

*The full press release can be read in the appendix on page 389.

While clearly condemning the attacks of September 11, the Prince says he felt it was important to point out one of the root causes of terrorism, and how it needs to be addressed: "So as a friend of the United States, I thought I should tell them, 'Please, just wake up!'"

Awaleed dismisses Mayor Giuliani's action as a natural consequence of his political standing in a place like New York, saying that, understandably, Giuliani has a constituency to consider. It becomes obvious that many of those people who could have a bearing on his political career would not be too pleased with the contents of such a press release, calling for a more sympathetic stance toward the Palestinians or a more balanced policy in the Middle East in general.

This idea is supported by the chairman of News Corporation, Rupert Murdoch, who is headquartered in New York. Smiling ironically, he agrees that there's a simple reason for the rejection: "I would say just one word . . . politics."

ACROSS THE GREAT DIVIDE

It was politics that angered many in the Middle East, who considered Giuliani to be bowing to pressure from certain groups in his community. One columnist in the *Al-Riyadh*, a Saudi newspaper, wrote:

> (Giuliani) sacrificed the public interest for a private interest, manifested in his desire to draw closer to the Jewish electorate . . .

It was not helped by Giuliani's comments in his book, speculating on the Prince's attitude toward Ground Zero—suggesting that he had a "smirk," for example, or describing his traditional robe as "opulent," implying that it was disrespectful attire for the occasion.

Giuliani certainly had many ready to support his actions. Renowned writer and commentator Tom Friedman started his column in the *New York Times*, a few days later, with the words:

*Three cheers for Mayor Rudy Giuliani for returning the $10
million donation . . .*

An article in the *New York Times* the day after the incident
stated that the U.S. State Department had been told by the
mayor's office of the Prince's remarks but had offered no opinion
on what Giuliani should do with the check, as it was not a matter
directly involving the U.S. government.

Alwaleed says that Giuliani requested the press release be with-
drawn, in which case he would still accept the contribution, but
the Prince was adamant: "We said no. The contribution was given
for the New York people and this press release was done for the
sake of the relationship between the United Sates and Saudi Arabia, and more globally between the West and the East."

The reaction to the events of October 11 drew a mixed response from people even back in the Middle East. Some believed
that the Prince should never have gone to the United States with
check in hand in the first place—though many of those conceded
that he had vindicated himself by issuing the press release highlighting the Middle East agenda and keeping it in the news.

Others believed that the gesture of a contribution to the Twin
Towers Fund was a great idea and an understandable show of
sympathy and unity from the Arab world. It was particularly important that a prominent Saudi—a member of the Royal family—
should show such unity with the United States at its time of
distress, especially as fifteen of the nineteen attackers on September 11 had come from Saudi Arabia.

Prominent Saudi newspaper journalist, Khaled Almaeena, the
editor in chief of the *Arab News,* is one of those who felt that the
Prince was premature in rushing to the United States. He believes
that in Saudi Arabia the vast majority of people were upset by it,
especially as the Prince was ultimately rebuffed by the mayor of
New York. Had the check been accepted, he thinks his countrymen might have seen the Prince's gesture more positively: "America was not in the mood to listen, and people said he could have

either waited or come up with some other kind of scheme, or done something to promote a foundation, or build a foundation that promotes dialogue between religions and societies."

Having said that, Almaeena, a respected and outspoken columnist, points out that the press release highlighting an imbalance in the U.S. Middle East policy did help the Prince's standing at home: "Yes, that gained him some points because he was frank, and one of the things that people said was that at least while giving this (money) he had the guts to say that you have to have an equal policy for the Middle East."

In Lebanon, where the Prince has a number of supporters due to his Lebanese heritage on his mother's side, the publisher and editor in chief of *An Nahar* newspaper, Gebran Tueni, was fully supportive. The fact that the Prince would go to New York when there had been so much talk about Saudi Royal family connections with the Bin Laden family was surprising to him, even though he's known Alwaleed's impetuousness since childhood days: "I think it was really very courageous of Waleed to go to New York, to try to help people and to tell them 'we are not all terrorists,' and he was able to face all the critics there—even critics in the Arab world."

The Prince himself feels vindicated by the feedback he had from a number of people: "After this incident I got bombarded with faxes, telegrams, letters, e-mails, even telephone calls from many thousands of Americans and even chairmen and CEOs of companies—and not only that—they were from the Jewish community. They were telling me they were sorry for what took place, 'what you did, it was right, and we are with you.' But clearly there were also some people who accepted what Mr. Giuliani did as right."

However, it seems there were some ripple effects in the business community as a result of the Prince's actions. An indication of this comes from the CEO of the Canadian Fairmont Hotels Group, Bill Fatt, who works closely with the Prince. Alwaleed is a major shareholder in the group and, pragmatically, Fatt believes that the content of the Prince's press release would have been less controversial had it not come so soon after the attacks when everyone was so sensitive.

"I think some viewed it as lecturing the American people on how they could better adapt their policy toward the Middle East. It was probably poor timing. From a company perspective I think that Fairmont was identified with the Prince, and we have some very important business interests in the United States. It created some degree of friction with some of our customers, which was relatively short-lived, but I think it was a difficult time for the Prince in terms of his reputation in North America, as well as a difficult time for some of the companies in which he invested, because of the high degree of sensitivity that his statements created."

In Alwaleed's support, though, Fatt does point out that the comments the Prince made regarding the Palestinian situation were actually echoed by world leaders in the months after September 11. In front of the United Nations, President George W. Bush himself talked, for the first time, about a Palestinian state, and British Prime Minister Tony Blair also equated the frustration of the Palestinians and Middle East, in general, with the growing resentment toward America and the West.

In this respect Prince Alwaleed again feels vindicated: "They have all started to say the same thing—that U.S. policy in the Middle East is behind the hate that drives the extremists and terrorists to battle the United States. There is no need for so much destruction and hate."

Comments of support for his effort came in from a number of areas in America, one of them being Congresswoman Cynthia McKinney, a Democrat from the state of Georgia, who wrote a letter to the Prince, expressing dismay at Mayor Giuliani's action. McKinney wrote:

> *Whether he agreed with you or not, I think he should have recognized your right to speak and make observations about a part of the world which you know so well.*

The Prince adds that, unfortunately, Giuliani—whom he still respects as a strong leader—politicized the issue by rejecting the money. On the other hand, the Prince's critics make the same argument about him, because he issued the press release in the first place.

Alwaleed rejects the idea that he had any political motive, stressing again that there were comments echoing his own, but made by Western leaders: "Just a few weeks after I returned to Riyadh, the exact same thing was said by (British Prime Minister) Blair, and then later by George W. Bush. Even two years after the attacks, the connection between the 9/11 events and how America deals with the Arab world is still being quoted. I'm vindicated. What else can I say?"

Being closely tied into the New York community, his friend, the Citigroup chairman, Sandy Weill, honestly feels the timing was inopportune: "I think it started fine and it ended in a very bad way, because it wasn't a question of what he was saying, or whether that was right or wrong, but it was the wrong platform to be delivering that message to that Mayor, in this city, at that time and it was taken poorly."

But one lesson that Prince Alwaleed learned from this incident is that there is some value in notoriety. He discovered that speaking out gets one noticed, even if not everyone is happy with *what* is said and *why* it was said. For his increased international recognition, he says, he has to thank Mayor Rudolph Giuliani: "Suddenly, everyone knew who Alwaleed was . . . people were asking who is this Saudi businessman, a member of the Royal family, who comes with a large donation, and gets turned down? Giuliani did me a huge favor, actually."

It is true that even if they can't remember his name, people do recall the "rich Saudi guy" who offered millions of dollars to the victims' fund—only to have it rejected by the mayor of New York City.

Seeing the impact his actions had, both in terms of publicity and in making a political statement, the Prince's appetite was whetted to be more engaged in trying to bridge East and West. It was a quick lesson in the value of public relations.

Ironically, it appears that the potential for bad PR among his New York constituents had prompted Mayor Giuliani to reject the Prince's donation.

Perhaps both sides walked away a little wiser from this strange and unique sequence of events that started out with good intention and ended in a political tangle.

As for the reaction of Sandy Weill—who helped connect his two friends, Alwaleed and Giuliani, in the first place?

He laughs philosophically and says, "I was glad I wasn't there."

CHAPTER 2

A Royal Beginning

When you suffer, it makes you a man.

—PRINCESS MONA EL SOLH,
MOTHER OF PRINCE ALWALEED

Look, look! You can see it in him, even at that age."

The elegantly attired woman raises a professionally manicured hand and points at the television set. For a moment she pauses, finger frozen in midair, and a small smile breaks out on her face, as her mind wanders nearly half a century into the past.

She snaps out of it and reaches toward a coffee table covered with everything from large picture books to expensive Patchi chocolates and an array of glass ornaments. On top of the books are old, black-and-white family photos, and a couple of intriguing letters handwritten in Arabic, one in numbered bullet points—like a list—and the other with lines written in different colored ink, also in a list.

Picking up one of the old photos, her smile widens and she leans back on the embroidered pillows on the couch in the tastefully decorated parlor lounge of her house in Beirut. She examines the picture carefully, remembering its story. A young mother, holding her baby boy in her arms. Both are looking in the same direction, and their common features are evident. Even after all this time, the years have generally been kind to her and her face doesn't reflect all the varied and interesting experiences she has been through. She remains ultimately poised and carries an air of sophistication.

In the background, an old black-and-white video continues to play silently. She looks back toward it and says, "Even as a child, you can see the determination he has. When he wants something, he wants to get it, and does not give up, even when he cannot walk!"

In the video, a toddler, barely a year old, dressed in a hooded, blue jumpsuit, stumbles in a clumsy fashion with his arms outstretched behind a small baby goat. Each time he reaches the goat and tries to grab it, it takes a few steps forward, eluding his grasp. So the child continues to chase the goat incessantly. With unsure footing, he pitches forward and falls over a couple of times, but gets up unperturbed, focused purely on getting the animal. After a couple of minutes, his little hands somehow connect with the goat's hind legs for a moment and he looks content.

The lady leans forward again, reminiscing for a moment before commenting, "I always remember this. It showed me even then how determined my son would be. He did not stop until he finally caught the goat."

Princess Mona El Solh has had a privileged life. As one of five daughters of Riad El Solh, she was the nearest thing to Lebanese Royalty. Her father, a popular man and charismatic figure, became the first prime minister of independent Lebanon, in 1943, after playing a major part in the withdrawal of foreign forces from his country. He was one of many determined nationalists who had opposed Turkish rule, and later the French Mandate in Lebanon. His visionary nature helped to bring together the quarreling factions to create a single, sovereign state. El Solh managed to head six cabinets until he was assassinated in July of 1951 while visiting Jordan. Gunmen of the Syrian Social Nationalist Party are believed to have been responsible for his death.

As they grew up, his daughter Mona and her four sisters were considered among the top, beautiful, elite socialites. As a young woman, she caught the eye of a handsome Saudi prince taking a short break in Lebanon.

Prince Talal Bin Abdulaziz Alsaud pulled up alongside her sporty convertible and before he could say anything, she raced away defiantly. He tried again, and again, she sped away. Intrigued, he had to know who she was, and he wanted to meet her. As a son of Saudi Arabia's King Abdulaziz, it didn't take long for Prince Talal to find out, and it seemed they were a perfect match. Princess Mona reflects on their pairing: "I married an intelligent man, and a handsome man, who happened to be rich. Many people thought I married him just because he had money, but he was intelligent and handsome."

Before long, they were together among the jet set traveling the globe, vacationing in Paris and Cannes in the summer, and heading for the Alps in the winter. Early film footage of them in the French capital shows them sporting the latest Western fashions, him looking suave with trendy suit and cravat, and her in a strapless summer dress, eating an ice cream in the shadow of the Arc de Triomphe.

Talal, the twenty-first son of King Abdulaziz, was always a modern-thinking and outspoken character. He was well traveled and had even been Saudi Arabia's ambassador to France, and briefly finance minister to King Saud. In some respects, he was too liberal-minded for the conservatives in Saudi Arabia in the 1950s. He had obviously inherited some of this attitude from his father, King Abdulaziz, who was also something of a reformer, pushing for schooling for women, and building universities in what was a new nation. The Kingdom of Saudi Arabia was barely three decades old.

Arab News editor in chief Khaled Almaeena believes that reforms were always going on in the Kingdom and that the only difference with Prince Talal was that he was a Royal making waves high up in the system, and he wanted reforms enacted in a speedier fashion.

"I think that in many ways, they were plodding on; I personally would have wanted it to be speedier. Maybe others, even in the Royal family, wanted it to be faster," says Almaeena.

Security concerns in the nascent country prompted the rulers to impose an authoritarian and fairly tightly controlled system. The openly vocal call for freedom and changes from Prince Talal was something unheard of in the Kingdom at that time. The young Talal became more organized, leading a group of liberal-minded princes who were pushing for reform. They named themselves, "Young Najd," after an area of central Saudi Arabia from where the Al Saud family came. Then the group changed their name to the "Free Princes." Their inspiration came from the "Free Officers" of the revolutionary Gamal Abdel Nasser in Egypt—an enemy of the Al Sauds. Toward the end of the 1950s, the pressure of Prince Talal and his group of liberals became more public and more active. They drafted their own version of a constitution, proposing more power to the cabinet, weakening the hold of the King, and demanding a partially elected consultative body, the Shura Council. These moves brought the Prince into conflict with King Saud and upset Saudi Arabia's religious leaders, who declared that he was violating Islamic law. It was also perceived as an embarrassing public rift in the ruling family. Looking back on it, Prince Talal remains diplomatic in his assessment. As far as what influenced him toward reforms at that time, he says, "There was no one single cause that made me take that direction. I'm always asked to clarify that issue, and there isn't one single answer. We just took that direction."

By 1961, Prince Talal was seen as a problem by some in the government, and they withdrew his passport in an effort to silence him. He ended up seeking refuge in Egypt, where he lived in exile for a couple of years. Even there, he continued his call for reform, earning himself the label "Red Prince."

BACK IN RIYADH

It took two years for Talal to reconcile with the Royal family and be allowed to return on the condition that he stay clear of political activity. Some people believed he came home, but that it took time for his relationship with his Royal relatives to rebuild. He turned his focus instead to what was a rapidly developing real estate and construction market in his country, and he soon started to make a fortune. In the meantime, his marriage to Mona collapsed in 1962. They stayed separated for more than five years, eventually divorcing in 1968. This left them with three children to juggle across two very different countries.

The first of those children, the baby boy who would go on to do so much, had been born on March 7, 1955, in Riyadh. He was only five when his parents separated and he went to live with his mother in Beirut, while his younger brother and sister spent most of their time with their father in Riyadh.

Princess Mona notes that in some ways, the weekend trips she took with her husband into the desert were a positive factor in their marriage, stalling the eventual separation. She felt calmed by the openness and peace of the environment. That love for the desert has been passed on to her son, who even now spends almost every weekend camping out there.

Early life for Prince Alwaleed was not particularly happy. Even as a child, the fire and determination was visible in his eyes, and he was by far the strongest character among his siblings. At a young age, he became very close to and protective of his baby sister, Reema, and his younger brother, Khaled. In those early years the children were so emotionally united that it was like they were welded together, according to their mother. She describes them as being like "mafia." Alwaleed grew to be closer to his mother than to his father, though he admired him greatly.

But after splitting from Princess Mona, Prince Talal went on to a second marriage, which upset the young Prince immensely. Talal is philosophical and understanding about this: "Any divorce will affect children, especially if the mother does not live in the same country and we see that so much so in the Arab world in general, not just in Saudi Arabia." He goes on to say, "We did notice that at the beginning it did have some effect (on Alwaleed), but we did catch that in time and we righted the relationship with his mother in Lebanon."

However, by all accounts, Alwaleed was rather indifferent to his father's second wife and she had no particular fondness for him, either. It got to the point where, even as a youngster, he would taunt her, and she would find ways to make his life difficult. Diplomatically, when asked about it, Prince Alwaleed evades details of any tension between them and only hints at the situation.

"The relationship with her was not ideal," he says, adding, "Whenever a father gets married to another wife, inevitably the son or daughter will always be more attached to their mother. That's inevitable. I was divorced from my first wife, and I had a second wife and third wife, and clearly the relationship between my son and daughter and my second and third wives can never be like the relationship with their mother."

He was also exposed to two very different countries: Lebanon, where he spent much of his early life with his mother and her family, and Saudi Arabia, where he returned for vacation. He was somewhat restless, affected by the disrupted family life, along with the cultural differences to which he had to constantly adjust.

His mother describes a child who, at the age of seven, "was really mischievous."

"He was fat! He used to open the fridge and put salt on everything, and when I asked him why, he said, 'I want to eat everything and I don't want anyone to touch it.'" She found this cute in a strange way and was always reluctant to reprimand him for it.

His first school was Pinewood College in Beirut. He hated it there and kept to himself to a large degree. Ironically, it was the same school attended by a beautiful little girl, Dalal, a cousin of Alwaleed's who eventually became his first wife and mother of his son and daughter. Another pupil at Pinewood was a close family friend, Gebran Tueni, now head of *An Nahar* newspaper in Lebanon. He remembers a shy young boy with a distinctive character: "He was not a spoilt boy. He was really a normal boy, and we used to go to his place, and he used to come to my home also."

But Tueni does note: "He was a prince. He was at the same time Lebanese and Saudi. So, different cultures, different ways of thinking, different minds. I think it was—even for him—very difficult to be Lebanese and Saudi at the same time, and to make the Lebanese feel that he is Lebanese and the Saudis feel that he is Saudi."

The Prince's rebellious nature manifested itself in his persistent habit of running away. He would play truant from school and show up a day or so later. While on the run, he would sleep in the streets, or often check parked cars for open doors. When he found one left unlocked, he would curl up and sleep on the backseat.

Another person very close to Alwaleed as a child was his first cousin, Riad Assaad, his aunt Baheeja's son. Living next door to him, Riad saw more of the Prince's lively side than did those at school: "Yes, he was a rebel; in all cases he was a rebel and he was always a fantastic man in argument. He would argue with you endlessly, until he got what he wanted."

Riad recalls the Prince's stubborn attitude through one particular story. Riad's father went to Thailand, around the time of the Vietnam War, where, at a flea market, he found some loose material in the design of a military pattern—combat fatigue. He returned to Beirut with it and told Riad and Alwaleed that they had to share it. Both the boys wanted to have it sewn into a combat outfit, but as there wasn't enough material for two full outfits, they ended up haggling for a long time over the single outfit that was made from the cloth. Finally, they decided Riad would have the jacket, and Alwaleed the trousers.

Then, a short while later, when an aunt went to Damascus, she bought similar military material, but with a different camouflage design. The boys had that sewn into another outfit, but Riad laughs as he recalls how, stubbornly, Alwaleed would not swap the trousers and jackets so that they could each have a complete outfit with matching top and bottom. He insisted on keeping the original one, and both were forced to wear mismatched camouflage gear.

Military outfits were of particular appeal to the young boys in

1967 because Lebanon was, at that time, directly affected by the Arab-Israeli conflict. The Palestinians had a fairly positive relationship with the Lebanese, and there were a large number of them living near Riad and Alwaleed's homes. The militants fascinated and impressed the young boys, but also seeing the conditions in which the Palestinian refugees lived in his neighborhood affected Alwaleed and planted the seed for his humanitarian contributions to Palestinians later in life. He went on to become the single biggest private donor of charitable funds to the Palestinian people.

Riad's mother, Alwaleed's aunt Baheeja El Solh, was close to the boy and remembers strong traits from his childhood years that have stuck with him to this day, she says: "He was always on the move. He was quite a rebel and he was different in his ways. Secondly, he was always in a position where he wanted to project leadership. He liked to buy military fatigues that would just project the image of a leader. And whenever he used to get his daily allowance from his mother, he used to go share it with the impoverished in the neighborhood and give them some of it. He would share his allowance with the poor people."

His mother confirms how, as a youngster, he would often answer the doorbell at home and find a small group of poor people outside. He would run back to her and insist she allow him money to give to them.

At the same time, he did not lead a life typical of many of his Royal cousins in Saudi Arabia. It was relatively basic for someone of his background, as his cousin Riad recalls: "It wasn't as comfortable a life, oh no, definitely not. Whatever you see now wasn't there, and I think this helped in the toughening of his character and his personality. He wasn't a Saudi prince like the regular ones—and there were lots of these guys around here. They were his friends, his cousins and my friends. They were all over the schools in Lebanon. Then Lebanon was *the* place, the boarding school for most of Arab elites. Waleed wasn't like that, definitely. He was a rebel, because of the divorce between his mother and father, and he took the side of his mother, more than once, and this made him, in a sense, an outcast. So he didn't enjoy the privileges of the other Saudi princes. But, on the other hand, whenever he really succeeded in his grades and his performance, his mother took care of him or his uncles took care of him and his father, from time to time, used to send him a special gift. I remember, for example, when he bought his first car. He was sixteen. It was a dune buggy. But that was the only thing, I think, that distinguished him from me in terms of money. It was never an issue of being a prince or being a Saudi, and I think it gave him strength, in that he wanted to become something. So this pushed him. He was always the man who worked more than most; he was a hard worker."

FAMILY ROOTS

Another of Alwaleed's aunts, Leila El Solh, sees many of the characteristics being passed on from her sister Mona to her son: "I think he is totally like his mother. His reactions, his way of talking, his gestures are from his mother. I think this restlessness is typically his mother."

Schoolfriend Gebran Tueni also sees a lot of influence from the Prince's mother and her family in shaping the young Alwaleed: "The Solh family is a major political family. His grandfather played a major role for the independence of Lebanon, so even after he was assassinated, the daughters of Riad-El Solh were really defending the independence of Lebanon. So Prince Waleed has been raised in that family, feeling the roots of Lebanon, understanding the meaning of being independent, being sovereign, being free, being able to understand different cultures, because in Lebanon, you know it's a secular society with different cultures. Christians, Muslims, people talking different languages, open-minded. So I think that this also changed Alwaleed and created a very unique personality within him, which is, I'm sorry to say, different than any other personality in Saudi Arabia. That's why, when you talk to him, you can feel that he's not like other Saudis. It is not that Saudis are bad or good, but for me, he is somebody who has been able to understand and digest these different cultures."

Reflecting on the factors that shaped his childhood and how he was affected by his parents' divorce, the Prince admits his dilemma: "Although I was very close to my father and very close to my mother, I always wanted them to be together. Like every child I wanted to be next to my mother and father, but since this could not happen, I had to bear the fact that I had to divide my time between my mother and father."

Even his mother recognizes that: "His childhood was touched by what happened. It changed his life, the way we lived. It was not a calm divorce."

As far as the impact on his brother, Khaled, and sister, Reema, Alwaleed feels they were a little more sheltered and didn't feel the same confusion: "They were very, very young, and they spent most of the time with my father. So I believe they were affected less because they had an element of continuity, whereby they were always living with my father in Riyadh. They did not have—I would not say disruptive—but they did not have this change in country every once in a while like I did."

Still, with his strong, defiant character, he was something of an anchor for his siblings.

His sister, Reema, remembers feeling the separation, with him being in Lebanon most of the time, and she and her other brother, Khaled, being with their father and stepmother in Saudi Arabia: "I used to miss him. He was older and my only security. He always left messages, 'I will take you out of this mess.' One time I was upstairs in my father's library and when I came down, the word *Reema* was written on the floor. My father said that only Waleed would do this. When he asked him, 'Did you do this?' and he said, 'No,' so he slapped him."

Reema says she believed this incident with graffiti on the floor illustrated the kind of thing their stepmother would do to antagonize the young boy and get him into trouble.

There was no real communication between his father and mother, and the young Prince had to play a difficult balancing act between his parents. He felt he acted like a bridge between them, although they did have to communicate on issues regarding the children, and particularly the antics of Alwaleed. The Prince recalls that for a long time the communication was strained, but it improved over time: "We have reached the stage now where sometimes they call each other. So I think they finally have a very good relationship. Previously the relationship was edgy, but in the last five to seven years it has become pretty good."

Looking back on how things were in the years after his parents divorced, Alwaleed says he saw things differently, and it was natural that there would be animosity between various characters in the family set up: "Tell me, how many divorces are calm and friendly? In most cases there are bad feelings, especially between an ex-wife and the new one, and often the children get caught up in the middle of it."

He believes that things were not quite as bad as his mother and sister recall and disagrees with their view on the degree to which it affected him.

Nevertheless, Alwaleed's mother, Princess Mona, blames much of the frustration that her young son went through on what she describes as the cruel intentions of his stepmother. Princess Mona and Alwaleed's sister, Princess Reema, believe that his father's second wife would often set up incidents that would cause Alwaleed to get blamed and punished by his father, such as the incident with the graffiti in the house. These experiences, particularly this suffering, says his mother, is what fueled a strong drive in the Prince to succeed and become independent. But that was not before he had a few more turbulent years at school.

CLASSROOM CAPERS

By 1968, a thirteen-year-old Alwaleed was having a disrupted education at Pinewood. He would run away and miss classes, and he would have to be forced to return to school regularly. It finally reached a point where his father intervened. The young Prince was dragged off to Saudi Arabia to attend the King Abdul Aziz Military Academy, in the hope of instilling some discipline in him. Looking back, his father asserts, "That was one of the causes; however, it was also his wish."

In effect, Alwaleed's day-to-day existence inverted. From a more relaxed lifestyle absorbing liberal, virtually European-style Lebanese culture and visiting Saudi Arabia during vacations, he was now in the rigid Saudi system, in an even more rigid military system, and only getting to see his mother in Beirut when school recessed.

Despite his father saying Alwaleed expressed an interest in military school, Alwaleed remembers it differently. He was being sent there to be disciplined, which went against all his rebel instincts. He even ran away from there once, but eventually began to settle down. He says he began to recognize some benefit from being a part of an efficient system, and that the experience was something of a crossroads in his life: "At first I was very much against it but after the first few months, I really began to like it. It was one of the turning points in my life, whereby I became very self-dependent, and very much doing things for myself—washing the toilets, bathrooms, having breakfast at six o'clock in the morning. Having lentil soup, and tinned spaghetti and Kraft cheese, and sleeping at six o'clock in the evening. So it really changed my life. It was very much structured, and my life became very much structured at that time, so it's one of those junctures that changed my life."

It certainly gave him time to reflect on the concept of a disciplined and orderly life. Interestingly, discipline is an obsession with him today and he exercises it in almost everything he does, from planning his day-to-day activities to overseas trips to even keeping absolutely strict time for meetings. A military precision is evident in Prince Alwaleed's system now, having found its roots in his time at the academy, although it did take some time to finally kick in, because back then, the Prince remained a bit of a trouble-maker and rebelliously unpredictable.

He would do things without thinking of the consequences, says his mother, remembering how at age thirteen, after watching action films, he tied a rope between two columns like a high wire ten meters (more than thirty feet) from the ground, and then tried to traverse across it like a commando. He fell from that height and broke his leg but did not seem too fazed by the stupidity or risk of what he had done.

Reviewing Alwaleed's lack of discipline, his father believes that Riyadh might have provided a better environment for his son. Prince Talal says, "I don't think having lived in Lebanon affected him much (in a positive way). We sent him to Lebanon for schooling, and it is true that when he was an adolescent he was somewhat of a rebel. I don't think that that affected him much, but I personally believe that he was more at ease in Saudi Arabia than he was in Lebanon."

But by 1973, eighteen-year-old Prince Alwaleed was getting restless in the military academy. His mother recalls him writing a letter to King Faisal, pointing out that there were 5,000 princes in the Kingdom of Saudi Arabia, and that if the King simply forgot about Alwaleed, he could do fine with 4,999. He asked to be released to resume his studies in Lebanon. According to Princess Mona, the King, a little offended, told Prince Talal that as his son did not want to study in Saudi Arabia he should be allowed to go back to Beirut.

Alwaleed's younger sister, Princess Reema, remembers looking up to her brother with awe. She said it seemed like he could do anything, and having the courage to write such a letter to the King shocked her. To this day, she remains very close to him, but equally amazed at his ability to continually surprise her.

THE RETURN TO BEIRUT

By 1974, the teenage Prince was back in Lebanon, enrolling at the prestigious Choueifat School, perched on a green hillside in the

suburbs of Beirut, overlooking the sprawling city. He was told initially that he was behind in his studies but would be allowed to
continue if he could catch up.

By now his confidence was growing and his adult habits starting to take shape. Even before he returned to Lebanon, a few ec-
centricities were marking him as an unusual character. The
Prince's mother recalls how he used to write his letters to her from
Riyadh. They would be bullet points, as opposed to a normal letter with flowing text, and they were mostly devoid of the usual
formalities of greeting and affection. In one, for example,
Princess Mona points out how he started by asking her to send
him a particular jacket, before going on to other requests. A few
bullet points down, he paused to ask, "By the way, how are you?"

Then he would occasionally write the bullet points in pens with
different colored ink so that they would stand out, and he could
emphasize certain requests. What is really apparent from the letters is that he was far ahead of his years, with a level of maturity,
irony, and a certain dose of sarcasm that would have eluded many
of his peers.

On the odd occasion, the Prince would make a critical comment about his father or his stepmother, and then make reference
to it later in the note, begging his mother to make sure his father
never got to see it. The Prince also developed a few habits while at
Choueifat that baffled his family. Almost daily, he would call his
mother in the morning and ask her to send food. Not just a sand-
wich or two, but large volumes, such as twenty-five chickens, and
fifteen kilos (thirty-three pounds) of meat, three casseroles, salads, and so on. He would then explain to his mother that he was
inviting students to have lunch with him. Quite often he would
specify that he was inviting only students from the Gulf region
(Khaleejis) because he felt they were the most decent and least
prejudiced. His mother says she indulged him with the large lunch
orders because she felt that if this was one way of keeping him at
school and deterred him from running away, it was worth it.

Alwaleed was starting to gain more confidence with his own

identity. He had a huge admiration for his grandfathers on both sides of the family. In fact, even from the age of ten, whenever the name of his paternal grandfather, King Abdulaziz, was mentioned on television, he would stand up. He even managed to erect a flag-pole with a Saudi flag flowing from it at his mother's house in Beirut. It caused a big fuss with the neighbors. Watching such things, Princess Mona noted that her child was very different from others an early age. His mother relates how one time Al-waleed turned up at an airport—London, she recalls—without any passport, money, or baggage. He told officials there that he was the grandson of Riad El Solh and requested that he be put on a plane to Lebanon. They eventually did, and his mother was asked to pay the fare once he had arrived.

Prince Alwaleed still reveres these key figures from his past family: "If you ask me the question, who were your role models in life, it's them—my grandfather Abdulaziz, in Saudi Arabia, and my grandfather Riad El Solh. Although they were not businessmen—they were politicians—they are role models from the point of view of being straight, clean, honorable, humble, loved by their people, generous, and they looked after the poor people. From this point of view I am very attached to them, although I didn't meet either of them."

The time at Choueifat School was a busy one for the young Prince. Although he remained a private person and had few real friends, he took up sports with a vengeance, often playing football nonstop from four o'clock in the afternoon until ten at night. He became crazy about soccer, but also found the time to take up vol-leyball, a game he still likes to play today. The Prince's mother was always terrified of her children being in the water, in case they drowned, so from an early age she discouraged them from swim-ming, telling them that the bogeyman would get them if they went into the water. By 1974, however, Alwaleed was forced into a pool by his father and eventually learned how to swim—a pastime he is still particularly keen on and in which he is quite accomplished.

Beyond the sports, reaching adolescence brought out a bit of

Alwaleed's wild side, and he was able to have fun from time to time with people close to him whom he trusted, such as his cousin Riad: "The scariest time in my life was in a car with Prince Alwaleed. When he was eighteen, he had a Ferrari, and we drove at 260 kilometers an hour (162 mph), and whenever I think of this I have goose bumps."

Even though he didn't have all the privileges that many of his wealthy Royal cousins had, Alwaleed was popular with many of the Saudi princes who were his uncles. Where his father was relatively strict on him and limited what he allowed his son to have, Alwaleed's uncles used to indulge him with gifts such as cars, watches, and some cash to play with. And play they did, says Riad.

"Yes, the dune buggy came, then the Ferrari came, then he had to go to the States. I think this is the period when he started realizing that he has to have his own niche and he can't be like others. But the drag racing, the wild life, oh yeah, we had ours. Beirut then was a place where the good life was all over. It was abundant, for somebody young, well connected, with some cash he could manage, there were beautiful places to be, lots of nice company; the parties were all over, the discotheques were all over, so we managed," says Riad smiling conspiratorially.

Even Prince Alwaleed grins as he reminisces about that time in his life: "Oh yes. You know, I was wild in all aspects of the word. I was definitely wild. Now, I am happy that those days are over, behind me, and all (the mischief) that was in my mind went away years ago. Now I am very disciplined, very structured, very religious, very straightforward. I am really happy that all these things happened when I was young."

There's no doubt that when he was young, Alwaleed was different and somewhat troubled, though Riad is quick to defend him: "He was a wild spirit, but he didn't lead a wild life for a very long time. I think it was outbursts of hyperactivity. But I think he realized early on that he can't be like others, he can't be like one of the other princes. He had to set himself apart, and I think he took the right way. By hard work early on, and by smart investments and by listening to others, he managed to make himself distinct from the other cousins of his."

SPIRITUAL THOUGHTS AND MONOPOLY

Alwaleed also started to develop a greater appreciation for religion after 1974. Until then, he had largely marginalized Islamic rituals in his daily habits and, despite his strict Saudi conditioning, stopped praying for three months. It was around this time that Alwaleed felt pangs of guilt that he had been neglecting an important part of his upbringing and life, and, slowly, he started to embrace Islam's values and disciplines more proactively. It evolved to the point where a lot of people who interact with Alwaleed nowadays comment on his religious devotion, particularly when he breaks away between meetings for prayer.

Along with Islamic values, the teenage Prince started to show more signs of a stubborn business spirit, competitiveness, and desire to succeed. Riad witnessed it: "I was the first person who detected this because after school we had a daily ritual. We had one hour of Monopoly and practically every time, he beat me. I think I had brains to be able to resist his onslaught, but he always managed to beat me in Monopoly, so I knew he was going to make money. He had a fantastic dream about building hotels, which he is doing now, and he had fantastic dreams of having lots of money, and once he lost, if he did lose, he would insist on having another game. So early on, I think, it was there, but it wasn't the issue of money, it was the issue of power. Money came later on, business came later on, but early on he was extremely interested in playing these games where he wanted to be the winner."

For now, though, the Prince hadn't quite kicked his habit of running away from school, and he still got into serious trouble a number of times: "Yes, I recall one time I ran away from school. It was very funny, really. My father sent six or seven people to look for me all over Riyadh, and actually I thought I would go to a place where they would never think that I would be, so I went to my bedroom inside the house of my father. I was there for three or four days and they looked for me all over the place except there, and later, only by accident did they discover I was there."

On another occasion, he went to his mother's house in Beirut, declared that he was running away, and demanded the use of one of her cars. When he asked what she had that he could drive, she explained there was a Volkswagen and a Chevrolet. Dismayed, he stormed off. A few days later, his mother was shocked to see the arrival of a Cadillac, a Rolls Royce, and a Lamborghini. He had called King Fahd and his uncles and requested they send cars for his mother.

Family turbulence became a preoccupation for Alwaleed during his childhood and adolescence: "They were not happy (times); they were tough. In retrospect, I think my father, when he reprimanded me, or my mother, when she censured me, they definitely had the cause and reason to do it."

But the real trouble began when he hit a teacher and made him bleed.

Prince Alwaleed was not a high-flying student. Though smart, his family distractions and the constant running away dented his capacity to concentrate on his schoolbooks.

Riad Assaad explains: "Well, his personal life—his family life—wasn't stable, and school required some kind of stability. I think between the boarding schools in Lebanon, between living at home, between Saudi Arabia, it became a bit of a turbulent thing for him. Definitely, I think that being in Lebanon, with his mother here and his father in Saudi Arabia, their divorce affected him in one way or another. But no, he wasn't good at school; I mean he wasn't the top student, definitely. He wasn't the top in math, the whiz kid, the physicist, but he always managed to pass. He always managed to make his way through."

By January 1975, the teenage Prince reached a low point in his education. Despite Alwaleed's embarrassed reluctance to recall the incident, his mother tells of how he was caught peering across at another student's notes in an exam. The teacher told him that he would be given a zero and ordered him to leave. The rebellious Prince argued that he was just looking, not cheating, and said the teacher could give him zero marks but could not ask him to leave. He pointed out that he was the grandson of King Abdulaziz and the first prime minister of Lebanon, Riad El Solh, so the teacher had no right to be rude to him. The teacher, not realizing how much this young man idolized them, said something like, "To hell with your grandfathers!"

So the Prince stood up and said, "Before I leave, I have a message for you from my grandfathers," and gave the teacher a tremendously hard blow to the stomach, bruising him badly. Other teachers at Choueifat School rallied behind the assaulted teacher. Having endured the rebellious behavior of the young Saudi Royal for some time, they basically said, "It's him or us." Even though the head teacher was a family friend, he had no choice but to expel the Prince.

This left Alwaleed in a very difficult situation. He was kicked out just before he was due to graduate and realized that this would badly affect his future. Through connections, his mother managed to find him a place at Manor School in Beirut, so that he could sit his exams and graduate. By now, most of his family and friends had little hope that he would manage to pass, but something had clicked in that teenage mind. Perhaps some of the discipline he had witnessed at the military academy was sinking in. His mother said, "I thought it would take ten years for him to catch up, but he achieved it in one year."

She notes that even the teachers at Manor School were surprised: "He doesn't forget anything. Even after ten years he remembers it."

Interestingly, that is a notable characteristic of Prince Alwaleed today. He doesn't miss a thing, and he certainly doesn't forget it.

Working with private tutors, and studying until five o'clock in the morning every day, pushed the Prince to the point where he was able to pass every exam and graduate. He was determined to prove himself, and he was desperate to study at the International

College in Beirut. But as he finished his exams and planned his further education, the civil war that would destroy so much of Beirut and separate communities began in earnest in April 1975. Princess Mona insisted that the situation in the city was deteriorating very badly and begged her son not to return to Lebanon, no matter how much he wanted to study at the International College.

CALIFORNIA DREAMING

The United States had always held a lot of appeal for Alwaleed and he had anticipated some sort of studies there at some point, so he enrolled for a degree in business administration at Menlo College, in Atherton, near San Francisco, in California.

He left in an anxious state, worried about his mother living in Beirut as the civil war raged and the city was pummeled into rubble by mortars, and also concerned for his younger siblings, who had looked to him for so much support.

He wrote a letter to his mother saying, "Don't worry, I will take care of my brother and sister."

Princess Reema spent two months at the end of 1975 with her brother, at his wooden, ranch-style house close to Menlo College. The house was a fairly discreet structure on the main El Camino Real road in Atherton, near the college. There were certainly no obvious signs or styling that indicated it was now the home of the nephew of Saudi Arabia's King. Having his sister with him was reassuring for Alwaleed, but he was now preoccupied with a new interest in his life.

The young girl, two years older than him, who had studied at Pinewood College in Beirut, was now about to become his wife. Dalal, a strikingly beautiful and particularly smart woman, also part of the Saudi Royal family, had caught the eye of the rapidly maturing Alwaleed. In 1976, the nineteen-year-old Prince found himself with a new responsibility . . . marriage.

He also found himself in a new and challenging environment, where his Royalty didn't count for much, as it had in Saudi Arabia or Lebanon, and one where the culture and habits seemed quite alien to him. Alwaleed describes it as quite a lonely time where he gained a lot of weight, shunned socializing with other students, and, beyond the need to look after his wife, didn't focus on anything except his studies. Quite different from the young boy who spent most of his youth ignoring schoolwork and running away.

During that time isolated from the Arab world, the Prince made a new and unlikely friend who is still a part of his life today, nearly three decades later. Charles "Chuck" Gulan was working in a department store when this tubby foreigner, fifteen or so years his junior, walked up to him and asked for help in choosing a stereo system. Chuck was in another department, but this stranger was confident and demanding and, as there was no one from the right department to help the young man, he thought, *What the heck.*

After looking around, as the Prince was leaving, he thanked Chuck and asked him for a business card. The American was surprised later that day when he got a call from a guy with a name he didn't recognize, and certainly couldn't repeat. When the Prince explained that he was the one who had needed help with the stereo, Chuck understood, but was then baffled when the Prince demanded that he pick one of the good stereo systems they had seen and bring it over. The tall, burly Californian, with slicked-back hair, looking something like a bespectacled cowboy, thought, *This guy is different*, and took directions to the Prince's house.

"When I brought the equipment over to his home, it went into a back room by the pool. There were a lot of people and he was in his thobe [a long shirtlike cotton gown worn by Saudi men], and we put all this equipment in the room. I gave him a bill and he wrote out a check, and as I was walking out he said, 'Who is going to put this up now?' I said, 'I don't know. I got the check, that's your problem, I guess.' If I had known then what I know now, I would never have said that. He just looked at me and I just realized I did something wrong, so I said, "Don't worry, I'll be back after I finish work and I'll help to put it together.' So I came back after work, a few hours later and we stayed up until 5 A.M. in the morning putting up that equipment on our hands and knees, on ladders—at that time there were wires and everything else—and that's really how the whole thing started."

That late night, chatting with the Prince, and getting to know and understand him, was a starting point for Chuck. For Alwaleed, it was the first local person with whom he had started to build a friendship. Their relationship gelled quickly, and Chuck became a person the Prince started to depend on fairly heavily for everything from advice to just companionship, especially at times when his wife was back in the Middle East.

"I think it was a lonely time for him as he was there by himself. There wasn't anyone else there, just him and me, and the phone calls to Saudi Arabia, and school. That was basically it. So it was a lonely life, yes," muses Chuck.

FIT FOR LIFE

On top of the loneliness, the Prince was uncomfortable with the weight he had gained over the previous few years. He was up to almost 90 kilos (close to 200 pounds), and at a height of 176 centimeters (five feet nine inches), he looked rather rotund. Chuck witnessed the comforts the Prince sought in his loneliness: "In the beginning he did a lot of things that he would never do at the moment, like strawberry milkshakes, donuts, ice cream. That's a no-no nowadays and hasn't happened for about twenty-four years. He's really on top of it and he stays with it."

The turning point came when the Prince was getting out of a low sports car he had bought in California. As he struggled to prize himself free of the tight seating with both his bulk and dignity intact, he realized that this could not go on. Chuck saw the change in attitude quite clearly: "Just all of a sudden, out of a clear blue sky. We went walking one day from a friend's home about four miles. Not everyone made it back to his home except the Prince. The rest of us kinda fell to the wayside. We didn't have the regular shoes and got trouble with our feet, so we kinda dropped off but he kept going, and ever since that point, it's been a walking and exercising situation for His Highness."

The Prince rapidly shed his weight and stabilized around 62 kilos (137 pounds). Fortunately, he had no particular excesses with cigarettes and alcohol while in California, despite the extra freedom in lifestyle compared with living in Saudi Arabia.

"Even back then, the smoking really wasn't that bad. It was smoking with a big long stick and a filter; it was no big deal," says Chuck, mimicking smoking lightly. "To me it wasn't smoking! As for drinking, I don't recall any liquor drinking in the home. I really don't. I mean he never was what I would call a playboy type."

Chuck sounds almost disappointed. If he had been hoping to hang out with a wild, partying Saudi prince, it seems that he had got the wrong guy.

One thing about the fairly isolated life Alwaleed led was that he was able to concentrate on his studies. Being close to the Prince, and spending a lot of time with him, Chuck noticed the drive the young man had to succeed. He says that Alwaleed was buried in books for five days a week and then would allow himself to relax on weekends, often visiting restaurants in San Francisco or somewhere in the Bay Area. He liked different kinds of food, such as Moroccan or Indian, but was now paying attention to what he ate. Walking long distances and participating occasionally in sports became his way of getting fit and shedding the excess pounds. He would also call his mother frequently, asking for advice on color schemes for his house, and checking whether or not certain shades would complement each other. His mother says that when she finally went to Atherton to visit him, she was surprised at what he had accomplished in interior decor, noting that he was partial to light colors.

His time in California marked another turning point for Prince Alwaleed. He became a father. When Khaled was born on April 21, 1978, he became very attached to his son, behaving like a nanny to the boy or, as his mother puts it, "both a father and a mother."

He was so thrilled by the arrival of his first child that as a gesture of thanks to the clinic where Khaled was born, he refurbished the suite where Princess Dalal had been staying, putting in new furniture and decor. The Prince's time in the United States gave him a affinity for the country, and he developed a far more pro-American attitude than he had while growing up in the Arab world.

So Alwaleed left the Middle East in 1975 a young, relatively undisciplined rebel and returned to the Saudi Kingdom in 1979 a very different person. He had married, had his first child, and passed his university exams with flying colors.

REMINISCING

A quarter of a century later, Princess Mona smiles quietly to herself as she folds up the old letters written in bullet points and colored pens. Collecting together the old black-and-white photos, she places the letters and pictures into a plastic sleeve to protect them. Her smile broadens as she reflects on how much has changed in her troublesome son, and yet how much remains the same. The old letters she packed away reflect much of Alwaleed's characteristics today, such as his obsession with being concise and employing almost military precision in everything he does.

The old movies reflect the same burning drive in the young Alwaleed as in the adult.

As she reminisces, Princess Mona, who carries a clear regal elegance into her mid-sixties, seems to perk up her ears as if to hear the echoes of those days gone by. So much has moved on, and the young man who persistently ran away from school and slept in the back of cars has proved himself to be the very distinct achiever he always said he would be.

Prince Alwaleed's relationship with his father has mellowed over the years. The boy admired Prince Talal's strong, outspoken character when he was a teenager, but the hurt of his parents' bitter separation was a lesson to him. When he and Princess Dalal divorced at the end of 1994, unlike his father, Alwaleed handled the divorce with far more tact and maintained a friendly and dignified relationship with Dalal. He encouraged his two children to remain very close to her, too, so they would not go through the same dilemmas and traumas he did during his childhood.

Prince Talal spent his postpolitical years developing humanitarian work, shedding the epithet "The Red Prince" and becoming known as "The Children's Prince" for his work with UNICEF, the United Nations Children's Fund. Talal admires his son's achievements and is glad about how things have matured between them over the years: "It's a father-son relationship and I feel that we have become friends because he is at an age when we can become friends. We have an old Arabic saying, 'When your son becomes older, befriend him'—and that's what I've done."

CHAPTER 3

The Black Gold Rush

That was like the great California gold rush. Everybody was here, everybody wanted to make money. There were a lot of opportunities.

—KHALED ALMAEENA, EDITOR IN CHIEF,
ARAB NEWS, DESCRIBING
SAUDI ARABIA IN THE 1970S

Black gold changed the fortunes of Saudi Arabia in the 1930s, when it was discovered there by American geologists. By the 1970s, that one commodity alone—oil—was shaping the economy of the desert kingdom that had the biggest known reserves in the world and soon became its biggest producer and exporter.

Oil gave Saudi Arabia global influence.

In uniting most of the wide, open plains of the Arabian Peninsula in the 1920s, the dynamic and forward-thinking King Abdulaziz shaped a nation out of bickering tribes with a long-running feudal history. Half a century later, his legacy supported the richest and arguably largest Royal family in the world, as they reaped the rewards of oil exploration and production. His grandson, a driven young man with a fixation on succeeding, was not going to miss out on this. Prince Alwaleed Bin Talal was itching to get back to his father's homeland in order to make the most of the booming business environment there.

He increased the pace of his studies at Menlo College, to the point where he finished half a year early. There is some irony in the fact that his father, having witnessed Alwaleed's reckless and generally irresponsible attitude to schooling in Beirut and Riyadh, sent an emissary to visit his son in his first year in the United States. The mission of the visitor was to assess whether or not the lad was paying attention to his studies, and to generally check on him in case he was not doing so well. What he found was a man approaching his twentieth birthday with his head buried in books.

Chuck Gulan would see it on a regular basis: "Intensely, yes. He was a real book hound and that came first. Even when I would come over, the maid would say, 'No, don't bother him. He's in there studying,' and that's what he was doing. He was different from a lot of Saudi princes that I've read and seen and heard about, altogether different."

The Prince now wanted to prove himself to those other Royals back home. Though financially comfortable in many ways, his life had certainly not been as privileged or as openly extravagant as the lives of many of his cousins, and he was anxious to prove himself an equal to them. By pushing himself through his studies, he wanted to get back and get down to business, but he needed his qualification from the United States—and good marks at that.

One of his tutors, Carlos Lopez, recalls the Royal student as the hardest worker he had ever seen. As the Prince's academic adviser, Lopez met with the emissary sent from Riyadh by Prince Talal. When the visitor asked if the Prince was having any trouble with his studies, Lopez remarked, "My God! Have you seen his grades?"

They were straight As.

Again, Chuck is not surprised: "Well, his drive was only for his schooling. I mean it was books. It was continually books. He had his nose in books all the time."

The rebellious student who had left Middle Eastern shores to explore the academic world of the United States was finally answering his critics. He had the qualifications, but now he had to do something with them.

REAPING REWARDS IN RIYADH

As he returned to Riyadh, Alwaleed saw the possibilities were end-less. Even without much seed money, someone with the right business sense could succeed in that environment.

Khaled Almaeena, of the *Arab News*, remembers it well: "That (time) was like the great California gold rush. Everybody was here, everybody wanted to make money. There were a lot of opportuni-ties, oil prices had risen, land prices had skyrocketed 8,000 percent maybe, so I think that was a time for those who wanted to make money, who wanted to invest in whatever deal or business venture they wanted to. It was a time when Saudi Arabia was buying any-thing. There was a building boom, infrastructure, so you could buy anything from plastics to steel to cement, so those who were clever, and those who knew, went to chip in and throw in their card, and became successful—and I think Alwaleed was one of them."

Added to the brainpower and drive of Alwaleed was the fact that he was a prince, a member of the Royal family, a man with connections. But his approach was different from other people with similar conduits to those in power making all the decisions. At that time, as in many other Arab countries—and even other non-Arab nations—opportunity and income were guaranteed by law for local Saudi businessmen in the form of official commis-sions. Some saw it as a way to spread the wealth and give as many people as possible a chance to benefit from the boom. To do busi-ness in the Kingdom, foreign companies had to have local part-ners and representatives. The percentage of the commission was usually understood to be 5 percent of the deal, but in some of the bigger and more competitive tenders, where much more was at stake, it was not unusual for particularly influential local middle-men to take as much as 30 percent.

How these local people used that golden opportunity varied very widely. For many, it was an easy meal ticket. With the size and financial scale of the projects taking place in Saudi Arabia during the oil boom, commissions were large and plentiful. Many of the businessmen partnered into these deals decided to sit back and count the cash as it came in, abundantly. They made lots of money, and spent lots of money. Western capitals such as London, Paris, Geneva, and Rome became flooded with Saudi visitors, particularly in the summer months as the locals fled the crippling heat of the desert sun. With pockets full of cash, literally, the Arab spending spree created a shopping frenzy at every location from designer stores to the best hotels and restaurants. Property markets in the trendy European capitals surged as Arab money poured in, and penthouse apartments and expensive town houses were turned over to Middle Eastern owners.

In some ways, the golden days of oil-boom spending hurt the Saudi image, as they were often dismissed by the snobbish Western elite as wealthy but uncultured and somewhat alien visitors. That image crisis was a result of easy money coming in fast.

However, not everyone was content with the idea of switching off the mind and holding out a hand for commissions. Alwaleed wasn't just going to sit there on the sidelines of big business. He wanted to actively participate as soon as his feet touched Saudi soil in late 1979.

"I finished my bachelor degree in two and a half years, which was a record, so I came back there (to Riyadh) toward the end of the boom and I wanted not to miss it. And thank God, I came at just the right time, whereby I was able to get several contracts on annual leases, and ploughed back the money I got into real estate, and just built it up as much as I could. I was trying to invest in companies where their turnovers were high. We had the boom here. You invest 1, 2, 3 million riyals, and within six months to a year this thing would double or triple; but sometimes you could be hurt if you didn't make the right investment. It was not easy to adapt but I did have to adapt."

By using the term "adapt," the Prince refers to using the business skills he had acquired from studying in the United States and then applying it to what was something of an immature and incredibly fast-paced business environment in Saudi Arabia.

Business procedures were often far from developed in the Kingdom at that time. Transparency and straightforward dealing was often clouded by the impact of "wasta"—influence—or convoluted connections and agendas. It proved challenging to implement a clear strategy and approach a contract with more established Western values and standards, as taught to the Prince at Menlo. Local expectations were not in line with that way of thinking, but he persisted, insisting that he would use what he had learned wherever possible. He could see the value of the connections he had, and was willing to be aggressive in using them, but he wanted the foreign firms he was dealing with to know that he had experience in how they generally did business.

Alwaleed says that his initial start-up sum was $30,000 from his father, which worked out to be just enough for him to set up his company, Kingdom Establishment, in 1980, just a few months after reaching Saudi Arabia.

His first major break came after a couple of tough years, in 1982, in the form of a deal he struck with a South Korean company. They had won an $8 million contract to build an officers' club at a military barracks near the Saudi capital. Instead of just taking a cut for facilitating the contract, and seeing it through the local regulations and bureaucracy, Prince Alwaleed took a stake in the project, and reinvested most of the money he was making. This philosophy of not simply taking and spending the money, but actually reinvesting it carefully and strategically, paid huge dividends for the sharp-minded and eager young businessman.

"You know, I never liked this issue of commissions. I always hated it! To me it was a very quick way to make money, and although I did participate with some companies and take some fees, I won't call it commission because I was earning it. Some (middlemen) would just sign with the contractors and go to home. They made money, they got paid, but I was a very active participant because I used to work *with* them; I arranged debts for them and worked very hard for them. So I earned my money with these contractors—contracts more specifically."

It was his extra work on the projects that made Alwaleed feel that they were more than simply commissions. He did actively seek contracts and was willing to be involved, but demanded a good percentage—as high as 30 percent—for fully taking care of the needs of the contracting company. He adds that by being more of a participant in the actual business projects he was able to make serious amounts of money quickly: "You can make more money by having a multifaceted operation, you know, debt raising, equity raising, assembly of shareholders with them, working on the visas, contacts with the government. So a wide area of businesses would mean you could generate more income, more fees."

But the Prince insists that commissions didn't account for more than about 15 percent of the money he was making in the 1980s, and that most of it—65 percent or so—was from real estate deals done with the commissions he was making. The wealth he started to build rapidly was helped greatly by the fact that Saudi Arabia has no income taxes. But even today, most people who know little about Prince Alwaleed are curious as to how he could have made so much money at such a relatively young age.

Many people assume it was simply "oil money," because he's Saudi and a member of the Royal family. Indirectly, it is perhaps oil money of sorts, because he made it from the oil boom taking place in his country. Oil fueled the deals taking place, and oil brought in the foreign business and investment. But Alwaleed didn't simply get a check for owning oil. He didn't actually have any oil.

The Prince insists his starting point was very simple and that he had relatively little money in 1980. Apart from the $30,000 Prince Talal had given his son, he also helped him out with a place from which to work: "He gave me a very small cabin that consisted of four rooms. One of them was my room, the other one was my secretary's, another one was the manager's, and the other one was the kitchen. It was very tough to begin with and in maybe two months or three months we ran out of money, so ironically I had to go to Saudi American Bank—at that time it was part-owned by Citibank. I asked them for a loan and they give me a million riyals, which was about $300,000, and I had to mortgage my house—the house that my father gave me. I still have the papers here with me, by the way. It's ironic because a decade later (in 1991), I went and I saved the day for the same Citigroup when I invested nearly $600 million. So, I went to them (in 1980), I got a million riyals, and this supported me for another year, year and a half. I was running a very small operation, and for the first two years, it was very difficult, but then things did pop up."

The Prince says that he still jokes with his friends now running Citigroup about how he had to go to them for a loan as he was starting out, and then had to bail them out when they were close to collapse ten years later. He keeps a copy of the loan agreement in a drawer in his office in Riyadh and gleefully waves it at people who question the origins of his money.

Less than half a million bucks to get started. And where did he end up? More than $20 billion in twenty-five years.

Impossible?

Many people think so, but when the numbers are examined a little more closely, it becomes evident that the Prince was using money in an incredibly strategic manner. He took some risks, but the overall environment in which he was working was all about rapid growth.

RISK TAKER

There are certainly critics of Alwaleed in Saudi Arabia and the Arab world. A number of businessmen from that time describe the Prince as an aggressive young man who was very direct in his desire to do a deal and use his Royal connections to the fullest. Some even saw him as a bully in insisting that he be an active participant in their projects. They needed the local connection to secure the contract and were pressured to do the deal because so much was at stake. These critics say that Alwaleed's ability to persistently lobby the decision makers, many of them his uncles, was

key to his early entrenchment in the business community. There
are also those who speculate that Alwaleed, being a favorite of his
wealthy Royal uncles, had an advantage in securing their blessings
and support.

Khaled Almaeena, a young journalist at the time, says that
everyone seemed to benefit in some way from the rapidly growing
infrastructure and economy of Saudi Arabia in the 1970s. He
points out that many people became very wealthy even though
they started with small sums of money, so for Prince Alwaleed to
make such a jump was quite possible.

"Well, I know a guy who started with $20,000 and ended up
with $8 million, so yes, it could be true," he says.

The Prince's suave, well-informed, and widely connected private banker and financial adviser, Mike Jensen, has spent a decade
working with Alwaleed as his dedicated Citigroup liaison. Jensen,
who has a long history with the bank, was first introduced to his
Royal client in 1993 and started working more directly with him
from 1994 on. Jensen says that his predecessor, the late Cedric
Grant, worked with Alwaleed from his very first deposit with the
bank, back in 1980. Grant, and then subsequently Jensen, witnessed every dollar coming in and out of the account over the following twenty years and watched its phenomenal growth.

Being so close to the numbers, Jensen says he has no qualms
about defending the Prince's integrity: "There is no question—
absolutely none—that that's his money and he's earned it. He's
earned it in construction and real estate in Saudi Arabia, he's
earned it in various industrial and financial companies in Saudi
Arabia, and he's earned it in his Western investments, whether it's
Citigroup or in his other, what we call portfolio, investments, plus
what he's earned on his hotel side, where he's managerially involved. So he earned his money."

A deep and probing investigation in February 1999, by the
highly respected British *Economist* magazine, went looking for dirt
on Prince Alwaleed's finances. A little annoyed at first, Alwaleed
later realized it was something of a blessing when, after turning

over every stone, they found nothing seriously untoward in his
dealings. They ended up reserving judgment on the Prince, stating:

> *However, his business empire has a mystery at its heart. The*
> Economist *has interviewed the Prince and his entourage, and*
> *examined the accounts of dozens of the companies in which he*
> *has a stake, as well as his filings with America's Securities and*
> *Exchange Commission (SEC). Our research raises two doubts*
> *about Prince Alwaleed. The first concerns the true extent of*
> *his success as a stock market investor; the second, the land deals*
> *that are the source of much of his income.*

He says that it was amazing that in all the time he had been doing business, all the articles about him were so positive, as he had
been very open with the media about his business dealings. Alwaleed was surprised at the approach of the *Economist,* saying it
was the only publication seemingly obsessed with trying to un-
cover something negative. All the others had been comfortable
with the answers they found when they did their research on him.

According to members of the Prince's staff, the investigation
by the *Economist* failed to dig up any evidence of wrongdoing and
pretty much vindicated the Prince, laying to rest any questions
about the origins or source of his enormous wealth. The feeling
among those close to Alwaleed is that in the end the *Economist* did
an article asking the right questions, but that the Prince answered
back effectively with a letter to the editor. The Prince believes
that the subject is finally closed because he feels the world now
understands he did make the money in a regular way. Alwaleed
also feels that holds for the U.S. government and the Federal Reserve, who studied him for a number of years and then closed the
case.

In actual fact, the big jump in Alwaleed's financial situation
didn't happen until he went international at the start of the 1990s,
but even his dozen or so years of working flat out in Saudi Arabia
proved very profitable. The Prince says he made his first billion

dollars by early 1989, a decade after returning home from college, actually achieving a net worth of $1.4 billion by then. Once he got going, he was able to accumulate large sums of money fairly quickly because of his strategy of striking joint-venture deals with companies, rather than skimming off simple, cold commissions. The risk was potentially much higher, but the rewards also proved to be much greater.

It is important to note that when the Prince says he started with less than half a million dollars, this money was used to launch the company and fund its activities at start-up. This was not money to fund his lifestyle, which was comfortable, although generally considered far less privileged than many of his Royal peers, but like them he was entitled to a minimum monthly stipend equivalent to $15,000 at the time, just for being part of the ruling Royal clan. Not a large amount by most Royal standards, but it was enough to give him a personal safety net; it definitely was not enough to bail him out of trouble if his business deals went wrong.

The business had to take care of itself, but with limited support from his relatives, and to some degree, his father, he was starting to create a more comfortable lifestyle in Riyadh. Plus, his own income was growing rapidly, although his focus was to reinvest most of the money into the lucrative projects of which he was now a part. That first sum of cash, $30,000 from his father, got him started with his own company. From the four-room prefabricated structure—the small cabin donated by his father—he started laying the foundations that would eventually make him one of the richest men in the world.

CHAPTER 4

A Drive to Succeed

A strategic workaholic— in other words he thinks way ahead and he is very, very aggressive working to accomplish what he wants in the long term.

—MIKE JENSEN, PRINCE ALWALEED'S
PRIVATE BANKER

Being a Saudi Royal conjures up images of a flashy lifestyle, a guarantee of unimaginable wealth.

In reality there is only a relatively small portion of the thousands of members of the Royal family who have significant pots of money. It's a large family. Even ten years ago, more than five thousand princes were reported on the books. So, when critics of Alwaleed attribute his current enormous wealth to him for simply being a Saudi Royal, they are making a fundamental mistake. The Royalty gave him connections and certainly status. It meant he was a target for businessmen looking to invest in Saudi Arabia because he had the ear of his uncles—the King and those who made the decisions as ministers of the cabinet. Once he started employing his Western-style business tactics, more Western businessmen sought him out because they could relate to him. They knew where he was coming from, and they were also more comfortable with the idea of engaging in joint ventures with someone who had studied business in the United States, and talked their language—deal making.

But being a Royal did not mean a regular delivery of buckets of money until he amassed a billion. It still meant hard work.

Although Khaled Almaeena is a vocal campaigner for modernization and reform in the Kingdom, the editor in chief of the *Arab News* believes the Royal family is generally misunderstood outside the borders of Saudi Arabia: "The Royal family here has a lot of goodwill, in all honesty, and I speak very clearly about it. Nobody says they are perfect, but on the whole, it is not a repressive society—I mean we lack many things, yes. There are many things that need to be reformed, we need more transparency, there's accountability in question. But it's work; I mean, you could be rich whether you are a Royal or whether you are not a Royal."

Not everyone, especially in the West, agrees with Almaeena's assessment of the situation in Saudi Arabia, particularly on the issue of being a repressive society, but the journalist qualifies it by differentiating between the restrictions imposed by culture and society and those directly imposed by the rulers. It seems much of the problem and conflict with Western values comes from the old-fashioned traditions and cultural sensitivities of the Arab, in particular the Saudi, world, not so much what the Royal family says you can and cannot do.

So did Prince Alwaleed benefit or not from being Royal? Almaeena feels it's a double-edged sword: "I think it puts him in a very tight situation. Every move is scrutinized by the media. You can't have a normal life because you are always surrounded, whether you are in a restaurant or whether you are in a boardroom. As far as he is concerned there are also skeptics, 'Oh, he got away with it because he is a prince.' But that may not be true in his case because what people know about him is that he is a tireless worker. He works hard and I think he had some successes."

The Prince has his own views on the benefits of being part of the ruling elite: "I cannot say it was an advantage, but for sure it was not an obstacle. I have to be honest with you. I was very ambivalent about that, so it wasn't a big plus, but it didn't hurt me.

Clearly, when a member of the Royal family asks to meet a contractor, you will meet him. When a member of the Royal family
asked to meet a minister, or asked to meet a deputy minister or
head of the project department in a certain area, I had access. It
helped me from the point of view of getting accessibility, sure, but
from the point of view of getting contracts, not really."

His close cousin, Riad Assaad, watched from the sidelines in
Beirut as Alwaleed started to build his empire brick by brick:
"This is a man who worked for his wealth, for a very long time.
This man believed that he could do it and he went all the way for
it, and he went all the way ever since he was a boy; I mean I know
it, I lived it. For example, in terms of money, he wasn't a spender,
he wasn't a lavish spender. He believed that things have worth and
value and this was abnormal for the culture that was—still is—
prevailing in Saudi Arabia."

His four-room cabin became home to the Kingdom Establishment for Trading and Contracting (it only later became Kingdom
Holding Company after a reorganization in 1995). It was certainly
far from Royal, and until the South Korean construction deal re-
lieved the financial pressure, it was something of a mundane daily
existence and routine starting with a trip to the office at 8:30 in the
morning. Unlike the large number of staff running his household
and personal matters now, it was a tight and financially efficient
operation, Alwaleed remembers: "It was really quite small. I mean
I used to have maybe six, seven, eight employees at that time only.
You know, actually my driver used to drive me during the morning, he used to drive my son to take him to school, and in the afternoon and in the evening he used to go and get the shopping."

The million-riyals loan from Citibank, representing the equivalent of about $300,000, was handled very carefully, especially as
the Prince had seen the initial $30,000 loaned to him by his father
disappear in a matter of months: "I had to make a rationing process whereby this million (riyals) would take me through two and
a half years, by spending just enough on my house and my office."

But even as significant sums started to fill his bank account, Alwaleed didn't get complacent. He was looking long term and was disciplined enough not to blow the money in the short term: "All the money I used to get from this construction, I used to plough it back into real estate, and in the stock market, both. So any money I used to get I'd just plough it back in immediately, and I used to take just enough for me to spend on my office and on my house, just enough. And you know what? I didn't travel for three or four years in the beginning of the 1980s because if I did I would have spent money. So I said 'No, I'm going to keep my money to plough it back.' I was very obsessed—*very* obsessed—with spending money very discreetly, and putting it back in the system. Each riyal or each dollar, I would like it to multiply, and sure enough it worked."

Another discipline the young businessman brought back with him from the United States was professionalism, particularly in meetings and dealing with people. Plus, he believed in putting in the hours and structuring his business carefully. His cousin Riad describes how most other businessmen in the Middle East are traditionally slack with time-keeping, saying that it is a cultural thing not to worry about being exactly on time. The approach to keeping hours in the office is similar, and tracking down executives and managers could be difficult. Alwaleed, he explains, was different. He was—and still is—obsessed with being on time. In fact, the Prince himself admits that he does not fully understand why punctuality is such an issue for him, and that he often reflects on how it dominates his day. Riad remembers that, first, the Prince was in the office early in the morning and ready to do business immediately. Second, if a person wanted an appointment at 8.30 A.M., they would get it, and the Prince would keep to the time. This alone, he says, made Alwaleed different from other businessmen around. Plus, his smart approach to doing business paid off in a big way.

"This man, early on, invested properly and his investment was smart. He also knew that the *best* way to make money was the banks, and before that, the *fastest* way to make money was contracting, and the *surest* way to make money was to be around cen-

ters of power. So he was there when the boom happened in Saudi
Arabia. He started contracting, he delivered, he delivered more
than once, being a contractor. Then buying banks, growing from
one bank to another, merging one bank to another, reaching
Citibank, this was just part of the story."

Riad emphasizes that although Alwaleed's bank account started
to grow rapidly, he made a point of not sitting back and being complacent. Even in one case where the Prince accrued around $200
million from one of the contracting companies, he did not think to
simply start spending it on lifestyle. Other businessmen also made
money, but many slowed down and sat back with their millions. Alwaleed started using the money effectively as an investor.

His first area of focus was construction and real estate. He
looked for opportunities and was not afraid of taking risks. He recalls approaching the owner of a large tract of land in the center
of Riyadh but was deterred by the high price the gentleman was
asking. It was not the kind of opportunity the Prince was seeking,
but he continued to watch the situation carefully. Sure enough,
when Saddam Hussein's Iraqi forces moved on Kuwait on August
2, 1990, many elsewhere in the Arab world were worried that it
wouldn't end there. The Saudi landowner was one of them.

The Prince tells what happened with a big smile: "This is
lovely story, I bought the land in the middle of the Gulf War. At
that time, the owner panicked and he sold that at one-third of the
price—one-third—to me. I mean, sure we had a war, but for anyone to tell me that Iraq was going to win against the United
States was just silly and stupid. Sure, in the middle of the war
everybody panicked, but I said, come on, this is going to take one
week, or maybe a bit more. In one or two months it's going to finish. So I bought the land at one-third of the price, and I took it, I
divided it into zones, and on one-third of it I built the Kingdom
Centre which is the tallest building in Europe, the Middle East,
and Africa. The rest of the land I sold three or four years later
and our return was more than 400 percent."

It didn't take long for the Prince's adventurous and strategic real estate deals to place him as the largest private landowner in the Saudi capital with twenty-five million square feet of prime real estate and fourteen square miles of property, according to some reports.

BANKING ON SUCCESS

By now, people were starting to sit up and notice Prince Alwaleed, who says it took four or five years before people took him seriously and did not simply dismiss him as a Royal player out to make a quick buck. His business dealings were getting larger and larger, and his aggressive push into the business community was starting to distinguish him from others in his family, but he could not ignore his roots. Khaled Almaeena gives his perspective of it in this way: "I think he's part of not only the Royal system, he's part of the business community, because I view him from the outside as somebody who has business connections. I view him as part of the business community. Now within the (Royal) family, there's a hierarchy and he has to be respectful to his uncles. He has to be nice, and there is that element of respect that flows from down to up and the cooperation that flows sideways and I think that is a tradition that will carry on."

As the Prince got into full swing with his business he found he was back home just in time to make the most of the progress the country was seeing. Oil prices were breaking records and Saudi Arabia's rulers were pouring billions of dollars into building infrastructure—from roads, buildings, and power and water desalination plants to telecommunications networks and military hardware. People were becoming multimillionaires overnight, and the Prince says that within a few years he was earning profits at the rate of hundreds of millions of dollars a year. The fact that he ploughed that back into Riyadh's real estate sector as it was booming made his wealth leap higher. But his mind-set was also changing.

Alwaleed's mother refers to his childhood letters written in bullet points as the sign of an organized and focused mind. He still works in bullet points today and hates fluffy conjecture around the cold, hard facts. Princess Mona says her young boy was always fascinated by Gary Kasparov, the long-reigning Russian chess champion famous for his remarkably strategic mind. That is the direction Alwaleed's thinking pattern started to take. Strategic, global, and long term. His drive to succeed was stronger than ever and the taste of such strong early results made him hungry for more.

Riad says he was sad to notice a change in his cousin once he had returned from studying in California: "He became systematic. With me it's a direct relationship, it's a very emotional relationship. You know we had a kind of a deal that whenever I call I'll find him, and until now this is the case and it's not for business, you know, there's this thing where you can call someone just to call him. But I think in Saudi Arabia, his business, managing this fortune of his, made him a bit less emotional, less sentimental, and more systematic as a person."

But Riad, himself driven more and more toward politics in his home country, Lebanon, accepts how things alter over time: "We've changed also. When you look at this person that you've spent your childhood moments with, things have gone past so fast that sometimes you don't realize that the person that you've known twenty years or thirty years is no more the same. On the other hand, there are so many other things that haven't changed, you know, a fantastic sense of humor if you know how to catch it, extremely shrewd and keen. The questions are amazing. The ambition hasn't left him, and most importantly the ability not to accept defeat and the ability to manage after defeat. Victory, it's amazing, it's still in him."

Riad points out that even at an early age, the Prince knew when to play to his strengths. As the two began to play more and more sports, Riad would prove his prowess with speed and strength, being physically bigger and fitter than Alwaleed, but the Prince would get revenge by continually beating his cousin during their daily ritual of playing Monopoly.

Alwaleed's ability to focus on what he was good at pushed him to learn more about business so he could make better-informed decisions, particularly in dealing with international companies. Plus, he soon came to realize that qualifications count for a lot in the Western world, and American businessmen, in particular, valued and respected someone with a master's degree.

In the middle of building a successful business the Prince set his sights on the United States again—this time, Syracuse University in upstate New York. He enrolled for a master's in social science and delved into the American lifestyle once more.

By now, his son, Khaled, was about four years old, and he had a new addition to the family. Princess Dalal had given birth on June 20, 1982, to a baby girl, whom they named Reem. As much as he tried to make time for family, he was also focused on where his business was going and was operating it remotely from U.S. shores.

Alwaleed's eleven months in New York State passed quickly, helped by the fact that he focused on his studies intensely, completing them in record time—a fact acknowledged by the dean of the college when he wrote to the Prince a little later.

By the time he was heading back to Riyadh, after graduating in 1985, he had already shaped a new plan of action. There was a new sector he had his eyes on, which would change the way his company operated.

Banking.

CHAPTER 5

Expanding the Horizon

Royals, in general, they earn their living by being Royal.
What made him different is that he earned his way.

— SALEH AL GHOUL, EXECUTIVE DIRECTOR
OF FINANCE AND ADMINISTRATION,
KINGDOM HOLDING COMPANY

Pursing his lips, Prince Alwaleed peers out from the shade of his traditional red-checkered Saudi headdress, or *gutra*. He can't resist a glance across to the bank of nine televisions to his left, flickering their colors across the dimly lit office. Most of the furniture in the spacious room is finished in black lacquer and so catches the reflections of the sets, which have their audio muted. Some are tuned to news from around the world, such as CNN, CNBC, or BBC World; others are supplying local information on channels such as Saudi TV. In contrast to the somber news presenters silently mouthing their scripts, vivid colors and quickly cut shots flick across the television tuned to the Prince's latest interest, his Arabic music channel, Rotana. A popular Lebanese singer, glowing from her heavy makeup, furrows her brow in a pleading manner as her ample figure lounges across satin sheets singing about a lost love. Atmospherically lit shots of a swarthy young Arab man staring into the distance, looking equally lonely, punctuate the rolling shots of the pining maiden who is so softly lit that she looks almost out of focus. In spite of her alluring manner, the

Prince is more drawn to the rapidly scrolling "tickers" on CNBC, updating stock prices and displaying the change in value of the world economy minute by minute.

"Financial intelligence! It's all about financial intelligence," he finally declares pointing at the screen. The one displaying CNBC, not the singer.

Financial intelligence is the reason why this man became a billionaire.

Despite the success of his investments in real estate and construction in Saudi Arabia in the 1980s, Prince Alwaleed knew he needed to leap to another level if he was going to be a serious player, someone who shaped the markets and was not simply led by them.

Following the basic principle that banks are the eyes of the economy, Alwaleed started researching the banking sector in the Kingdom: "That's a turning point in my business career in Saudi Arabia, when I began really growing up. This issue of companies doing construction and real estate, this was still going on but I really wanted to get into the heart of the business community and get into a bank, so I evaluated all the banking entities in Saudi Arabia."

Careful scrutiny gave him a clear picture of what was happening in the country's financial sector, and he was surprised with what he found. Saudi Arabia's local banks were generally over-staffed, poorly managed, overleveraged, and staggering along on tired legs: "Once you evaluated all these banks in Saudi Arabia, there were two types. In one type of bank you had foreign share-holders, like Saudi American Bank—you had Citigroup there—you had the Hollandi Bank, Fransi Bank, Saudi British Bank, HSBC, so all those banks were eliminated (in the evaluation), because you could not control them; that control was by foreign partners. Plus I did not have enough money to be able to control any of these banks. Then there were other banks like NCB (National Commercial Bank) that were worth a huge amount of money, and I did not have the money to finance these. So we were only left with two or three small banks. I took the worst bank, which was on the verge of bankruptcy, but obviously I did my homework and analyzed it. We analyzed that maybe we will not sink with it, and sure enough we bought it and we cleaned up all the bad loans. We did not inject any more riyals into it."

The particular bank he refers to is the United Saudi Commercial Bank, or USCB. Of all the ones he looked at as possible candidates for a takeover, it was the worst one in terms of performance—unprofitable for years—and virtually on the point of collapse. For the Prince, this was the perfect candidate, because with the minimum amount of equity he was able to control it. In 1986, quietly and swiftly gaining a substantial hold on the enterprise, the Prince shocked the Saudi business community by announcing that he had control, with around 7 percent, and the endorsement of the major shareholders to run the bank. It was effectively a hostile takeover.

It had never been done before in Saudi Arabia. The business environment was relatively young and no one there had witnessed such an aggressive and strategic tactic before, especially in an area as sensitive as banking. The Prince remembers the reaction: "At that time, they were shocked because I was a member of the Royal family, number one. Number two, because all of a sudden I came into this very high-profile area, because construction, you know, is low profile; doing business in the real estate is also low profile, but to come to a nationally oriented bank—because they had branches all over Saudi Arabia—all of a sudden you are on the radar screen, the 'takeover Saudi Prince.'"

The Prince's tactic was to gain control and clean up the bank, which he did by getting into virtually every little operational detail. Banker Maher Al Aujan, who later went on to head up the United Saudi Bank under the Prince, was one of those who witnessed the arrival of Alwaleed into the financial sector. He says people didn't know what to expect as he was such an unlikely candidate to suddenly turn up and take charge. First, he was a member of the Royal family, which Al Aujan believes caused immediate suspicion because it seemed like the governing ruling family were stepping in and taking over with bully tactics. Second, Alwaleed was young and didn't have any visible experience in the banking sector, so people were completely baffled as to how he was going to go about fixing its problems and how his long-term plans might shape up. Third, many local businessmen feared that being in charge of a financial institute, the Prince would have access to a lot of private and personal information about their companies and that they might be vulnerable.

The Prince remarks: "Yes, it was a U.S.-type hostile takeover of USCB. We took it over because at that time it put me in the middle of the business community, because in the bank you see everything. You get involved in construction, in agriculture, in manufacturing, in trade, in commerce, in everything. So we became the eye of the hurricane, seeing everything—and not only that, we began building connections with the business community, with who's who in private banking, in corporate banking, investment banking; it was very important to create this."

The Prince does admit it gave him a distinct business advantage, but he was more concerned about how he could grow his own businesses, rather than worried about what others were doing with theirs. Before he grabbed USCB it was a slack operation with many of the staff underperforming and producing little, as they were aware of the lack of control and regulations.

Maher Al Aujan also confirms the business advantage the Prince found himself having as chairman of a national bank but stresses that Alwaleed did not use any inside information for personal benefit. The Prince's position did create a problem for USCB at first, though, because in trying to market the bank to big companies, he found them hesitant to give out any information for fear that the Royal might utilize it against them. It took patience to convince the business community of the Prince's agenda, and to win their confidence. The credibility of this new, young bank chairman took some time to build, but his handling of USCB and the way he turned it around—particularly his emphasis on transparency and good corporate governance—helped a lot.

Al Aujan believes that it showed many in Saudi Arabia a new way of working: "I think it was a blessing for the bank to have somebody like the Prince come and take it over. You had a young man who was hardworking, intelligent, who spent the time and the energy with the people. The first few months, he spent time with every single individual—I'm talking about officer level and above. He talked to them. He listened to their problems. He listened to the bank—what was going on at the bank, at different levels. He didn't make rush decisions. He took his time until he had a very good feeling of what was going on, and then he started taking action. The first thing he did was to start stringing the bank to the wall with regard to expenses. The bank was very loosely managed. There were no controls on how money was spent. So that was his first priority—to cut down on expenses, and he did a very effective job on that. In fact (laughs), he was very difficult on that part. He also stopped all hiring. He himself was interviewing every single individual that came to the bank at officer level and above. He made sure that good-quality people were joining the bank—not like the old days where just anybody could come and join. So the first thing was the expenses and placement of staff, and then we started working on the five-year business plan. It took us a very long time to come up with a realistic business plan that defined what this bank would be—how we were going to build the name and get our credibility back."

From the outside it looked merciless, and to a large degree that is how the Prince was in his approach. His justification is simple: "If a company is sleeping, not doing good, if you have bad management and you have paid management not doing good, then it should be a candidate for takeover, and that's what we did. We gave a message to companies that, 'If you don't wake up, then you are a candidate for takeover, and we'll take you over, we'll fix you up and the price of stocks should shoot up.'"

BOOM TOWN

Saudi Arabia in the 1980s was in the midst of a boom and expanding rapidly, so firing of workers was a rare event. Suddenly, at USCB, a staff numbering around six hundred was drastically axed. After Alwaleed checked the quality of the people around him, only two hundred fifty remained. Al Aujan says the Prince's decisive chopping was needed because the people working there before the Royal took charge were well below any acceptable standard. In his words, "We only had the rejects."

Al Aujan describes the atmosphere at the bank as being very tense in the wake of the Prince's arrival: "It was, you know, very, very negative. People didn't know what to expect the next day. They might be fired, they might be moved around, and so on, so there were rumors and there was gossip. But what the Prince did was warranted, and there was no other way to turn around this bank without taking the actions that he had taken at that time. But at the same time, when he was cutting down on staff, we were adding—we were adding quality."

In spite of the fears and negativity, Alwaleed was guilt-free and up-front about it all: "They really didn't accept it, but I told them, you know, business is business, charity is charity. We're here to make money. We're here to have profits. On charity you get things for free, but here business is business. If you're not productive, you have to leave. For the first year all the money we made was not from increased revenue, not from reduction of loans, but just from cutting costs, just from cutting expenses. There are two sides to profit, you either increase revenues, or cut expenses."

But the Prince saw his action at USCB as multipronged, attacking a number of areas at once: "We worked on several fronts. Front number one, we cut costs. We had a lot of overheads. If you looked at the expense-to-revenue ratio, it was just crazy. It was the highest in Saudi Arabia, so the first year we just cut costs—by 70 or 80 percent—and this caused the profits to go up, not from increasing revenues but from cutting costs. On another front, we were working on the bad debts. On the third front, we were working on getting new business. Clearly, the first two were easier because they were under my control. Cutting costs was my decision. For example, I made the decision whereby no one could buy even a pencil without my approval—my personal approval. So this was under my control. Lowering the ratio of bad debt was also under my control because some of these people that had debts were never called upon. Management was very loose. So I followed up, and we went to sue them. We went through the legal system and we were able to get the money from them. So these two fronts enabled me to generate more cash flow in the entity, whereby we were able to get a better reputation, whereby I was able to have more business come to me through corporate banking and investment banking."

At that stage in his business career, Prince Alwaleed introduced something that he was to continue as part of his management style. He created incentive schemes and bonuses. Even now, the Prince believes in rewarding work that is done well, and equally, reducing bonuses to indicate his displeasure with poor performance. For those at the USCB, it was another world. Suddenly, what they did on a day-to-day basis and what they achieved on the books was directly related to the rewards they received.

Khaled Al Thukair became the board secretary of USCB under Prince Alwaleed and was also responsible for managing special accounts for the chairman, especially those of significant clients who needed any special attention. He believes the Prince set an example to the staff by putting in serious office time and being there to personally deal with problems: "He was very aggressive on it, and he worked very long hours. People were doing fantastically with him. They were rewarded very generously on their performance, and he cleaned up a lot of mess there."

It was made clear to those who survived the axe and were along for the ride that it was up to them to make their own success within the bank and that hard work would be rewarded. Failure was not an option. Staff meetings were held regularly, and performance-related incentives included cash bonuses as well as new cars. The managers there also described it as a very aggressive system—very capitalistic. It was leadership with a clearly stated objective—"you deliver, you receive."

Al Thukair says that Prince Alwaleed is far from a conventional Saudi businessman, a sentiment echoed by Maher Al Aujan: "He set new standards. He changed the way to conduct business in Saudi Arabia. He was the first to come up with mergers. It was unheard of in Saudi Arabia before his time. The way he approached his businesses, the dedication, the time he spent, the effort he put in, the support he gave, all of those were unheard of. I mean, you don't hear of a Royal who comes and spends fourteen hours a day working—you don't see that—except for Prince Waleed—and people realize what this guy has done."

At first, the staff at the bank couldn't figure out why this member of the Royal family, who was by now comfortably wealthy, would spend so many hours at the office, nitpick every detail, and push himself physically to near exhaustion every day. What they didn't realize was that this was Alwaleed's first real hands-on project, where everything he did, every decision he made, had a direct impact on the business and his own experience and reputation. From the Prince's perspective, he wasn't going to sleep, almost literally, until he had proved himself to all his detractors.

Mustafa Al Hejailan, who was working closely with the Prince as his investment adviser, recalls being enlisted to help turn the bank around. Al Hejailan says that part of the secret to a quick turnaround in the bank's fortunes was that, apart from working long hours, the Prince did not miss a trick when it came to saving money. He would even ask Al Hejailan to reduce the wattage of the bulbs lighting the building, to save on electricity costs—often requesting him to remove some of the bulbs in the ceiling lamps altogether. Alwaleed was determined to make this bank work, whatever it took.

Sure enough, within two years, by 1988, the United Saudi

Commercial Bank was back in the black. Not only was it showing profit once again in such a short period of time, it also became Saudi Arabia's most profitable commercial bank by the next year. By then, the Prince had increased his stake in USCB to 30 percent.

Al Aujan saw everything firsthand but didn't expect it all to turn around so fast: "It was like a revolution. The way things were approached in this bank was unheard of—unheard of! I mean, everybody had started realizing that it was time to do business. After a couple of years, when people started—when the business community started—seeing results, we had a much easier time penetrating the market and building a good name for ourselves."

A NEW TARGET

Having won the respect of the banking community and businessmen at large, the restless Prince was ready for his next adventure. If he could create such a dramatic turnaround in one bank, why not in another. His careful study of the banking sector had revealed a number of weaknesses, and he was now in a much better position financially and as far as reputation, to exploit them. Several years later, Alwaleed set his sights on another struggling financial institution, Saudi Cairo Bank, SCB.

Having introduced the Kingdom of Saudi Arabia to the concept of hostile takeovers, he was now looking at another business practice that was, up until then, uncommon in the Middle East—mergers: "With USCB the main problem was bad loans and bad management. We fixed both, so we had a good learning curve and, guess what? Saudi Cairo Bank had the same thing, had very weak management and a very high amount of low-performing loans. So we issued a document describing 'the urge to merge,' and we went to Saudi Cairo Bank and told them, 'Look, we have good experience, a good track record the last year—look back at what it was and look at what it is like now—without adding one dollar or one riyal for equity.' They accepted our idea that we merge them together and we started the same thing all over, but on a bigger scale."

The maneuvering was a little more complicated this time. First the Prince acquired a substantial stake in SCB, again keeping a relatively low profile.

The advantage the Prince—or any investor—had in Saudi Arabia was that there was no limit on shareholding, unlike in many other countries, where anyone owning above a certain portion of a company has to declare that ownership publicly. In the United States, for example, the threshold for revealing a holding stake can be as low as just 5 percent. Once visible as a significant shareholder in SCB, the Prince had the task of personally negotiating with the bank's management and convincing the shareholders, who were from around the Arab world, of the benefit of such a merger. The Prince lobbied hard on that front, while at the same time going to the Saudi government to get its permission, too. Nothing would move without the blessing of the Saudi Arabian Monetary Agency (SAMA), whose job it was to monitor and regulate the activities of the country's banking sector. Plus, since the banks were joint-stock companies, they also came under the auspices of the Ministry of Commerce, which also had to clear the proposed merger. As part of the evaluation process, Alwaleed and his team hired two independent consultants, one to assess the situation for USCB and the other examining circumstances for SCB. Based on the assessments and the clearance by SAMA and the Ministry of Commerce, the shareholders finally agreed. In 1997, USCB and SCB merged and the newly formed United Saudi Bank—USB—quickly proved to be a very successful venture, and a wise investment for the $335 million the Prince had put into it.

By now the financial intelligence was kicking in, and the Prince was seeing opportunities in other sectors. One area that caught his eye was food and livestock. He expanded his empire to include majority stakes in one of the Saudi Kingdom's largest supermarket chains, Al-Azizia Panda, which he later merged with another large group, Savola. He also took over the large, joint-stock National Industrialisation Company, which specialized in industrial investment. It was headed by Khaled Al Thukair before the Prince moved him over to USCB. With profitable banking and hugely successful investments in almost all sectors of Saudi Arabia, Prince Alwaleed was now influential, widely networked, and a billionaire.

With few legislative limitations and regulations in his country, issues of monopoly and market control did not limit what the Prince could achieve: "I'd created what you could call the 'Nestlé of the Middle East'—the Savola Group, which is a very dominant force in its field. We have 45 percent of all such food group products in Saudi Arabia through one of our subsidiaries. For example, we have 80 percent of the edible oil, 90 percent of the sugar (market) in Saudi Arabia. Among many other things, we have 40 percent of all the supermarket industry in Saudi Arabia. This group was established by me and some of my allies."

Allies is a key word here. The Prince had become much more confident of his skills as a manager and an all-round investor, and he was beginning to discover something that would become an increasing part of his business style—relationship building with key people.

The executive director of finance and administration at the Kingdom Holding Company, Saleh Al Ghoul, has been with Prince Alwaleed since the time he was focused on Saudi's banks in 1989. A quiet, urbane man with an eye for detail and a sharp financial accounting mind, Saleh was introduced to the Prince while he was working as a manager of an off-shore bank in Cyprus. As chairman of the new USB, Alwaleed was looking to build a new team to join him in building the strength of the bank, which had been diluted by the merger. By September of that year, Saleh had packed his bags and was settling down in Riyadh: "He [Alwaleed] would go out of his way. He went out into the desert—at that time he used to go every Wednesday—and he would take two to three top clients either in private banking or corporate banking and he would personally take the time to build a relationship with them. That was unique. No other chairman in the (banking) community would do that and go out of his way. He would call the big customers and visit them in their offices. Also the bank had inherited a big portfolio of bad loans. He worked endlessly—at the time they called it remedial management—in collecting a lot of these bad debts."

That relationship building paid off. Saleh could see the effect of it: "I don't know if I should say this but Royals, in general, they earn their living by being Royal. What made him different is that he earned his way. People will not give you their money as depositors or have a special banking relationship with you because you are a Royal—you have to prove yourself and this is basically what he has done. He showed them he is a serious man. He learned the business very quickly and he could negotiate with them very deeply, and I think most probably what made us the best bank is the response time. In other banks it would take, let's say, a few days to make a decision, but in that bank (USB) you got it in a few hours. So people would appreciate the service, and that helped him in proving himself as a real businessman, not only a Royal."

By engaging people and working on professional terms the Prince was able to win over much of the business community to his camp. Deals became easier and trust was building. Although his own confidence in what he was doing grew, and he was developing a lot of relevant experience, Alwaleed was also concerned with creating good management teams, because as his empire grew, his ability to reach every part of it diminished. He needed people he could count on, and he would be very careful to hire and foster the kind of talent that he felt could implement and continue his strategies once he stepped back from the day-to-day operations. Considering the kind of person he was, that approach didn't come easily. Alwaleed was not only a tireless worker and a multi-tasker, but he also paid attention to the minutest detail in every transaction. He was now also convinced of the value of financial intelligence, and the benefit of being properly briefed on news and current affairs, particularly if there were events that might impact his businesses in one way or another. He began the habit of extensively reading a broad range of topical publications and continued thoroughly researching the various sectors in which he was invested. There were not many managers, no matter how smart, who could keep up with that kind of example or pressure from him, so he had to learn to work with people in the most engaging way possible. In an effort to accommodate his staff's needs, he focused on paying attention to what the workers had to say—the same habit he had first adopted when he took over USCB—even though he could be hard to convince on some matters.

"The Prince is a very intelligent individual. Extremely intelligent," says Al Aujan. "He learned from that (USCB) experience. He learned how to deal with people at different levels, he learned how to listen. He wouldn't make rushed decisions. I have worked with the Prince for over ten years and he has never, ever imposed any decision on me. We sit together, we talk, we discuss, and I either convince him, or he convinces me. So he has good managerial qualities. It's not like, 'Okay, I own this bank, I'll do whatever I want.' This has never happened, and people realize that. Even with the customers, even with our clients—clients we have problems with—he would spend the time to help them out, to work out their problems. He'll do whatever it takes."

Going from strength to strength only increased Alwaleed's quest for more successful projects. USB, which had come out of the USCB and SCB merger, had grown into the fifth-largest bank in Saudi Arabia. Alwaleed was stretching himself on all fronts now, but after carefully investigating the prevailing circumstances, he felt that there was at least one more bank merger he could achieve. This time the target was even more ambitious: Saudi American Bank, known as SAMBA, where again, the Prince saw good management as an ideal acquisition for his own bank.

At that time, Citibank was in one hundred nations, and Alwaleed happened to be in direct competition with it locally. Even though he was the force behind SCB, he was, ironically, also the biggest shareholder in Citibank by then. He says he saw the deal between SCB and SAMBA as a chance for him to officially get his two, competing banking interests to hold hands in partnership: "Our appetite was to get even bigger. Now, clearly in the first merger between Saudi Cairo and USCB, I became a bit diluted. I went down from 40 percent ownership to about 25 percent, but that's fine, because you have a bigger bank, that's okay. Then in the second merger between USB and Saudi American Bank, I became even more diluted. I didn't mind being diluted, and the price of that merger was that I had to sacrifice my chairmanship. I gave it up for the sake of creating a big entity. We created the biggest bank, not only in Saudi Arabia, but in the Middle East—Saudi American Bank."

As it was the third bank he was reshaping, it was easier for Prince Alwaleed to make quick decisions based on his past experience. Khaled Al Thukair, who had seen USCB completely restructured and then merged with SCB, was also around for the merger of USB with SAMBA in 1999: "He always repeats this thing, that when he gets into some business, he goes into details at the beginning and he's very much concerned about the management element. He buys things not only for their value, but he cares a lot about the management team running the show. He cares a lot about it."

Thukair adds that that is exactly why USB and SAMBA were put together and why some of the other mergers the Prince enacted at the time also happened; for example, when he brought together Al-Azizia Panda and Savola, creating the country's largest food conglomerate chain.

As Al Thukair puts it, "He bought the management."

When he looks back on it, Prince Alwaleed believes that his biggest success in Saudi Arabia in the 1980s was probably his real estate ventures, because those fueled much of what he later did in the banking sector, but he is particularly proud of how he turned the financial sector on its head in the Saudi Kingdom. SAMBA effectively became the biggest and most successful bank in the Middle East, he proclaims—and in such a short time.

Along with his significant hold on other business sectors, such as supermarkets, retail, livestock, agriculture, industrial projects, and real estate, the Prince's portfolio was proving hugely diversified and universally successful. His personal financial situation was strong, and he felt the urge to invest more and more of what he had into areas that would bring higher returns. The burning drive he had for achievement was now in full flow, to the point where some of those close to him started to worry that he was starting to close off emotionally.

Riad Assaad, the cousin who had grown up with Alwaleed and witnessed his wild years in Lebanon, was one of those concerned. He acknowledges that it is difficult for him to put himself in Alwaleed's shoes, to get a true judgment of the Prince's personal and business situation, but he does feel that success has come at a price. He described seeing the change in the Prince's character as becoming more logic based and less emotional: "There are certain things that Waleed has chosen to distance himself from, and this is something, I fear, in the long run will make him maybe feel regret. Being systematic is a tough thing. A mind that doesn't allow for emotions, doesn't allow for regrets, doesn't allow for lethargic time; it's a doing mind, it's the 'go do' mind. It's a case of, 'do it and then ask questions.' I think it shows in the relationship he has with his past; it shows in the relationship that he has with people."

Riad's explanation for why Alwaleed might become more distant is that the world of business at his elevated level is particularly pressured and potentially damaging. One wrong step can have disastrous consequences. As a result, the Prince had to become more cautious in his dealings with people, especially as most people who approach him have a business deal in mind. People are drawn to his success and are naturally looking to benefit from it: "His understanding of people who are in contact with him has become a bit, with time, more tough—harder. It's not as flexible, and more guarded, definitely."

Riad might have assessed the Prince as more guarded emotionally, but in business Alwaleed was opening up.

CHAPTER 6

A Prince, a Kingdom, and a Citi in Trouble

Any investor has to be a risk taker, but he should to be a prudent risk taker. . . . If you become too much of a risk taker, you become a gambler. I'm not a gambler; I'm a risk taker—a calculating risk taker, for sure.

—Prince Alwaleed Bin Talal

Those who don't know the story of the desert Prince might be ready to dismiss him as the lucky, rich guy who had that one big hit with Citibank, the one where he put in a few hundred million that turned into a few billion.

It's a little more complicated than that. The story didn't begin with a pot of oil money lying around waiting to be invested in some fluke deal. The years between 1986 and 1990 were very important in educating Prince Alwaleed in the value of banking and the potential rewards from it.

When critics question the Prince's skills as an investor, they are failing to look at the bigger picture. Citibank might have been a big hit for the Prince, but it came through considered research, not a random bet. More important, though, that assessment neglects the wide-ranging success he has had across the board with what might best be grouped as his investments in countries of the OECD (Orga-nisation for Economic Co-operation and Development), which includes stakes in Canary Wharf, Four Seasons

Hotel Group, and News Corporation, among others. On top of that, there have been phenomenal results with his Saudi investments.

Even if Alwaleed had achieved only one big hit with his Citi deal, not a single investor in the world would complain about winning such a jackpot.

Interestingly, beyond his interest in the actual profit he makes, the Prince is now also concerned with the kind of impact he can have as an investor.

From an early age, the Prince had a different relationship with money, compared with many of his rich, Royal cousins. Although his father became one of the wealthiest businessmen in Saudi Arabia through real estate and construction in the 1960s, and though he was from a Royal family on the Saudi side and virtual Royalty from his mother's side, as grandson of the first independent prime minister of Lebanon, the young Prince was more preoccupied with the issue of his family life than anything else. Money—sometimes a respectable amount—came sporadically in the way of gifts and handouts from various members of the family, but it never played a central part of his early existence, though his mother, Princess Mona El Solh, affectionately remembers how Alwaleed would behave when he received any cash.

As a young child, he would take the money he was handed and routinely joke around, making an act out of kissing it and respecting it, as if it was the most wonderful thing he had ever seen. Princess Mona laughs when she recalls how he would exaggerate his expressions, clutching it close to him with a big grin on his face and then smothering the banknote with kisses, declaring it was the best thing ever.

As an adult, Alwaleed realized the power of money in achieving goals and, rightly or wrongly, how it is universally used as a measure of success. His cousin Riad had noted how the youngster was determined to succeed.

Alwaleed's next steps put him a lot closer to that goal.

He had assigned his financial experts to start studying the international markets as far back as 1987, while he was still preoccupied with turning around the operations at USCB. In 1989, he felt he had assessed the global market fairly thoroughly, and he started buying shares of a handful of banks overseas—Chase Manhattan, Citicorp, Manufacturers Hanover, and Chemical Bank. In all, he had placed around $250 million into those particular companies, but he realized he needed a more dramatic strategy than that to achieve a proper, high-value return.

Although he is so closely associated with Citigroup nowadays, back then it was a fairly open plan of action, he recalls: "Toward the end of the 1980s, we were still pretty well entrenched in Saudi Arabia, we were diversified, we began really assembling quite a bit of money and equity at that time, and we began looking internationally. There were four big banks and they were all hammered badly. At that time, I had a lot of experience and expertise from my knowledge in USCB, so I was really ahead of the curve. I began evaluating these banks and I thought, my God, the price is so low, ridiculously low, so I bought in to all four banks. But then, seven months later, I said, wait a minute, I should really concentrate on one bank only. So after evaluating all four, I decided that I would sell all my stakes in the others and I put everything in Citicorp."

That bank's share price was suffering, and by spending $207 million at $12.46 per share, Alwaleed's maneuver allowed him to acquire 4.9 percent of the bank—just enough to keep him under the radar of federal regulators in the United States. That share price, adjusted to 2004 levels, means that the Prince bought in at $2.49 per share.

On paper, Citicorp was the worst performing of the four, at the time, but Alwaleed believed that it had the best potential. He valued the fact that it was far more global than the others, which were mostly focused on their operations in the United States. He felt that Citibank's truly international brand and presence gave it the most potential for future growth.

Citigroup's Mike Jensen has always paid close attention to the Prince's strategy and methods when working a deal. Looking back, Jensen says, there were obviously tactics the Prince developed when going into the Citibank deal: "He was very well prepared because he'd been studying the industry for three years, during which time he didn't make any major purchase. He was waiting for an attractive 'price entry point.' This is an approach we've continued to refine. Essentially, we initially study a company, at his request, to determine whether or not it's a 'good company'—meaning an excellently managed company with a worldwide brand name and other competitive advantages. Then we determine a potential 'purchase entry point' at which, if a purchase were possible, the investment would be a potentially excellent investment. A good company is not necessarily an excellent investment—the share price is almost always too high."

Jensen goes on to explain how the Prince tracks any company he has identified as interesting: "If, as generally is the case, the price is higher than the price entry point we have set, we follow the company in the hope that its share price might drop down to that set point. For example, a company might be at $80 per share and we'd like to be at a price of $50. If the price does ever drop to $50, it may look like we are jumping in opportunistically, but the reality is that the Prince did his homework months or years in advance and has been poised to move if the price entry point is reached. One of the critical factors for success—in his opinion and mine—is how cheaply one buys a good asset."

The key to the Prince's investment goals are summed up by Jensen in an assessment of good versus extraordinary deals: "The price of acquisition is the single most important criterion in an 'extraordinary'—as opposed to 'good' investment. 'Good' investments are what brokers generally offer, and a purchase will definitely make money for them, but these are not sufficiently attractive for Prince Alwaleed. We don't want 'good' investments, we want 'extraordinary' investments, and His Highness is willing to wait one year, two years, or even five years in between investments. That's exactly what's going on right now. We see a lot of good companies, but their prices are above our entry points, so we're sitting back and waiting."

A BANK ON ITS KNEES

The full story of the Citicorp deal unfolds as something of a drama. It is still almost inconceivable that one of the most powerful financial institutions in the world could end up in such a vulnerable position. The sequence of events illustrates how Alwaleed's research, patience, and then negotiating skills paid off.

As the Prince scrutinized the international banking sector, Jensen's predecessor, the late Cedric Grant, prepared the stage for his Royal client: "After March in 1989 the Prince asked for copies of the annual reports of ten different banks which Cedric got for him—the reports were for the year 1988. Cedric got the accounts and sent them to the Prince who studied them. Then in mid-1989 the Prince narrowed down his study."

Having carefully read the reports on the four he targeted, the Prince was ready to purchase heavily into whichever one of them proved to be the weakest. As Jensen puts it, that "dubious" distinction went to Citi: "So the purchase of Citibank was not an accidental situation; it was something where the Prince had actually done his homework in advance, made up his mind that he wanted to invest in a U.S. bank, and then was waiting—and that is still what he does today, does his homework and then waits for the right share to come along at the right price."

Citibank's position was perhaps far worse than many people outside the financial world actually realized. It was virtually on its knees, and then knocked to the ground by the events around it.

In late September 1990, one of the other overseas banks in which the Prince had originally invested made a move that had an impact across financial institutions. As the chairman and CEO of Citibank at the time, John Reed, remembers, Chase Manhattan Bank took out a reserve to protect itself from a series of questionable loans largely in the real estate sector. Citibank had the same kind of exposure as Chase, and the markets knew it. Credit losses through real estate activities the late 1980s, plus exposure due to severe developing world debts, particularly in Latin America, prompted financial regulators to declare a problem for Citibank. They evaluated that it needed more capital than it possessed.

Reed says, "We were undercapitalized and immediately the market reacted to the Chase decision by dropping the value of our stock, importantly signaling to us that they knew we had a similar exposure and therefore we must have problems, but there was a feeling—which was correct—that we didn't have the financial capability to respond by simply setting up reserves."

Reed was just on his way to Tokyo and had taken off from an airport in the Carolinas in the United States, when he got a call onboard the aircraft. He was told of the Chase move and responded immediately to save his bank by trying to reassure the markets that he had a plan. He got his people to issue a statement that Citibank intended to raise capital and take steps to make sure it could deal with any potential problems.

The couple of days of meetings in Tokyo were a tense time for Reed. Far from his home base with so much at stake, he was counting on the resourcefulness of his vice-chairman, Paul Collins, who was in London. Collins, being a close friend and trusted adviser to Reed, was also very conscious of the fact that Citibank had been undercapitalized, and the two had already been discussing how to resolve that situation. It was a particularly tricky one because they knew it wasn't simply a matter of raising capital. That capital had to be generated as part of a clearly defined program that would indicate to the markets there was a longer-term strategy, rather than simply recovering as soon as possible from the immediate problems. Reed was in close contact with Collins: "I said to Paul, I will come to London on my way back from Japan and we'll spend some time, and we'll start talking to investment banks, because investment banks presumably have their own views of what you should be doing, and their views reflect the market-place and it's a way of making sure you get into sync."

Winning the confidence of the market would at least allow the Citibank bosses to start talks with prospective investors. Reed and Collins met in Britain, as planned, and spent a tough and extended period trying to follow up on their announcement that they were dealing with Citibank's impending problems.

Collins put his mind to it straightaway, pressured by the fact he had already seen a poor response to his efforts to get support in the United States. He found that normal domestic investment sources were too wary to get involved and turned down Citibank for various stated reasons. He now feels that many of them were opportunistically waiting for the situation to deteriorate further, offering them a better price on a stake in the bank.

Things were looking very shaky by the time Reed had landed in London to join Collins.

"We met with some of the investment banks," the former Citibank chief executive recalls, adding, "We wondered if a rights offering might be the best way to raise new capital. We met with some investment banks in London and we started interviewing investment banks, and listening to their various comments, trying to figure out who we were going to use for this transaction. It probably took us a couple of weeks, and in the meantime, we were trying to understand just what the portfolio looked like, trying to get our minds around how much money we were going to have to raise and how big a problem we were facing. I would say that at the end of a couple of weeks, we had decided that we were going to use Morgan Stanley as our investment bank. One of the important reasons for deciding that was that Lord Richardson—who had been head of the Bank of England—was head of their international bank and we had a high regard for Lord Richardson. He was a tough but fair regulator and we valued his views, because obviously you have to get this right; you don't have a lot of opportunities to go back to the market—and you don't want to have to recast your plan two or three times. People will begin to lose confidence in you. So we really felt we had to get it right the first time round and we felt that Lord Richardson, given all his experience in the banking business—plus Morgan Stanley was clearly competent in their investment banking business—would be good advisers. So we did select them and immediately started working with them. We decided that we probably wanted to do what's called a 144 offering, which is a capital offering for professional investors, not a public offering to stockholders, to allow us to raise some money."

At this stage, neither knew exactly how much they needed to raise. They were simply trying to get their minds around the numbers, but at least they had decided on the plan of action—approaching *private* investors, rather than going *public*.

Even today, Reed believes the advantage of this approach is that first, such private investors are around in significant numbers, and second, they take the trouble to examine the books of the company into which they are buying. With a public offering, there would have to be a prospectus, which would be the responsibility of Citibank. It would mean pressure on the company to get it right, and even then, the assertions and contents of the prospectus would be assumed to be correct. With professional investors, the scrutiny is far greater. Their people look through the company books and develop their own point of view, the conclusions of which may differ considerably from those of the bank. They will try to find all the problems they can because, ultimately, these investors want to bid down the price and get a better deal for themselves. Their interest is to get a better stock price and pay less for capital, and so on. This means the offering company gets a "worse case scenario," as Reed puts it, and the benefit of very intelligent, capable people giving their own point of view. He adds that when so many professionals with a vested interest look so closely at the contents of a portfolio, there is very little likelihood that they will miss any details.

It was quite an enlightening process for John Reed, who admits that what he learned from that experience now prompts him to advise his clients to take the same route. If they get in trouble, he says, he encourages them to seek an offering to private and institutional investors to raise capital, not so much for the money itself as for the discipline it takes to really analyze the depth of the problem, which good professional investors are likely to do.

Reed recalls: "We were actively sounding out investors in this November (1990) time frame. One of our people in the Middle East indicated that there was some buying in our stock we had noticed, and that it came from His Royal Highness the Prince. We knew his family from historic banking. I didn't know the Prince at all, but we asked our people in Saudi, who did, and first asked, was he in fact buying our stock? The answer was yes. Second, would he have any interest in a private placement? He said, yes, he would."

A SAUDI SAVIOR

Since the amounts needed to bail out the bank were quite high— placed at first around $2.5 billion and soon after increased to an estimated $4.5 billion, Citibank believed that it would take a number of key high-end investors to save the day. The world's leading insurance company, AIG, was approached along with General Electric and General Motors. Citibank was hoping to forge a group of investors who could, between them, provide for a capital offering. Citi's vice-chairman, Paul Collins, disappointed from the lack of U.S. support, still had his hopes on international sources: "We basically went round the world talking to people and trying to encourage them to become investors, and in the process of that, put together what appeared to be a consortium of truly international investors, principally from the Middle East, and we included the Prince as one of the investors."

As this was an American bank, there were some concerns about who was getting involved, and who might potentially have a strong stake in the institute. As would be expected, Citibank had thoroughly done its homework on the Prince, in the same way he had been researching them: "Because there were some relation-ships that preexisted in the bank, we knew a fair amount about him and his family. Sources of money are always some concern, but the reality was, there was considerably less concern on *our* part in terms of his being an important investor—in fact the largest single investor in the company—than there was on the part of some of the regulators in the United States."

Citibank's finance chief got on a plane to meet Prince Al-waleed, an arrangement made following an introduction by Cedric Grant, one of Citibank's private bankers who handled top clients in the Middle East. Collins was immediately impressed with the Saudi Royal: "The conversation with the Prince was pre-cise, brief, to the point, disciplined, and it was perfectly clear he was willing to be an important participant in what we were trying to do. The other thing that impressed me was, at that stage, he was a relatively young man—still is—and he had really done his home-work. He understood what we were, he understood what our weaknesses were, strengths were, what the opportunities were, and so on, so there was no need on my part for a long explanation of where we were going, and why. He knew it."

Once again, it came down to financial intelligence, and the Prince was on top of it.

He felt relatively comfortable with what he was getting into because by now he had spent about four years immersed in the banking environment. Alwaleed was starting to draw comparisons between Citibank's situation and that of USCB when he first started targeting that ailing institute: "They're all banks; the core business of all of them is the same. So I decided that Citibank had a future. Although it was facing difficulties and the price was very low, I thought that with some adjustment this thing could happen. I told them let's make a deal. At that time they needed money badly."

Reed was just glad to have a committed investor: "Well, the Prince initiated it, in that he had decided for his own reasons—and I never asked him why—to be buying our stock. We approached him and asked would he like a private placement; he said yes. He might have said no, he might have said 'Look I am going to buy a little stock on the market, but I don't want to get engaged in a major effort' at that point, of course, but he had sort of indicated his interest by being in the market buying stock."

Another potential investor was the Kuwaiti government, and at that stage it was expected to lead the consortium. Reed's memory of those dealings are not particularly happy ones: "The Kuwaitis were very engaged, and it turned out not seriously. The people with whom we talked wasted a lot of time, but you don't know that at the time. The Kuwaitis had an investment office in London and I spent an awful lot of time with them, trying to understand what they wanted, but once the Prince indicated, A, that he had been buying and, B, that he was interested, Morgan Stanley and Paul Collins were on it. The Prince appointed some advisers, and our advisers and their advisers got together and they started putting together what turned out to be a package. In the meantime we were talking to all these other people, too, because we understood the Prince alone wasn't going to be able to do this."

Reed's deputy, Collins, was also involved in the negotiations with the Kuwaitis and gives a bit more of an understanding assessment of the situation: "The thing that unfortunately happened is that the Gulf War started and diverted their attention from a possible investment in Citicorp, to obviously coping with the war and what was going on, and when that happened we lost our lead investor—and that's when we had our second conversation with the Prince, which was to say, "What now?" and he said, "I'll do it all."

These words brought hope to Citibank's management because they desperately needed to clear the logjam. It was a catch-22; until there was a group of investors, no one was willing to invest, and basically it was impossible to get such a consortium without someone being the first to step up with money in hand. Having the Prince break the circle paved the way for the next steps. Even though it sounded so easy, and the Prince appeared like a knight in shining armor coming to the rescue of the struggling bank with little reservation, it had actually been far more carefully thought out by the Royal investor.

Still, it caught Collins pleasantly by surprise: "As often happens, over a period of time the other investors disappeared, for good reasons or bad, but they disappeared, and we went back to the Prince and said, 'It's not so good—this is not where we expected to be,' and he said to us, 'I will be willing to step up and do it all.' It surprised us to know that he had that capacity. We did a lot of checking around and found that he truly did, and that then led to the set of negotiations that, in turn, led to his making a very important investment. As so often happens, once he made the first investment, that broke the logjam, and within a few months we were able to do another issue within the public markets within the United States."

DESERT DECISIONS

Alwaleed remembers very clearly the evening he decided to make that commitment to put so much of his money into such a potentially risky venture. He had gone out to his desert camp, as he still does while at home in Saudi Arabia. To some degree, it was a weekend like any other and he participated in his usual activities, meeting with Bedouins who travel great distances to have an audience with him, gathering large numbers of people for meals under the desert stars, and sitting on cushions around a crackling log fire in a dug-out pit in the sand. He and around two dozen people wrapped in blankets huddled around the flames, trying to fend off the chill air of the open plains. True to his commonly used epithet, the "Desert Prince," Alwaleed went out walking a number of times. He likes to go for particularly long walks in the desert—often for hours in one go. The fast-paced strolls are partly for exercise and partly to give him time to think about things on which he needs to focus. Usually, an entourage of up to a dozen people follow him closely as he treks across the sand and sparse shrubbery around the camp, which is located about an hour's drive from Saudi's capital, Riyadh. The entourage keeps close, and keeps up with his rapid pace, ready to provide him with attention for anything he needs. On this day, the Prince intentionally kept them a little farther behind and paid them no heed as he strode along in his typically upright gait, swinging a long, thin walking stick in his hand, more for ceremony than the usual task of tapping a camel or horse along.

As the night drew in, and he sat in front of the log fire, he kept staring into it for long periods of time, concentrating. His staff knew very well not to disturb him. The Prince says despite having his team around him at the camp, he felt alone. He had not been able to find moral support from any of the people on whom he counted for advice. They all thought getting involved with Citibank was too risky.

Alwaleed was aware of Citibank's dire position. In some ways, it was almost perfect for him: a custom-made investment—grabbing a top-brand global stock just when it was reaching the point of sinking beyond recovery. But this was a particularly big deal, and he had a lot to lose. He spent the weekend in the desert being unusually quiet and distracted.

Should he go for it or not?

He had a nagging feeling that this was an opportunity of a lifetime, and it fit in almost ideally with his plans to grab a chunk of an overseas bank when the timing was right. But how big was the risk? And *was* the timing right?

The Prince was putting up a big part of his accumulated wealth—about half of it—for this deal, and had it gone wrong, it would have financially hurt him to a degree, but he would not have been—as some reports speculated—ruined: "Not wiped out, you know, I could've been hit badly, but not wiped out. But I was ready for this great leap forward and I believed in it but, at that time, no one was with me—no one. My committee was against me, my advisers were against me, my father was against me. Everybody said 'Don't do it,' but I went to the desert for two, three days. I was completely alone. I thought it through very thoroughly. I did my homework and out of the four banks I said, 'No, Citibank *can* do it,' and I did it."

Even though he had proved himself to be a canny investor and businessman in Saudi Arabia over the previous decade, the stakes here were much higher. As he mentioned, he was warned off this venture by most of the people around him, including his father—a businessman whom he respected greatly: "There were people saying Citibank was on the verge of bankruptcy. My father was so scared and worried. He said, 'Don't invest there.' 'No,' I said, 'I'm going to invest because I believe in it.' So I invested $590 million in Citibank."

Saleh Al Ghoul, who worked with Alwaleed at his bank, and later become his executive director of finance and administration, witnessed the reaction of one of the senior bank customers, whom the Prince was entertaining out in the desert on a weekend, as he often tended to do with his valuable clients. It was around the time of the negotiations with Citibank, and word was out that the Prince was looking at this large, risky venture: "One of these clients told the Prince, 'You are making a big mistake, these people are just going to take your money. This bank is going to be bankrupt, you will not make it, and so on. The Prince started explaining to him that, no, he believed it was a good investment. He told him what he believed the performance would be in two years, three years, five years. By the end of this meeting this guy bought five million shares—the same person who was trying to convince him that it was a bad deal."

Finally, after a long, quiet period of turning over the numbers in his head, and calculating possible outcomes, he reached his decision. He jumped up, grabbed one of the numerous satellite phones rigged to the desert camp, and told his financial advisers to make the move. The negotiations began in earnest.

Though he was not to meet the Prince in person officially for another two years, Mike Jensen was following events from within Citibank. One thing he now knows about the Prince, being so close to him, is that as a businessman, Alwaleed is a dealmaker and does not like to hang around. He may spend years researching. He may even sit patiently for years waiting for the right price and the right moment to buy, but once he makes the move, he is impatient with negotiations. As Jensen points out, this was a big deal, and took some intricate and extended contract work: "They actually negotiated for some period of time—I think we are talking weeks. The Prince had made up his mind he was ready to invest, and then Citibank stalled the negotiations—stalled for some reason—and the Prince said, 'I've got better things to do—we're either going to do it or we're not going to do it,' and so wrote a letter to Reed—or maybe addressed to Paul Collins—saying, 'Put up or shut up! You've got to move on this!'—saying, 'Do we have a deal or don't we—and if we do let's move it.'"

TURNING UP THE HEAT

As the temperature of the negotiations went up, there were many sleepless nights for people like Paul Collins, who was in the thick of things: "There clearly were! The final negotiating sessions were actually held in Washington at his lawyers' offices and we were down there (from New York), and we had Morgan Stanley working with us at that stage, and he had his own lawyers and people like that in the room. It was like one of those negotiations—joint meetings in the rooms, somebody would go out and talk to the Prince—and then I'd go and talk to John (Reed), but we got it done. I mean, yes, of course, there is always angst in this, but it was professionally managed, I mean, it was professionally done, and we both knew that we were so close and were going to get it done—and we did."

But Reed recalls the Prince's impatience, particularly as Alwaleed likes to deal face-to-face, while in this case most of the talking and haggling was done by advisers on both sides who had to keep going back to consult with the people they were representing: "I do think, as there always are, there were some ups and downs in the negotiations. I think we were frustrated that Morgan Stanley was trying to be cute. The trouble with professional investment bankers is that they always want to get that last one-eighth (percent) because they are professionals, and they are going to look at a plaque on the wall and say we got that one-eighth. From a businessman point of view that one-eighth doesn't mean anything. It's either a good deal or it's not a good deal—it isn't that last little nickel that makes the difference. So I do recall there was a little frustration there, that maybe we weren't reaching an agreement as quickly as maybe we should have."

It turns out that at the same time the Prince was being engaged more proactively by Reed and Collins, Citibank hadn't managed to close the chapter with the Kuwaiti government deal. Plus, before their investigation into his finances had been completed, they were worried that Alwaleed might not actually have the resources to take on such a big venture. Even though he had made so much money in Saudi Arabia, he was not a significant player on the radar of the international business community. As Mike Jensen explained, Citibank didn't know he had the money and numerous checks had to be performed by the U.S. Federal Reserve regulators to get the clearance.

Things were dragging, and it seems that the Prince's frank and rather direct letter to the head of the bank might have been the necessary pressure needed to make things finally move. Despite his impatience with the situation, Alwaleed felt his position getting stronger and stronger: "With the Gulf War the stock went even further down, and no one was going to invest in them. I was the only one around—no one would invest at that time. Actually my investment was announced the same day the American ground troops went into Iraq in 1991. So, we did the deal, and now, thank God, the return on this deal is more than 25 percent, annually compounded."

Reflecting on the situation, it's interesting to note the irony

that as American troops were in Saudi Arabia, helping the Kingdom against Saddam Hussein, a Saudi prince was helping an
American bank against the risk of bankruptcy.

The demands the Prince set out during the negotiations were
straightforward, but firm, according to Collins: "From my perspective he was after a good investment. He wanted to make
money. He was after a fairly regular set of reporting so that he
could be kept informed. He wanted to have complete access to the
senior management of the company, which would have been myself, but particularly Mr. Reed, which is obviously something that
we agreed to without any difficulty. And then there were the expected negotiations in terms of price. This was a convertible security, you know, how much is the premium, what is the current
return, what kind of dividend are we going to put on this return.
He loves to negotiate (laughs). He is indeed a tough negotiator.
He was a particularly tough negotiator when, you know, he held
most of the cards at that particular point, but I did not believe—
and I still do not believe—that he was out of line. He didn't try to
drive such a hard bargain that made the bank even weaker. He understood the value of trying to build confidence, build the fran-
chise, and make his money because of the equity holding that he
had, and it worked out very well for him."

Reed recalls that the basis of the deal with Alwaleed finalized as
follows: "I guess it was around January (1991) that an agreement
in principle was struck as to the terms and conditions, which was
basically a five-year convertible; I think we were paying 11 percent
interest for five years, and then it was convertible at a price of $14
or $16. The stock got down as low as about $9 but at the time we
were talking I think was around $12 (equivalent to a bit less than
$2.50 adjusted to 2004 levels), so it represented capital we needed.
It was going to be the transaction that would trigger others to
join—which it did, and so it was very important to us."

He adds: "When you look at the total number of shares we issued to the Prince, plus everybody else—and we eliminated the
dividend totally, and the dividend had been about $1.72—we had

diluted the stockholders by 35 percent. We reduced staff by 18 percent, and we sort of improved the earnings of the company by 50 percent, which is why once the danger subsided, the stock went way, way up and the Prince did well."

But there were hiccups along the way. In the first instance, the Prince was told by Citibank that the dividends from the convertible preferred stock would be tax free, but that turned out to be wrong. This gave the Royal investor the chance to strengthen his position even more. The bank needed the deal, so the Prince was able to squeeze the negotiators to increase his percentage, and he leveraged a high dividend rate.

Considering that Citibank's future was pretty much at stake, no one was going to argue too much with a man holding a check for $590 million. Even though tensions were raised briefly, Collins knew that this mix-up would not break the deal: "It turns out that what we thought could be done effectively from a structuring point of view couldn't be done, and it could not be structured as tax free. It had to be taxable, with the net result that there was a modest increase in the dividend to compensate for the fact that it became taxable instead of tax exempt. At the time it seemed like a major issue, but with the benefit of hindsight, it probably was not that important."

The deal was completed, and both the Prince and the bank were happy, although there must have been a few doubts in Alwaleed's mind when, by July, the price of Citicorp common stock had fallen by almost 10 percent. By the end of the year, it was back up.

However, there was to be one more stumbling block, this time not the fault of either party in the negotiation.

A FOREIGN INVESTOR

By February of 1991 Alwaleed's investment of $590 million to bail out the bank, plus the common stock he had already bought a year earlier, pushed the value of his investment to a total of $797 million. The Prince was now left holding close to 15 percent of Citicorp.

Any investor acquiring 10 percent or more of a U.S. bank requires clearance from the Federal Reserve. A temporary waiver was granted to the Prince by the Fed, and by the end of 1991, he formally filed an application to be allowed to keep his entire stake of 14.9 percent. Normally the Federal Reserve approves such applications within sixty days, but Alwaleed found himself waiting and waiting. In 1993, after fourteen months, he said he "got the message," and withdrew his application because the Fed had still not given its approval. Alwaleed sold off enough shares to take his stake in the bank to just below the 10 percent threshold. He got $364 million for them—making a nice profit—and tries not to think about how much they might be worth if he had been able to hang on to them long-term. If he had sold them in late 2004, for example, that 5 percent would have been worth more than $2 billion. The Prince does point out, however, that he put the profit to good use, reinvesting it in other areas, so, overall, the potential difference is not as painful as it might first sound. He still made money.

The Fed did publicly investigate the Prince but never gave a reason for not giving the approval for him to hold the entire stake. The Prince himself pragmatically accepted the decision as part of playing by the rules in America: "We said this could be an uphill battle. We decided we did not want to ruin our relationship with the American government, so we decided to sell some shares."

Ironically, at the time of the Citibank bailout, there was some speculation that it may actually have been the Federal Reserve who had made the first approach to Prince Alwaleed to step in and help the bank as a significant existing shareholder, a claim the Prince dismisses as "nonsense."

When the Fed failed to give approval to the Prince to hold more than 10 percent in the bank, there was a belief that the circumstances were not ideal for such a decision following a high-profile banking scandal in 1991.

At that time, the financial world had been shaken by the collapse of the Bank of Credit and Commerce International, BCCI, with a loss of more than $23 billion. Before it folded, BCCI was run by one of the ruling elite of the United Arab Emirates, although it was incorporated in Luxembourg and based in London. It was discovered that the bank had made an illegal purchase of First American Bank shares in 1982, in a crooked deal backed by Saudis. Suspicions were already high, especially when it came to Arabs with money.

It seems the Prince almost expected there might be problems: "To invest $590 million I had to get approval from the Federal Reserve—and they approved it because they had nothing against it, but they were very worried. Worried about the media, worried about the press coverage following BCCI. Unfortunately, we had Saudis immersed in a scandal, and they were allowed to escape by the government and authorities. All of a sudden you have a member of the Saudi Royal family invest $590 million. Wow! That was very worrying to them, so we had to go to them, put everything on the table, be very transparent, utterly transparent, with them."

Still, the BCCI incident had left a lingering cloud of suspicion over Middle Eastern and other foreign investors sporting large sums of money. Even though the source of Alwaleed's money had been cleared to the satisfaction of U.S. federal regulators, it was not the ideal climate for a rich Saudi investor to be holding such a large chunk of an American bank.

The Citibank senior management professes to having had absolutely no qualms about the Prince owning more than 10 percent of the bank, and Reed says they lobbied for him to be able to keep the entire amount he had: "The Federal Reserve were concerned— I don't know if they were really concerned, but they acted as if they were concerned—about having a Saudi investor and they were very tough on him. They made him cut back to 10 percent. I would have been quite happy if he had 20 percent, it didn't bother me any, but the Fed was tough on him. But we always tried to help him convince the Fed that they needn't worry."

Paul Collins believes it wasn't so much the Prince that they were concerned about, or the fact that he was a Saudi: "I think this was at a time when there were some other problems in the banking industry and they were concerned for people fronting for consortiums—not related to Citicorp but related to other institutions—so the regulators perhaps justifiably were a little nervous over who is this and what is this. We were very supportive. If 15 percent was the right number and that gave us the amount of capital that we needed to get everything done, God bless, but it didn't work that way. It was not personal, I think it was the regulators trying to do their job, trying to deal with the fact that they had just been stung badly on a couple of other institutions, and saying they would rather have this be at the under 10 percent level. I really don't think it was pointed at him, it could have been anybody—and it didn't even have to be Saudi, it could have been anyone else."

No bitterness seems to linger on this final outcome. When reminded how much more the Prince would be worth if he had been allowed to keep such a big chunk of Citigroup, as it is now, he says it's not important. He points out that as Citibank had continued to issue shares, his stake in the bank was diluted to under 13.5 percent, during nearly a year and a half of waiting for the Fed to decide. He felt he didn't want to keep it dragging for the sake of about 3.5 percent, and certainly didn't want to politicize the situation and confront the U.S. Federal Reserve. He may have decided to back down but points out that, officially, the Fed never refused permission; it simply didn't grant it. That may sound academic, but the Prince feels that it was a significant difference from an outright refusal. So Alwaleed moved on philosophically and still proclaims publicly how Citigroup is the linchpin of his investments—almost half his wealth is tied up in it. He claims that he will never sell it outright because he feels it still has a long way to go. If it was a one-hit wonder for the Prince, it was a one-hit that took years of preparation. Dedicated studying of the markets, careful planning, a healthy dose of ambition, and ignoring conventional wisdom all went into making this a key deal for Alwaleed.

It certainly earned him the respect of the Citibank chairman and chief executive, John Reed: "It turned out in retrospect to be extremely successful from the Prince's point of view, but I must say I never had any doubt but that he earned it because there were a lot of people around, and it was he who first committed and it wasn't as if we hadn't been talking to other people. My view is that whatever money he made on the transaction, he certainly deserved to make and I was happy to get the (investment) money, and happy that it triggered more. As soon as we did the deal with the Prince, within twenty-four hours we put together a package, I cannot remember the number, but with eight or ten other major investors. The other investors got somewhat of a less good deal than the Prince because they were sort of second, but they all did extraordinarily well."

In fact, following the Prince's lead, with renewed confidence in the bank, a secondary set of international investors put up $600 million for the new preferred shares within two weeks.

Ironically, the Prince didn't get to meet with the bank's chairman face-to-face until after the deal was completed. Just through circumstances, the two never had the chance for a formal introduction, plus much of the negotiation was being done while the Gulf War was taking place, and Alwaleed was obliged to show support for his country. He didn't travel out of Saudi Arabia much and handled the negotiations remotely from Riyadh through his lawyers and financial advisers.

Once the deal was done and the relationship was sealed, Reed and the Prince would consult frequently. In 1993, Reed even took his son to visit Alwaleed at his desert camp—the scene of decision making on the deal—and the Americans had the chance to fully experience Bedouin culture and the peaceful desert environment that the Prince finds so alluring.

For Reed it was interesting to witness the contrast of the Arab culture kept by a man who is so comfortable in the West, too. Paul Collins also noticed it when he had to negotiate with the Prince over the bailout. He recognized the Western influences that have shaped Alwaleed's business decision making: "No doubt that that made a great deal of difference. I mean, he's very familiar and comfortable with Western standards, and you have to think that had something to do with the fact that he was willing to make a very, very major bet with an American company. I think he also recognized that this was quite a unique American company. It was probably the most global financial institution in the world, and one that had that type of focus, so his having *been* in America— and not *being* in America—made it one of the things that made it come together."

Collins points out that, as a deal, it put Alwaleed on the map by virtue of its magnitude, its profile—this was an American bank, after all—and the returns he achieved on it in a relatively short time: "Well, it took him from being unknown to obviously very, very well known, because all of a sudden here is somebody completely unknown to the normal individual becoming the largest shareholder in the largest financial institution in the United States, and in the process of that he obviously had increasing exposure to a lot of investment bankers. All of a sudden he is front page."

Perhaps more important, it gave the Prince credibility on the international scene. From there he was able to start targeting other global companies and get endorsements from people who counted, particularly as he developed a reputation for sticking by his investments. John Reed recalls one particular occasion: "Oh, he's a perfect investor, and it was funny when he invested in Euro Disney—which I don't think went as well—I got a call from (Michael) Eisner at Disney, saying he was concerned. I said, 'Look, the Prince is a businessman and he invests not because he likes you but because he thinks the numbers are right.' I mean he's not a relationship investor, he's a financial numbers investor, and he has good people working for him and they know what they are doing. He does what he says he will do, and he's totally loyal when he makes an investment. We went through some bad times after the Prince had made his investment and he was very good, he was professional. He wanted to know what was going on, he gave me the benefit of his point of view, but he didn't jump up and down and yell at me and say, 'Hey, you should do this and you should do that.' He was very good and he's exactly the type of investor you would like to have."

LOYAL ROYAL

The Prince had ridden the ups and downs in recent years. At the start of the new millennium, American corporate scandals hit the economy hard, and Citigroup was one of those dented. Alwaleed says he watched the share price more than halve at one stage, from around $55 to $24, but he stood firmly in place, and sure enough, it bounced back.

His fondness for his Citigroup shares is also reflected in the relationships he has had with the bank's leadership. Once the bailout deal was done, and Reed and Alwaleed met, the relationship grew. Even though Reed's replacement at the top, Sanford "Sandy" Weill, clashed badly with his predecessor—the Reed-Weill confrontations were almost legendary in the banking world—the Prince built a close bond with the successor.

Sandy Weill actually became a lot closer to the Prince than Reed, who always kept the relationship fairly professional and didn't delve too much into personal life. Weill first and foremost respects what the Prince did for the bank in 1991, before Weill was even a part of it: "I think the Prince really stepped up to the plate at a very difficult time, with enough money to make the whole transaction very believable. I think that what he did really saved the bank."

Over the years, Weill's interactions with Alwaleed grew into a close friendship, which helped build confidence on both sides when it came to investment issues: "I think my relationship is fantastic, I really like him as a person. I think he is a caring person. He has been supportive of our company through all types of issues. He is encouraging from the point of view of our doing more and better things and he is really a long-term investor."

Mike Jensen, who also communicates with Weill at Citigroup, believes the chairman and the Prince share a fundamental characteristic that bonds them: "They both like to do deals—they have both done big deals together, and from the first day they met they did a major deal. The Prince has a lot of respect and admiration for Sandy, and Sandy, over the last five years, has developed an appreciation for the Prince, for what he has done, and as he's the largest shareholder, is glad to have someone who supports him so strongly and vocally."

It has turned out to be a balanced and mutually beneficial relationship between Alwaleed and Citigroup. He made it clear from the start that his desire to take such a large stake in an overseas bank was not to have control of it, which is one possibility people like Paul Collins had to consider when they first approached him—especially as he had taken the United Saudi Commercial Bank in a hostile takeover just four years earlier: "Sure we were concerned about that, because when you have a shareholder who has 10 or 15 percent of the company, you have to wonder, is there a risk that he might try to take that further and might try to take over? The reality was that at that stage, with the regulatory issues and things like that, it wasn't a big concern."

Even Sandy Weill points out that the Prince believes in investing in good management, and although he actively monitors what is going on at Citigroup, he avoids interfering in the running of the company: "I don't think he tries to influence the board decisions of the company at all. I think he'll talk about things, we'll know where he really stands on something, but he expects you to tell him where you stand on that thing. But I have found him to be flexible and not be dogmatic about positions, and really supportive of management. He's not trying to run the institution but he's trying to be not just a shareholder, but a helpful shareholder."

During his time as CFO of the bank, Collins remembers occasions that the Prince would get in touch regarding the financial condition of the company: "He had the entitlement of any major shareholder to know what was going on; he did not have any quote "control position," and in fact, as you recall, the regulators were very concerned that he did not have a control position. His focus from my perspective was—'let's step back a bit.' It was clear that, not only did he talk to us, he talked to a lot of other people who knew the company, knew what was going on—and not just analysts, but customers. He has, or he had, a very good read, a very good set of sources of information, that kinda kept him informed, but the focus was, 'Are you doing what you said you were doing? Are you delivering on your promises? What is your plan?' I can remember him once coming in and saying to us, 'Now, I am not sure you are being aggressive enough on costs,' and coming back and saying, 'What about this and what about that?' and frankly, we took that very seriously. We thought we were doing it well, but we probably could do it better, so we listen and try to respond."

The Prince is not shy about making sweeping statements, particularly when it comes to his entrenchment with Citigroup: "It is not a relationship, it's an alliance. We are there forever with them. That is an investment we will not sell—ever—because of where Citigroup is right now (2004): the fact that they have $1.3 trillion of assets, they have almost $110 billion of equity, they are available in 105 nations, and they have 200 million consumers. And I'm telling you, you ain't seen nothing yet, because Citigroup's market is not yet saturated. If you look at the market share in each country they have only 1, 2, 3 percent so far. The sky is the limit. So this investment is forever."

Understandable, really, considering his position. With the stake he owns, the fluctuations in the market mean big changes to the numbers in Alwaleed's bank account—he estimates a change of about $200 million for each dollar variation in the share price: "Sometimes we went up $600 million a day. If Citigroup went up or down $3 or $4, we could lose or gain $600 or $700 million!"

Millions to billions. Doesn't happen very often.

CHAPTER 7

Beyond the Citi Walls

When I take a wrong turn in business, it's not a mistake—it's a blunder. Losing a hundred thousand or even a million dollars is a mistake. When I lose two or three hundred million— that's a blunder!

—Prince Alwaleed Bin Talal

Warren Edward Buffett is America's most successful investor. In fact, he is the world's most successful investor.

Operating his company, Berkshire Hathaway, from the relatively small town of Omaha, Nebraska, his eye for a bargain and ability to select winning stocks has placed him in the top ten list of the world's wealthiest people for almost a decade. In the *Forbes* magazine list of wealthiest people in 2004, he was second only to Microsoft's founder, Bill Gates, who was valued at $48 billion. Buffett clocked in at $42.9 billion net worth, while Prince Alwaleed Bin Talal was positioned at number four, weighing in at $21.5 billion.

It amused the Prince to see a *New York Times* article in March 1999, describing him as the "Arabian Warren Buffett." Chuckling, he started quoting the phrase in media interviews, saying that he was very honored to be compared with such a respected investor. Then he dropped Buffett a brief note stating the same. Imagine his surprise when he got a letter back from Buffett declaring that the senior investor was touched by the Prince's comments.

Buffett wrote, on June 15, "In Omaha, I'm known as the 'Alwaleed of America'—which is quite a compliment."

Buffett also wrote to him a couple of times, congratulating him on the quality of the Plaza Hotel, in New York, in which Alwaleed had a 50 percent stake. The Prince said a friendship started between them and that Buffett even mentioned he would be delighted to consider any projects on which they might team up. That is a formidable team—billionaire investors who are friends.

It tickles the Prince that Buffett is happy to have the exotic title of "Alwaleed of America" (he was previously the more parochial "Oracle of Omaha"). Alwaleed is more than comfortable being referred to as the "Arabian Warren Buffett."

Buffett's financial wisdom is legendary. Over the years, he has certainly become a guru to many investors, and for over thirty years averaged close to 25 percent returns through his Berkshire Hathaway investments. Remarkably, the company's stock stands out from the average pick due to its high cost. Even by the end of 2004, it was around $86,000 *per* share.

After originally taking control of Berkshire Hathaway, a textile firm that he bought cheaply, Buffett turned it into a holding company. Reports say that it was only through a sense of duty and loyalty to the workers at the company that he kept a downsized textile operation going, because the company was soon making far more through its investments in other areas. Success came quickly, and in ten years Buffett made his partnership portfolio grow by 1,156 percent, at a time when the Dow Jones Index showed a 122.9 percent growth. Applying a principle of "being fearful when others are greedy, and being greedy when others are fearful," Buffett went on to even greater successes, snapping up shares in key companies when they hit rock bottom.

If anyone can feasibly compete with him at a global level, it is Prince Alwaleed. Interestingly, Buffet and Alwaleed share some common traits and a similar investment strategy. On the surface, both are ambitious men who know the power of money, and they are able to apply it effectively. Looking deeper, both clearly be-

lieve in the value of research and careful strategizing. Buffett, like
the Prince, studies not only specific companies, but whole industries. Where the Prince looked at banking and later media, technology, and hotels, Buffett had successes with insurance, banking,
and retail, among others. Both value good management. Buffett
has been more active in his companies over the years, while the
Prince, after turning around Saudi Arabia's banking sector, only
really applied hands-on management skills to the hotel industry
and then entertainment television.

Buffett was taught by his mentor, Ben Graham, at Columbia
University in the 1950s, not to simply look at the markets, but to
pay attention to buying the underlying worth of the stock—its
"intrinsic value"—and to snap up the stock if it was selling at way
below that value. "Buy low and hold"—it seems both men follow
that principle, but critics of the Prince say that where he differs
from Buffett is that he's not as sharp and skilled in knowing when
to sell and has been burned a few times through his stubborn desire to hang on to plummeting stocks in the hope that they will
eventually recover. In a few articles the Prince is quoted as saying
that, unlike companies that have a five-year or ten-year plan, he
has a "forever plan," to which even long-term investors like Buffett would probably never commit.

In reality, Buffet suffers the same criticism—someone who finds
it hard to let go of his investments. It is a judgment many long-
term investors have to endure, often unfairly, particularly when
their overall results are examined and found to be exceptional.

In the case of Citibank, the "buying at rock bottom and waiting
for recovery" certainly worked for Alwaleed, as it has in the case
of other key companies in which he started investing in the 1990s.
Again, not all of them went the way of Citibank, but, by and large,
the Prince spent the next decade taking his game global and dis-
proving the claims that his Citibank deal had been a one-hit wonder: "Look, I'm not going to defend my record. Thank God, I'm
very happy with it. My record says—and it's public—for all our investments internationally from ten years ago—*from twenty years*

ago—to now, our return was 23.5 percent. Nationally and regionally (Middle East), our return since we became established has
been more than 35 percent. So if these two results don't conclu-
sively say that we have a very good track record, I rest my case."

The Prince's private banker, Mike Jensen, says it sounds easier
than it looks: "Apart from his trading portfolio, which I think is
the exception, he's not in for the short term. He's looking at seven
to ten years and so it's a difficult goal. It's easy to compound and
make a 20 to 30 percent return over one or two years, but if you
are trying to make a 20 to 30 percent return compounded for
seven to ten years, you will have to have exceptional investments,
and you can't do it if you just buy at any time in the market. You
have to buy when the share price is very low. If we believe the
market is significantly underpricing a particular security versus
what we value it at—and if we think the intrinsic value is much
higher than what the market says—that's what we are looking
for."

So, checkbook in hand, the Prince started trawling the international markets for good deals. He had suddenly become a major
player in the financial world because the business press had covered his Citibank bailout in great detail, but he was still not that
well known to the general public and other sectors. On top of
that, although his major investment in Citibank had opened his finances to close scrutiny—including the investigation by the U.S.
Federal Reserve—there were still some in the global business
community wondering where all the wealth came from, and that
maybe he was fronting for other wealthy investors.

The Prince is dismissive about such claims: "Oh, I heard more
than that, I heard that I was an arms dealer, also. I can assure you,
I work for myself, and all my money is for me. It is for my sake
and my son and daughter's, and I have trusts in the Cayman Islands and in Saudi Arabia, showing that I am a beneficiary with my
son and daughter, and some others obviously. So I work for myself
alone. I work with no one's money, at all, period."

There was even one media report suggesting that Alwaleed was a conduit for the American Central Intelligence Agency, funneling money to the Taliban, on behalf of the CIA, at a time when the Taliban was still in favor with the United States, in order to fight communist Russian troops in Afghanistan. On that one, the Prince smirks and says that he won't even venture the phrase "no comment," as it implies there is something to hide, suggesting that the question might be more appropriately put to the CIA.

STRATEGY, STRATEGY, STRATEGY

Trying to describe and analyze each and every one of Alwaleed's numerous business dealings from the start of the 1990s to the new millennium is an almost endless task. There were so many of them in so many areas of business, from banking and hotels, to real estate and media, that it is actually hard to understand how he has managed to keep them all under control. Plus, they were often negotiated or managed over extended periods, with the Prince deftly weaving from country to country and deal to deal.

The easiest way to get a clear look at Alwaleed's investments is to split them into what he sees as either *Saudi-based* investments—covering the Saudi Arabian and Middle East market, where he started and now remains a serious force—and the *international* market, where he is associated with some of the world's leading companies. Then the international market interests are subdivided into "core" and "noncore" investments.

Essentially, what determines whether or not an investment is core is how central it is to the Prince's business, how large it is, and how long he plans to hold it, or how actively involved he is with them.

By splitting the huge number of Alwaleed's deals into these categories, it is easier to examine the basic principles involved in those investments, hear the often remarkable stories behind them, and then assess how they worked out in the long term—or in some very rare cases, the short term. The Prince himself admits that there were some serious lessons learned by the time the new millennium started to unfold.

So, essentially, the picture can be examined as follows:

1. Core international investments

2. Noncore international investments

3. Saudi-based (Saudi/Middle East) investments, which are subdivided into public holdings and private holdings

In a very general overview, it can be seen that the *core international investments* are centered around banking, hotels, media, real estate, and technology, with the leading players including Citigroup, Four Seasons Hotels, Fairmont Hotels, News Corporation, Time Warner, Disney, Canary Wharf, Apple, and Motorola, to name just a few.

The *noncore international investments* have included Planet Hollywood, investments in Korea, and what he calls his "Millennium Bug," where he invested in old and new economy companies—some of which were dot-com deals.

The *Saudi-based investments* are actually split into subdivisions of private holdings and public holdings. The *private holdings* are mostly centered around the Prince's "Kingdom" projects—Kingdom Tower and Shopping Centre, Kingdom Hospital, Kingdom City (a residential compound), Kingdom School, and Kingdom Hotel Investments, which Alwaleed sees eventually becoming a public company. The *public holdings* include banking, media, real estate and construction, food and agriculture, and hotels. The brand names under that category include Rotana music and entertainment, The Savola Group, Saudi American Bank, and the National Industrialization Company.

Although he clearly came out on top, the 1990s must have felt like a roller-coaster ride for Prince Alwaleed. That time period started

off with a world-class banking deal that was to become the lynch-pin of his huge wealth and ended with the loud pop of the dot-com bubble bursting, and a few bitter pills to swallow.

This decade also marked a coming of age for the Saudi Prince, who, remember, was still in his early thirties. The decade leading up to the new millennium marked not only his arrival as an inter-national investor, but also saw the development of a global empire that rapidly diversified to include some of the biggest brand names on the planet.

His private banker, Mike Jensen, watched as big, established brands became a target for Alwaleed over the years. Jensen began to see the reasoning and said the Prince recognized their value: "He is looking for companies that are worldwide—or at least regional—brand names with excellent management, whose share prices are very low because of some market-perceived weaknesses. He then buys and holds, and is always a 'friend of management.'

"For example, a company might have overleveraged itself so the market has hammered its share price. The Prince particularly likes this situation because, if he believes in the value of the brand, and trusts the management, his investment—if in specially issued com-mon shares or convertible securities—can be part of the solution, an increase in equity. Concerning management, the Prince views himself as an allocator of equity, rather than a manager. He regards himself buying management expertise and, consequently, is very concerned about the quality of a company's management. On the issue of brands, he believes that a worldwide brand name is evidence of past and present brand management excellence, which is a both a barrier to competitors, and a sign of future product longevity."

The way Alwaleed sees it, money goes into establishing, build-ing, and promoting big brands, so they have a future. That fits in with the Prince's principle of "buy low and hold," when it comes to investing. With so much effort and development behind them, top brands are looking long term and aiming to be around for a while. If the timing is right, and the brand is down in value, it is the perfect target for Alwaleed.

1. Core International Investments

In some cases, the Prince would see a *good* brand as one that could be built into a *great* brand. In these cases, he would follow his strategy to buy in as low as possible and then, once involved, push the company very hard to realize that greater potential. In other cases, he would see a *great* brand simply going through a terrible time. This is how he got his hands on an American bank— one of the most established and globally visible banks at that. He had confidence to back it when no one wanted to touch it.

Since then the Prince has stuck through thick and thin, and describes his relationship with Citigroup as a marriage. Of course, like a marriage, it has involved ups and downs, especially as things never stand still for long in the financial world.

For example, the end of 1997 was a testing time for the Prince. Being the biggest shareholder, he suffers immense changes in the value of his stake for every dollar that the share price moves. The Prince says if it wasn't for the fact he was in it for the long term— that Citi's his flagship investment—it would have been easy to lose his cool when he saw his wealth drop by $640 million *in one day* that December.

On the other hand, 1998 proved to be a momentous year for Alwaleed's most significant holding, which was worth around $5 billion by then. It was the year that Sandy Weill's Travelers Group went through a $72 billion merger with Citicorp, coming out of the other side as Citigroup, a strong global company with a hundred million customers in one hundred countries.

It was something of a coup for Weill, later described by *Time* magazine as a "consummate dealmaker," because he had managed to persuade U.S. federal regulators and lawmakers to ease restrictions that prevented U.S. companies from offering both commercial banking and insurance. The success of that lobbying opened the doors for the creation of U.S.-based global financial conglomerates.

At first, there was a lot of painful surgery on the merged entity.

Between July and October, in the wake of the merger, Citicorp shares fell 56 percent, as the new company struggled to realign its commercial and investment banking business. It was not helped by a $1.33 billion trading loss at its Salomon Smith Barney securities unit, which dented profits by 65 percent in the third quarter. Alwaleed watched his account rapidly falling to the tune of hundreds of millions of dollars. At one point, it was costing him $1.5 billion on paper, but the Prince sat through it all patiently, concentrating on his other numerous businesses.

Sandy had only met the Prince briefly in the early 1990s, while he was still with his own company, Travelers Group. They had talked over some common business interests but hadn't really gotten to know each other. Sandy wasn't to fully understand the Alwaleed experience until he took over Citigroup soon after the merger in 1998. But even before then, the Prince was starting to build a reputation as one of the most active people in the U.S. financial markets. Those who got to know him realized it came down to his meticulous research and planning and patience—traits that Citigroup's CEO, Sandy Weill, could clearly see in the Prince as the two men bonded: "He is a very good thinker. He spends more time than most of us doing that, because he doesn't need much sleep—but he's also a good listener and a good partner with people, and supportive, and he takes a very long-term perspective, which is really rare. I find I enjoy being in business with him. He's got a wonderful smile, and when you do something that he really appreciates, he doesn't have to say a word because you can see it on his face and the body language, and you know how he feels about what you are doing."

Room to Grow

1994 was a busy year for the Prince on the international front.

Having crunched the numbers in the world of banking and finance, he was ready to book in to the hotel world.

Bill Fatt, the CEO of Fairmont Hotels and Resorts, which the

Prince was eyeing as a prospective buy at the time, believes that Alwaleed may have developed his interest in the hospitality sector at an early age: "I have heard a number of different stories, including the fact that he spent a good part of his middle-teen years in the George V Hotel with his family in Paris and came to appreciate and love the hotel industry. I can tell you from personal experience it's an easy industry to love, so I think that was a part of it. I think, though, with the Prince, he never lets his emotions go too far, and a potential investment has to be backed by a solid business case and a prospect for reasonable returns, and I think in the hotel industry he was able to marry all of those things together. It's worked out quite well for him."

Alwaleed did, indeed, have a very clear business perspective on the industry. He was looking to buy into management more than he was interested in the actual real estate he happened to be acquiring: "During recessions, hotel owners are hurt. By owning a percentage of the management company, I continue to earn money."

Sarmad Zok is CEO of Kingdom Hotel Investments, created in 2002 and originally named The Kingdom Hotel Investment Group, which oversees the Prince's Middle East hotel ventures: "His debut in the hotel business was not at the real estate level. He took an interest in Four Seasons Hotels Management Company and with Fairmont's Management Company. It was very much driven with a vision, and the strategy around it was not an opportunistic, ad hoc accident; it was very well calculated. He built a vision around this investment, and then as his investments in the hotel sector expanded and developed, the composition of his portfolio changed in nature. You had investments in management companies and real estate, and today it's quite a substantial portfolio—one of the largest private equity portfolios throughout the industry, but it was built around a strategy and a very focused approach."

Sarmad's take on what made the Prince jump into the sector is that it was more the business opportunity than it was emotions dating back to childhood: "The hotel business has attributes that comply very much with the Prince's investment criteria; accessing an industry that had strong branding, great distribution pattern, operational and real estate components. The hotel industry fits all these profiles and criteria; it is a very international business."

Bright-eyed and sociable, with a big flirtatious smile, Sarmad is typical of the kind of people Alwaleed hires at his Kingdom Holding Company. Young, loyal, and willing to take on a challenge, he was ready to be thrown in the deep end soon after meeting the Prince in 1995. Back then, Alwaleed had been looking for someone who spoke both fluent Arabic and English and was presented with Sarmad Zok: "I was twenty-four or twenty-five years old—that young—with limited experience, but I had the background for this. I studied hotel management, I studied law, real estate law, and I had worked in the field of hotel acquisitions with some background in hotel operations, so I was gearing myself for this position from the time I was at university."

A three-hour grilling session by the Prince, during which he covered strategy, growth, and acquisition, among other things, secured the position for the young Sarmad, who was working in the area of development for the British Forte Hotels, which was subsequently bought by another British company, Granada. Interestingly, it was Forte that outbid the Prince on one of his early attempts to get into the hotel business.

In 1994, the Prince had joined forces with the co-presidents of the French Accor Group, Paul Dubrule and Gérard Pélisson, with the aim of buying Le Meridien hotels from Air France. His main competitor was the Forte Group, which was bidding 1.8 billion French francs ($323 million at the time) against his consortium's 1.6 billion francs ($287 million).

In the media coverage of the bidding war, the Royal suggested that even though the offer from his group was a little lower than that of Forte, he felt it was in the interests of Air France to take it because Accor owned a lot of travel agencies, which provided the airline with a lot of business and significant revenues. Plus, he pointed out, by allowing Accor to buy the group, Le Meridien would effectively stay under the French flag.

At one point, Alwaleed was willing to raise the bid, but after close consultation with his partners, withdrew. Pélisson had told him Le Meridien was not worth a single franc more than their assessment, and the Prince trusted his advice.

As it was, he had his feelers out for another hotel chain that he felt was an underutilized brand. The San Francisco–based Fairmont Group fit the profile of his investment goals—a company with solid potential that didn't seem to be going anywhere. The five-property chain had about 3,075 rooms, and he felt the brand awareness could be raised, and standards established, to utilize its luxury placing.

Alwaleed took a 50 percent controlling interest in Fairmont, which was later reduced to a 4.9 percent stake in the surviving company, Fairmont Hotels and Resorts, when Canadian Pacific bought Fairmont and took its name.

Overseeing hotel deals in North America and Europe, the Prince has two key people, Chuck Henry and Simon Turner. Both principals at the New York–based Hotel Capital Advisors, they are a contrasting pair and almost typify their nationalities. The large and jolly American, Henry, was formerly the director of real estate at Credit Suisse First Boston bank. He is more outgoing and willing to express his comments, critical or otherwise, to the Prince with good humor and a chuckle. The tall, willowy, bespectacled "Englishman in New York," Turner, carries the urbane manner of a British city gent and demonstrates an equally English reserve when it comes to discussions, providing mostly backup to Henry's commentary. Both witnessed the Prince grow his hotel portfolio while developing an active interest in the mechanism of the industry. The Prince likes to know how things work, in case he needs to take them apart and put them together again. Henry says that it was natural for the Prince to take a hands-on approach with hotels because it suits his character, especially as the Prince pays a lot of attention to detail.

Following the Fairmont deal, Alwaleed was on a bit of a roll, and was quite proactive in the next acquisition.

The chairman of the prestigious Canadian Four Seasons Hotel Group, Isadore "Issy" Sharp, spent April of 1994 looking to raise cash. He instructed the financial firm Goldman Sachs to approach any companies and high-net-worth individuals whom they thought might want to invest, so among others, they contacted established and recognized players such as the Sultan of Brunei, who already had an extensive property and hospitality portfolio. Although Alwaleed was not in their sights, *he* made the move to invite Sharp for a preliminary meeting. The Prince had done his research and had zeroed in on the luxury hotel sector. By the time the two men sat face-to-face, Alwaleed was spending his August, as usual, onboard his yacht moored off Cannes, in the south of France. As soon as Sharp was in front of him, the Prince laid down the ground rules. He would be willing to pay 50 percent over the market value for shares in Four Seasons, but he did not want to be treated like other bidders, otherwise he would withdraw the offer straightaway.

For a self-made, independent, and decisive character such as Sharp, who has a tough reputation in the hotel business, it came as quite a shock to be confronted so boldly by such a young man, who had obviously done his homework: "I think his interest was piqued in Four Seasons when he heard of our objectives, the focus we had in terms of only operating medium-sized hotels of exceptional quality. I think the key word I said to him was, to be the 'best' in each market. At this point in time our brand was building, and I think he looked upon this as the beginning of a company that could prove itself and invest in people. I think his ability to make judgments about people and rely on them is quite remarkable. He gets into the detail, to understand what he needs to understand, but not to be able to run a business. He's leaving that up to the people who he has trusted who have obviously learned their trade."

It was this trust in good management that allowed the two men to quickly realize they had a working partnership in the making, with common goals.

"He's a man who gets into the detail (of a deal) himself, makes his decisions based upon his thinking of the future, and is a long-term investor," according to Sharp, who had challenged the Prince very directly on his motives. "When we first met I said, 'What are your objectives of buying into the company? Is this something of an investment you buy and sell?' and he said, 'No. This is something I will keep, and I will not share with anyone else. It's for my family and the future.' I think he's kept up to that, and I think he's as proud of it as we are proud to have him as one of our investors."

It must have been this long-term view that made the Prince go after Four Seasons so aggressively: "We believe in the hotel industry; it is very lucrative. The key issue is that we enter at the right price. Even Citigroup, I mean, it's a home run because we entered it at a very low price. Entry point is very important."

So it is curious that he would have paid above the market rate for his initial stake in the Four Seasons Group. Obviously, Alwaleed was planning something more complex than simply buying into a hotel management company. He was weighing the potential synergy between being involved with those who run hotels and actually owning all or part of the real estate itself.

He had one or two ideas on properties he wanted to own, and this eventually led to some friction between him and Sharp, but at the time, the Prince was willing to hand over a check for $120 million and take a 22 percent stake in the prestigious brand. The price came as a surprise to the industry, but Alwaleed made it clear that he and Sharp were already talking about an active expansion plan that would increase the company's holdings by 50 percent in the first five years and double them within ten. As it happens, $120 million initial investment ended up being worth $250 million by the start of 1998—double in just three and a half years—and by the end of 2004 worth over $600 million.

The Prince was enjoying his hotel shopping spree of 1994, so much so that he didn't stop at Fairmont and the Four Seasons. He did actually get his hands on one prestigious place through a deal with an investor from Singapore, Kwek Leng Beng. Teamed up, they bought the landmark Plaza Hotel on the edge of New York's Central Park, a stomping ground for not only Manhattan's elite but also the rich and famous from all over the world. In that complex deal structure, agreed at the end of the year and completed early in 1995, Alwaleed secured the equivalent of 42 percent of the property, valued then at $325 million. He had sent his private jet to London to fly Kwek to see him in Riyadh, where he convinced him to let Fairmont Hotels manage it.

Chuck Henry recalls what a smart move it was for the Prince to get Kwek onto his private jet, where Henry and his negotiating team effectively had a captive audience in the Singaporean. The deal negotiations were stuck on nine specific points, which the Prince had told his team to sort out by the time the plane landed in Riyadh. A big smile crosses Henry's face as he remembers how Kwek, realizing he could not simply "walk out" of the talks onboard the jet, was stuck with having to find a solution. The pressure was on him to give way, and not make the whole trip a waste of time.

In 2001, Alwaleed increased his stake in The Plaza to 50 percent, and then in August 2004, he and Kwek Leng Beng agreed to part with it for $675 million, in a deal Kwek described in the media as, "Too good for us to refuse." The Prince admits that it had been a prime holding for him, and that he had not intended to sell it, but was surprised at the offer. He does, however, plan to keep his association with this New York landmark by retaining an interest in the hotel.

Just a year earlier, Alwaleed had met the Fairmont chief, Bill Fatt, for a late-night dinner at The Plaza, after which the two strolled around a couple of the empty rooms discussing what they might do to renovate the place. For such a premiere but old property, the rooms were considered too small, and the tiny bathrooms a particular issue for Alwaleed, who talked about the possibility of knocking rooms out to reduce the total number of beds, but make each room far more comfortable. A very ambitious project.

The Prince had wanted to bring the hotel up to its former glory and wanted Fairmont's buy-in on the idea. He had yet to talk to Kwek and was pessimistic that he would agree to the cost, which he and Fatt had put as high as $200 million to let The Plaza rule New York once more.

Sure enough, as the hotel was sold in 2004, Kwek told the media that the hotel needed renovation, and that he did not want to spend any more on it. He wanted to maximize shareholder value for his London-listed Millennium and Copthorne Hotels Group, M&C.

"Why do I want to be emotional about it?" Kwek said in the newspapers.

The sale of The Plaza was slated to be finalized at the end of the year, to an affiliate of the U.S. property investment company, El Ad Properties NY.

Kwek added that both he and the Prince had already taken out some money from the asset.

The loss of that flagship property would not hurt Alwaleed's plans to push the Fairmont brand and presence much further. As soon as the deal was signed for The Plaza, the Prince was eyeing London's prestigious Savoy Hotel and considering it as a flagship location for Fairmont. The deal on that property was as good as sealed by the end of 2004, as part of a massive boost to Alwaleed's hotel investments announced at that time.

The Prince secured a joint venture with the Fairmont Group and the Bank of Scotland, focusing on the hotel sector and valued at $1.5 billion.

The Prince always saw Fairmont as a group that could grow quite a bit more internationally through his property deals. He toured Latin America during 1998, following which he announced expansion plans for the Fairmont Hotel group. The seven-property chain he had bought into had originally specialized in 400 to 600-room landmark convention properties. The Prince said that may change to accommodate smaller ones.

Meanwhile, Four Seasons continued to grow from strength to strength, and by February 1998, the Prince's investment in the group had more than doubled since his initial $120 million purchase in the autumn of 1994. Prince Alwaleed was finding his involvement in hotels paying off. His private banker, Mike Jensen, believes it goes deeper than that: "I believe that the Prince changed the direction of the hotel industry, at least the luxury end of the hotel industry. He was, to my understanding, the first one to come up with a different strategy on hotels—and this was in the early 1990s—when he decided that the objective shouldn't be to own real estate, but rather to own the management company which earns off the gross (income), as opposed to the real estate where you get the net (income). So, he's got part ownership of the Four Seasons, part ownership of Movenpick, part ownership of the Fairmont Hotel chain, and he's been an active developer for these chains. That change in strategy is changing the industry. Now other people in the industry are switching around to his approach and he has made a killing."

Jensen adds one other thought. In being so widely networked in a wide range of industries from real estate to banking, the Prince adds more value to the hotel management group: "He doesn't just put money in, but he uses his connections to be a catalyst for developing new hotels for his companies."

In fact, the hotel industry in general has proved to be one of the Prince's strongest core investments, and by April 2004, the overall value of the Prince's hotel holdings was more than $1.3 billion.

The World's Best Hotel

There was one deal that Alwaleed pushed for very heavily, despite some initial resistance from the Four Seasons chief, Issy Sharp, and people thinking the Prince was crazy.

In the heart of the French capital stood a hotel that had fallen into disrepair and could only look back on its days as the grand dame of Parisian style. The George V, just off the Champs Élysées, not far from the Arc de Triomphe, had been the Paris home to the world's elite up until the last two decades of the twentieth century, but by the 1990s was run-down and a sad shadow of its former self. It was not until 1996 that the Prince got his hands on that hotel and put it through a radical transformation. Some people believed that it was one of his rare emotional decisions. It certainly might have seemed that way at the time, although Alwaleed can now declare the definite business sense in that particular purchase.

The Prince had been pondering endlessly on the idea of buying the George V, and toward the end of 1996 there was a lot going through his mind. He had wanted to get his hands on another top brand, a landmark property that he could use as a showcase.

The head of his Kingdom Hotel Investments, Sarmad Zok, explains the Prince's logic for securing such a visible asset: "It's very important. This business, the hotel business, constitutes a significant part of the Prince's overall portfolio but really, in terms of its capital amount, it's not a major part. It's probably 10 to 15 percent of his overall net worth, but it provides substantial visibility."

Sarmad says that unlike the Prince's banking, media, or technology holdings, which are not directly noticed by the average person, hotels are places that people visit, stay in, and experience personally. It again comes down to the importance and value of being linked to a top brand: "The visibility is substantial and that clearly affects the branding, and this is how you build a brand, by having the right properties with the right curb appeal with the right management with the right flag on them. It adds value to the brand—value the Prince benefits from because he is a shareholder in that brand. So he benefits from both ends, the real estate and the brand."

The George V was owned by a British company, Granada, which was taken over by the Forte Group. In the bidding for the run-down hotel were a number of French groups, plus Alwaleed's friend and co-global Royal billionaire, the Sultan of Brunei.

Alwaleed had decided that this famous property in the heart of

Paris, near the Champs Élysées, would be ideal as a Four Seasons Hotel. The company's chairman and CEO, Issy Sharp, didn't think so, and it created some friction in the partnership: "That went on for some time. He'd always had a desire to own that hotel and we had a bit of a difference of opinion because did it make financial sense? Was it a good economic investment, to buy it to fix it? The process you'd have to go through? So we explained what he'd have to do, because he wanted to make it the world's best. That was his primary objective—'Can we take the George V back to its former glory?'— and I said we could, but it would be at great expense, and was that warranted in view of his investment criteria? But I must give him credit. He listened, made the decision, and then supported that decision right to the end. So he paid the price to buy it, he restored it according to what we believed was necessary—which meant closing the hotel and literally gutting it and restoring it *beyond* its former glory. What you see today is much better than it ever was, and he allowed management to do what was necessary to compete in a very, very competitive market to bring it to the top."

To do that, the Prince splashed out $185 million to buy the building outright in December, snatching it from the Sultan of Brunei's Audley Group and the other bidders. He had given himself a Christmas present of what he considered to be, "the best hotel in the world."

Then Alwaleed wrote another check for a further $120 million to renovate it. Plus, he had to shoulder the cost of lost revenues from closing the hotel for two full years while it was torn apart and put back together piece by piece. Critics in the media commented that Alwaleed had paid over the top for a has-been hotel. They described it as a trophy brand for someone with a big ego, but Sharp commends the Prince for his persistence, and what he believes was trust in the Four Seasons management for advice on how to view the project long term, and then providing financial backing for that advice: "I am not sure there are that many other people who would have had that longer-term outlook, and desire to make it work, and as a result of it, it not only became the best in Paris, but one of the best in the world. Economically it turned into an outstanding business investment for him. So he created value where no one else could and relied on us to do that."

In spite of the initial dispute he had with the Prince, Sharp believes that, looking back, it was a positive outcome: "It turned out to be one of those unusual situations that turned out to be a golden opportunity for Four Seasons as well as an excellent investment for Prince Alwaleed."

Prince Alwaleed likes having the upper hand, however, and did manage to get in one last financial jab.

Even once the deal was struck at the end of December 1996 for the Prince to buy the hotel and Four Seasons to run it, the two stubborn businessmen were wrangling over what the front of the hotel should look like. Alwaleed's goal was to have the George V name stand out as an individual piece of historical and elite branding. Sharp wanted it to clearly display the Four Seasons label. The Canadian laughs as he remembers the tension: "Well, we had that as an argument because George V was always part of history, but again, to get the hotel to compete worldwide, we explained the importance of having our brand recognized—and the only way to do that was to put it on the building, top billing. So it had to be Four Seasons Hotel, George V, and he went along with that. As a result, that is certainly one of the reasons why we've been able to market the hotel successfully, because it does bring all the Four Seasons marketing force to help the hotel."

In reality, the Four Seasons brand was kept visible but relatively subtle on the front of the classically ornate façade, although literature promoting the hotel clearly brands it as Four Seasons. Essentially, the Prince had things his way, keeping George V as a distinct brand to the eye of those who pass by it.

The property, which reopened in December 1999 after renovation, has won numerous accolades for both the high level of service it provides and the remarkable renovation that was achieved. From 2000 on, it was voted the "Best Hotel in the World" by a number of the industry's publications, achieving the premier status for an unprecedented four years in a row.

The hotel's unusual floral displays elicit many comments. Not surprising for a feature that costs around $1 million every year and draws people off the street simply to take a look. There have even been documentaries on the subject. The lobby and walkways are lined with massive chest-high glass vases with tall flowers propped at the lip in erect, close formation, lit by numerous candles, creating an elegant and unusually warm atmosphere.

Alwaleed also had the magnificent stone foyer refurbished to include two discreetly carved stone plaques he commissioned with short verses from Islam's holy book, the Koran. It is out of respect and thanks to God, he says, for what he has been able to achieve in life: "I am a Muslim, I am an Arab, I am very proud of my heritage and my culture, and I just put two verses of the Koran that are very relevant, and very close to my heart, and I put them in the main entrance in the lobby. They say that if you thank God, God will give you more. That's one verse; now, the other verse says, all this is for God's blessings."

The Prince likes to take his long, fast-paced strolls along Parisian streets when he stays there a couple of times each year, and it is with something of a smug grin that he frequently pauses outside the front of the hotel under the large awning with the name George V. He points to how the wall sign near the entrance of the hotel has the name George V with the Four Seasons lettering just below it—something Sharp's group had fought hard to secure.

"That cost Issy $27 million," Alwaleed mischievously muses, before pacing off into the distance.

The Canary's Song

What do billionaires talk about over lunch?

It certainly isn't how much tip to leave. Actually, in this case, Alwaleed was having lunch at someone's home in the chic Italian city of Milan, so it's unlikely that the subject of a tip would even arise.

It was the end of May 1995, and he was with one of the most influential men in the media in Europe. In reality, Silvio Berlusconi's influence went far beyond just the media, as he had stepped in and out of the country's prime minister shoes a couple of times.

Just a couple of years earlier, Awaleed had started his own interest in media by investing in Arab Radio Television, ART, and had said it was the start of something big. Now he was looking at how he could participate in Europe's media scene.

Something about Berlusconi's setup obviously impressed him, because by the next month, he had joined a consortium to buy into his communications company. Alwaleed spent $100 million acquiring a 2.3 percent stake in Mediaset S.P.A., a subsidiary of Berlusconi's Fininvest media empire.

By the time the autumn of that year came around, there was another big, and very high-profile deal on the horizon.

In the heart of London's Docklands, to the east of the city center, lay the ruins of an ambitious plan put together by a Canadian businessman, to rejuvenate the area and create an 86-acre (34.4-hectare) landmark office park known as Canary Wharf.

It was the largest European real estate and land development project at the time, but unfortunately, it had been completed just as a slowing economy and high vacancies hit home. In 1992, Vienna-born Paul Reichmann lost the project he had conceived, as the company went into administration, leaving it in the hands of a third party, whose responsibility it was to either run it, turn it around, or sell it. With around 1.7 million square feet of unrented space in the Docklands, Canary Wharf was looking more like a disastrous white elephant, but Reichmann's luck bounced back in October 1995. Prince Alwaleed and a consortium of investors paid off the bankers around $1.2 billion for control of the riverside development, and then hired Reichmann as chairman to run it, which a few people seriously questioned at the time. Citigroup's Sandy Weill, sees it differently: "I think he (Alwaleed) is a very good businessman; he is extremely practical. He made the investment in Canary Wharf, and he reached out to Paul Reichmann, who really came up with that whole concept and built it, and got overleveraged and lost it. He brought Reichmann in to be a partner in that venture, because he thought he knew where every screw was, where every nail was, he knew and loved the operation better than anyone else and it was a very smart thing to do."

The rescue of the massive real estate project won Alwaleed's investing group the praise of the British establishment, which had been suffering a large degree of embarrassment over the problem.

Alwaleed got ownership of 6 percent of the company in the deal. Canary Wharf went public in 1999, and shares in the company reached their peak in 2000. Fortunately for the Prince, he ended up selling two-thirds of his initial investment of 63 million euros (then $66 million) for 192 million euros in January 2001 ($204 million)—an estimated return of 47.7 percent per year over five years. Soon after, the shares started a downhill slide, and a battle for control was under way again by early 2004.

So the Prince timed it right with his Canary Wharf involvement, making a large profit by selling when he did.

A Handful of Gems

From the moment he turned his eye seriously to the international market, in the early 1990s, Prince Alwaleed focused on opportunities that involved established brand names going through hard times.

Soon after the Citicorp venture, Alwaleed got his hands on 10 percent of the high-class New York fashion retailer Saks Fifth Avenue. That deal in 1993 cost him $100 million and gave him a piece of a top-class retailer. It was good for Saks, too, as the Prince opened up great opportunities for the company in major shopping areas in the Middle East, starting with a flagship store in the Saudi capital, Riyadh.

One deal that had less media attention but was significant came a year later in the Netherlands. Alwaleed had personally seen the growth potential of the Middle East's infrastructure, as well as in-

creased construction in other regions of the world. He himself
had benefited to the tune of tens of millions of dollars from construction contracts, so he sought to get a more formal foothold in
the construction industry and bought into the established European company Ballast Nedam. Based near Rotterdam, this company specializes in large-scale projects such as dams, bridges, land
reclamation, causeways, and stadium and arena structures. This
association came in handy when the Prince started to contract de-
velopers for various construction projects he undertook in both
the Middle East region and beyond.

Other core international investments during the 1990s included
the information technology sector. Alwaleed had concluded 1996
with a ten-day tour of the United States ostensibly looking at real
estate prospects, but while on the West Coast, he ended up having
a late-night meeting with Oracle's founder, Larry Ellison. At the
meeting in Ellison's home near San Francisco, the two billionaires
talked about the dot-com world, companies such as Netscape and
Microsoft, and the future of the Internet. Alwaleed, though someone who always utilized the benefits of technology to the full, was
not a hard-core "techie," but his business sense was tingling.

By March of 1997, he had quietly started to buy into Apple
Computers, as he conducted business from his office in Riyadh.
Ellison, unaware that the Prince was already picking up stock in
the company, tried to call him to ask whether or not he was interested in joining forces to launch a takeover bid for the ailing Apple. The Prince discreetly had his lawyers handle the call, avoiding
talking directly with Ellison, for fear of breaching U.S. regulations controlling insider trading.

Publications watching the deal reported that Alwaleed had
spent $115 million, picking up 6.23 million shares, giving him
about 5 percent of Apple, although, until now, the Prince has
never spoken publicly about the percentage of the company in his
hands. His initial 1997 deal was done at a time when the stock had

fallen to about $18 from almost $50 in mid-1995. By December 1999 the Prince had every reason to smile every time he read the papers and saw Apple shares up to $96. A profit of $500 million in only thirty months is enough to make anyone smile.

For his part, Ellison later commended the Prince for his smart decision to buy 5 percent of Apple back in 1997, pointing out that he himself had thought of buying control of the company and decided against it. Alwaleed had ended up as the biggest shareholder in the computer company.

On the media front, in the same year, the Prince targeted another big name he had been researching and closely watching.

Rupert Murdoch's News Corporation media empire was struggling around this time after a generally bad start to the 1990s, and Alwaleed saw the opportunity to buy into what he described as, "the only truly global media organization, with interest in nearly every country of the world." News Corp. certainly covers a lot, overseeing more than eight hundred companies of film production, press, editing and television, including top names like HarperCollins, FOX TV, Sky TV, STAR TV, and the respected British *Times* newspaper.

Alwaleed did his homework, then walked away with 5 percent of the company, paying $400 million for the limited preferred shares, making him the third-biggest shareholder in News Corp. after Murdoch and John Malone's Liberty Media. The Prince and Murdoch have developed a good working relationship, and the Australian-born media man appreciates the Saudi prince's direct manner: "We are very friendly. Our paths cross two or three times a year, and he is very outgoing, and very forthcoming with his opinions. As far as a shareholder is concerned he couldn't be more passive or more supportive."

Murdoch is grateful for the fact the Prince stuck with News Corp. through thick and thin after committing to it: "He certainly had a ride with us up and down and back up again and never sold a share."

In fact, in April 1999, the Prince boosted his News Corp. stake

with another $200 million, bringing the total up to $600 million.
Although Murdoch's media empire included major companies in
the United States, such as FOX TV, the Prince stayed away from
any direct investments in the U.S. media market. He said the
prices were too high, but to some degree, there was speculation
that he wasn't sure how an Arab investor would be received in an
industry treated with such sensitivity by Americans.

Alwaleed was also drawn to a couple of other brand names in the
tech sector that went through some ups and downs, which the
Prince had to ride out to see real returns.

His purchase in November 1997 of slightly less than 1 percent
in the giant cell-phone and electronics systems manufacturer, Motorola, at a cost of $287 million took a roller-coaster route over the
next two years. He bought in at $76 per share, watched it plunge to
$38 over the next twelve months, and then rocket back up in the
following year to $90, leaving him $82 million better off and
holding a $538 million stake in the wireless communications com-
pany. Subsequently, Motorala took some hits, leaving the Prince
around breakeven in 2004, according to his financial advisers.

Netscape also rode up and down after Alwaleed purchased 5
percent in the same month. He spent $146 million for four mil-
lion shares in the Internet company, which started to fall, until another dot-com stepped in. The announcement, a year later, by
America Online (AOL) that it was buying Netscape sent the stock
back up in November 1998. The next step in its fate came in January 2001, when the merger between AOL and media giant, Time
Warner, got an approval to go ahead. That deal, creating the
world's largest media-Internet company, named AOL Time
Warner, was completed in the spring of 1999, and the Prince's
Netscape holdings were exchanged for four million AOL Time
Warner shares, which went up to $600 million in value.

The Prince raised that investment in 2001 and 2002, by $540

million, bringing his total stake in the company to more than \$1 billion.

2. Noncore International Investments

The Prince admits he has made a few mistakes—indeed "blunders" to use his own word—in his international dealings, although defensively emphasizing that they had the impact of a "mosquito bite" on him financially. A hundred-million-dollar loss to the Prince is a very large number, but relative to his stated net worth of more than \$20 billion, it represents less than one-half percent of that worth.

However, the danger that comes with high-profile investments is that they receive high-profile media attention whether they succeed or fail, and the media, usually focusing on the negative, is always drawn toward the failures and gives them disproportionate coverage.

There were a couple of these, which the Prince has filed as "noncore" investments in his overall portfolio. One in particular, in all reality, is not a complete bust yet, but it surprised Wall Street at the time because it seemed to be folly in some experts' eyes, who believed it was doomed for failure.

The Prince had been carefully studying struggling blue-chip companies in the United States and Europe during the early 1990s, following his Citicorp deal, and saw that another American brand was in need of help, but this time far from the shores of the United States.

Le Wonderful World de Disney

Mickey Mouse was in trouble—or at least his French counterpart was.

After a grand opening in April 1992, Euro Disney's \$4 billion theme park at Val-de-Marne, just outside Paris, was struggling.

Disney's most ambitious resort project had seven hotels with five thousand rooms. World-class designers, such as Michael Graves, Robert Stern, even Frank Gehry, who had designed an entertainment village for the park, had been brought in to add a touch of class. The venture had kicked off with a relatively healthy ten million visitors in its first year, but it was burdened with heavy debts just as recession was kicking in. By the summer of 1994, it was more than the Parisian sun bringing a sweat to the brows of Euro Disney's bosses. There was $3 billion owing, and instead of the desperately needed crowds, all that came flooding in was criticism. Defensively, the company gave a host of reasons for the evident failure of the theme park, ranging from recession in Europe to anti-Americanism in France. Many believed the location, thirty-two kilometers (twenty miles) east of Paris, was to blame.

The idea of having a theme park in Europe had come up after the successful launch of a similar venture in Tokyo in 1983, but initially there was some confusion over where to place it. Spain, with its consistent, warm climate was considered, but the French, keen on securing the large number of jobs such an investment would create, went about making the conditions as favorable as possible to win the bid. The forty-four hundred acres of parkland now housing the site was sold at a discount, low-interest loans were provided, and it was agreed that the Paris metro train would be extended to the site.

Many people in Europe, however, felt the American bosses sitting at Disney headquarters in Burbank, California, had totally misjudged their market. For a start, the French, and most Europeans taking vacations, believe in long lunches, often up to two hours long, not the clinical but efficient conveyor-belt restaurant service that operates in most theme parks in the United States. Euro Disney's restaurants were not prepared for the crush, and flustered staff was left to handle large numbers of frustrated, overheated customers. Second, it may be a no-no to drink alcohol at lunchtime for Americans, but banning wine inside the park was a big mistake for the French, young and old, who enjoy a light tipple with their meal.

With the prospects of such a potentially unappealing experience awaiting at Val-de-Marne, few were inclined to leave the trendy street cafés of Paris.

From his own location in the desert, far removed from the lights of the Champs Élysées, the Desert Prince was busy planning his next move. Once again, over a weekend at his camp in the sands just outside Riyadh, Alwaleed was doing what he considers to be his clearest thinking. At the end of 1993, he had been approached by Steve Norris, one of the Wall Street financiers who had worked on the big Citicorp deal, and in their discussions, one particular brand name came up that got his attention. Disney. Norris had met with the American giant's chief financial officer, Richard Nanula, and was trying to connect the Prince's investment pool of money with the needs of Disney. Alwaleed looked into it, and all the pieces of the puzzle seemed to fit, so by the late spring of 1994, he summoned his then closest business adviser, Mustafa Al Hejailan. He told him that he had studied the Euro Disney situation carefully and saw no major issues that couldn't be resolved: "The problems weren't permanent. It wasn't that people hated Paris or the weather, or Disney. The problem was simple overleveraging. They just didn't have enough to cover the debt."

In addition, Alwaleed could see a positive future for the park for a number of reasons. First, the Euro Tunnel was opening, which he believed would encourage a flow of British holidaymakers across the channel to visit an attraction more or less identical to the one they loved so much in the United States, only much nearer. Second, the French train service was now stopping right outside the park, and third, the hotels were lowering their prices as an incentive.

He told Al Hejailan to get the ball rolling on a potentially large buy-in, and by June, negotiations were under way. Al Hejailan says it was the most difficult and complicated deal making he had

ever had to do. After sixteen days of intense and often heated discussions, the Prince managed to secure a tight agreement that involved a number of compromises on the part of Euro Disney and
the parent Walt Disney Corporation in the United States. Disney
had originally spent $100 million for a 49 percent stake of the new
publicly traded company—which was reduced to 39 percent following the deal—and had a complex arrangement guaranteeing it
regular income through royalty payments and management fees
for operating the park.

Using the park's desperate situation as leverage, the Prince and
his team managed to get the banks to forgo interest payments until 1997, possibly worth as much as $500 million in itself, and he
persuaded Disney to write off $70 million a year in royalties and
fees until at least 1999.

A satellite phone call was arranged between Disney's tough
boss, Michael Eisner, in California, and the Prince sitting by a fire
under the desert stars. It was described as a bit clumsy at first,
partly because they got disconnected a number of times, and to
some degree because Eisner could not figure out why he had to
use the protocol of calling Alwaleed "Your Royal Highness"; after
all, it's not an expression one gets to use regularly in Burbank.

Before long, with final adjustments, Alwaleed's $345 million
bought him a 24 percent stake in Euro Disney.

The media splashed all the regular clichés across the front
pages, mostly making references to Alwaleed being a "fairy story
prince" conducting a "fairy-style" rescue of the theme park that
was on the brink of bankruptcy.

Even minus the "fairy story" steed, the Prince was riding high
on the deal.

"Any investor who subscribes to Euro Disney at ten francs today (then 1.8 U.S. dollars) is going to be very happy in three to
five years," he declared, in his confident, bullish manner. The
Prince was looking long term, as usual.

A few cultural concessions were made by Disney. The top of
Sleeping Beauty's Castle, the landmark of Disney theme parks,

had its turret changed to resemble fifteenth-century French design, rather than the Bavarian look used at Disneyland in the United States. Plus, now, the French were allowed to reflect on such cultural joys with a glass of wine in hand. That did not appease all the critics, and fearing American influences were becoming too all-pervasive, one labeled Euro Disney a "cultural Chernobyl," while one British satirical magazine nicknamed it "Euro Drinkey" for serving alcohol.

For Disney, though, things seemed to be turning around and with tight management, new marketing, discounted tickets, and better-prepared dining venues, the company managed to show its first profit by 1995's second financial quarter, and Alwaleed had doubled his investment. By the end of the 1990s, the theme park had become one of Europe's most successful tourist attractions and had been renamed Disneyland Resort Paris. Encouraged, the American entertainment giant decided to build a second park outside Paris, based on the success they had witnessed with a multi-park strategy in the United States. The hope was that visitors would stay longer, eat more, and spend more money.

Walt Disney Studios opened in March 2002, just six months after the terrorist attacks of September 11. To everyone's dismay, it was back to square one—in particular, the serious problem of a lack of numbers attending. This time, Disney blamed other factors, including industrial action in France, which led to severe transportation problems as workers went on strike, then extreme weather conditions that made planning a trip uncomfortable or unpredictable. Plus, it wasn't long after that traffic from Asia petered out due to panic over SARS, severe acute respiratory syndrome, and Middle Eastern and American travel was curbed by the war on Iraq. Those looking a little more closely say the second venture was simply overpriced. The tickets cost the same, but instead of having forty-five attractions to visit, as in the original, there were only eight major features at Europe's Walt Disney Studios.

By 2004, the situation for the company had slumped again. Even a full decade after that initial 1994 rescue, with the Prince now owning a reduced 17 percent of the company, Euro Disney was struggling to service its debts in excess of $2 billion. It had seen the occasional surge in visitors, with a record-breaking 13.1 million in 2002, but it needed something closer to 16 million, and attendance figures did not seem to be on the rise.

Articles critical about the Prince's stubborn loyalty to the project can't seem to figure out why he persists. But he does: "Euro Disney is an investment that is more than worth it for me. It is the number one tourist attraction not only in France but also in Europe. Almost 13 million visitors come there every year, and it is a development that is way ahead of its age. Clearly there is an issue with the capital structure because it has too much debt on it. We have restructured once and we are on the verge of another restructuring with it. Euro Disney is a force and power to be reckoned with; its best days are yet to come."

For his part, Michael Eisner, Disney's long-standing boss, who has faced his own struggles for control of the parent company, is grateful for the Prince's backing: "He has been amazingly loyal, and it's not just that he said it to me personally, he said it in the press."

As it has proved to be one of his more questionable investments, at least according to the media, the Prince has looked for more support and guidance from the parent company in Burbank. Alwaleed invested the time in building his relationship with Disney's CEO over the years since the initial cash injection. Even though they are both direct men—Eisner is often described as abrasive and dictatorial—their communication is friendly. The Prince even proved to be a useful resource for Eisner at the turn of the new millennium, when there was a potential problem over the design of a pavilion at one of Disney's theme parks in the United States: "I have seen him quite a few times, and I would say that the most interesting (incident) was the unsolicited advice he (Alwaleed) gave me about this pavilion that we were building in Florida. It may not have been totally sensitive to the Arab world, it may not have been totally sensitive to the Israelis, and we had a mini diplomacy issue there. He was very, very helpful. He quickly called me and said, 'Let me explain what you have to do,' and then he explained to me what was necessary."

According to some reports, Alwaleed had been under pressure to intervene and use his contact at the top of the Disney empire to try to have the pavilion altered because, to the dismay and anger of the Arab world, it was planning to feature Jerusalem as the capital of Israel. The matter even went as far as The Arab League, which called a meeting at the United Nations to discuss boycotting Disney. Alwaleed said he was assured by Eisner that Disney had "no religion" and passed that message on to the Palestinian leader Yasser Arafat, adding that any Arab boycott of Disney would be seen as "Mickey Mouse." The Prince says that Arafat personally asked him to fix the problem, so he put in calls to a number of senior figures in the region, including the Arab League secretary, Egypt's foreign minister, to explain the situation, and finally diffused the tension.

The Prince also backed Eisner in January of 2004, as he became embroiled in a power struggle for control of the company he had headed for two decades. Roy Disney, the grandson of the company founder, Walt Disney, resigned from the board after a falling-out with Eisner, who held the position of both chairman and chief executive officer. The former board member then launched a campaign questioning Eisner's ability and tried to have him removed.

"I'm a friend and ally of Eisner's. I'm no Roy Disney," the Prince bellowed down the phone to a newspaper reporter who tracked him down during his vacation in Jackson Hole, Wyoming, in the United States, in that first month of 2004.

In the ensuing battle of the board, Eisner lost his chairmanship in March, but stayed on as chief executive officer, only to declare in September 2004 that he would be stepping down as the CEO at the expiration of his contract in 2006.

As 2004 came to a close, the future of Euro Disney was still hanging in the balance. The Prince mulled over a number of possibilities to revive its fortunes. Another cash bailout was possible, but the Prince would look for support from other investors, possibly even the French government, who would have to participate, even if indirectly, so as not to anger the French public over the use of any tax money. A better option was for Alwaleed to consider buying some of Disney's French hotels at a significant discount. That would give him some prime properties, fitting in perfectly with his hotel portfolio, and give him the opportunity to bring his Four Seasons and Fairmont brands to Disney's resort—a possibility he started debating with his hotel team.

In ten years, Alwaleed's original investment was down by nearly a third in value, but his optimism remained high. The way he saw it, "We faced crisis number one, now we have to face crisis number two."

Testing Deals

Prince Alwaleed had a few high-profile deals in the late 1990s that had very little impact on him financially but were substantially covered in the media.

The Prince's learning curve took a leap in April 1997 when, despite his successes in so many other areas, he made a business decision in April that was to bother him for years to come.

Alwaleed spent $57 million for a 4 percent stake in the Planet Hollywood restaurant chain linked to action movie stars such as Arnold Schwarzenegger, Sylvester Stallone, and Bruce Willis. As the stock tumbled, the Prince made a further commitment eighteen months later, in November of 1998, to buy another 16 percent of the company for $45 million, and then when the company said it needed more money for restructuring in August 1999, he put his hand into his pocket once again, only to witness Planet Hollywood file for bankruptcy a few months later, in time for Christmas. The star of Planet Hollywood had certainly faded, at a cost of around $80 million to Alwaleed from his total of $112 million invested for a 20 percent stake.

Alwaleed says he stood by the company because he believed in it, describing it as an excellent brand with great potential, with numerous untapped markets to explore. Planet Hollywood was a relatively low-cost investment for him, but a very high-profile global name that the media was keen to exploit.

The turn of the millennium was the last time that the Prince really steered away from his investment strategy of heavily researching a company, setting a price target, and then sitting and waiting until it is achieved.

By the turn of the millennium, *The Guinness Book of World Records 2000* listed Prince Alwaleed as the "Richest Businessman in Asia."

Not bad for a forty-five-year-old.

It was also the last time he spent a substantial amount of money investing in largely untried territory.

He put close to $2 billion on a selection of "old economy" and "new economy" stocks, including WorldCom and Priceline.com on one hand and Coca-Cola and Ford Motor Company on the other. It was a mixed bag, including some established blue-chip companies that had solid track records, and some shining stars of the Internet boom. The results were also a mixed bag.

Unfortunately, for the Prince, the biggest single amount was the $200 million on WorldCom, which went bankrupt in late 2002, and Priceline.com also sank with the dot-com sector collapse. The old economy purchases proved to be a good bet, however, and countered the new economy losses.

Alwaleed thinks of this particular investment spate as his "Millennium Bug," when he effectively strayed from his usual, rigid, long-term strategy of investing. There may have been an element of not wanting to miss out on the dot-com boom, which would explain why he put aside his meticulous research and investigation prior to committing his money.

On a relative scale, these investments were very small for a man who has a portfolio exceeding $20 billion. Over time, he gained in some and lost in others and learned a few lessons on the way.

A Debt Repaid

Although Alwaleed's diverse range of companies now included de facto investments in almost every corner of the globe, he had never really concentrated on East Asia.

That changed when he went on an investment mission to the Asian markets, just as the financial crisis there was erupting. While everyone else was shifting their capital out, stock markets were dropping rapidly, and currencies were collapsing, the Prince was traveling in the opposite direction to the panicked investors, declaring it would be the first of many investments to come in the region, as he had great confidence in it.

There was a little more to the story than people realized.

The Prince was particularly anxious to invest in Korea for reasons that went back to the start of his business career in the early 1980s.

When Alwaleed had returned to Riyadh from his studies in the United States, he was essentially an unknown player trying to secure business contracts. The first to give him a break were the Koreans, who were looking at a construction project in the Saudi capital. By giving him the chance to prove himself as an enthusiastic and particularly efficient liaison, the Korean contractors had essentially publicly validated Alwaleed's abilities.

As Asia struggled with its financial crisis in 1997 and 1998, Korea was in serious trouble, and the Prince realized that he could show, publicly, that he had confidence in the Koreans by making some high-profile investments there and elsewhere in Asia while he was focused on the region.

He started in early October by spending $50 million on Daewoo Corporation convertible bonds, securing him 5.9 percent of the Korean car manufacturer and conglomerate at a time when the

Korean economy was struggling. That stake was increased the following year to a total of 18 percent when he pledged another $100 million.

November saw him splashing out $46 million for a 3 percent stake in Malaysia's car manufacturer, Perusahaan Otomobile Nasional-Proton, and late in December, he bought 3 percent of Hotel Properties Ltd., a Singapore real estate development company controlled by local businessman Ong Beng Seng, who was a fellow shareholder in the ill-fated Planet Hollywood.

A couple of months later, he put up $50 million for Hyundai Motors convertible bonds.

By now, the business world was curious about the gung ho attitude the Prince had taken while investing in Asia. They were waiting to see whether he would prove to be a visionary and strategic investor, or go down in flames.

Alwaleed had obviously invested believing that Korea and other Asian economies would bounce back, which they did.

According to the Prince, by 2004, his Asian investments had proved to be a break-even venture. They were not quite the Eastern gold rush that some expected, but they left no visible dents in Alwaleed's bank account. Philosophically, the Prince says that, either way, he did achieve his objective of returning a favor to the Koreans . . . that it was a debt repaid.

Ill-Fated Deals

For several years, Alwaleed had been looking for a big deal in the tech sector. In April 1998, with a lot of media noise, Alwaleed invested $200 million to get 13.7 percent of Teledesic, a company set up by investors including cell-phone pioneer, Craig McCaw, Microsoft's Bill Gates, and aerospace giant Boeing. The Prince had discovered Teledesic through an article he had read a few months earlier in a business magazine, profiling the company's president, Russell Daggatt. The media speculated that as Alwaleed has always been obsessed with being connected globally, through phones, televisions, the Internet, faxes, and so on, this "Internet-in-the-sky," as it was dubbed, was the ideal investment for him. Teledesic announced it would be providing global Internet access, video conferencing, and computer networking through 288 low-orbit satellites. A year earlier, Boeing had paid $100 million for a 10 percent stake, meaning Alwaleed was paying a premium of 43 percent, but he argued it was still worth it and would be ideal as a service he could introduce into the Middle East as new and cutting-edge.

Telecoms industry analysts were not so sure, but it was the early days in this pioneering field, and Alwaleed wanted in. Unfortunately for the Prince, the analysts were proved right and the whole of that pioneering industry collapsed.

Media investments had proved successful for Alwaleed, particularly in the case of News Corp., but he stayed away from any direct investments in the U.S. media market, largely because he believed the prices were too high.

Instead, toward the end of 1999, he helped to broker a joint venture that was aimed at creating the first Pan-European TV network. With his 3 percent stake in Silvio Berlusconi's Mediaset in hand and a serious stake in News Corp., he agreed to buy 3.19 percent of Kirchmedia for $200 million. This amount was more than matched by Mediaset and boosted by an even bigger investment by News Corp.

Mediaset, Italy's number one commercial television company, would be teamed up with Germany's second-largest media company, owned by Bavarian magnate Leo Kirsch, pooling assets of more than a billion dollars.

It was an ill-fated marriage, as only two years later, in April of 2002, Leo Kirsch was forced to declare the bankruptcy of Kirchmedia, in which the Prince was already invested, and a month later, the collapse of Kirsch Pay TV, shortly after the Prince had parted with another $150 million or so to acquire 3.3 percent of it.

Not all the noncore investments were failures.

The Prince had promised to invest in Africa, and in 1998, he made good on that promise.

He took time out to tour sub-Saharan Africa and proposed investing $500 million there over a period of time. On subsequent visits to the continent, he continued to check very carefully to see what he was getting into, because he found there were some countries with great opportunities but investing in them needed patience and tough business practices to get them in order.

Through an initial public offering he bought a 10 percent equity stake in Senegal's national telecommunications operator, Sonatel, in which a French company had a 33 percent stake.

EcoBank, which was operating through branches in west Africa, also became a target for Alwaleed's investment plans on the continent, and he bought 10 percent of that financial institution.

Soon after, he became the biggest shareholder of the Nigerian United Bank for Africa by acquiring 13.7 percent. He rounded out his interests in Africa's financial sector a year later when he bought 14 percent of CAL Merchant Bank Limited in Ghana.

By 2004, his investments there totaled about $50 million total investment, although he continued to donate several times that amount to charitable causes in a number of African countries. Alwaleed was also in the process of creating an African fund management company and a joint-venture investment company to expand and institutionalize his investments in the region.

3. Saudi-Based Investments

Riyadh was still a boom town in the mid-1990s. It had stolen away some of the thunder from the large port town of Jeddah, which had been Saudi Arabia's main hub of business. Despite seeming more remote, and being in the middle of the desert,

Riyadh's climate was less humid and a lot kinder to the people, who were starting to settle there in large numbers. According to the government, the population had increased tenfold since the oil boom twenty years earlier in the mid-1970s. A few hundred thousand were now 3.5 million, and the Riyadh Development Authority estimated that figure would more than triple over the next twenty years. The Saudi Royal family's presence ensured it was the hub of power, not just the official capital city of the Kingdom.

Irrespective of his wanderings around the globe in the private jets he now possesses, Riyadh is home to Prince Alwaleed, and he has watched it grow, and he has grown along with it.

The Prince is proud to use Saudi Arabia, and its capital, as his base.

Riyadh is, to some degree, Alwaleed's town, where he has a lot of presence.

His Kingdom Holding Company is headquartered there and handles his Saudi-based investments, which actually cover not only the business he does in his home country, but also in the Middle East region.

These investments are effectively run as two subdivisions—privately held and publicly held. Both have been very successful for Alwaleed, particularly as the Saudi market has been booming solidly since the mid-1990s.

The privately held investments have largely been centered on the Prince's ambitious, high-profile Kingdom projects.

Building a Kingdom

Land and construction had played a major part in making Alwaleed rich and influential, and he still saw the potential for more. He had spotted a substantial tract of undeveloped land in the Olaya District, an area of the city that was fairly low-key commercially, being littered with only a handful of small shops selling anything from electrical appliances to ornaments. When he had first approached the owners about buying the land at the end of the 1980s, he had been taken aback by the asking price of 6,000 Saudi riyals ($1,600) per square meter—or $487 per square foot. Always on the hunt for a bargain, Alwaleed was willing to walk away. He kept an eye on it, though, and when things went haywire in Kuwait with the Iraqi invasion in 1990, he revisited the prospect of buying the land. Capital was flooding out of the country, as panicked Saudis and expats feared the Kingdom was next in line for an attack. The owners were now willing to part with the land for just 2,000 riyals ($533) per square meter—$162 per square foot. At a third of the original price, it was just right for the Prince.

"It's typical of us. If it's dirt cheap, we buy it," he reflects. "I always look for a weakness and then hammer the heck out of it."

And that's exactly what he did. Scooping up the vacant space, he decided to develop half of the site and held the rest for either future development or sale. He did eventually sell some of it off, as the price rocketed back up.

The crisis had served his purpose, and he had secured a bargain, but he looks back on the reaction of the landowner and is baffled: "What did they think—America was not going to defeat Saddam?!"

Based on the premise that Saudi is an ally of the United States, he took the calculated risk of committing to the purchase, believing, quite rightly, that America would take decisive action.

That land in the Olaya District is now the most expensive in Riyadh, and the site of one of Alwaleed's most ambitious projects. Thrusting out of the ground at 303 meters (994 feet), Kingdom Tower's cool, space-age monolith has transformed the capital's skyline. Riyadh is, otherwise, a 713-square-mile sprawl of very low-level, flat-topped, cream and white blocks. The city actually has strict local planning laws limiting the height of buildings to thirty occupied floors, and there are not even many of those. That would have limited the Prince's pride and joy to only 180 meters (590 feet) in height. Alwaleed rejected more than one hundred designs from international architects because none of them struck the right chord with him. He dismissed them all, and cleared away all the models they had sent in, which he had been forced to store on his basketball court at home because he had run out of space in his office.

Alwaleed then asked three companies specializing in skyscrapers to submit designs. When he saw the one from American designers Ellerbe Becket, he clutched the drawing to his chest and said, "This is my tower."

The original design was in stone and glass, but the Prince insisted that was too representative of old Arabian values, and he wanted something futuristic and forward-looking. He insisted on it being constructed entirely in glass and metal. The managing principal of the company, William Chilton, described the Prince as having a very critical eye, but the real ingenuity came in how he got around the planning regulations. If 180 meters of *occupied* floors was all he could have, then that is all he would have—but the rest of it would be empty. All 120 meters (394 feet) of it.

So the top third of the tower became a vacant metal frame, housing just the reflective glass that coats the whole building. The top fifth looks like the eye of a needle, or, according to a few commentators, a bottle opener. A "sky bridge" walkway runs along the very top, with a viewing deck that gives unparalleled views of Riyadh.

Back when the structure was being built in the late 1990s, Alwaleed joked that he had designed his tower with a cutout big enough to be able to fly his Boeing 727 through it. Any reference to such possibilities were soon hushed after September 11, 2001.

It is hard not to find the award-winning design of the Kingdom Tower very striking, and fortunately for those who conceived it, most people also consider it to be quite beautiful. It catches the light in remarkable ways depending on the time of day, often reflecting cloud formations as surreal patterns along its structure. At night, the softly lit necklace of the tower's cutout section, topped by the slim sky bridge, is visible for miles, slowly cycling through changing colors.

Alwaleed could not have found a more distinct landmark. In bright daylight, the broad monolithic needle made of glass and chrome looks like it has been planted there from outer space. Almost supporting that idea, the only other tall structure, the Al-Faisiliah tower is nearby, and looks like a space rocket. If aliens did ever land in the district of Olaya, they would have to see Prince Alwaleed about any prospective land deals.

As it is, the 1.7 billion Saudi riyal ($453 million) Kingdom Tower, and Kingdom Centre around the base of it, was not the only construction announced by Alwaleed in 1995.

He had grand plans to establish his company name across the city, and in the process make some more money. Four projects were announced around the same time.

Kingdom Centre and Tower served as the landmark project, and certainly the most visible. The design of the shopping center allowed a separate driveway for ladies to embark and disembark, with direct access to a floor exclusively for ladies shopping at certain times. This was necessary to conform to the cultural sensitivities in Saudi Arabia where single men and women rarely mix in public places.

At a cost of 400 million riyals ($107 million), Kingdom Hospital, modeled on the Mayo Clinic in the United States, would have some of the finest facilities in the country for the 120 beds in the first phase.

Kingdom School, a project costing 330 million riyals ($88 million), would compete with the top three private schools in Riyadh and serve the needs of four thousand fee-paying students at $5,350 per semester. Bemoaning the lack of English language and technology courses in the curriculum of national schools, the Prince decided that his school would actually emphasize these subjects. Alwaleed also pointed out that Riyadh's private schools were turning away five thousand to six thousand applicants a year due to lack of space, so there was great demand for a project such as his.

Finally, Kingdom City, a 400 million riyal ($107 million) residential compound starting with 333 units would offer modern high-end properties, with comprehensive community center facilities.

The Prince's relative holdings in the schemes were announced as 32.5 percent in Kingdom Centre, 39 percent in Kingdom City,

36.4 percent in Kingdom Hospital, and 30 percent in Kingdom School.

As these projects were just being announced publicly in 1995, Alwaleed was already planning how he would combine his brands. For example, Kingdom City, the school, and the hospital would be very close to one another, to create a minisuburb. Sixty-five percent of the properties at the housing compound were pre-let to major companies such as Ballast Nedam, and also to staff at Kingdom Hospital. The school would be ideal and convenient for the expats in Kingdom City, especially as they could afford to send their children there. The hospital would service their needs, too, as they don't have easy access to the public hospitals. On top of that, Apple Computers was called upon to supply the school with its equipment. Back downtown, the Prince had planned to involve two of his brands at Kingdom Centre. Four Seasons would manage a hotel located in the tower, and Saks Fifth Avenue would be the lynchpin of the high-end retailers located in the shopping center on the lower floors around it. The United Saudi Bank, of which the Prince was chairman at the time, was committed to office space in the Tower (although by the time the bank moved in, it had become the Saudi American Bank, SAMBA).

Like someone putting together a jigsaw, Prince Alwaleed was making his brands work together.

Expanding the Business Empire

Real estate was still very important to Alwaleed, and watching his hotel portfolio grow prompted the Prince to structure his strategy a little more formally, at least in the Middle East.

In March 2002, he set up the Kingdom Hotel Investment Group (KHI), with capital of $211 million, and a list of fourteen hotel properties either existing or under construction, worth a total of around $1 billion. As part of the expansion plan, Alwaleed traveled to Libya, strengthening his already good relationship with President Muammar Gaddafi by entering into a partnership to start a hotel group. The initial capital was worth an estimated $20 million, and the first project in the cards was to develop a Movenpick resort in Libya. The country's president was already looking to improve his international standing and wanted to end his isolation from Western business, thereby creating a massive investment potential in Libya.

Alwaleed's interest in Switzerland-based Movenpick had begun in October 1997. Having already bought into an American and a Canadian hotel group, the Prince had this European company in his sights. Movenpick lacked focus, as far as he was concerned, but fit perfectly into his plans to invest in a different range of hotel types. He wanted a brand that fit well with the full-service segment, but he didn't want to duplicate or compete with his existing holdings. He had the top brand in the luxury Four Seasons, and something close to that in Fairmont, so Movenpick provided him with a flexible brand that could range from three to five star, depending on the property and its location. Being small and aggressive, it was the ideal company to expand in the Middle East and Africa, because it could enter a variety of cities that might be ruled out by the luxury names.

He personally visited the majority shareholder of the chain, Baron von Finck, in Munich and Germany, and reportedly told him, "your brand is going nowhere."

Never one to beat around the bush, Alwaleed certainly had the attention of the German businessman, who after prolonged debate on the matter was convinced by the younger man's argument. As a sign of good faith, in signing the deal for 27 percent of the chain, Alwaleed also signed a contract to put a hotel in Beirut under Movenpick management.

Soon after, he kept to his word by buying 50 percent of the Meridien Hotel in the Lebanese capital and turning it into a Movenpick. He used the brand aggressively over the next few years, bringing the management group in to develop and run hotels in Saudi Arabia, Jordan, Egypt, Qatar, Morocco, Tunisia, and Libya. In 2003, Alwaleed raised his stake in Movenpick to 33 percent.

The Prince also spotted greater opportunities for growth of his other brands, the Four Seasons and Fairmont Hotels among them. He made good on his promise to push expansion aggressively for Four Seasons. A $70 million venture with the Arab Jordan Investment Bank was secured in order to develop the Four Seasons Amman, at a prime location in the Jordanian capital. Set on a small hill, with panoramic views of the city's sprawl, the luxury venue boasted 175 rooms and extensive restaurant and banqueting facilities.

Another big check that year secured him 50 percent of the Cairo Nile Plaza Complex, a high-end $300 million hospitality center that housed not only a Four Seasons, but luxury apartments, too. He also set his sights on establishing a Four Seasons resort in the popular coastal destination Sharm al-Sheikh, which happened $120 million later, in 2002.

Awaleed's media foray began while he was still in his mid-thirties.

During the Gulf War in 1990–1991, another Saudi billionaire, Sheik Saleh Kamel, about fifteen years senior to the Prince, was busy building a media empire. He was one of those who helped to create the Middle East Broadcasting Corporation, MBC, which was bought later by the brother-in-law of Saudi Arabia's King Fahd, Walid Al-Ibrahim. This prompted Saleh Kamel to team up with another of his countrymen who was eyeing the media market. By 1993, he and Prince Alwaleed had worked out a deal for the younger man to buy into his Arab Media Corporation, AMC, owned by his Dallah Al-Baraka Group. AMC controlled the Arab Radio and Television network, ART, headquartered just outside Rome, Italy. ART broadcast a bouquet of five channels catering to Arab viewers, from a 7,000-square-meter (75,347-square-foot) studio space,. The network had also acquired almost 50 percent of the Lebanese Broadcasting Corporation satellite channel, LBC-Sat.

Parting with $240 million dollars, the Prince took a 30 percent share of ART and became fairly active in overseeing parts of it. He was particularly interested in the network's music channel, and while supervising it, he enjoyed mixing with, and getting to know, the top singers and entertainers regularly featured on the station. Even at that time, Alwaleed started to indicate that this first foray into the media was the beginning of something much bigger down the line, which it did eventually prove to be, but for now, he watched as ART established itself as a regionally successful television network.

He did, however, plant footsteps in other areas of the industry over the next year or so, a significant one being the purchase of 100 percent of the Rotana Audiovisual Company. It was the largest recording label in Saudi Arabia, with most of the top Arab artists, around one hundred, on the books at the time.

As a progressive Saudi, particularly with his Lebanese background, the Prince was keen to break new ground with the media, but he had to watch out for issues that might conflict with local and regional sensibilities.

By 2002, his interest in Rotana was growing, metaphorically and literally, as he invested more money to increase his stake to 48 percent. By the following year, he made the step of taking 100 percent control of the label.

As it is, by 2003 he had become a little disgruntled with the lack of progress at the ART network and agreed on a deal with Sheik Saleh Kamel, whereby he could reduce his ART shareholding to only 5 percent, but take on the 49 percent of LBC-Sat, and convert ART Music to a new Arab-language music and entertainment channel fully under his control. Rotana Music Channel was then quickly developed as a twenty-four-hour, free-to-air service playing the latest clips from his Rotana artists. Once more, his brand synergy was at work. Based on the rapid success of the first music channel, within three months, there was Rotana 2, known as Rotana Clip, which added the unique feature of a Short Messaging Service (SMS) for viewers, via a system agreed with mobile phone networks. Just a matter of months after that, Rotana 3—Rotana Classical—provided classical Arabic music.

"My channel pays for itself with just these messages and advertising," the Prince declared, pointing to a screen that rapidly scrolled not just one, but two lines of short comments and affectionate remarks from Rotana viewers over the air to each other. Having the media bug, and working it so well, the Prince soon started planning a whole bouquet of specialized Rotana channels. A movie channel was up and running soon after Rotana 3, pushing him even closer to his target of six Rotana channels in total—for now.

Around the same time as his media investment in the region, Alwaleed was closely watching another Saudi company. By 1993, the Panda supermarkets in Riyadh were well known, but suffering severe annual losses. Buying up majority shares in the chain, he took over control and started to apply the same turnaround skills he had displayed at the United Saudi Commercial Bank in 1986. Alwaleed then noted that there was a synergy between his brand and its units, and those of another large chain, Al-Azizia supermarkets. He brought the two together in a merger and injected $267 million in capital he raised, creating Al-Azizia-Panda United Inc., APU, controlling 49 percent of the supermarkets in the country.

With the strength of the combined companies, Alwaleed realized there were still more steps he could take to develop the brand and the assets. APU invested in Herfy, a local fast-food chain that, with dozens of restaurants, dominated the market.

1995 remained a busy time for the Royal investor, who was getting his Kingdom company projects organized in Saudi Arabia and also planning the purchase of one of Saudi Arabia's largest companies. He did, in May of that year, take a majority holding in National Industrialisation Company (NIC), a joint-stock conglomerate with forty-five subsidiaries focused mostly on industrial projects. The Prince appointed a new board and a major restructuring of the company.

Then in March 1996, he invested $133 million—half a billion Saudi riyals—to set up the Al-Azizia Commercial Investment Company as a vehicle to handle real estate investments and stock exchange deals in Saudi Arabia.

By now he was developing a mantra that he would carry with him to other ventures: "mergers are the future."

So, by 1998, he was ready for another merger, the largest one to date in this sector, in Saudi Arabia. APU, which had come out of the first supermarket marriage he performed, now teamed up with the Savola Company, bringing together the Kingdom's two major food producers, into one entity, Savola-Azizia, or the Savola Group, as it became known. Alwaleed now controlled the largest food production and services conglomerate in Saudi Arabia.

Banking on Success

After frantic activity for nearly two decades, it seemed like the Prince was easing off big deals in 1999—until he created the biggest bank in the Persian Gulf region.

Two years earlier, he had taken steps in Saudi Arabia's banking sector, which continued to impress the financial community there. His huge success at bringing the United Saudi Commercial Bank (USCB) into profit had given him a good idea on how to turn around banking institutions, at least in Saudi Arabia. Monitoring USCB's competition in the market convinced him that rival Saudi Cairo Bank (SCB) was ripe for a merger, because it was struggling with an estimated $400 million in bad loans. From the deal that brought the USCB and SCB together, the United Saudi Bank—USB—was created.

Heading up USB, the Prince took time to monitor the competing, and more powerful, Saudi American Bank (SAMBA) and decided that it had an excellent management team. It was, he decided, the ideal candidate to merge with his bank.

In 1999, that is precisely what he did. USB came together with SAMBA, which, incidentally, had a history and connection with Citibank. In the 1970s, the old Citibank branch system had been partially nationalized, and Citibank retained a 30 percent stake in the new entity, as well as managing it.

The Prince had seen the percentage of his stake dilute with every merger, but he had seen massive returns on his initial investment by now and was proud of what he had achieved in an industry of which he initially had no comprehensive knowledge. The outcome of this second merger was that Saudi American Bank, known as SAMBA, kept its name, and Alwaleed volunteered to relinquish his position as chairman. He said at the time that he was more than happy to do so.

The diversity of his investments in the Middle East was serving Alwaleed well. He covered so many different industries, and he was getting good at making them interact to direct more returns back to his own financial pool. He now had massive stakes in key industries including real estate, construction, agriculture, food and agricultural projects, retail, and, of course, banking. Even though the size of the prize on the *world* stage was potentially much greater, Alwaleed did not stop investing in his national and regional markets in the Arab world. Still, there were some who feared that with his sights set on the multinationals the Prince might lose interest back home. That is dismissed by Maher Al Aujan, who managed the United Saudi Bank under the Prince in the late 1980s: "He had not given up on the Saudi business society, because he had invested in so many public-listed companies in Saudi Arabia. He invested in the retail business, in Azizia Panda, he invested in Savola, he invested in National Industrial Company, besides his private investments in the (Kingdom) Tower, in a school, Kingdom City and hospital, so it was a good allocation. He did not abandon Saudi at that time and did not reduce his exposure in Saudi."

Regionally, Egypt came onto the scene.

Alwaleed bought a hundred thousand hectares of land in Tushka, in the south of Egypt, near Aswan. That total area is bigger than Bahrain, Qatar, and thirteen other countries. Through his Kingdom Agricultural Development Company, KADCO, he was looking to initiate agricultural projects worth $500 million. According to Alwaleed, as an incentive and reward for resuscitating large areas of land, KADCO was provided with water and power free of charge, adding that it was a project that provided opportunities for thousands of Egyptians and was looking to serve Egypt. The Prince highlighted this as an example of a project that was not just agricultural, but also political, socioeconomic, and demographically influential, as it was aimed at providing a sustainable environment into which millions of Egyptians could move from the north delta. It was, says Alwaleed, a venture that brought together the strengths of the Egyptian government and private business.

During the summer of 1997, Alwaleed was quite focused on the Middle East. He had always supported the position of the Palestinian people, particularly having grown up around the homes of refugees during his childhood in Lebanon. He had developed a close relationship with Palestinian leader Yasser Arafat, but rather than getting embroiled in the politics, he was focused on the economic situation the Palestinians were facing as a result of their prolonged conflict with Israel.

July saw the debut of his Palestinian investments, with a $10 million stake in the Palestinian Investment and Development Company (PADICO), which has been engaged in development and construction projects in the West Bank and Gaza Strip.

He also cofounded the Jerusalem Development and Investment Company (JEDICO), to enforce and leverage the Palestin-

ian presence in the disputed city of Jerusalem, mostly through
housing and hospitality projects.

BLUNDERS—NOT MISTAKES

Being a catalyst in business becomes incredibly demanding for
someone spread across so many interests in so many countries.
One impact of the increased pace of his investing in the 1990s was
to push Alwaleed harder and harder, and to demand longer hours,
because as one market was closing, another across the world was
opening. Alwaleed's ability—and drive—to keep on going without
a break and little sleep served him well during this busy time. He
would almost crave the nighttime—not for rest, but for reading
time, so that he could focus on accumulating information and
catch up on international news.

If Alwaleed wasn't keeping himself busy enough with real estate, hospitality, the food industry, agriculture, and banking until
now, he was certainly about to increase the pace in 1997. He revealed that he logged more than two hundred fifty thousand miles
on his private jet during that year. Plus, with all the business he
was doing, Alwaleed says his phone bill was now in excess of
$80,000 per month. The thing is, when the Prince wants informa-
tion, he wants it now, any time of night or day (frequently night)
and in any location—on his private jet, on his yacht, or even in the
middle of the desert. If time is money, Alwaleed was certainly
making money by saving time.

But he was also stealing time from sleep periods and what
would be, to ordinary people, rest time.

His close cousin, Riad Assaad, who grew up with him in Beirut,
is not surprised to hear that Alwaleed often doesn't reach his bedroom until dawn: "It was always like this, always like this. I never
remember him sleeping more than five or six hours, never. This
was when he was young. I don't know about when he was in the
States, I don't know about Saudi Arabia, but when he was here . . .
super active. Super, super active!"

Issy Sharp, of the Four Seasons Hotels, also noticed this about Alwaleed from day one: "He's always had many things going at the same time, and that's what is most remarkable, the diversity of interests. But he has the ability to comprehend and retain that which he hears or reads. If he gets an article in a magazine, he will underline and send you it, and say you might be interested in some of this. He is what I call an excellent reader, meaning he quickly comprehends that which he is reading, and I think that's part of his brilliance, his ability to understand and then make his judgment."

Those who deal with him always describe Alwaleed as a strategic thinker, doing business like someone moving pieces around on a game board. The Prince's Saudi financial adviser for many years, Mustafa Al Hejailan, once remarked, "With the Prince, it's like playing Monopoly with real money."

It's an interesting analogy when one remembers the story of how competitively the Prince used to play Monopoly as a young man with his cousin Riad in Beirut.

As shown by his investments, both successes and failures, Alwaleed is willing to take risks in business: "Any investor has to be a risk taker, but he should be a prudent risk taker with calculating that risk. If you become too much of a risk taker, you become a gambler. I'm not a gambler; I'm a risk taker, a calculating risk taker, for sure."

For this reason, if nothing else, Mike Jensen believes it is wrong to assume that the Prince is a one-hit wonder with Citigroup and that nothing else worked out: "There have been mistakes, and critics are picking them up as they should, but there have been many major successes, any of which would have put him in the headlines again—they're just dwarfed by the Citigroup megasuccess. Canary Wharf was a major home run by any standards, and the same holds true for the News Corp. and hotel investments. These aren't seen because the actual amount he has in these companies is not publicly known, but he has done extraordinarily well."

The Prince points out that in nearly a quarter of a century, there have been many positive articles on his investments and business acumen, and, essentially, only one that was negative in its approach.

In assessing his performance in its critical and probing February 1999 article, the *Economist* magazine concluded that beyond Citigroup, most of Alwaleed's wealth has come from property deals, and it rated his stock market investing between 1992 and 1999 as below standard. In fact, it called him a "brilliant short-term property trader (who) has become an average long-term stock market investor."

Alwaleed, although originally upset by the magazine's assertions, is now philosophical about it. He says he clearly addressed these issues in a letter to the editor and had heard nothing else since from the publication. More important, he has seen his wealth growing consistently, pushing him up the *Forbes* list of the world's wealthiest.

The Prince finds it almost amusing to reflect on his losses. He remembers being interviewed by a journalist who asked him, "Do you ever make mistakes?"

He says he replied with a definitive, "No!"

When the journalist looked at him surprised and said, "Isn't that a bit arrogant?" Alwaleed replied, "No, I don't make mistakes . . . I make blunders! When I take a wrong turn in business, it's not a mistake—it's a blunder. Losing a hundred thousand or even a million dollars is a mistake. When I lose two or three hundred million—that's a blunder!"

LESSONS LEARNED

Blunders apart, Mike Jensen believes that success and failure are both important parts of the learning curve: "In the initial years there was talk of 'King Midas'—that everything he (Alwaleed) touches turns to gold, and I think now we've seen that that is not the case. He has had some failures, whether it's Planet Hollywood or Euro Disney—which is still an investment that's not up to par from the Prince's point of view. We do make mistakes, and I think the good news is he learns from his mistakes, really."

That learning curve was a part of the 1990s decade for Alwaleed. From an assessment point of view, Jensen sums it up as follows:

> Core investments, both international and regional—superb, excluding Euro Disney and Time Warner, which haven't yet come up to scratch, although Alwaleed believes they still have great potential.

> Noncore investments—overall mediocre and small, where a few hard hits are softened by successes in other areas and therefore have had little effect on the Prince's overall IRR (internal rate of return).

Also, Jensen points out, the Prince realized that his mistakes occurred mostly when he strayed from his otherwise firm strategy of researching major names in distress and stepping in only when the set target for buying in was reached. The venture into East Asia did not produce the high results he had hoped for, but Alwaleed came out even, if nothing else; in addition, he feels that he helped lift South Korea out of the doldrums.

Straying from the "buy and hold" road, it seems, is the only thing that led the Prince to wander into the desert of financial loss.

Alwaleed says that he is fortunate that he learned major lessons and was certainly not financially debilitated by his losses in any way. His lessons include:

1. Don't chase the market.

2. Don't make "good" investments. Be patient and make "extraordinarily attractive" investments. Be patient and buy really cheaply—or don't buy.

3. Have a strong preference for liquidity, especially on larger investments.

4. All investments should be at least 1 percent of the Prince's and his trusts' net worth. This way, they actually make a significant difference to the overall portfolio.

When hearing any criticism of the Prince's investment strategy, Citibank's boss, Sandy Weill, comes directly to the defense of his friend and biggest investor. He says, "You can't argue with the results." Even if he was lucky in the past, Alwaleed's current status speaks for itself: "I think luck is a very good thing to have, who cares how? What he did in the Citicorp investment, at the time, was a very big thing to do. But he's had a lot of big investments, he made a lot of money in Canary Wharf, his investment in Four Seasons Hotel is terrific. He has stayed with things like Apple, which has come back, and he has very good relationships with a lot of people. I mean everyone has to make some mistakes, you're not going to be a good investor unless you are willing to take risk and are willing to make a mistake, I mean no one is perfect."

Mike Jensen says the Prince is incredibly structured in his investment planning, and as a result has not only generated extraordinary wealth, but has also institutionalized his business and diversified both geographically and by industry. He adds that although Alwaleed's net worth and strategy were resilient enough to ride through the 1998 and 2000–2001 market storms and crashes, the Prince and his portfolio are even better prepared for the future.

Jensen does admit that the stubborn nature of Prince Alwaleed sometimes serves him well, and sometimes compromises his returns, but it is not a trait found in just the Prince: "If you look at the two most successful investors around—some would argue they are Warren Buffet and His Royal Highness—neither of them get out (of an investment) soon. Both of them, many people argue, are stubborn investors."

As it happens, the relationship between the world's two most powerful and influential investors gelled a little further in December of 1999. *Forbes Global* did an article entitled "Buffett: What Went Wrong?," questioning the investment skills of the "Alwaleed of America" and suggesting that he was not all that people made him out to be. Quick to his aid came the "Arabian Warren Buffett," who countered with a curt letter to the magazine that the article was narrow-minded and an unfair assessment. Alwaleed, himself more than familiar with probing questions and critical analysis, ended his note with the comment, "When all is said and done, Buffett is still great!"

The fax that landed on the Prince's desk a couple of days later had the Berkshire Hathaway Inc. letterhead and started with the line, "You're terrific!"

Omaha's investment guru expressed his gratitude to the Prince for coming to his defence so publicly and promised, "If the press ever takes you on in Saudi Arabia—which I sincerely doubt—call on me to reciprocate."

Even billionaires appreciate friends.

CHAPTER 8

Family Time

*I was on a jet ski and I did one of those stupid moves. . . . I
ended up crushing my skull and paralyzing my right side.*

—PRINCE KHALED BIN ALWALEED BIN TALAL ALSAUD,
THE SON OF PRINCE ALWALEED BIN TALAL

Whats the best thing about being a princess?"

Princess Reem answers without a pause: "Nothing!"

Then a moment of reflection, and a glimpse of mischief on her
elfin face.

"Well, when I wear a T-shirt that says 'I'm a Princess' . . . it's
true!"

Then what's the worst thing about being a princess?

"I don't get a single moment to myself. The only time I'm
alone is when I go to the toilet."

Reem looks a little glum as she says it, but then her usual demure elegance sets in. Even to the casual observer unaware of her
actual regal status, the twenty-one-year-old would still appear unusually composed and somehow beyond her years. Her quiet disposition reflects her tendency to be someone who thinks a lot and
says only what needs to be said. Her angular, slim, and strikingly
beautiful face is topped with large, almond-shaped eyes that are
very dark and intense, and almost secretive. For someone like her,

so private and poised, to be surrounded by people constantly, particularly the impersonal presence of security, steals her peace of mind: "It's like you have eyes always on you, bodyguards always around. It's hard to have a normal personal life, like a family life. We do have it, but it's around other people."

Reem then pauses and reflects for a while on the fact that it is the price she has to pay for who she is and the privileges she is granted. She says that she is willing to accept that price.

Then, aware that she might have given away too much in her answers, she changes the subject with a crafty smile, and begins talking about her father, who is seated next to her.

It is a bright and comfortably warm August day in 2003, and the narrow pavements of the Cannes seafront are playing host to a stream of idle pedestrians casually strolling up and down, mostly trying to spot famous faces in the open café terraces. As there's a rather healthy dose of visitors from the Middle East in the parade, the occasional hushed mumble is heard as people notice the Prince. It's usually just one word: "Alwaleed."

In the Arab world, everyone knows who is being referred to when someone says "Alwaleed." Every summer, Alwaleed takes his holiday in that particular part of the Côte d'Azur, along with half of the Arab elite who have been patronizing these shores for decades.

The Prince and his entourage have appropriated the front section of a café, leaving little room for others, as the party consists of more than thirty people. Alwaleed and his daughter sit in the center of a long group of narrow tables, pulled together to fit about ten people on either side. The remaining dozen or so take smaller tables placed in satellite positions around the main one.

Keeping the subject off herself, Reem reveals how her father will always move anything placed in front of him at a dining table to the sides. He does this subconsciously, says Reem, indicating that she will be proved right very shortly. Her cheeky humor kicks in.

"Let's see how long it takes for him to move this lot," she says, pointing to her wristwatch, and then to the silverware, condi-

ments, napkins, and glasses that the waitress had just been placing
directly in front of the Prince. When he turns toward her, she
looks away wearing a mock-innocent expression, while waiting for
him to return to his conversation with one of his advisers sitting
on the other side. As soon as he's back into his debate, she glances
at her watch to begin the timing.

Knowing her father as well as she does, she grins as the transfer
of plates, knives, forks, and beverages begins and is completed in
less than thirty seconds, as an animated Alwaleed distractedly
starts pushing items to the periphery, in between emphasizing
points he is making with his hands.

Game over. Reem smirks. That was too easy.

Before she can start highlighting another quirky habit of her
father, the food starts arriving. A wide variety of salads start filling
up the blank spaces on the white tablecloth. Alwaleed grabs the
first two items nearest him, scoops a mouthful of each with a
spoon, pauses for a moment to reflect on the taste, and then distractedly pushes the dishes to the side . . . in front of his daughter.
Reem glances around at those who had witnessed her prediction
earlier, as if to say, "See!?"

Two–nil.

Suzan and Nahla, her two assistants—each a modern-day
equivalent to a "lady-in-waiting"—both smile quietly. They have
come to know the Princess very well, and despite being in her employ, have a low-key and mature friendship that lends its support
whenever Reem needs it. Here, they were amused by something
they have witnessed a hundred times but have rarely heard the
young Princess comment on publicly.

It is the closeness between Alwaleed and his children that allows them to be able to joke around in such a way. The Prince
feels that he has been able to build up a trust by allowing the interaction between them to be relaxed and mature: "It is very important for me to have a very close relationship with my son and
daughter. It is really based on friendship now, because they are
both over twenty. I give them a lot of discretion to do what they

want to do, because I think they have the basic foundation that I built in the relationship with them over the last two decades."

In contrast, he says, his childhood was different because of the lack of continuity and the distance he sometimes felt from his father. He spent the early part of his youth shuttling back and forth between his mother's house in Beirut, Lebanon, and his father's in the Saudi capital, Riyadh: "My relationship with my mother and father was also good, but I was left alone to handle my own business. I went to the United States when I was very young also, so I think my father's policy with me was to have a laissez-faire situation, whereby I used to depend on myself a lot."

But one thing Alwaleed feels that he did learn from the time he got to spend with Prince Talal was the value of religion in teaching and enforcing a moral code in young people: "If you give them the basics of integrity, of ethics, of high morals, and you instill these into them, then they can function well, and I think this has been happening so far."

THE LITTLE PRINCESS

Reem carries a lot of latent energy that remains subdued in the presence of her father. Partly out of respect, and equally because she has been brought up to be poised, the Princess generally remains demure in front of Prince Alwaleed. He, on the other hand, turns to her at regular periods throughout the lunch, to joke, ask questions, and make comments, eliciting mostly nods and the occasional soft reply from his daughter.

Reem has a very close relationship with her father and sits beside him with a visible sense of security and comfort: "He's an amazing father. He's very close to my brother and I. We talk to each other very openly and there are no barriers, nothing. Sometimes it's hard to think about it, I mean, him being very busy, you know, loads of things to do, but he actually has time for his family and he just gives a lot to us."

Alwaleed does actually make it a point to have lunch with his children every day if possible. Lunch, it should be pointed out, is usually between 5 P.M. and 7 P.M. Apart from when they were traveling or studying overseas, both Reem and her brother, Khaled, would be at the table daily, in time to eat with their father.

Sure enough, just as everyone is in the middle of the starters, Prince Khaled shows up with his small entourage. They had been running late shopping in town. Khaled walks up to his father, pays his respects and apologizes for the delay in his arrival, and then settles at a separate table nearby with his guys, rather than sit at the main table with his father. It's something he does from time to time, and more as a sign of his growing up and being a little more independent as a young man in his midtwenties—he had actually just turned twenty-five in 2003. Still, the closeness of the relationship he has with his father is evident, and he puts that down to good communication: "The quality I like the most about him is listening. He is an extremely good listener; he may not show it, but he is an extremely good listener. He'd be looking somewhere else, and he'd still be talking, so you'd think, 'He's not listening to me,' but at the end of the day he even noticed your cough, your hiccup . . . he got it. Caring is definitely an important aspect, and I mean, the values that he showed us in life. There is respect for the elders, there is respect for the family members, there is Islam. He basically taught me everything. When I was a kid, I'd pray next to him, and then we'd go to lunch; it was never lunch first and then that (the prayers). He's a perfect example for me."

It was Reem who got her father hooked on sending SMS (Short Messaging Service) messages on his mobile phone, by showing him how convenient it was for quick and brief communication and generally for staying in touch without having to make an actual call. Until 2004, the Prince rarely carried a mobile on his person, simply calling on his communications manager to hand him one when he needed it. Once he got the texting bug, he would fold his clamshell-style Motorola phone over his belt and keep it with him, frequently flipping it open to start messaging or answering messages he had received—often from his daughter and son.

It would have been unusual prior to this to see Alwaleed sitting hunched over his mobile, smiling to himself as he got absorbed in SMS conversations. Texting is something he has come to enjoy wholeheartedly.

It is hard for many people to reconcile the notion of the tough, aggressive businessman who has achieved so much in twenty-five years with the idea of a warm and gentle father figure who remains so devoted to his offspring, but, in actual fact, Alwaleed is constantly concerned about the day-to-day welfare of his children. It has to be seen to be believed.

He is also somewhat careful that his daughter is not too exposed to the media. That largely comes from respect for Saudi culture, where there is extreme sensitivity to women being photographed and filmed, and it is something he keeps an eye on for all the women around him, including his mother and sister. Having said that, he says ultimately the choice is theirs.

The year 2004 marked a turning point where he positioned himself as a champion for women's rights and freedoms in the Saudi Kingdom, saying there is no reason why the increasing number of women who work for him should not be free to talk to the media on their areas of expertise. He does check with them first, in case they do have traditional sensitivity to that kind of exposure.

Alwaleed's family is central to his life. Of course, with huge financial resources at his disposal, the Prince is able to make sure that he can conduct his business around family events, or the other way around. The main thing is that he meticulously ensures it happens by managing a tight timetable. On Reem's twenty-first birthday, just a couple of months earlier, in June, the Prince flew into Pisa, Italy, and drove his entire group in a bus to Florence, to visit his daughter, who was on an extended trip to the city as part of her college studies. Alwaleed had built the final leg of his business trip to allow him to visit Reem actually *on* her birthday, before returning to Riyadh.

Even though the Princess knew he was coming to see her, the excitement was visible on her face as he walked into the hotel at exactly midnight, smiling to himself about the precise timing, to wish her a happy birthday. The setting was reminiscent of a moody, but romantic Italian movie. It was a beautifully ornate, old hotel, overflowing with character, located in the center of Florence, and the Prince joined Reem and her handful of friends in the building's tiled courtyard, near a tall, well-lit fountain. Beautifully chic young people were milling around in the background, near the bar, including the actor Adrian Brody, who had just received accolades for his performance in the hit movie *The Pianist*.

Alwaleed sat and joked with his daughter and gave her a birthday present of an expensive watch he had selected during a stopover in London the day before. She seemed to appreciate him taking the trouble to travel all the way over to see her, if even for just a couple of hours. The young woman's school friends seemed equally excited at meeting the legendary Alwaleed, and Reem reveled in this, too.

Knowing her father's strong drive and commitment to manage his business interests, she still finds it surprising and a little amusing that he will break off from what he is doing across the other side of the world, just to get some time together with her: "I remember six or seven years ago, I was still going to high school and my dad came back late from Uncle Abdullah's farm (the Saudi Crown Prince). He came in at 7 A.M. and I'd just woken up to go to school, so he's like, 'Oh you're going to school, what time?' and blah, blah, blah. Anyway, he says that he's going to take me to school—for the first time. I was so excited, you know, 'My dad is taking me to school!' "

Reem goes on to relate how, when they got in the car, the Prince covered his face by wrapping his traditional Arabian headdress around it, leaving only the sunglasses showing, in the hope that no one would recognize him. At the school, the system was such that cars bringing students had to drive in to a drop-off lane, allow the student to disembark, but then move on rapidly, allowing the next car to move in and do the same, keeping a smooth flow going. As Reem recalls it, her father was too preoccupied with his daughter: "I was walking toward the gate and I look behind me and the car is still there, so I just walk a little more and I look behind me, and he is still there. So I wave to him and he waves back and he is still there. I get into the gate and I peep outside and I still see his car standing there, so then he opens the window and waves, and he makes sure I'm really in there. I'm like, 'There's 200 cars waiting behind you!' but he just had to make sure I was in. I thought that was funny, but what was really fun was, all my friends were like, so excited about it, and they didn't really believe that my dad would take me to school."

A secret the Princess has confessed is that she has a birthday gift in mind, but feels a little strange asking her father for it. Instead of a material gift, she wants him to take her out on her birthday to Pizza Hut and have a simple and quiet dinner with her there. He certainly does not seem to be snobbish about such ideas and has often succumbed to the requests of his entourage when they want to stop at McDonald's or other fast-food places, although he himself gave up eating any kind of fried foods a long time ago. Until now, however, the Princess had not got around to asking for that particular gift.

Ironically, as her father finally got up to leave the hotel in Florence on Reem's twenty-first birthday, he might have reflected on the fact that he had come to see his daughter in the land that can genuinely claim to be the home of the pizza.

BOYS WILL BE BOYS

The south of France is looking a little tatty according to its critics.

The original charm of an exclusive, elite, and well-maintained resort has given way to hoards of people parading themselves, or sometimes their expensive cars and accessories, in a congested mass on the seafront. Many of the hotels and cafés look like they've seen better days, and forgotten them. The voice of the genuinely chic is drowned out by the mediocrity of new, upstart designer labels.

For someone like Prince Alwaleed, who can go literally any-where in the world for his vacations, there is something of a mys-tery as to why he continues his regular jaunts to Cannes, St. Tropez, and the neighboring resorts. For a couple of weeks every August, the Prince's yacht moors off the coast at Cannes, and he commutes between the vessel and the shore daily. The area cer-tainly holds many memories for Alwaleed, going back to the early days when he was taken there on summer holidays with his father, for a rare chance to spend some quality time with a man he ad-mired and quietly respected.

He might want to reminisce about his childhood days there on the beach, but there is one trip—the summer of 1993—the Prince would rather forget. His personal physician, on the other hand, remembers it quite clearly. Dr. Jihad Aoukal has been with Al-waleed since the Prince was in his late twenties: "In St. Tropez we heard an ambulance passing by, and I swear to God he (Alwaleed) said, 'God forbid that someone has had an accident or something.' Ten minutes later, I had a phone call from the captain of the boat telling me that Prince Khaled had a jet ski accident, and that he is on the shore at St. Tropez now. So I told the Prince, 'Your High-ness, Prince Khaled has had an accident.' We went over there, and saw Prince Khaled on a stretcher, and he said "I can't move my arm, I can't move my leg.'"

Alwaleed's close friend from California, Chuck Gulan, was also visiting the Royal on his vacation when the fifteen-year-old prince had the accident: "It was very dramatic. We got down to the beach and got out of the car, and at that point they were bringing Prince Khaled up on a makeshift stretcher. Khaled was lying there in no pain and kinda like smiling, but he was all bloody. It was a close deal and Prince Alwaleed said it could have gone either way. We were together in the (hospital) room and I told him don't worry, God will look over your son and look over you and everything will be fine. It was a very, very close—millimeters away from death."

It is hard to imagine such a close call for Khaled, who stands just a little taller than his father, but sports a stockier, more sturdy frame from his early interest in sports. Khaled's handsome and gentle face is broader than his sister's, and he is more prone to grinning and laughing with the inherent mischief of a college boy, throwing high fives, donning hip, baggy clothing when not in a traditional Saudi thobe, and displaying elements of the American "dude" culture. Even his small goatee and moustache resemble youth of the West, though they are kept more out of respect for Islamic values, which recommend that a man should maintain at least some facial hair. For all intents and purposes, Khaled could pass for any other young American, down to the accent, and his love of the American Dallas Cowboys football team. (He used to like the San Francisco 49ers, but transferred his loyalties when his favorite player, Deion Sanders, moved from the 49ers to the Cowboys.) Look a little deeper, and you will see a very kindhearted and gentle fellow with strong cultural values, who carefully balances the strict demands of being a prince from the Saudi Royal family and the magnetic pull of a free and expressive Western lifestyle.

His good nature is evident on first meeting with him, where his genuine, warm smile is offered generously, and his philosophical attitude to life is clear when he talks about the accident he had when he was fifteen. Although left with a slight limp and a handful of scars on his scalp, he laughs about it now: "I was on a jet ski, and I did one of those stupid moves, which had worked pretty well before. I don't know why it didn't this time, but anyway I ended up crushing my skull and paralyzing my right side, and I ended up in the water. One of my friends got me out of the water and got me into the boat. My sister was the first person who saw me when I came out of the water with blood on my face and everything, you know, not a pretty sight. She saw me, and she was freaked obviously. She went berserk."

Reem shudders at the recollection: "Yeah, I saw him; he was unconscious in the water for quite a while, and I just went crazy. I couldn't believe what I saw, and they (friends) just talked to me and got me back to the boat. He had a white T-shirt on, which made things worse; blood was all over it. I couldn't think for a couple of hours. It's a miracle that he's . . . ."

She pauses, disturbed at the thought of how terribly things might have worked out.

Although it was simply an accident, Reem feels guilty and blames herself to some extent for what happened to Khaled: "I got on his jet ski and I told him to just go fast, and that I would jump off, and that's what happened. So he thought to himself, 'If my little sister could do that, I should do it in a crazier way.' So he gets on his jet ski, zooms so fast and he wanted to jump into the water headfirst. By the time he was standing on the jet ski and had jumped into the water, the jet ski went a little slower, so his head bumped into the back handle of the jet ski."

At the time Khaled didn't know the severity of the accident and found himself trying to calm his family down, even though *he* was the injured one. He couldn't move his right side as they dragged him to the shore at St. Tropez. After about ten minutes, the sensation in his hand started to come back, but his leg was still paralyzed. He was rushed to the local hospital with his parents in tow, along with Jihad, the family physician. The local doctor who examined the injured prince said that the facilities at St. Tropez were not adequate and that Khaled needed to go to Marseilles or Paris where he could get better treatment. Alwaleed, distressed at seeing his son on a stretcher, covered in blood, contemplated the idea of rushing his son to specialists in the United States, but was told that there was no time to delay as the boy had a fractured skull. Alwaleed told Jihad to go back to the yacht to get a small suitcase of clothing prepared, as he was going to take his son to Hospital de la Timone at Marseilles, by helicopter.

Khaled's mother, Princess Dalal, was back on the yacht, and Alwaleed instructed the doctor not to tell her the full extent of the injury yet: "I went back to the boat and his (Khaled's) mother was having some of her relatives visiting. He (Alwaleed) had told me not to worry Prince Khaled's mother because the boat would take twelve hours to reach Marseilles. I said 'Your Highness, it's okay, we're going to take him to Marseilles, it's a small accident.'

I took the Prince's things and I went by car, four hours driving, to Marseilles."

There he found the worried Alwaleed beside his son's hospital bed. In a quiet moment, the Prince turned to his physician and asked if he thought Khaled would walk again. Jihad said he would, if it was God's wish.

Khaled later learned the extent of the damage he had suffered: "The injury was a concussion and a crushed skull, (a piece of) which basically landed on my brain and did some nerve damage, to the extent that it paralyzed my right side through the left part of the brain. My leg was paralyzed for, I think, a week, then I had an operation. I was blessed, my father prayed for me. My mother didn't know about the operation, the severity of the operation until the day after. My dad told her after I came out of the surgery."

Reem feels that her father had to carry a heavy burden, keeping the possible risks from his wife, and planning what to do by himself: "He made a very big decision, because there was a doctor there saying he had to do this operation. He didn't even ask my mum, he just made the decision. He said, 'Just put him into surgery, just do it,' and he acted very strongly. It was a terrible time . . ."

Alwaleed said he couldn't imagine his son not being able to walk and remaining wheelchair-bound. He then spent the early hours of the morning praying.

Chuck witnessed the extent of the Prince's focus: "Nothing else mattered, that's where he stayed, and that's where his concentration went, and I am sure he talked to God and asked for help for him and his son. I mean he was a scared person at that time."

After a while, Jihad took over the vigil and spent a full week with Khaled, as Alwaleed came in and out daily. Local surgeons had operated on the young prince to the best of their ability, but Alwaleed wanted his son examined by specialists from around the world. He instructed his doctor to contact a number of physicians in different countries: "We got two from Germany, six from

Britain, and about four or five from the States. Most of them said he will never walk again. One doctor, Joseph Malone, from Pittsburgh—a neurosurgeon—examined Prince Khaled, and said, 'Your Highness, it is 95 percent you will walk again.'"

It was a tough rehabilitation for the teenager at first. For the first ten days after the operation, he still could not move his right foot. It seemed like an eternity, and his optimism was fading, but the two physiotherapists assigned to help him persisted.

Reem lent her support to her brother and feels that the strength of his willpower helped the recovery: "All the doctors said, there's no way he'd walk, there's no way things will get back to normal, but he just thought about it, 'Oh, my God, how? I won't be able to play football, no walking, no nothing,' so he just put it in his head and actually, a couple of months after that, he was better than before. He started working out and he really, really put lots of effort into it (recovery)."

Jihad, who spent twenty days nonstop at Khaled's bedside, got to break the news to Alwaleed that his son was making progress, that there was hope for a full recovery: "During the physiotherapy, I was with them sitting, and he moved his toe. I jumped up and I went straight to the Prince, who was in a big meeting, but I went inside, and said, 'Your Highness, Prince Khaled moved a toe,' and he said 'Thank God,' because they told us if he moved his toe, he would move other toes and he will walk again."

Alwaleed and his entourage decamped and moved on to Paris, as they normally do each year from the south of France, taking with them a full-time physiotherapist to work with the injured prince. Even once the family returned to Riyadh, Alwaleed hired a physiotherapist to spend a whole year with his son.

BUILDING BONDS

One noticeable outcome of the accident for most of the family and close friends was that it showed them a soft side to Prince Alwaleed. Priding himself on not showing reactions during business dealings, the Prince has learned to keep a straight face during even the most challenging situations.

When his son took his first steps after the accident that had paralyzed his right leg, the emotion was too great for Alwaleed. The bonds between the father and son strengthened, and Khaled, being a natural optimist, certainly sees a positive outcome: "Ironically, the best thing that ever happened to me was that (accident). I know the value of life, I value life more, I'm much closer to my family, I'm much closer to myself. I know the value of a tear—that my dad teared up, and it was the first time I'd seen my dad cry. I remember it like yesterday. The first time I walked—and I had a cane—I saw my dad walking away and I thought why is my dad walking away? He went just behind the corridor, and just held his head down, and he cried."

Khaled was shocked because even though he had an open and trusting relationship with his father, he had never felt it as a particularly soft one, especially as he was aware how much his father hated to let other people witness him displaying any reaction, particularly an emotional one: "After I saw that—I've never seen my dad cry before—that was a breakthrough for me. I was like, 'Oh my God, my dad's human,' you know, by the way he's emotional, he actually cried for me—oh my God.' So I got very close to my father and my mother. My mother and father showed me a lot of love and affection, and they pretty much gave me the pump that I needed to just start walking again, which I did, thank God."

The incident also took Khaled's relationship with his sister to another level, especially as she had witnessed the horrible sequence of events: "After he had his accident, that was when we really got close, and we really looked at life as something that we really have to live every day and not just do things that waste it."

Fortunately, they were already quite close, as both Alwaleed and Dalal had made sure their divorce did not adversely impact either the relationship between them and the children, or between the children themselves. The parents encouraged the youngsters to spend time with them both and kept open a line of communication that showed the children there was no anger or ill-feeling. They weren't forced to take sides or show more loyalty to one parent or the other.

Reem believes that was crucial in helping to build the bond between brother and sister: "One thing is very surprising . . . we were never jealous of each other. I mean, to have two kids—just the two of us—one of us could be jealous of the other, but my parents always treated us the same, equally . . . we were like rascals."

Watching from the sidelines as Khaled slowly recovered, Chuck says that he could see Alwaleed was determined to get past this difficult experience and get the family back to normal. He says the Prince made it his goal to bring his son back to full strength and ability following such a traumatic experience: "After all this was over, he did everything in this world to regenerate him (Khaled) and get him back to what he was—and that's where he is today."

MARRIED TO WORK

Alwaleed's ability to focus on his son's needs at a time of trouble answers the critics who say he cares about nothing but his work. His devotion to his children manifests itself in his paying constant attention to his timetable to make sure they all have time together wherever possible.

In retrospect, the Prince's relationship with Khaled and Reem has been far more successful than his marriages.

Marrying Princess Dalal in 1976, when he was only just turning twenty, meant that his children were born while he was still a very young man. Now, as Alwaleed approaches his half-century, Khaled and Reem are adults in their twenties and mature enough to have developed a friendship with him. On the other hand, his relationship with Dalal, who is also his cousin, and a couple of years older than him, gradually suffered over the next eighteen years or so, but Alwaleed refutes that his first marriage failed because he was too young when he committed to it: "Not necessarily, because I stayed with her quite a bit of time, and we had a very good time in America and a very good time when I came back to Saudi Arabia. I do not think it was because I married when I was young. Actually, it helped me a lot when I got to the United States, because I married her one semester after I got into the university, so it helped me stabilize a lot, and be more home- and family-oriented."

The Prince also points out that as a young couple they were very supportive of each other. When he was determined to prove himself as a self-starting businessman, despite his Royal background and connections, his wife was behind him. Alwaleed remembers that he was touched by a gesture Dalal made four years into their marriage, as his company funds were running low. He was stubborn, and not inclined to request or accept any assistance from his rich relatives, so she sold a valuable necklace that she had been given as a gift, in order to provide her husband with some cash.

Alwaleed wags a finger of respect for her as he recalls that the exquisite necklace had been worth nearly a million riyals (around $300,000 then), but she had not hesitated in parting with it to help him. He smiles when he adds that, as his fortunes changed, he took great pleasure in replacing the necklace for her with a jewelry set worth twice as much.

Looking back on his relationship with Dalal, Alwaleed says that she added a lot of stability to his life and helped his maturity curve upward rapidly, but he remains fairly tight-lipped about the reasons for their divorce, saying that "sometimes, there are secrets that remain between man and wife."

Princess Reem describes how she sees her parents differing in character, and how her mother approaches life: "Stubborn and strong, she really looks a lot to the future. She really treats us like her friends, I mean she's not like an ordinary mother, like 'do this, do that,' you know, stuff like that."

Dalal's more random lifestyle obviously contrasts to the finely managed daily routine employed by Alwaleed: "My father's very systematic and he plans everything in advance. I'm sure he has to

do that for who he is, but my mother's different in that way. She
doesn't really like to do things like that, she doesn't like planning
things, she doesn't like to have everything so perfect; she just likes
to live life easily." Alwaleed says he believes that was not a factor in
why they ended up parting ways.

Chuck Gulan, whom the Prince befriended soon after moving
to the United States for his studies, was there to witness the early
days of the Prince's marriage. He saw the young couple building a
life together and coping with the difficulties of being in a very different culture from what they were used to at home in the Middle
East. From what he could see, Alwaleed and Dalal were pretty devoted to each other. Chuck remembers how he received a call at
home early one morning from the Prince, who urged him to head
over as quickly as possible. The large, jolly Californian sped to the
house, and as he pulled into the Prince's driveway, he noticed Alwaleed standing on the porch steps. He had called Chuck over, excited over the news of a medical test result the couple was
anticipating: "They got the notification that she was pregnant. Oh
my, he was just happy! And then when he (Khaled) was born at
Stanford University, I was there. He had a private room that they
arranged—it was never done before—and the Prince's mother was
there, and then the baby came."

For the laid-back American, the only strange part of the relationship between the Prince and his wife was the lack of public
displays of affection. Coming from a place like California, he was
used to more expressive behavior between young people in love,
and he did not fully appreciate that both Saudi culture, and the
fact that they had Royal standing, dictated a little more reserve.
He found it a little amusing, especially from two such strong characters: "He was more dominant than she, of course, but the part
that was kinda funny to me was, once in a while, we'd all three of
us be in a limo, and we'd be going out to eat and coming back to
the house, and I am sitting in the front and they are sitting in the
back, and they weren't even holding hands or anything, and I'd
say, 'Come on now, let's get together and give each other a kiss

once in a while,' but they shied away from it, and there wasn't any closeness, and I was (thinking) what the hell's going on here. I couldn't figure it out, but anyway, they got along real fine as far as I know."

The Prince is reluctant to reveal the source of their differences later in life, and why they eventually parted ways: "I cannot tell all the secrets between me and my first wife, but at the end of the marriage, we decided it was time to separate and still be friends, and obviously I still meet her sometimes. She comes to me and I go to her, and we have communication—maybe not on a monthly basis, but at least twice or three times a year, so at least we are on good terms. Sometimes it is easier to separate and have a good relationship, rather than have pressure and strain and have a bad relationship. We chose to separate and have a good relationship, especially as we have a beautiful son and daughter."

Eighteen years after taking their vows, Prince Alwaleed and Princess Dalal divorced. It was December 1994, not long after Alwaleed had signed his momentous deal with Disney for a big stake in Euro Disney. Even as the "fairy story" Prince was riding in to save the day for Mickey Mouse, Alwaleed and his own princess were having far from a fairy-tale ending.

Alwaleed did, however, apply the experience he had from his own childhood to the way he handled his divorce from Dalal. He did not want a repeat of the situation he had faced as a child with the split of his own parents, and the difficulty it had created for him and his siblings. They had been split between their mother and father, and the cultures of Saudi Arabia and Lebanon. Alwaleed made sure that Khaled and Reem remained close to their mother, and he made the most of the fact that both he and his ex-wife are in the same city, fairly close to each other. The children spend large amounts of time with both parents.

When Princess Reem graduated from New Haven University, in Connecticut, on January 17, 2004, Citigroup chairman Sandy Weill was the guest of honor and featured speaker. As the good friend of Alwaleed stood at the podium on the stage, the Prince was seated directly opposite, in the front row, with Prince Khaled on his left, and Princess Dalal next to her son. Blessed with mature sophistication but very youthful looks, she complemented the Prince's own young features. This could easily have been a scene from ten years ago, when the couple was still together. Although not particularly chatty with each other, it was clear that they had made their peace for the sake of their children, and as a result, their children certainly had peace themselves.

TYING THE KNOT ONCE MORE

Following the divorce from Princess Dalal, Alwaleed stayed single for a couple of years, but by 1996, he took the plunge into the marriage pool once more and, soon, Princess Iman Sudairi was by his side. This time it was not destined to last longer than a year or so. It seemed almost like this particular marriage came and went without fanfare.

In 1999, at the age of forty-four, Alwaleed decided to try once more. This time, it was the glamorous young Kholood who caught his eye. Only a year older than his son, Khaled, the twenty-two-year-old beauty joined the Royal circle, becoming Princess Kholood and taking her place at Alwaleed's side. Although not originally from Royalty, she was considered to be from a respectable enough background for the Prince to commit to the relationship.

To some degree, it was jumping "in at the deep end" for Kholood, as she became part of the Prince's life. They married just as his business deals were ramping up, and he was expanding his empire rapidly across the world. The young wife would travel with Alwaleed on his incredibly packed trips from country to country, and city to city, and despite having her own small entourage, including three ladies-in-waiting and a couple of bodyguards, it became more and more challenging for Kholood to keep up with the human dynamo she had married.

She did her best to play the part of a Royal consort and would always appear in Alwaleed's company at the appropriate moments. Knowing her husband's strict time-keeping habits, and his need to organize his time meticulously, Kholood was kept on her toes as far as planning her time around his. In fact, he often planned it for her in his usual, highly organized way. In the more open moments they shared in front of others, she would joke around and tease him a bit, claiming that with his four or five hours of sleeping a night, and action-packed schedule year-round, he was definitely not a normal person.

The issue of her not being of Royal descent certainly seemed to play no part in how their relationship progressed. The only point at which she seemed put on the spot, and a little uncomfortable, was one summer on Alwaleed's yacht moored off Cannes.

The Prince was having his light dinner, in the early hours of the morning, close to 4 A.M., on the large open deck of the huge vessel. As usual, he had a large group seated around the big table set at the end of the deck, including one or two visitors. Various people would come and see the Prince onboard almost daily, either for casual business meetings or to socialize. Dinner was usually the time when the Prince's travel team would distribute the itinerary for the following day, especially as most of the key people who needed a copy would be seated at the table with Alwaleed. On this occasion, one of the visitors looked at the sheet and spotted the separate sections that highlighted the schedules of Prince Khaled, Princess Reem, and Princess Kholood. Quite innocently, the guest commented that the prefix for Alwaleed and his children was "HRH," as in His or Her Royal Highness, while the one for Kholood was "HH," denoting Her Highness, and asked whether that was intentional or a printing error. Alwaleed fidgeted and shifted in his seat, aware that Kholood was watching him closely, and after an uncomfortable mumble, the prince dismissed the issue as simply a matter of Royal protocol. It took a little while to get conversation back on track at the table.

Still, the Prince, for his part, seemed to enjoy Kholood's company and considered her an exceptionally patient person,

but it seems that after five years on the "Alwaleed Diet," her energy reserves were depleted. By 6 A.M. in the hotel lobby of the
George V, in Paris, Kholood could be seen trying to show loyalty to her husband by staying awake, but struggling to keep any
semblance of interest in his nocturnal lifestyle. It's not like Alwaleed did not notice: "You know, living with me is not easy—
not because I am a difficult man, but because I am structured.
The way my life is proceeding, the way I am on twenty-four-
hour call for business, the way I am immersed in so many aspects
of life—be it business, economics, finance, politics, charity,
philanthropy—there is not much time for a marriage, let alone
another child."

This in particular might have been a sticking point in the relationship. Alwaleed already had two children to whom he was devoted, and he made it clear to Kholood that he wanted to keep it
that way: "It is a decision I made after I got my daughter, Reem,
more than twenty years ago. I decided not to have more children,
and I have been pretty consistent, and my perseverance is pretty
stable on that subject, so I do not see myself having any more children at all. I don't know why, but I am against it completely."

It actually surprises many people to find out that such a prominent Saudi, a Royal at that, has only two children and has actively
decided not to have any more. In Middle Eastern culture, as in
many others, children have traditionally been considered a blessing, and large numbers indicate a sign of spiritual prosperity. It is
true that modern Saudis are not inclined to think that way, and the
progressive ones follow the Western trend of having just two or
three children at most. For Alwaleed, there may have also been the
consideration that having more children from a different mother
might create intrafamily tensions. Competition between different
branches of the Saudi Royal family is already well documented,
where princes with the same father but different mothers vie for
control of the family fortune or seat of power. If this holds true
for Alwaleed's situation, then he is clearly avoiding any risk of dis-
putes and succession issues in his family line.

Either way, by early 2004, the Prince's travel itinerary no longer included a section for HH Princess Kholood.

Alwaleed's mood seemed a little lighter, almost mischievous by the time he took his winter vacation at the American ski resort of Jackson Hole in Wyoming in January. He had only his son and daughter and regular entourage with him, and he was in particularly good spirits. One or two of his party observed the subtle change in the Prince and put it down to him not having to carry the responsibility of looking after a wife and her needs. Alwaleed tends to feel very responsible for the people around him and actively takes an interest in making sure everyone is participating and having fun. The long hours and nocturnal sittings were obviously a strain for his ex-wife. It could also be that there is an element of insecurity in him that makes him feel that unless he is orchestrating a good trip with fun events, he is not being a good host—a characteristic considered crucial in Arab culture. Either way, he is also a very demanding boss, husband, father, and friend and realizes that the pressure he places on people takes its toll.

Reflecting on the latest failed relationship, the Prince offers a candid assessment and something of a confession: "I think in the last two marriages, I played a role, somehow a big role, in not having it succeed, unfortunately. The way I am structured, the way my life is proceeding, may prohibit me from ever getting married (again)."

Alwaleed does not rule it out altogether, and in wistful moments reflects on the need for a man to have a wife, but he feels that it has to be a secure relationship, which he is not sure he can manage with his lifestyle: "I am going through a period in my life of discussing that with myself and evaluating it. I think the fast pace that I am going through may be in conflict with having a stable marriage, potentially, but I have not reached a final conclusion yet. I am undergoing an evaluation of that, and I am trying to be honest on that subject."

Back in 1999, when Alwaleed married Kholood, a line in the

newspapers stated that she had ended his reign as the world's most eligible bachelor. It seems he started the year 2004 by reclaiming that title.

THE NEXT GENERATION

"Who's going to take over the business?"

It is a question that plagues any successful company or organization.

In the case of Prince Alwaleed, there is a lot at stake. His Kingdom Holding Company is a massive, global empire of investments that can dramatically impact financial markets if the Prince decides to buy or sell in large amounts. He has spent the past two decades almost micromanaging that empire, so naturally the question arises as to what happens when he passes the reins on to his successor. Who might that successor be? His son or daughter, or both, perhaps?

That would seem most likely, and Alwaleed has become more vocal about the part his children will play in moving the Kingdom Holding Company on in the future. Prince Khaled, for example, started to receive more and more major projects to manage by the end of 2004 and took on the responsibility with a serious and professional attitude.

Princess Reem started to find her way around the company quickly after graduating in January of 2004, although her immediate goal was to follow in her brother's footsteps a couple of years earlier and ensure she gets enough outside experience.

Judging by the unnaturally high amount of energy Alwaleed still has, it is likely that most people asking questions about *full-time* succession at this point in time are likely to be too old to care by the time it actually happens. Still, the issue does have an impact on the way the Prince introduces his children into the family business and delegates power to them in the coming years. Their upbringing has been radically different from his own, and no doubt that has shaped their hopes and ambitions in its own way.

Alwaleed's own drive developed early by his own admission: "I've been very committed from a very young age, always wanted to win, always liked to be at the forefront, always liked to be number one. I think it's part of me. The dependency I had on myself, I think, played a role in making me very independent and motivated and counting on myself a lot."

This raises the concern that his personal aspirations may be pushed onto his children, pressuring them to succeed to the same elevated levels as himself. In his own defense, Alwaleed says that he has consciously made the effort to keep his hand out of their goals and ambitions: "I have done my duty with them and I am very happy with the way I raised them. They are very religious, and ethically they have high morals, and that's good enough for me. The rest, I leave it to them; whether they are as motivated as me or not is academic. I think I have set the basic foundations in them and that is very important to me, but the rest is up to them."

It sounds too easy, and pushed a little further on the matter, Alwaleed admits that deep down, he hopes he has influenced them by example: "To be honest with you, yes, the fact that they are around me, and they know I am driven by work, by being motivated, inevitably they are going to be affected by what I am doing. It is not bad to be motivated, to do better, to improve and always be number one, so that's a motivation that they are going to inherit from me, and I would not discourage them, but I will not really push them through brinkmanship. I will not pressure them to reach the point where they get nervous and upset."

Alwaleed also says that it is unlikely that they themselves will do anything radically diverse, or controversial, because of the way they were brought up. The level of understanding and communication the family has built and maintained will ensure they follow a straight and successful path, believes the Prince, ideally within his company.

Reem confirms that there is a sense of trust between them all, and that she and Khaled were told repeatedly by their father that they have the responsibility to manage their own destinies: "Deep inside, it takes guts to say that, because he does trust us, he does give us a lot. I mean, he doesn't order us around, he doesn't make us do things, he just gives us advice and we choose what's right to do."

Alwaleed stresses that he has always had a relaxed approach with both his children from when they were young, and he focused only on making sure they had a solid understanding of Islam and the value of having high morals and meeting their duties and obligations.

Khaled remembers clearly how his father dealt with him when he was a troublesome youngster. He describes a family trip to Orlando, Florida, where, at one point, his mother and father left him and his sister under supervision while they traveled elsewhere for a couple of days. The young prince says he was only nine or ten years old and decided that he would throw items off the eighteenth-floor balcony at the people below. He secretly collected a variety of projectiles, from ashtrays to water-filled balloons, and sneaked onto the balcony so he could send them hurtling down a couple of hundred feet to the ground. Even with such unruly behavior, Alwaleed was careful with his disciplining when he returned and found out what had happened. Khaled recalls there was never any threat of him being hit by his father: "He never, never, laid his hand on me, ever, but you know, his look . . . for me you don't have to hit, you just look at me that way and it's finished. You know, I'm terrified. So he punished us. He pretty much put me in a corner, facing the corner, and I think I stood there for like twelve hours, man! You know, it was like military style. It was good for me. It was an experience, and it was something I'll never forget because it was the first punishment I ever got from my father for being bad, and I was never bad after that."

Fortunately, such military measures were not needed to get Khaled through his studies, and he graduated from the University of New Haven at Connecticut in 2000 with a degree in Business Administration, Marketing, and Finance.

Wanting to get some experience outside Saudi Arabia, Khaled joined Citibank's Geneva office under Mike Jensen, who heads a team of private bankers there specifically to deal with Prince Al-waleed's rather significant account. Khaled explains that, even though this job had a tangential connection with his father—Jensen is close to the Prince—his personal role at the bank was clear of any influence from his father: "I had nothing to do with my father; I never reported back to him. It was always Michael, and Michael did everything by the book. I'm his employee and he knows it. So I did not feel pressured into working with him (Al-waleed), because he left me alone, 'Don't work for me, do whatever you want to do.' Citibank. That's what I wanted to do, and I did it. I then went into other silly things, and I say silly because when I think about it now, they were. I wanted to get into Formula One, I wanted to buy into a team, I wanted to enter that boom. I wanted to get into this Internet boom thing, and there was this company I wanted to acquire. So little stuff like that that I wanted to do was silly, but at the end of the day nothing was ever really fruitful, nothing ever came out of it. Everything was bad. The company in Formula One went bankrupt, the technology, well I don't need to talk about the Internet boom, because we know what happened to that!"

Being a genuinely modest young man, and even shy about his own abilities, Prince Khaled is a little hard on himself. He did, in fact, do quite well dabbling with online trading at one point. From his own money, he used $66,000 to open a brokerage account with E-Trade, and joining forces with a friend boosted the amount invested to $100,000. Then, later borrowing $50,000 through a service to trade on margin, Khaled was investing a total of $150,000. He was only twenty-one years old and experimenting in what started as a hobby. After lunch, every evening, he would head up to his bedroom and fire up his laptop, preferring the flexibility of being able to lounge on his bed, instead of being stuck at a desk. Logging on, he would start trading, just as business folks in the United States were getting their late-morning coffee. Up until then, his father had not gone heavily into Internet and technology stocks, so at the time, Khaled was quite cutting-edge with his foray into shares in America Online, Lucent, Intel, Compaq, and Dell, among others. He says he did not day-trade, because of the slow Internet connection he faced in Saudi Arabia, and, after being stung a few times, set a firm 5 percent rule, where if a stock either gained or lost 5 percent, he sold it, plus he generally stayed a maximum of three weeks in a company.

From opening the E-Trade account in December 1998, he doubled the amount invested to $300,000 within eight months. According to periodicals at the time, his father had gained 21 percent on his investments in the same period, and both had beaten the Dow Jones Industrial Average, which had risen 18 percent. Having said that, in cash terms, Alwaleed's account actually increased by around $2.5 billion during those eight months in 1999.

It was natural that a couple of years later, as he was approaching his mid-twenties, Khaled would join the Kingdom Holding Company, to work with his father: "I tried to do things on my own and at the end of the day—you know what?—I grew up, and I thought, you know, you have the best teacher you could ever have, a job that's pretty challenging, what the hell are you doing?"

An early assessment of their working relationship is offered by Khaled: "Right now it's working great, because there's no crossing roads between father figure and boss, and at his office, believe me, he's my boss and I'm his employee and he knows that. So if I screw up in anything—excuse my language, but if I do—it's handled professionally and it's handled right. So I feel very comfortable and I feel very challenged, which is what I've been wanting to feel for the past three years. I mean, I was challenged differently in my previous job, but I feel much more challenged now working for him in domestic investment, which is where I'm working now."

Princess Reem found herself at a similar junction as her brother as she graduated in January 2004. Also wanting experience overseas for a period of time first, she knew that, inevitably, working with her father was the best option. In her case, that might eventually be with the company's charity division, handling the $100 million or so that Alwaleed donates each year.

By 2004, it was not clear where the young princess would place herself to get the broad international experience she had been seeking, but she certainly did not feel in any way forced to join the Kingdom Holding Company eventually. Like her brother, she feels it is a step she would actually *like* to take because she can gain valuable experience from tapping into her father's business acumen. Plus, she says she is already fully aware of what she is letting herself in for, working with him: "I'm sure he's just going to guide me with whatever I want to do. Having spoken to my brother, and how he (Alwaleed) is with him, I know it won't be a father-daughter relationship when I work with him, and I hope it won't because I don't want it to be; I just want that to be at home only— I am his daughter, after all."

Having explained how different her mother's and father's characters are, Reem initially assesses that she is like her mother and Khaled is like her father, but confronted with Khaled's assessment as the opposite, she acquiesces: "From my brother's point of view, I can see why he thinks he's more like my mum and I'm more like my father and I think that's very true."

But she does have one big difference compared with her father, who is a consummate long-term investor and planner: "As a person, it's hard for me to commit to something. I mean, if I start to do something, I get very bored easily. I'm also easygoing; I'm very quiet. I don't really like to plan things like my dad does; I just like to do things day by day."

In giving their candid views about their father, both Reem and Khaled come to the same conclusion regarding the high speed of his lifestyle. He seems to be getting faster and more driven as he gets older, and though his energy levels show no sign of fading, both of the children worry that it will eventually take its toll on his health.

That view is shared by some of the people who have been working with Alwaleed a long time, who believe that the increased pace and pressure have worsened the physical tic the Prince displays from time to time. Under pressure, and during high-powered animated deal making, the twitching of his facial muscles increases and, in contrast, relaxes when he is calm. Their worry for the state of the Prince's health is dismissed by his personal physician, Dr. Jihad Aoukal, who attends regular checkups on the royal at some of the world's leading medical establishments. According to the doctor, Alwaleed couldn't be in better health, and his bio-indicators, such as blood pressure and cholesterol levels, are well below any significant thresholds. In line with his youthful appearance, the Prince has an extremely healthy body. It is helped by the fact that he exercises regularly and is incredibly fussy about what he eats.

His children would still like to see him slow down a bit. Reem sometimes finds it hard to relate to the pace of it all: "Sometimes he's just too harsh on himself. He hardly sleeps, he reads the whole time, he's talking on the phone for business . . . I sometimes just want to tell him to relax, you know, 'Just take everything off your mind, just go out, and have something to eat.' I think he'd be happier if he tried to cool down. He's so stubborn; he would never think about sleeping more; he would never think about relaxing."

Khaled expresses a similar wish. He gets bothered by his father's persistence in trying to defy his body's need for rest. He relates one particular story that his sister told him about on the journey back to Riyadh from their winter vacation in Jackson Hole, Wyoming, in the United States, in January 2004. They were on their private Boeing 767 on a long flight back across the Atlantic. Khaled was fast asleep on the floor of the bedroom on the aircraft, while Reem was lying awake on the bed. Their father came in and lay down next to Reem, apparently intending just to rest, but she noticed that he accidentally dozed off for a few minutes. Suddenly, he opened his eyes, sighed, and starting getting up making, a "tut, tut," sound, disapproving of himself for letting himself slip into sleep. Khaled says that, one day, he would like to list "the ability to chill" as one of his father's qualities: "Nobody is perfect in this world, but I would love him to relax more. He is a very hard worker, he is very dedicated to his knowledge, to his reading. He is always learning, he is always striving to be the best. Even though he gets there, he's never there; he wants to go on further. The rest time in the desert (on weekends) isn't enough, so I would say more leisure time, more fun time, more relaxtion and much more time alone—spend some time with friends."

Reem adds: "He has an aim, he has a goal, and he has to reach it no matter what. I don't know what his goal is; it's not really to be the best or the number one, but it's just to be good in everything he does."

On the subject of his energy, pace, and drive, the Prince is a little defensive: "It's fast but not out of hand, at all. Very fast, the fact of the matter is that we (Kingdom Holding Company) have been like this for the last ten years—that's where the acceleration took place—but we are able to work on so many fronts because we have a very good staff. Each one in his area is an authority, so this creates a good foundation. I don't think I will calm down or cool down, because I think what I am doing is right and is providing benefit for me and my community, and I think I will do what I am doing for a long time."

Alwaleed has yet to become a grandfather, and many among his family and friends are waiting to see what impact that will have on him. On one hand, he is happy encouraging Khaled and Reem to explore the world, and engage in careers, particularly through the Kingdom Holding Company, but on the other hand, he is keen to see them settled in other directions, too. Alwaleed says he is keeping his former house for Khaled to move into when he is settled. The young prince now lives in one of the wings of the new palace, which is actually located pretty much next door: "He would like to be living next to me and his sister, so we are very much a close family. I kept that house for him, and whenever he gets married he can refurbish it the way he wants."

Being so close all the time, both in terms of being together almost daily and being open to each other emotionally, might create a sense of separation when the young prince and princess finally get married. The only criteria Alwaleed insisted on, in giving his approval for marriage, is that his children's spouses should be practicing Muslims and Saudi. A little ironic, some might say, considering his own mother is Lebanese. As for Khaled and Reem marrying other Royals, the Prince says he is not concerned about that. In fact, he says he would almost rather they don't marry Royals, as that might only compromise the kind of open expression and freedom that his children are used to at home right now. Reading into that, it seems Alwaleed is wary that they might end up marrying overly conservative people if their spouses are part of the Royal elite.

Still, he does give his children the benefit of the doubt to some degree and recognizes their independence.

The Prince's longtime friend, Chuck Gulan, who has seen Alwaleed welcome both of his children into the world, believes that the father is now mentally prepared to see his son and daughter move on to the next step in their lives and ready to cut the umbilical cord of their close dependency: "As a parent you never want to see your children leave, but the cord eventually has to be cut. I don't think the Prince hates to see this happen—that they are going to get married and leave, and be on their own—but he knows it's going to happen, and he just hopes that everything will go in the right manner when it does happen."

As 2004 came to an end, Prince Alwaleed witnessed his son taking that next step and getting engaged. The introduction was made by none other than Princess Reem, who was friends with the young lady, Moneerah Ibrahim Al-Assaf.

Being close as siblings, it appears Reem and Khaled support each other in almost every aspect of their lives.

CHAPTER 9

An Extended Family

It's a family. I feel when I'm with him, I'm safe.

— DR. JIHAD AOUKAL, PRINCE ALWALEED'S
PERSONAL PHYSICIAN

The clock was about to strike midday, and, sure enough, precisely on time, Prince Alwaleed appeared at the top of the sweeping staircase and made his way down rapidly, with two valets trailing behind clutching items their Royal boss might demand on short notice—a box containing sunglasses in different shades, grooming kits, and any personal bits and pieces the Prince is reluctant to put into his pockets as they would ruin the trim outline of his expensive, tailor-made suit. It is actually something of a luxury not to have to carry a single item on one's person. No wallet, no comb, no pens, no keys, and no mobile phone. Clothes do look a lot better without the protesting bulges of our material manacles.

By the time the Prince had reached the bottom of the staircase, the crowd of a dozen or so people arranged in a semicircle were already standing, as protocol required, and greeting the Royal with mumbles of *"Salaam-u-alaikum"*—peace be upon you. Their eyes followed the Prince, who, in one smooth movement, plopped himself down in the middle chair, signifying that it was now okay for others to sit.

His travel manager, Robert El Hage, stepped in discreetly to the side of the Prince and slightly behind, stooped toward him, and silently handed him a piece of paper containing the day's schedule. The Prince glanced at it briefly, toying with the end of his moustache as he did so, and then handed it back to Robert, nodding. Suddenly, Alwaleed jumped up to his feet and shouted, "Ready?"

Everyone else, caught by surprise, struggled to get up as quickly as they could, adjusting their clothes as they stood.

The Prince stepped out of the circle and strode toward the front door of his palatial home, where two tall, robed men waited patiently. One held a pot of burning incense, with the fragrant scent pouring from it in a stream of wispy, light gray smoke. The other held a tray containing small but ornate perfume bottles with dark brown liquid in them.

The Prince went up to the tray, selected one of the bottles, unscrewed the top, which drew out a thin applicator coated in the thick liquid, and then he dabbed it onto his wrists. Closing the bottle, and replacing it on the tray, Alwaleed moved over to the man with the incense, leaned forward into the smoke with his face eight inches away from the burning ember, and then wafted the billowing gray cloud with one hand, directly on his face and torso.

He then stepped out toward the dark limousine parked in the forecourt.

Behind him, the trail of people followed the same ritual: dabbed the rich Arabian scent, "aoud," onto their wrists—some then rubbed their wrists behind their ears, spreading the scent to their neck—and then wafted the fragrant smoke onto themselves, to add a dusky but clean smell to their clothes and hair.

Within moments, the limousine, and a number of cars waiting behind, streamed out of the large front gate.

It was a typical Alwaleed trip, departing his home in Saudi Arabia on the afternoon of June 14, 2003, and scheduled to land back in Riyadh in the early hours of June 20. Just five days, but not one spare moment at any point in the itinerary.

From the time he boarded his private Boeing 767 at Riyadh Airport's VIP terminal, to the moment he landed in Paris that evening, Alwaleed was focused on the days ahead. His overseas trips were getting more and more ambitious in terms of scheduling and travel routes.

His company, Kingdom Holding, is run by very few people, who are already stretched to the limit, and any increase in the workload is felt by them quite severely. Aware of the need to release the pressure valve a bit, the Prince had added a couple of extra staff; one extra valet to cope with the longer days he now keeps, and one extra member of the travel team to help Robert and his assistant, Hani Agha, with the packed schedule. The aircraft was now starting to get a little crowded with the expanding team, but Alwaleed was dealing with this. He had bought a Boeing 747, with almost three times the volume of his current jet, to make the long trips more comfortable for all. The bigger plane was due to be refitted according to Alwaleed's interior layout and design preferences and—almost as important—in the standard Kingdom company colors, beige and green.

For now, almost all seats were taken as the Prince and his wife, Kholood, and their entourage made their way to Europe. Only two key people were absent, Prince Khaled, who was traveling, and his sister, Princess Reem, who was on a college study trip to Florence, Italy, for a couple of weeks.

Even then, the number of people traveling with Alwaleed was listed at thirty.

FAMILIAR FACES

Certain members of Alwaleed's corporate and personal teams almost always travel with him.

Dr. Jihad Saad Aoukal is a tall, slim, fair-skinned man in his early fifties, with hair streaked heavily with silver and gray and thinned out on top. His close and neatly cropped moustache reflects the color scheme on his head, giving him a slightly Einsteinian look. He first met the Prince soon after he moved from Lebanon to Saudi Arabia in 1987 to work as a private physician for a company operating there. It turns out that Alwaleed had been looking for a doctor to care for his family and travel with them when needed. The Prince's office got in touch with Jihad after hearing about him through a local contact. A fifteen-minute first interview with the thirty-two-year-old Alwaleed was uneventful, and the doctor was told he would be contacted soon. Two months passed before he was called to see the Prince again.

This time, as he sat chatting with him, Alwaleed pulled out a sheet of paper and handed it to the doctor, telling him it was a list of physicians, and asked if he recognized any of them. The doctor spotted his name among them: "I said, 'Yeh, I know one.' He asked, 'Who?' and I said 'Number 25.' He said, 'What is his name?' I said, 'Jihad.' He said, 'This is your name!' and I said 'Yes.' He told me, 'You have a sense of humor, I like it.' I replied, 'I know, I like it, too.'"

Alwaleed then invited Jihad out on one of his so-called "big" desert trips, where he heads out to a remote camp in the sands for about two weeks. That gave the two men time to get to know each other, and the Prince's wife and young son and daughter to get familiar with him. Soon after returning to Riyadh, the doctor was contacted by the Prince's palace staff. He was told that the Alwaleed wanted him to continue in his current job with the company, but to see his family at the same time, ideally traveling for weekend desert camp trips every Saudi weekend—Wednesday and Thursday.

So, for about eight months, Jihad led a split life between his company work in Riyadh and the Prince's desert trips at the end of the week. After that period of time, the Prince invited the doctor to have dinner with him one Friday evening, where he told him that he had narrowed down his list of prospective family physicians to just three names. Teasing him, Alwaleed said with a straight face that one of his staff would contact the doctor tomorrow and tell him the name of the person chosen. Jihad's response was a simple, "Okay, Your Highness."

Surprised at the doctor's nonchalance, Alwaleed asked, "Don't you want to know who it is?"

Again, the doctor replied, nonplussed, "It's up to you, Your Highness."

Alwaleed was a bit baffled by the relaxed attitude of Jihad, but at the same time admired his calm nature.

The next day the doctor was told that he should resign from his company and join the Prince full-time. Since that time in late 1987 Jihad has witnessed many of the twists and turns of Alwaleed's life, becoming as much a friend to the Prince as his doctor: "It's a family. I feel when I'm with him, I'm safe. To be honest, when I have my vacations sometimes, after four or five days, it becomes so monotonous. With him there's action, it's not standing still, it's just on your toes. You can't just sit and relax like on my vacation, where I can sit for two three hours doing nothing, but with him, we do this, we do that, we go there . . . it's action with him."

Sometimes, as the Prince's day comes to an end in the early hours of the morning, and the entire entourage disbands, the doctor, like everyone else struggling to keep up with Alwaleed, marvels at his resilience. The checkups Jihad arranges annually show the Prince to be in great shape, so he believes Alwaleed has more or less trained himself to survive on less sleep: "Four hours or five hours of sleep for him is like when you sleep for eight hours or nine hours. His body's adapted to this period of time of sleeping, and there is, in his five hours of sleep, the feeling that he slept for eight or nine or ten hours."

But feeling the stress on his own body in trying to keep up with the Prince's tough schedule, the doctor realizes exactly how demanding it can be on a person. As the Prince's physician, he does worry when he witnesses the rare moments of strain: "Sometimes he exhausts himself, and I can feel that he is tired and he has to relax or go to sleep, but he pushes himself to a certain limit. He feels it sometimes, and he stops, but sometimes he overdoes it, like on his trips, when he goes from six o'clock in the morning to eleven o'clock, midnight, then he comes back to the hotel and stays in the lobby till four o'clock in the morning. He wants to read the papers, he wants to see the magazines, to eat something, he wants people to be around him."

Out of respect, the entourage is obliged to stay with the Prince until he retires, so it gets tough for those who cannot cope with the eighteen-hour days that are common during the Prince's trips.

While on those travels, it is rare to see Jihad without the company of another person close to the inner circle of the family.

Mohammed El Amine, another of the large Lebanese clan among the entourage, is the Prince's personal barber and hairdresser. A very athletic man, standing at medium height, a little shorter than the doctor and a few years younger, El Amine's wavy locks are almost always gelled back, and left longer at the back, in a style almost reminiscent of the 1980s. His gray moustache is trim and gives him more than a passing resemblance to the actor Omar Sharif, particularly as his smile is very similar. Every couple of days, Alwaleed starts his morning with a traditional hot towel, brush and lather, and then open razor shave by El Amine, just like in the old western and *Godfather* movies. Awaleed usually lets his beard grow for a couple of days, preferring not to shave daily, unless he has an important meeting. Plus, every week or so, El Amine gives the Prince's hair a trim, maintaining the coiffured look that Alwaleed had sported consistently for the past couple of decades. El Amine's history goes back that far, from when he used to be the hairdresser for Alwaleed's first wife, Princess Dalal, of whom El Amine is a great fan, describing her to be one of the most elegant and sophisticated ladies he has ever met. He is very devoted to the family, and although quiet and gentle in nature, is always nearby to lend support. Alwaleed pretends envy of El Amine's lean physique, especially as the hairdresser seems to wolf down masses of food and never gains an ounce in weight. Alwaleed on the other hand, counting every calorie obsessively, and exercising daily, is all too aware of the dangers of his sweet tooth. The Prince jokes that one time, after watching El Amine guzzle four hamburgers and still complain that he was hungry, he said to him, "Isn't it terrible that I can't even look at food without gaining weight, while you eat as much as you want and it doesn't change your body?"

The hairdresser smiled back in between mouthfuls of French fries, and joked, "Your Highness, if you care to give me $10 million, I would be more than happy to put on weight for you."

Ever since he shed around twenty-eight kilos (sixty-two pounds) during his college years in California, the Prince has been careful with every morsel that passes his lips. His personal chefs in Riyadh always make very low-fat foods, with almost no oils used in the cooking process, and sugar-free desserts. When on the road, the kitchens in his regular haunts know the Prince's preferences, and the George V Hotel and others include Alwaleed-compliant cooking in their menu for him and his entourage. The Prince often curbs his hunger by starting the meal with low-calorie Melba toast, packets of which his valets carry for him when he is eating out. In 2004, he discovered another product, which he added to his valet's collection, low-carb tomato ketchup. Alwaleed has always loved ketchup but has been bothered by the high sugar and carbohydrate content. Finding the new "one-carb" version—and liking the taste—was the perfect answer. He now has that sitting close by at the dining table. In addition, his diet involved him sticking with salads, eating small amounts, and only picking at other dishes, such as grilled fish, as he does not eat meat at all.

The Prince has succumbed to his love of apple pie, but manages to order it sugar-free, preferring diet sugar products, such as Splenda. He has a routine with that particular dessert, which he will have made at the hotel and delivered to any outside restaurant he is visiting if he is out and about. Alwaleed takes a slice of apple pie, lifts the crust off the top, eats the apple filling, and then replaces the crust lid and leaves that uneaten. When asked why he does not simply order the stewed apple that fills the pie, without the crust, his reply, quite sincerely is: "But that wouldn't be apple pie, then!"

Following the lead of their boss, many of the entourage now do the same thing, leaving restaurant waiters across the world confused at platefuls of apple pie crust scattered around at the end of a meal hosted by Prince Alwaleed Bin Talal.

Jihad points out that the Prince has been obsessive about his eating habits since his twenties: "Before I knew him, before I worked with him, he knew everything (about food). He'd calculate each calorie in everything—everything! As a doctor you are not necessarily a nutritionist, but you are a doctor and you know many things about health and health products, but he used to tell *me*, 'This has these calories and this has this many,' and I was surprised that he knew a lot."

The large group that the Prince travels with needs managing, particularly with protocols such as the seating arrangement and access to the Prince at various times. The man in charge of that is Hassan Moukhtar. A dark Saudi of medium height and frame, he has also been with the Prince for around two decades. Hassan is not inclined to say much, but keeps a very close eye on the behavior of the entourage and makes sure that those who the Prince wants access to are available promptly.

Media inquiries go through Amjed Shacker, the managing director of corporate communications at the Kingdom Holding Company. His very light complexion and American accent often confuse those who meet him when he is part of the Prince's entourage, where he is often mistaken for a Western Caucasian until he turns to speak to the Prince in Arabic. Prior to his arrival in the middle of 1997, there had been no formal public relations or communications department at what was the Kingdom Establishment for Contracting and Trading. He arrived just as the company completed a restructuring under the auspices of Arthur Andersen and had been renamed the Kingdom Holding Company. One of the gaps the Andersen analysts identified was a lack of in-house public relations, and Shacker was interviewed for a manager's position in that area. The young Saudi, who had studied and lived in the United States extensively before moving full-time to the Saudi Kingdom to work in television, remembers exactly what happened on that July 21: "Ten minutes after they had showed me where my office was, and they had given me a password to log on to the computer, and another password to start dialing and making toll calls, I got a big pile of files from the press that he (Alwaleed) wanted me to sort out. Eventually I sorted out thirty to forty requests from various media around the world to interview him, and slowly the interaction between me and the Prince gave me insights into how the Prince thinks and what his strategy is, what he likes to achieve, and how he utilizes the media."

DUSK 'TIL DAWN

The first meeting in Paris on June 15, 2003, started unusually early, at 8:30 A.M.

While traveling Prince Alwaleed normally schedules meetings beginning at 12 P.M., the time he winds his way down from his room on the first floor of the George V Hotel to the back lobby area that is reserved exclusively for him whenever he is staying there.

That morning it was too early for there to be a piano player tinkling away in the background. Normally, at midday, the Prince comes down to the sound of a professional pianist, mellowing the mood in the tastefully decorated, exclusive lobby setting. For some time, the pianist performing around midday was Jean-Claude Orfali, a tall, suave man of Egyptian descent, in his fifties, with a clean-shaven look and swept-back silver hair.

Every day, during previous visits, as the Prince came down the steps with his team behind him, Orfali would quickly segue into the theme from *Mission Impossible*, playing it wonderfully with remarkable style and texture.

After this happened a number of times, the Prince, slightly baffled, went over to him and asked in a firm tone, "Why *Mission Impossible*? It is not 'impossible'—everything is possible!"

Though the reprimand was in good humor, for choosing a song with a pessimistic title, the nervous pianist decided against playing that particular tune in the presence of Alwaleed again.

As it is, this particular morning in June, the Prince was actually *not* heading to the lobby for his first meeting. Citigroup's chairman and CEO, Sandy Weill, was briefly passing through Paris and due to depart on a lunchtime flight, and the Prince wanted to see him before he left for the airport. Alwaleed met Weill in his plush suite, having made sure first that the hotel was giving his special guest top priority and service. In greeting his friend and biggest shareholder, Weill commented on how well the staff at this Four Seasons landmark property had treated him. It should not have surprised him, considering he was having breakfast with the owner.

Once they had bid each other farewell, the rest of the morning found the Prince catching up on his notes and briefings until the first set of meetings began in the early afternoon. Alwaleed had asked his aviation team, led by his head pilot, Duncan Gillespie, and consultant, Brett Lindsay, to assess the rather tricky negotiation he had in front of him. Four groups were bidding for the project to refit the Boeing 747 the Prince had recently bought. The bids were ranging from nearly $90 million to over $120 million. Over a two-hour period, the Prince had slotted them in for a half-hour meeting each, to explain exactly what they were proposing, and to justify the amount of their bid.

The first group walked up, all smiles, to the crowded arrangement of chairs alongside and opposite the sofa on which Alwaleed always sat, the ubiquitous television screen beside him tuned to CNBC. Orfali had started working up a gentle melody to accompany the bright afternoon, which was visible through the high glass windows overlooking the hotel's central courtyard.

Bidding the men to sit down, the Prince decided to kick off the afternoon playing hardball. Company A—let's call them that to preserve their dignity—had naturally sent their top managers to meet with such a special client. They had proposed one of the midrange bids, coming in close to $100 million for the job. After a little informal chatting and greeting, Alwaleed took them completely by surprise by starting off asking how much profit they had built into their bid. Flustered, they hesitated and stuttered, turning repeatedly to one another for some sort of help. No one had anticipated having to address such an inquiry. After allowing them to brew a little more discomfort, the Prince offered a suggestion, "$20 million . . . $25 million?"

The four executives, one of them clutching a large portfolio of design work he hadn't even opened yet, looked even more sheepish.

Before they could speak again, the Prince offered a price, "Okay, how about we say you do it for $80 million?"

"But Your Highness—" one of them managed to say, "we wouldn't make any money at that price."

"That's okay," Alwaleed replied confidently, "but at least you get to tell everyone that you are working on the most expensive private jet owned by any individual. Imagine how much more work that will bring in for your company, and how much publicity it can generate for you."

Having hardly had the chance to debate the issue, or explain the details of their bid, the executives of Company A found themselves completely stumped.

Following a moment of silence, the Prince interjected, "Why don't you go over there and think about it, and we'll discuss it in a little while," pointing to a distant corner of the lobby.

Quite innocently, in the background, Orfali sitting at the piano, had started playing "Waltzing Matilda," as Gillespie and Lindsay led the confused executives over to the corner table and beckoned one of the attentive serving staff to take any orders they might have for tea or coffee. They looked like they needed a strong drink.

When Gillespie and Lindsay returned to Prince, he asked them to bring in the next group, if they had already arrived. Fortunately, with such a big job at stake, Company B was already waiting in the front lobby, eager for their audience with Alwaleed.

They had probably been camped outside since early morning, just in case.

Following the smiles, hellos, and handshakes, the Prince faced the seated group of executives and immediately berated them for having the highest bid, at just over $120 million.

"I can get it for $80 million," he mused to what looked like a bunch of rather skeptical faces. "You should be able to match that."

His reasoning was the same—that they would be working on such a prestigious project, it would be worth their while treating it as a loss leader and looking to the long-term benefits they could extract, including getting the maintenance contract for the jet.

There were still echoes of "Waltzing Matilda" as this second group was led off to another corner to think about it.

Company C had the fortune, or as it turned out, misfortune of having worked on the Prince's current Boeing 767 jet. Alwaleed was not entirely happy with the way they had conducted the work, or the quality of the finish, although, in reality, he later confessed that it was not as bad as he was making out. The problem with the Prince is that he does not miss a single detail, so even one screw out of place, and it is going to be mentioned, and an explanation required. This bid was the lowest, closer to $90 million, probably because these executives carried the scars of the last negotiations with Alwlaeed and realized they would have to give him obvious value for money.

"You should be doing this for free for me, because of the faults I have on the 767."

It was an afternoon for aviation industry executives to look sheepish.

"You made a lot of money from me last time and have made a lot of money from the maintenance contract. Think about it."

The George V lobby was running out of corners to place harried businessmen.

The final group, Company D, was the second-most expensive, coming in around $110 million, but one that carried a particularly good reputation. The first thing that caught the Prince's eye was the large model of a jumbo jet under the arm of one of the executives. It was painted in Kingdom colors. A wise move, as Alwaleed found his eyes straying to the beige and green livery on the model, which the executives had placed strategically right in front of him.

Having put them through their paces with the same arguments as the others, Company D was also forced to retire, leaving the model behind. Apart from the fact that the Prince liked seeing what his jet would look like, he wanted the returning executives from the other companies to notice it, so he could emphasize the competition they faced and that they had not been smart enough to bring a model.

A brief meeting with Gillespie and Lindsay was convened to discuss where things now stood, and to get their take on other ways in which the Prince might leverage a price reduction.

"Am I the only one who thinks they are asking far too much?" Alwaleed asked, leaning back on the sofa and spreading his arms for emphasis.

"Am I the only one?"

The pianist was playing "O Sole Mio."

Coincidence or force of nature?

Either way, the next hour or so was spent shuffling around groups A, B, C, and D, to negotiate the best price. The Prince did not reveal the final bid value at the end of the day, but it was clear that he had secured a much better price than any of those he had originally heard.

Aviation matters were rounded out with two interviews for potential flight attendants. That was almost light relief after the earlier battle of the bid. One of the questions the Prince posed to the young women, who were both white Western Caucasians, was whether or not they were happy to be based out of Riyadh. Security tensions had been high in the Kingdom in recent months, and Alwaleed was adamant to show support for his country by not moving his operations or staff outside Saudi Arabia. It would be business as usual.

Neither candidate had any reservations, both having lived in the Middle East at various times in the past.

By now it was approaching evening, and time for lunch. With such a packed itinerary for this day, the Prince opted not to stroll to one of the restaurants on or near the Champs Élysées, as he had originally planned. He decided instead to stay put and arranged food for the team at the George V Hotel. This would keep the meal brief and clear him up in time for his 6 P.M. meeting with Neil Bush.

Bearing more than a passing resemblance to George W., the younger man has no political profile, unlike his brother, the president of the United States, or his other brother, the governor of the state of Florida. This Bush was in Paris to talk about possible business ventures with Alwaleed, who concluded by saying that he would examine any specific ideas if Bush forwarded them to him.

Half an hour later, it was the head of *Al Watan Al Arabi* newspaper, Walid Abu Dahr, in the hot seat for simply an informal courtesy meeting, followed by a more intense discussion with the recently recruited head of Rotana Music, Michel El Murr. A half hour was not enough to discuss the progress of Rotana with El Murr, so the Prince invited him to continue the conversation as he took his evening walk along the Parisian streets.

Before long, the soft-spoken and gentlemanly El Murr was struggling to keep up with Alwaleed's high-speed strides and to talk at the same time.

This particular evening, it was not to be the routine couple of miles up and down the Champs Élysées. Instead, the Prince wanted to walk to his next appointment, at the house of his aunt Alia, at 8:30 P.M.

His mother's sister lives part of the year in an exclusive home in the heart of Paris's diplomatic district. Decorated heavily in an ornate romantic rococo, the place is filled with artifacts collected through years of travel. A cup of tea later, Alwaleed was back walking the streets at close to five miles per hour, continuing his daily exercise routine, and heading to the Gaumant Marignan, one of the cinemas along the Champs Élysées. Here, those of the entourage who were not on the walking program or listed for the visit to Alia El Solh's house, were waiting for Alwaleed outside.

As it was around 10 P.M. by now, the timing was right to catch the regular movie showing. Robert and Hani, in managing the schedule, also have to make arrangements such as restaurant bookings for the large group, or securing eight to ten rows at the back of the cinema for the Prince and his party to sit in privacy and security.

Ending around midnight, the cinema emptied onto the street, and the Prince and his party headed toward one of his favorite haunts in the French capital.

Alwaleed has a prime corner reserved for him at the world-famous Fouquet's café on the Champs Élysées, near his George V Hotel. Fouquet's is a bit run-down and faded for many people's taste, but it is still one of the landmarks of the Parisian night scene and a location many of the elite head to when visiting the city.

Here, from his vantage point beside the large open window, Alwaleed watched the world go by and conducted his informal nighttime meetings.

By two in the morning, the café was closing up, and it was back to the familiar, cozy corner in the lobby of the George V Hotel for his intense reading session.

As usual, the newspapers, including the *New York Times, Washington Post, International Herald Tribune, Wall Street Journal*, and a handful of Arab ones, were already printed out from the Internet and waiting for the Prince upon his return to the hotel, and he spent the next couple of hours more or less in silence, absorbed in them.

By about 4 A.M. it was time for a nocturnal dinner, with the Prince choosing his usual soup and salads to keep the intake light. Then back to the reading.

Bedtime arrived well after bakeries were delivering breakfast croissants to most places. In fact, this was one of the rare occasions that the Prince decided not to go for another walk at 6 A.M.

before going to bed. Perhaps it was because of the early start he had had to the day—nearly twenty-four hours ago.

This was just day one.

WATCHING THE CLOCK

The schedule is particularly punishing for the travel team that has to coordinate the tight timetable set by the Prince.

Robert El Hage and Hani Agha are the first to wake up and the last to go to bed. Both start to show the wear and tear after a couple of weeks into an overseas trip, although Robert explains that he tries to find ways around the demands: "I have trained myself, and I know how to cope with His Royal Highness. I know when to have ten minutes of sleep in order to keep going. If I have two hours of nonstop things to do, I know how much to eat, when to sleep—if I ever have time to sleep—and I know how to preserve my energy."

Robert stresses that they have to make sure that every minute is accounted for in each day, especially as the Prince is fastidious about punctuality and doesn't like to waste time: "There is a lot of effort involved, especially as His Royal Highness is a perfectionist and wants everything done 200 percent. To cope with him you have to put in a lot of effort. It needs a lot of concentration—a lot—and a system."

That system includes going on scouting trips to locations beforehand, to make sure everything is in place for when the Royal party arrives. Robert or Hani often travel the world while the Prince is spending time in Riyadh, looking for the ideal spots for him to visit or stay. They have to check transportation and security and even liaise with the Saudi ambassador or consul general in that location to alert them of the Prince's impending arrival. Returning to base, they write a detailed report on their travels and the options open to the Prince if he chooses that location. They know that he will go through it carefully. Sometimes, according to Robert, even all that meticulous planning goes out of the window:

"The worst part in my job is when something goes wrong, because I am a perfectionist, too. I am surprised when something goes wrong after all my preparation. This is when I have to be quick and have to have the initiative and reflexes to solve the problem on the spot."

There is actually a lot at stake for the young Lebanese pair. If the Prince is happy with the way the trip was executed logistically, it can mean a big bonus. If not, and there are problems, Alwaleed is known to reduce the quarterly bonuses to indicate his displeasure—and he does not forget a single incident, good or bad, as his media chief, Amjed Shacker, explains: "He pays a lot of attention; he more or less has a photographic memory—he does not forget anything; I mean nothing! Nothing escapes him; the minutest detail—he will make a mental note of it and when good things accumulate all of a sudden you get a bonus—three months, six months, one full year's salary as a bonus, or just a big lump sum; you get it for doing superb, exceptional work."

Many at the company believe that after Robert performed a near miracle in getting the Prince through ten African countries in five days, in the spring of 2003, he received a bonus equivalent to a whole year's salary.

However, when a restaurant booking went wrong in Cannes, in the summer of the same year, consternation was written all over Robert's face. He could feel his bonus being whittled away as the Prince's frustration grew.

Planning is everything, but as Robert and Hani know all too well, the only certainty in life is that everything is uncertain.

Day two began at the Prince's usual time of midday, by which time he expected his staff to have had their breakfast and be ready to go—nonstop until dawn.

After a quick follow-up discussion with Rotana's Michel El Murr, he gathered his hotel people for the Middle East region—Sarmad Zok, Ramsey Mankarious, and Tim Hansing, another motivated young team with a strong drive for success. They had flown in especially for a meeting with representatives of the Movenpick Hotel Group, including the young Luitpold von Finck of the founding family, and Jean Gabrielle Perez, the company's CEO. The Prince wanted to express his unhappiness at what he considered the poor quality of the property the hotel chain had undertaken in Jeddah, Saudi Arabia's main port city. His concern, he told the gathered group, was for prime quality and image in building up the Movenpick brand, not just a quick run for a good revenue stream.

Within an hour, the meeting was over, and Alwaleed was rescheduling his agenda to shuffle around a couple of the items on the itinerary. As a result, lunch came a little early, closer to 4:30 P.M., at a Chinese restaurant off the main drag of the Champs Élysées. It was essentially a working lunch, though, as Alwaleed was preoccupied with hotel-related events, talking this time with his U.S.-based consultants, Chuck Henry and Simon Turner.

Not long after the Prince had returned to his sofa in the George V, around 6 P.M., he spotted the head of AOL Time Warner, Dick Parsons, in the lobby of the hotel. Quickly, he sent one of his team over to ask Parsons if he had time for a quick hello. With the Prince being a such a big shareholder in the company, the tall African American media boss was more than aware of Alwaleed's importance. The heavyset, but urbane Parsons said he would be more than happy to meet, indicating he would be over in a moment.

As Parsons walked toward the reserved seating area in the rear lobby, the Prince quickly turned his back to him, and was desperately jabbing buttons on his remote control, trying to change the channels on his television from CNBC to CNN.

Parson's opening line—with a big smile—was, "I saw that!"

The conversation centered on where Parsons was hoping to take AOL Time Warner in the short term and the long term. The media giant had seen a drastic drop in its shares over the previous couple of years. Conversation was kept brief, but the two men agreed to meet early in the new year. Once Parsons had gone to his room, Alwaleed instructed Robert to make sure that the hotel bill for the AOL Time Warner chief was charged to the Prince's account. A week or so later, Alwaleed received a courteous thank-you note from Parsons.

The spontaneous encounter did not throw the day's itinerary too far off, and before long, Alwaleed was talking with his nautical division, who were currently working on plans for a new, custom-built yacht for the Prince. Actually, it is hard to call it a yacht when it is rumored to be at least double the size of the current one, housing two helicopters (the Kingdom 5-KR has only one). Initial designs of the new yacht would have one of the helicopters land on a platform jutting out of the side of the vessel, which would then retract into a hangar inside the hull.

The Prince wants it to be the biggest and most luxurious yacht in the world. Overseeing every detail himself, Alwaleed was paying attention to even the smallest things, like the type of wood for the handrails and the type of glass being used, and keeping his design team very much on their toes. Supervising the project, Mark Binnie, who looks after the Prince's current 5-KR yacht, tried to reassure his Royal client that it was still in the early stages, and that all the Prince's requirements would be met. Alwaleed seemed to nitpick even the smallest issues in front of the designers. He later turned to his advisers and explained that his tactic was to be tough on the small contracts in order to set the tone on the big ones, especially when a bigger contract is to be negotiated with the same company at a later date. This way, he can manage their expectations from the start and get added value.

After all the large blueprints and design drawings were rolled back up, and the handful of people involved in the yacht had departed, Awaleed sat back for a moment, content in his day of deal making so far. With only his close advisers around him, he declared, "I was born to get everything cheap!"

It's a phrase he likes to use from time to time to emphasize his confidence in his negotiating skills, and to illustrate that even he likes to save money. In real terms, when a yacht costs hundreds of millions of dollars to build, the savings alone can run in to tens of millions . . . but "cheap" is still a relative term when building a high-class floating palace.

By 8 P.M., the day was not even halfway through according to AST, Alwaleed Standard Time. He was still going strong.

Over the previous half hour, the Prince had managed to squeeze in a meeting with the assistant to the French prime minister, along with a couple of his investment advisers from the Kingdom Holding Company, to discuss, among other things, the fact that Euro Disney was sitting stagnant and suffering financial woes again. The Prince was looking for some tacit support from the government of France, since it had lobbied so hard to have the site placed on French soil, instead of another European country like Spain. The difficulty for the French government was that they knew their politically active public would not tolerate a bailout with taxpayers' money. It would take President Jacques Chirac's full diplomatic skills to be able to help without putting a political noose around his own neck. Nothing specific was resolved at the meeting, but Alwaleed was able to make the point that he was watching the situation closely, especially as he was expecting Disney to turn again to him for further investment before long.

At 8 P.M., on the dot, the Prince was ready to receive the wife of the president of Senegal, and his son, Karim Wade. Alwaleed's successful trip to Africa earlier in the year had triggered some business opportunities in the country, particularly in the hotel sector, plus the Prince had endeared himself to the First Lady of the country by donating $1 million to her pet project, education. Alwaleed was told that his donation was assigned to fund the building of about ten schools in Senegal.

Pleased that he was already making significant progress in at least one of the African countries he had visited, Alwaleed was looking charged and restless after the meeting with the Senegalese delegation, but he had just one more, quick item on his itinerary to deal with before he could take his exercise.

He kept the meeting brief with his head lawyer, Mark Mazo, of the American firm, Hogan and Hartson, and communications director Amjed Shacker, regarding a plan to create an advertising campaign for the Kingdom Holding Company. The Prince wanted to be able to use the logos of the top brand companies in which he was heavily invested, as part of both a print and television commercial campaign, illustrating the successes Kingdom has had in backing global names such as Four Seasons, Saks Fifth Avenue, Apple, Citigroup, and so on. For this he needed permission from the various companies, as their logos are trademarked and copyrighted. Anxious to get on with his evening walk, he decided to continue the discussion on this issue later that night, at Fouquet's café.

BODYGUARDS AND BEDOUINS

It's not unusual for people to parade up and down the Champs Élysées, either to shop, or to exercise, or to simply see and be seen. When Alwaleed's entourage steps out of the George V Hotel every evening, it's very different from anyone else on the street.

Though lacking long legs, the Prince's stride has even his taller associates huffing and puffing to keep up. With as many as twenty people pacing behind him, the Prince is an obvious sight on Paris's trendiest avenue. When visiting the city in August and September, the Prince gains the added stares of recognition from his countrymen, who flood into the French capital for part of their summer vacation. On occasion, his speedy perambulation is curtailed by an encounter with another member of the Saudi Royal family, such as one of the sons of King Fahd, or the offspring of another of his uncles, but otherwise, he cuts through the crowd almost like a bowling ball rolling through the pins.

It's the duty of his bodyguards to make sure his path remains as clear as possible—a tough task when most people barely have time to see the Prince coming, let along react by clearing the way.

Nasser Al Otaibi, one of the Prince's closest bodyguards, and the one who travels most with him overseas, guides the other members of security in what to do. As a matter of diplomatic courtesy, the French government offers a bodyguard to the Prince, and one each to his son, daughter, and spouse, while the Royal party is in town. It is usually the same security officers, so as to keep continuity and familiarity. As a result, each year, the bodyguards from Saudi Arabia greet the French ones with warmth and camaraderie . . . and no doubt compare firearms when they get a little free time.

Nasser paces along with the Prince, a few feet in front, but remaining close, while just a fraction behind, but also just in front of, Alwaleed, the French bodyguard follows his lead. The two anticipate obstacles such as crowds of people milling around in the middle of the footpath, or the changing of traffic lights at intersections, and, above all, potential threats to the Prince's safety. Licensed to carry guns, which they try to do unobstrusively in hip pouches when wearing casual clothes, the bodyguards always seem on edge. Perhaps that's to be expected with a loaded pistol pointing near one's groin.

In his position, Alwaleed has a number of security issues to consider, but he takes them in his stride: "There's a price we have to pay eventually, and that's a price I am paying obviously. I like to be alone, I like to be free, but that's the price of being what I am right now. I have to pay being a member of the Royal family, being a Saudi, having the wealth that God has bestowed on me. You have to pay the tax on that, and that is something I am willing to do."

But even if his wealth makes him and his family a target for kidnappings and ransoms, or his nationality and Royalty has its own deadly political implications—in light of tensions in his country—Alwaleed says he is not obsessed with the idea of personal protection: "I have one security guard from Saudi Arabia,

Princess Mona El Solh with Prince Alwaleed five months after he was born on March 7, 1955.

Prince Alwaleed with his father, Prince Talal Bin Abdulaziz Alsaud, and mother, Princess Mona, 1959.

Prince Alwaleed with his mother in 1959 in Beirut, where they lived after the divorce of his parents.

Prince Alwaleed in Beirut in 1960.

Two inspirational figures for Prince Alwaleed were his grandfathers: King Abdulaziz Bin Abdulrahman Alsaud (left) was the founding father of the modern-day Kingdom of Saudi Arabia. Riad El Solh was the first Prime Minister of independent Lebanon.

A birthday celebration in Beirut for the young Prince with his sister, Princess Reema, and his parents. The cowboy outfit was a present from his mother.

Wearing traditional dress, Prince Alwaleed is accompanied by his mother as his aunt Leila El Solh carries his sister, Princess Reema. His aunt now runs the Alwaleed Bin Talal Humanitarian Foundation in Beirut.

The three siblings would often reunite in Lebanon. Here, in 1962, a seven-year-old Prince Alwaleed with his sister, Princess Reema, while his mother guides her youngest son, Prince Khaled.

Attending the King Abdul Aziz Military Academy in Saudi Arabia 1968 to 1973. Prince Alwaleed describes it as: "one of the turning points in my life, whereby I became very self-dependent."

Graduating from Menlo College, in California, with a degree in business administration.

Three generations together: Prince Talal joining his son, Prince Alwaleed, and grandson, Prince Khaled, as the young boy celebrates his fourth birthday on April 21, 1982.

No one is closer to Prince Alwaleed than his children, Prince Khaled (left) and Princess Reem, seen here as youngsters with their father.

Summer vacation in 2000 saw the Prince with his children, Princess Reem and Prince Khaled, as they approached adulthood.

Home is a 460,000-square-foot palace in the heart of the Saudi capital, Riyadh. Prince Alwaleed shares the 317-room property with his children, who live in private wings on either side of this central section.

The global investment empire of the Kingdom Holding Company was built from this office in a two-story building near the center of Riyadh, pictured in February 2004.

The striking Kingdom Tower dominates the Riyadh skyline at 303 meters (994 feet). When it opened on October 23, 2003, it became the tallest building in Saudi Arabia.

A close relationship has grown between Prince Alwaleed and the Citigroup Chairman, Sandy Weill, seen here meeting at the bank's headquarters in New York City.

Prince Alwaleed is joined by his son, Prince Khaled, during renovations of the George V Hotel in Paris in 2000. Alwaleed took a personal interest in many of the renovation details.

Prince Alwaleed leads a gathering of world leaders around the Four Seasons hotel in the Egyptian resort of Sharm al-Sheikh in 2003. From left to right: Palestinian Prime Minister Mahmoud Abbas, Egypt's President Hosni Mubarak, Saudi Arabia's Crown Prince Abdullah Bin Abdulaziz Al-Saud, Bahrain's King Hamad bin Isa Al-Khalifa, Prince Alwaleed, Jordan's King Abdullah Bin Al-Hussein, U.S. President George W. Bush.

New York Mayor Rudolph Giuliani is presented with a $10 million check by Prince Alwaleed a month after the terrorist attacks of September 11, 2001. The rejection of the check later caused an international incident. *(Photograph by Mike Jensen)*

Prince Alwaleed has developed a close relationship with most of the Middle East leaders, including President Bashar Assad of Syria. The two men are seen here meeting in 2004.

Prince Alwaleed receives the Bethlehem Medal, the highest award from the Palestinian Authority from its late leader, Yasser Arafat, in Gaza in 2000. The Prince is the second largest contributor of aid to the Palestinian Authority after Saudi Arabia.

Prince Alwaleed congratulates Britain's Prince Charles after a polo match in Windsor attended by Queen Elizabeth and sponsored by the Kingdom Holding Company. England, 2003.

Boarding his personal Boeing 767 during his summer vacation to the South of France in 2003. In the meantime, the Prince was already fitting out its replacement—a Boeing 747 jumbo jet.

Making business calls on a flight to Paris, August 2003.

Prince Alwaleed's personal 747 jumbo jet on a test flight in 2004, prior to coming into service in June 2005.

The 83-meter (283-foot) *5KR* is used by Prince Alwaleed during his summer vacations. Its name comes from the initials of his children, Prince Khaled and Princess Reem. This yacht, previously owned by Adnan Khashoggi and Donald Trump, is also being replaced by one estimated at twice the size.

Keeping a close watch on financial developments while on vacation, August 2003.

Prince Alwaleed took up skiing in his forties so he could enjoy winter vacations with his children. Intensive lessons made him proficient by this trip to Jackson Hole, Wyoming, in January 2004. The Prince's private banker, Mike Jensen, joined him.

On the slopes of Jackson Hole with Prince Khaled and Princess Reem, January 2004.

The Prince has declared his strong affinity for desert culture and heritage, and spends every weekend at his desert camp just outside Riyadh.

The Prince's entourage is used to his weekend long walks in the desert, seen here green and lush after heavy rains in February 2004.

and the French government supplies me with some security, so really to me that is not an obsession at all. I believe in God, I am doing my best for my society and my region, and my best between the Arab world and Western world, so I don't believe I am a target."

His American friend of twenty-five years, Chuck Gulan, disagrees and insists bodyguards are a necessity for Alwaleed: "He should have them; I mean, he's no longer low-key. He's now high-key, and he has to have this protection because it's a must. You don't want anything to happen to this man, or any man of this importance, because that would hurt a lot of people."

Chuck's perspective is interesting, suggesting that the man who has enough investments to move markets needs to be protected not just for his own sake, but for the peace of mind of others, who would not want anything to upset their financial stability.

Security has been a part of the Prince's life since he was a child. Even if his time in Lebanon was free and easy of such concerns, his life in Saudi was woven into the Bedouin traditions, where firepower meant strength, and tribal friction dictated the need for armed desert warriors protecting the tent camps. Even now, when Alwaleed is in the desert, he is surrounded by traditionally robed Bedouins, many of them sporting bullet belts diagonally across their torsos, and ornamental pistols or rifles. In many cases the weapons are kept and worn more out of tradition than security, and often look like collectors' antiques that would present more of a liability to the person trying to fire them than to any potential target.

Still, it is symbolic and all about tradition, and that is something the Prince values.

While at the desert camp, Nasser Al Otaibi is obscured by his thobe and headdress, but his posture and constant proximity to the Prince clearly identify him as his protector. While traveling with Alwaleed, he dons suits and casual Western clothing, but his stance is still the same. Nasser, a thickset, ex-military man of medium height but wide, muscular frame, cannot afford to take chances. He will not let anyone near the Prince randomly in the street, unless he sees Alwaleed is making a move to allow it. Even with his dark sunglasses on, which he seems to be wearing most of the time, it is obvious that Nasser is looking around constantly. Apart from the pistol, he carries any devices he is allowed to, depending on the country or location. One of the most useful, he finds, is a device the size of a cigarette packet, capable of delivering thousands of volts to stun a would-be assailant. This stun gun, he says in a cautious voice while pointing to the device, will knock down even the biggest man and leave him helpless on the floor for at least a few minutes.

On the odd occasion where the bodyguard gets to wear shorts, for example, following the dress code of the Prince when he takes a stroll along the seafront in Cannes, it is possible to see the huge scars that Nasser has around both his knees. When asked about them, a lopsided grin parts his trim beard and moustache: "Parachuting in the military. Bad landing."

An economic description of what must have been a visual nightmare.

When the Prince does stop to talk to people in the street, Nasser moves in close, hands held in front of him near his hip pouch, watching every move directly around Alwaleed, while the taller, leaner-built French bodyguard with close-cropped blond hair, stands farther back, surveying the surroundings.

Usually, it is just a mixture of Arabs stopping to say hello, a glint of awe in their eyes, or distant relatives who are obliged to pay their respects. Interactions are kept short, largely because the Prince does not want to lose the flow of his walk, and also because the clock is constantly ticking toward the next item on the itinerary.

On this evening, the Prince had made the unusual decision to watch a movie again. Normally, the cinema visits are scheduled on alternate nights when Alwaleed is traveling, but presumably, because he had put in such long days with so many meetings since arriving in Paris, it was an opportunity to relax for a while.

By the time the walking group has reached the cinema, it had grown in size—first, because members of the entourage who had not joined the walk from the hotel spotted the Prince pacing the Champs Élysées and fell in line behind and, second, because some simply opted to meet the exercising group at the Guamant Marignan Cinema directly. This latter group included the older Bedouins in the entourage.

It is interesting for the average spectator to scrutinize the lineup of people constantly around Alwaleed. He always has, beyond his doctor, barber, and close company staff, a rather strange-looking crowd of older men with heavily weathered skin and remarkably craggy features. These half a dozen or so Bedouins who travel overseas with him seem so out of place. Their Western clothes fit them uncomfortably, particularly formal suits, which they wear with the ease of a straitjacket. Their ties hang like a colorful nooses dragging down from neck to the waist—or often halfway in between—as they are usually tied so clumsily. When visitors ask who these men are, and what purpose they serve, the explanation given is that Saudi tradition keeps the Royal family close to their Bedouin brethren who are referred to as *khouyeah* in Arabic, translating to mean something representing a "circle of friends." Apart from having deep-seated roots in Saudi tradition, the relationship between the Bedouins and Royals, such as Alwaleed, is based on respect for the passing of knowledge, values, and cultural strength. It may have a deeper significance, such as providing a close and direct connection with their desert kinsman, and protection in volatile days gone by, but essentially, they are a valuable part of an extended family now.

These wise old Bedouins often provide an alternative perspective on things and offer advice or counseling, but being familiar with Alwaleed's mischievous sense of humor, this particular band of cheeky rogues loves to joke around and jest with their relatively young prince. Many of the men are in their late sixties or midseventies, and one or two of them are approaching eighty, although that is hardly evident considering how sprightly they are, both physically and mentally. Unlike many of their aging Western counterparts, these men have led active lives, eaten mostly natural foods, and remained relatively close to nature. As a result they seem to bypass modern illnesses common elsewhere. They somehow keep up with the Prince's crazy schedule and maintain a high level of wit and energy. Alwaleed values them highly for their ability to keep the mood of the entourage positive and level, and for their natural sense of humor and perspective on what is otherwise a very demanding lifestyle for him.

Some of them acknowledge him as Abu Khaled, "Father of Khaled," using an honorific term. In the Middle East, a man is often affectionately named as father of his first son, so in the case of Alwaleed, with Khaled being the name of his boy, his title becomes Father of Khaled. Equally, his mother may be called "Umm Khaled," or "Mother of Khaled." The Prince's father, Prince Talal, would have been "Abu Waleed" according to this tradition.

One Bedouin in Abu Khaled's entourage stands out in particular—Aghsain Al Shaibaini. Coming to the end of his eighth decade, his remaining wispy gray hair, bushy moustache, and leathery skin etched heavily with lines still fail to hide the fire in his eyes. He bears the marks of someone who has been constantly beaten by the sun, and yet emerged the victor. One or two of the entourage members jokingly say he resembles an old version of the surrealist painter, the late Salvador Dalí. Perhaps a sun-dried version.

Nothing seems to faze Aghsain. His jolly cackle, coming from a wide mouth displaying a total lack of teeth, resembles the happy laugh of a child. He seems to fear nothing. One time in Cannes, he was seen speeding off into the distance on a jet ski. It was his first time on the machine, and despite not being able to swim, he was happy to crank up the power and head for the wide, blue yonder. Fortunately, a couple of the yacht's staff had managed to strap a life jacket onto him, in case he did fall off, and then others happened to be in a small powerboat nearby, enabling them to quickly chase him and steer him back to the yacht. He climbed off the jet ski visibly excited by his maiden voyage, and he celebrated his nautical first with all those observing from the deck by displaying a huge, gummy grin.

Aghsain and his companions provide endless entertainment for the Prince by their pseudoarguing and taunting of each other, and a constant stream of witty remarks, often peppered with Arabic folklore or proverbs. Most important, having spent so much time with the Prince—some of them joined the Prince's family before he was born—they know his moods through a sixth sense. Accordingly, they either keep quiet, allowing him to concentrate, or pipe up to lighten the atmosphere when it seems a bit dull.

Alwaleed acknowledges the value of their contribution to the mood of the entourage and says it is very important to stop negativity spreading when things get tough: "I am under tremendous pressure, there's no doubt about that—I acknowledge that very openly—so it's very important for me to handle things very discretely and not to have a problem or issue in one area be contagious in other aspects of my life. It is very diverse, so I try to take everything with laughter, with fun, and with joy, and not to load myself with too much pressure."

From watching him over the years, Chuck has this take on it: "In my opinion, he wants to make sure everyone else is happy and satisfied more so than himself—maybe a crazy statement, but he wants to be sure they are happy with the food they are eating, happy with what they're doing, what movie they are seeing, and if everyone isn't happy, then I think he's not happy. So he is very generous in that way—he wants to see his whole group happy."

The Prince's personal doctor, Jihad Aoukal, has seen the rare occasions when the pressure gets to the Prince, or something is bothering him: "When he is in a bad mood, I don't come close to him. I know he is in a bad mood, so I keep away unless he calls me to stay and sit down, because I know if he is in a bad mood, you can't negotiate with him, you can't say anything to him."

Chuck says the Prince has learned to separate business from

play in order to control any tensions: "He has a good sense of humor. When it's time for business, it's business, and there is always
time for fun, and there's always time for family, and always time
for his clan to be together and have fun. But when it comes to
business, then, I mean, it's business."

So the group gathered outside the cinema in Paris at 10:30 P.M. on
that warm summer night in June 2003. On this occasion, the
Prince had instructed Hani to book the entire theater for an extra
screening of the movie, as they couldn't make it in time for the
regular show.

One thing about the Prince is that he puts time before money.
Or rather, knowing that time is money, he will spend money to
make time for his money matters. Confused?

Perhaps Robert explains it better: "We don't do it always, if the
movie is playing at a time suitable for us, we go with everybody
else and see the movie, but if it is not, and His Highness would
still like to see the movie we can book the whole cinema. Although
he has billions, he doesn't spend a penny without getting something in return. He doesn't throw (away) his money. He can help
someone with a million dollars, (but) at the other end he can refuse to spend ten dollars that is going to waste."

Basically, knowing that his important meetings would run past
the regular film show times, the Prince found it more convenient
to continue with his itinerary of important business, and then
spend a bit more cash booking the entire cinema screen to see the
film at the time that best suited his own schedule.

Once the entire group had collected outside, the Prince and his
entourage strolled in to the empty theater. The bleary-eyed staff,
which had stayed on to keep the cinema open for the extra show,
did not look particularly surprised. This was something the Prince
did quite regularly while in Paris.

If he was willing to pay, they were willing to work.

NIGHTS AT FOUQUET'S

The waiters at Fouquet's, just along from the cinema, toward the George V Hotel, were also used to the needs of Prince Alwaleed. Robert and Hani had built up a good working relationship with the management of all of the establishments the Prince regularly favored on his trips. The prime corner at the front of the café was always at the Prince's disposal. In fact, he took over the entire small room that comprised that section of the café. Even then, it was a crowded and musty setting of tables jammed too close, and it reeked of better times. The waiters served as much an air of diffidence—for which French service is famous—as they did the contents of the limited menu. Surviving on nostalgia, and the memories of the wealthy who still patronize it, Fouquet's is considered more of a tourist experience than anything else for most people. For Alwaleed, it is strategic, being close to his hotel, and it is riddled with the memories of his childhood, so he easily looked past the faults inherent in the famous old establishment and set up his usual evening camp there.

One bodyguard stood outside, next to the window where the Prince sat exposed to the street, while the other sat at one of the satellite tables nearby. On the occasions where the Prince was at the café with his children or spouse, the various bodyguards could be seen inside grouped together, chatting and catching up on the day's events, and no doubt comparing potential life-threatening situations they spotted here and there.

Looking back on it, Alwaleed seemed to enjoy the movie, unlike some of the science fiction or action adventure he has sat through. He has a system whereby he asks Robert or Hani to get a list of all the movies playing at the cinema, with a brief synopsis of each. Then he gets them to pass it around the entourage for a vote. The movie with the most votes is the one democratically selected. The Bedouins are usually not consulted as they don't speak English, and often give the movie a miss—especially as they are probably disappointed to find *Lawrence of Arabia* is never among the listings.

Anger Management, a comedy with Adam Sandler and Jack Nicholson, was more the Prince's style of film. He had found it amusing. Not that the Prince needed any tips from the movie's theme . . . it probably had content more relevant to the aviation executives he had hammered the day before.

Sitting in Fouquet's, sipping Perrier after the film, he started off by getting an update on the Boeing 747 situation from Captain Duncan Gillespie and consultant Brett Lindsay. It seems his pressure had worked, and they were close to finalizing a decision and contract. The Prince would be kept updated.

Then he continued his look at the advertising campaign with lawyer Mark Mazo and his associate, Dan Macoby, based out of Hogan and Hartson's London office. It was decided that they would start off by writing letters asking for permission to use the various corporate logos in the Kingdom Holding Company advertisement. They would contact key people at the various corporations, such as Saks Fifth Avenue, Apple Computers, and AOL Time Warner, the latter helped by the fact that Alwaleed had earlier met the chairman, Dick Parsons, for a friendly chat.

As for the request to Citigroup, the Prince's flagship investment, where about half his wealth was held, that would be left in the hands of the man sitting very close by, Michael Jensen.

THE MAN WATCHING THE MONEY

A financial magazine once explained that Mike Jensen could tell you a lot about the Prince . . . but he'd have to kill you. Though far too much a gentleman to contemplate homicide, the tall, suave private banker is actually governed by some of the strictest regulations in the financial world. He can serve a long term in prison for revealing the wrong thing, and, as an extended period of incarceration is not one of his goals in life . . . it would be easier to kill you than tell you.

Jensen, who has more than a passing resemblance to a James Bond figure, being well groomed, slim, athletic, and dressed stylishly, has spent a decade working closely with Alwaleed. It had started with a two-minute introduction in April 1993, when the Prince had been to visit his personal banker, Cedric Grant, at Citibank. Grant was the long-term unique relationship partner for Alwaleed, while Jensen was doing corporate finance for Citigroup at the time, and so had little to contribute to the Royal client at that point: "In April 1994 the Prince had some technical questions for Cedric, and Cedric was not able to answer them because he was a private banker, so he came to me with the technical questions and I got the answers and gave them to the Prince at Cedric's request. Then the Prince came back with some more technical questions and I responded to them, and so that led to me doing some work for His Highness on some corporate issues. Over the year, Cedric and I became a team working for the Prince—Cedric was the account officer and private banker and I was the technician, the corporate finance technician, who was called in periodically."

As the Prince's business was primarily corporate finance and not banking related, Jensen's relationship with the Royal investor grew rapidly. Equally important was his ability to fit perfectly into the manic pace of the Prince's business and private life.

First of all, Jensen is remarkably fit, despite approaching sixty, sharing the Prince's enthusiasm for regular exercise and careful diet. A trained pilot, and something of a sports car fan, he is happy to parachute out of airplanes and take on physically challenging tasks. The Prince, however, is more interested in his sharp, analytical mind, and his ability to rapidly assess investment opportunities. Jensen also shares Alwaleed's addiction to information and research, allowing him to have a sound base from which to work. Still, it is tricky, because Jensen knows that when he is presenting material to the Prince, his client is often as well read up on the details as the Citibank financial team: "One treads cautiously. Though we do much of the research for him—that's part of our role, to generate research for him and sift through research on his behalf—he's got other sources. But we're a major source, and we send him the raw data, as well as a short synopsis of it, and then I will give my opinion based on the analysis, which the Prince can either agree with or disagree with."

As is typical of Alwaleed, it took time for him to trust the banker: "I think it's easier today than it was in the past. Part of my job in the past, when I was the corporate finance head working with Cedric—he was the relationship manager—was to tell the Prince some of the things that maybe he didn't want to hear, but should hear. So, over the years that has led to the Prince gaining some trust in me, because generally we have been more often closer to right than wrong."

Right enough times to allow Jensen and his team of five in Geneva to oversee the Prince's global stock investments and manage his cash accounts—which often total well over a billion dollars. They also assist in monitoring Alwaleed's family trust, in which he has placed most of his assets.

Even by the time the Prince first met Jensen in 1993, he already had a lot of experience under his belt. He had clocked up twenty-six years at Citibank, having started straight out of university at UCLA, and rapidly moved on to a series of senior postings including São Paulo, Manila, Seoul, Bogotá, and Tokyo, before finally heading to London and then Geneva.

It served him well and he doesn't look any worse for wear and tear from such extensive global travel. His full head of silvery-gray hair does not detract from what is still a boyish face, and easy laugh, but it is his methodical manner, and ability to know when he has to get down to serious business, that allows him to be the perfect filter for the Prince. He takes proposals, reports, and pitches from the big investment banking houses, sifts through them, and then only passes onto Alwaleed what he believes would be worthwhile for the Royal investor to consider. Jensen says that in his research of a prospective buy-in deal for the Prince, he checks out the condition of the company, and then sets an entry point that is tailored to Alwaleed's growth requirements, which according to the banker is usually an internal rate of return (IRR) of 20 percent.

Jensen's top job at Citi, taking care of such an important client, put him in the ideal position to approach the bank's bosses for permission to use their logo in the Kingdom advert, which is what the Prince now wanted.

Having agreed to a plan of action, the Prince's group left Fouquet's café as the place closed down at 2 A.M. and sauntered back over to the George V Hotel, just a five-minute walk away. It would only be a brief session of reading and an "early" light supper, as there was a big day coming up.

WIRED FOR BUSINESS

There would be no sleep for Raouf Aboud that night.

His room on the first floor of the hotel looked like a cross between a printing shop and an electronics store. The tables in the lounge area were littered with a selection of walkie-talkies sitting in charging bases arranged in rows, plus mobile phones, and computers rigged to the Internet. Alongside the wall, a large professional printer was sitting silent for a change. Normally, it would be chugging out multiple oversized A3 paper prints of newspapers and magazine.

In the bedroom just off the lounge, there was very little space left to move around, because a dozen or so empty, large professional travel cases with superhard shells were piled up.

Raouf's room was the nerve center of communications for the Prince and his team.

Conversation with the tall, stocky Algerian is difficult, because every few moments, one of his many phones goes off, having him fumbling between pockets for the right one. When the Prince calls, his hand goes automatically to the one clipped at the front of his trousers on his belt. No time for fumbling that one.

Raouf's shiny, shaved head and olive complexion give him the air of a henchman from a James Bond movie, even more so, if he is next to Jensen, but his big, relaxed smile reveals the gentle side of this constantly harried telecommunications expert.

He has every conceivable type of telecommunications gadget, including a variety of GSM mobiles, satellite phones, and walkie-talkies. His job is to make sure that wherever in the world the Prince is, he can be reached, and more important, he can reach out and still do business. Raouf is the link, so he himself is permanently connected to the Prince and responds quickly. When any new location is reached, Raouf replaces the telephone set in the Prince's hotel suite with a duplicate of the one Alwaleed has at home and in his office in Riyadh. The buttons are preprogrammed and labeled to allow him to connect with ease. By simply pressing button number one, he gets directly through to his palace in Riyadh. Equally, there are preprogrammed buttons to get his family, security, Raouf, the travel guys, and any other key personnel. In most cases, Alwaleed will simply call Raouf and ask him to locate the person he needs to contact.

According to Raouf, the telephone connection is crucial to the Prince, but so is television: "Every place the Prince sits, we set up a TV for him, and a telephone—*wherever* he is, he has to have telephone, and he has to have access to TV."

Even when the Prince is not in front of the box, he is still indirectly connected, says Raouf: "When he's walking he's connected by the telephone, and we have someone in Riyadh who is watching TV all day, and if something happens on TV, he just lets us know and then we can tape it, or they can send it to us."

In fact, Raouf was asked by the Prince to look into a new system, which, he explains, uses satellite and the Internet to transmit video via the MPEG4 format, allowing Alwaleed and his team to receive and send video wherever they are in the world.

Raouf says his job is particularly busy when the Prince is on the road, away from his Riyadh base: "He gets people on the line all day, especially when he's walking. This is the best time for him to do deals, by the way, and sometimes he has two or three conference calls a day just while he is walking. He says, I want a conference call with this guy, and this guy, and I have to get all the people on the line, and he talks to them and he makes deals."

Alwaleed's heavy investment in the tech sector and telecommunications sector has failed to make him a "gadget freak." He still prefers to use small, palm-sized index cards on which his itinerary is marked with color-coded appointments. Throughout the day, Alwaleed will make corrections with a colored pen. He favors green ink, as green is the color representing Islam.

His low-tech method is something he adopted many years ago, as a youth. His cousin Riad Assaad remembers that Alwaleed always used his index cards. One time, years later, when they bumped into each other in Saudi Arabia in 1992, Riad asked him a question: "I said, 'What has happened to the amount of your wealth now?' He said, 'Wait a minute.' So then he takes out these index cards. 'Ah! I have . . . in Citibank, USB . . .' Then, meeting three years later, I ask, 'What has happened with the index cards?' 'Ah, sorry! The index cards.' So he takes out the index cards again, and we are talking two index cards, and he has written them with his own handwriting."

Despite stubbornly sticking with his index cards, Alwaleed demands the latest technology to stay in touch, and it's Raouf's job to be on top of it: "You'd be impressed if you talked with the Prince about all this technology, because even though I am a professional in telecommunications, he knows things, and you cannot tell him anything new, because he reads so much, and he knows how everything works. Every week I receive articles from His Royal Highness on new technology, asking where is this, why didn't you tell me about this, you should tell me about this. He's following up on technology and aviation telecommunications."

Raouf says there is not a single moment when Alwaleed is not connected somehow: "No, it never happens—24 hours a day, 365 days a year. He does business wherever he is—even in his sleep he does business."

This fateful night, Raouf had to forsake his own sleep in order to pack up his extensive collection of equipment for the crazy day ahead.

PARACHUTE PRINCE

Among all the Prince's people, Mike Jensen may be the only expert at high-altitude parachuting (apart from the bodyguards), but Alwaleed certainly knows how to parachute in and out of countries, metaphorically speaking.

Tuesday, June 17, 2003, was a tense day for the Prince's travel manager, Robert El Hage, from the moment he woke up at 7 A.M., on only three hours of sleep, until his head finally hit the pillow almost twenty-four very tough hours later.

This day was an Alwaleed Special. Six cities in four countries— in one day.

Robert would travel with the Prince's party at 9 A.M., while Hani would accompany Alwaleed's then-wife, Princess Kholood, along with the Bedouin entourage and Dr. Jihad, as they departed later in the day at 3 P.M. for the EuroStar train that would take them directly from Paris to London, the Prince's final destination.

The Boeing 767 was waiting ready to depart as soon as Alwaleed and a relatively compact team of about ten people boarded at Le Bourget Airport on the outskirts of Paris. That is the location used by most private flights and also is the site of the annual Paris Airshow.

By 10:30 A.M., Captain Gillespie was climbing to 32,000 feet, en route to Amsterdam Airport. As soon as the plane had leveled off, the Prince jumped up out of his seat and went over to one of the porthole windows, looking around outside with a puzzled look on his face. He then beckoned to Raouf and asked if the "other jet" was behind.

Raouf said he would check with the captain, and returned a few moments later to confirm that the "other jet" was indeed on a flight path following close behind, and that the Prince simply couldn't see it because of its relative position.

It turns out that Alwaleed had hired a small, eight-seat private jet to follow his Boeing 767 on its travels for this whole day. He explained that he did it as "insurance," in case his Boeing faced any problems, messing up his tight schedule with all those high-powered meetings. In such an instance, he would simply be able to hop onboard the smaller jet with a core team of people.

At $30,000, that was expensive insurance for one day.

From Paris, a short hop in the air, and the Prince was greeted less than an hour later by Saudi Arabia's ambassador in Holland, Waleed Al Khuraijy, and was soon heading with him in a convoy of limousines to Soestdjik Palace, to meet with Prince Bernard of the Netherlands.

Shortly after midday, the Prince emerged from the stately home and was heading by road to Nieuwegein, near Rotterdam, to pay a courtesy call to the top executives at the world-class Dutch construction firm Ballast Nedam, in which Alwaleed is heavily invested.

That was not a long visit, either, as the Prince then had to head by limo to The Hague, where the minister of housing was due to bestow a national decoration upon the Prince, the "Officer in De Orde Van Orange-Nassau" award. After she made the presentation, the Minister cracked open a bottle of champagne in celebration, but the Prince declined, explaining he did not drink alcohol, requesting a glass of water instead. As photos were being taken with the Prince and the ministers together, glasses in hand, Alwaleed suddenly hesitated. He asked the photographer to hold on a moment, and then asked if he could have his water in a straight glass, not a wineglass, as he had originally been given.

The minister was baffled, but quickly arranged it, while the Prince explained that if the pictures were printed in black and white, it might appear as though he had a glass of white wine in his hand, since only the shape of the glass would indicate the contents. Not wanting to send the wrong message, he opted for a more obvious straight glass for water.

As the Prince and his team shuttled back and forth in the large black limousines, his Boeing 767 and the "other jet" had made their way to Rotterdam Airport and were awaiting his arrival at 3:45 P.M. As would be expected, Alwaleed was on schedule and was in the air by 4 P.M., on his way to Dublin Airport to meet with the Irish president, Mary McAleese.

Even while keeping to his tight time schedule, the Prince was able to be composed and relaxed as he sat with Ireland's leader. He surprised her by discussing changes in the Irish economy in detail, and the country's positioning within Europe, and the two even traded some humorous stories. Half an hour later, at 5:30 P.M., the limousines left the presidential palace and merged with the rush-hour Dublin traffic, threatening, for the first time, to dent the Prince's otherwise perfect time-keeping.

The limousine driver, with a typical laid-back Irish attitude, said not to worry, it would work out fine. Looking out onto the stationary cars clogging the narrow streets of the Irish capital, Alwaleed was not so sure.

WATCHING THE CLOCK

Promptness is essential to the Prince, to the extent that if he arrives at a location early, he will either sit in the limousine, or preferably go for one of his power walks, until it is the exact moment of the appointment.

He even admits that he cannot explain why he has such an obsession with being perfectly on time, and that sometimes he spends time wondering how he became like that.

On one occasion, when he was due to meet with Steve Jobs, of Apple Computers, near San Jose in California, the Prince and his team arrived twenty minutes early. Without hesitating, the Prince strode off at full speed around the campus-like building, until he was due to appear for the meeting. As he walked through the front door, straight to the person waiting to greet him at reception, he looked around at members of the entourage, tapped his watch, and smiled, before being led upstairs to Jobs.

In another light moment in Atlanta, Georgia, while on his way to meet with the former U.S. president Jimmy Carter, Alwaleed, Mike Jensen, and a couple of others from the team found themselves stuck in a stretch limousine parked in slow-moving traffic on the city's downtown highway. The Prince shouted to the small and elderly, but wily, African American driver that he would give him $300 if he could make it to the Carter Center by 5:30 P.M., in time for the appointment. At first the driver stared back at his passenger through his rearview mirror, wide-eyed and disbelieving. This would be a full week's salary in one afternoon—as a tip.

"Now, are you playin' wid me?" he asked in a slow, heavy Atlanta accent, not taking his eyes off Alwaleed, as the car languished in traffic, clock ticking desperately.

Alwaleed looked bemused: "Why are you wasting time?! Thirteen minutes left!"

The driver quickly swung the elongated car out of the line of traffic and toward an exit slip road off the motorway: "Ah hope yowh a man of yowh word. Ah'm a man of mah word; Ah hope yowh a man of yohwz."

Within moments the large limousine had found its way onto the city's backstreets, and was winding its way rapidly toward Jimmy Carter's low-rise office, which is set in small park to the east of the city center.

Realizing the pressure was off as the Carter Center approached, Alwaleed teased the driver: "It's your lucky day. You're going to get your $100 dollars."

The driver's eyes shot to rearview mirror, where he could see Alwaleed trying to keep a straight face.

"You said $300! Ah'm keepin' mah word. Ah hope yowh gonna keep yohwz. Dhon' be playin' wid me."

As the Prince stepped out to the greeting party at the Carter

Center, thirty seconds early, he turned to Robert and told him quietly to make sure the driver got his $300.

Whether it is through planning, or luck, or occasionally the added incentive of a large tip, Alwaleed is rarely off his time-keeping, and sure enough, he pulled up to his jet waiting at Dublin Airport in time for the scheduled takeoff at 6:15 P.M.

The next stop was the city of Exeter in the west of England. Landing shortly after 7 P.M., it was only a short drive to Exeter University, where the Prince was meeting with the vice-chancellor; attending a seminar at the Institute of Arab and Islamic Studies, to which he was heavily donating financial support; and attending a brief reception that would include an interview with a local journalist.

Spending nearly two hours in Exeter seemed like light relief compared with the rapid buzz of the earlier part of the day. The Prince was more relaxed. He had met most of his high-level commitments and could let the "other jet" go, as his insurance was no longer needed.

The day was easing up by 9:30 P.M., when the Prince's 767 took off from Exeter Airport to London's Stansted Airport. It was not the most central location, and involved a lengthy road journey to get into the center of town, but was the most convenient airport where he could get permission to fly in with his large private jet.

It was 11:15 P.M. by the time Alwaleed walked into the Four Seasons Hotel off Park Lane in the heart of London, and he had only two meetings left, starting at midnight, including a representative from a charity, and a magazine journalist.

Before they arrived, he called over Hani and asked what time the last movies were playing, and what specifically was showing, and then requested that he get a vote from the entourage.

Hani returned a few moments later and told him the preferred choices, but indicated that the last showing had already begun.

"Okay," the Prince said looking at his itinerary card. "Tell them we'll be there at 1:30 A.M."

If Robert and Hani snored through the movie, no one could hear them, and no one could certainly blame them. The day had gone without a hitch, and their boss was happy.

As the ambient light of the big screen flickered onto the faces of the two dozen people occupying the massive Empire Leicester Square Theatre, it was clear that many of them had shut their eyes, oblivious to the adventures of the British actor, Rowan Atkinson, as the spoof spy "Johnny English." Better known to the world as Mr. Bean, the comedian would have been disappointed to look out from the celluloid to spot a near-empty theater where even the few occupants were making up for lost time in their beds. Fortunately, Johnny English was too busy saving the world.

It didn't end there, either. The Prince was fully charged from his successful day and had made Hani book the theater next door so that the entourage could watch another film of their choice, *Matrix 2*. Some woke up enough to enjoy this but didn't notice the Prince leave shortly after the film had started. It was not his favorite type of movie, but he knew that if was spotted getting up and going, the entourage, out of respect and protocol, would have followed him. He chose instead to sneak away, back to the hotel, where he could get on with some reading.

The Prince reads a lot. There's the daily dose of newspapers printed out from the Internet by Raouf, who plops the latest *New York Times*, *Wall Street Journal*, *Washington Post*, and *International Herald Tribune* in front of his boss every night. Raouf says that getting them from the Internet, he is able to get them to the Prince before even most New Yorkers have their hands on them. There are also all the worthy magazines, such as *Newsweek*, *Time*, *BusinessWeek*, and the *Economist*.

Then there are the books. Alwaleed says that up until 2003, he had been reading a lot of political books, including biographies of political players, analysis of political scenarios, and so on, but had then shifted his focus to finance-focused publications, such as *Yes, You Can Time the Market* by Ben Stein and Phil DeMuth.

He admits to getting anxious as he approaches the end of any book, confessing that he starts counting how many pages are left as he is close to finishing and feels the urgency to read faster to complete the book.

The Prince was already deep in his nighttime reading and research by the time the rest of the group returned from Leicester Square, to a buffet meal laid out in the lobby seating area of the Four Seasons Hotel.

Outside, dawn was breaking.

ROYAL CIRCLES

If variety is the spice of life, than Prince Alwaleed's life is the equivalent of a bustling Eastern spice market. Having spent the previous day trekking across Europe and the United Kingdom, holding business meetings, receiving awards, and donating to charitable causes, he was now preparing to mix with Britain's Royals at a sports tournament.

The GCC (Gulf Co-operation Council) Polo Cup 2003 Final was being held in Windsor, close to the home of Queen Elizabeth II, and Alwaleed was one of the sponsors of the match. Players on the Prince of Wales's team included Prince Charles himself, and his younger son, Prince Harry, who had apparently become something of a whiz at the sport.

A 2 P.M. lunch at the Four Seasons preceded the bus trip over to Windsor, about thirty miles outside the center of London. The Prince enjoys traveling by bus, as it keeps him close to the entourage and allows him to either deal with any outstanding matters or concerns of particular individuals, or simply joke around with various people.

Between 4 P.M. and 7 P.M. the match was played at the Royal

Guards Polo Club at Windsor, with a presentation of the trophy and awards jointly by the Queen and Prince Alwaleed, in the presence of the Duke of Edinburgh, Prince Philip, and the Queen's second son, Prince Edward.

As it happened, Prince Charles's team won and collected the trophy.

In their casual chat over a glass of orange juice immediately after the match, Alwaleed told a still flushed and perspiring Charles about the time the Queen personally drove his uncle, Crown Prince Abdullah, around her private estate, while he was over in the United Kingdom on a visit. On his return to Saudi Arabia, the Crown Prince had related to Alwaleed how he grew increasingly nervous as Her Majesty spent most of the time behind the wheel of her car looking at *him*, deeply in conversation. It did not take long before a frightened and anxious Crown Prince Abdullah kept pointing ahead, indicating to the British monarch that she should be watching the road.

Alwaleed told Prince Charles that his uncle's memory of that tour was how nervous he had been about the Queen's driving.

Prince Charles smiled and nodded knowingly.

Shortly after, charity checks were presented, followed by a brief afternoon tea with the Queen and Prince Charles, before Alwaleed made his way back into central London.

The large bus got stuck in traffic for a while at Knightsbridge, opposite the world-famous Harrods department store, owned by the Egyptian businessman, Mohammed Al Fayed. Looking over at the distinctive building through the bus window, Alwaleed talked about his interest in buying the exclusive British landmark, but explained how the high price Al Fayed was seeking made it anything but a bargain. Still, he did glance back at it a couple of times as the bus moved past.

Getting stuck at a traffic light a little over half a mile from the hotel, near Hyde Park, the Prince glanced at his watch.

8:05 P.M.

Looking at the row of car taillights in front of the bus, he shook his head and asked how far away the hotel was from the current location. When he found out, he ordered the driver to open the door, and hopped out, causing a scramble among the entourage to join him on the street. Before long, he was striding toward the Four Seasons, off Park Lane. He pushed through the front door at precisely 8:15 P.M. gloating.

His 9 P.M. exercise walk through the streets of London proved to be a little more challenging than on the Champs Élysées, because the narrow footpaths and winding roads with many intersections become a nightmare for the security trying to flank the Prince. Still, he would not be deterred, and his walk took the entourage to the cinema once more. The Prince opted for a meal by 2 A.M., a little earlier than usual, but carried on reading until dawn.

Quite often, his habit is to stay awake until it is time for the dawn prayer of the day, according to Islamic schedules. The Prince points out that it is worse for him to go to bed for a short period of time, and then get up to pray, and return to bed again. Instead, he often opts for a predawn walk, returning in time to pray, and then going to bed.

Alwaleed's daily timetable has built in gaps for the various prayer times, which are distributed to the Muslims in his team along with the itinerary for the day.

The next day was the last of this short trip, but it was to be no less busy.

The standard midday gathering soon set off as the Prince led everyone to an early exercise walk, before departing in the bus for Stansted Airport, an hour or so drive north of London.

The 4:45 P.M. flight to Geneva took off on time, landing around 7:15 P.M., and Alwaleed took his team straight to the Hotel Des Bergues, a property he had identified for purchase and refurbishment.

The entourage then stayed in the hotel lobby to have a buffet meal, while the Prince, escorted only by his security, set off for the Genolie Clinic to visit his ailing uncle, Prince Mishaal Bin Abdulaziz Alsaud.

Alwaleed then returned to the hotel for a proper tour and assessment of the state of it, before heading back to the aircraft.

By 9:30 P.M., the team was back in the air, heading for the Italian town of Pisa.

There was another large bus waiting at Pisa Airport to take the Prince to Florence, but the delay in the journey had the Prince wondering if he was going to be on time. As it was, he walked into the hotel in Florence just as the clock struck midnight. He had arrived exactly on time to wish his daughter, Reem, a happy twenty-first birthday.

She was glad to spend the time with her father, who took a tour of the hotel with her and visited her room to make sure it was up to scratch, and that she was comfortable. Reem's trip to Florence gave her a break away from her schooling environment and the routine of life at home in Saudi Arabia, but it did not take her away from some of the issues that bother her deep down. She was still manacled to the need for security and constant vigil for her safety, no matter how low the perceived threat.

Reluctantly, Alwaleed bid his daughter farewell around 1:30 A.M., and boarded the bus to drive back from Florence to the airport at Pisa. As the vehicle approached Pisa, the Prince got a wild idea.

He asked the driver how far the Leaning Tower of Pisa was from the route the bus was taking to the airport. The driver indicated that it was not that far, so the Prince decided to contact the aircraft and delay the takeoff and make a visit to the world-famous tower in the early hours.

At 3 A.M., two local policemen, sitting huddled in a lone car parked close to the tower, were baffled to see, strolling along the path, a crowd of about two dozen foreign-looking people, including some surly old guys with sunburned faces.

HOME ON THE DESERT PLAIN

Relief was clearly etched on the faces of the Kingdom Holding Company staff as they made their way down the steps from the jet into the bright Riyadh sunshine. The high temperature of the desert sun is made more bearable by the fact that Riyadh is known for very low humidity, so although the danger of overheating still exists, the immediate discomfort of stepping into the summer sunshine is far less.

It was close to midday, and fortunately, it was a Friday, the main weekend day in Saudi Arabia. The team could finally rest after successfully getting the Prince through his whirlwind tour and back.

The employees of the Prince feel satisfaction when such an event goes so well, but they feel the burnout, too. What makes them persist with the job when it is so tough? The Prince has his own perspective on the matter: "The way we run our business is very professional, yet very personable. The hiring process here is very difficult. To hire someone here, no matter how small the rank is, we go through a difficult process; we screen them, we talk to them, we have a dialogue with them, and we show them that they come here to stay. We don't have people leave within a month or two months or a year or two, three years. Most of the people have been with me for five, seven, eight, ten years, and we have a very good relationship, but it's very professional. We have a very small number of people but there are some common things among them, for example, they are all in their thirties to forties, they are all American-educated or English-educated, they are all technologically oriented, they are all fast, and they all have good, high IQs. They are all dynamic and they mesh together."

Alwaleed confesses that he uses his system of bonuses as a strong incentive to get the most out of his people. He had seen it work when he took over the United Saudi Commercial Bank in the late 1980s, and turned it around by using such incentives: "It's very much balanced. Our salaries are not very high, but the incentives are always relatively high. So we tend more toward awards and rewards than salary, because if you are guaranteed to have that salary at the end of the month or at the end of the quarter—you will just work normally."

He prefers a much faster pace with more drive, and he adds that with a quarterly bonus scheme, people stand to make much more than a standard salary, if they prove themselves consistently. That is a tough call considering what are, for most people, very long days and eccentric work hours. Alwaleed refutes that: "Eccentric to whom? To the people here—to me—they are normal. At the end of the day, when you have success, when people are seduced by success and results, they just love it, they feel part of it. No one wants to be associated with failure. We are the number one company in Saudi Arabia and the Middle East. We are ahead of many government-owned companies—with only about thirty-four people."

Amjed Shacker, who handles the Prince's public relations and has spent nearly a decade in his service, believes there is more direct contact possible with Alwaleed than with the heads of many top companies: "How many bosses in this world would allow you to talk to them very openly and very freely, and how many bosses care to know what your family problems are? How many bosses would care to know the names and ages of your children? How many bosses will try to resolve any marital problems you might have, or family issues? How many bosses will try to help you sort out financial problems that you might have? So he doesn't become just a boss, he becomes a friend."

Even then, Amjed admits, Alwaleed does not open up to everyone: "You have to gain his trust, and he believes in the (Ronald) Reagan principle of trust over time, and he does that. He trusts a lot of people, but he trusts different people with different issues. To trust a person with more issues than others is a privilege that, I would say, only two or three people around him have."

The Prince's personal physician, Jihad Aoukal, adds that it takes a long time to win Alwaleed's trust, but that once it gets there, he rewards the loyalty of extended service. He says that the

Prince sometimes spontaneously shares his good fortune with the people around him: "He would have stocks going up, showing a good investment, and he would write on a small piece of paper and give it to me, and two or three guys from the entourage, (promising) a big amount of money . . . like gratitude, like, 'Guys, I'm doing good, so you have to be in good shape too,' sharing the good fortune."

Jihad says that the most *expensive* thing that Alwaleed gave him was a house worth a million dollars . . . but the most *valuable* thing was his trust.

When asked how hard it is to have real friends, being in such an elevated position financially and socially, Alwaleed, does not elaborate but simply says: "It is not very hard, really. I have very good friends in Saudi Arabia, in the region and internationally, even in the United States. I have very good friends from various communities and various religions."

But although Alwaleed pays attention to every detail concerning his people, he himself is not an easy person to get to know intimately. Even those who can catch up and then keep up with him on his accelerated trips around the world still have to invest a lot of time in getting to know him properly, as well as winning his confidence. His life is one where he takes his family around with him, but it is cocooned in the confines of an entourage and security. His generation may be comfortable with such traditions and rituals, but it will be interesting to see how far the next generation will take it, particularly the constraints of living with an entourage and security.

His son, Prince Khaled, takes it philosophically: "Look, it's difficult, but that's the hand we were dealt with from God, not from anyone else. So I accept it, my sister accepts it, my father accepts it, we deal with it, and we make the best of it. I can't complain. Okay, I'm going to complain about time off, I'm going to complain about time alone, (but) other people are complaining about not having dinner tomorrow, or not knowing what tomorrow has to offer. I do thank God, so I'm not going to complain about that. I'm blessed and I'm very thankful."

But a small spark of defiance comes from Alwaleed's intelligent and independent-minded daughter, Reem, who says that, for sure, she can see herself living without bodyguards: "Yeah, and I definitely will, eventually. It's too much; I don't really like to be around people a lot, and actually being out there with people that are always watching you, it just gets on my nerves. So, yeah, one day, I will. You'll see me walking alone, and I'll be looking all around me—and have no one behind me."

CHAPTER 10

The Kingdom of Business

He does business wherever he is—even in his sleep he does business.

— RAOUF ABOUD, PRINCE ALWALEED'S
HEAD OF COMMUNICATIONS

If Prince Alwaleed's lifestyle was a song, it would be heavy rock. It has a solid beat that stomps through everything else in an orderly fashion, with little or no spontaneous variation. He likes to plan it in a clear, linear manner and follow through with no diversions.

But look into his mind, and the tune is definitely jazz. It goes in every direction, with changes in speed and volume, and can be unpredictable. It's the sound of many instruments complementing each other, or often competing to be heard, and is a multilayered audio-fest.

It is hard to believe that the jazz in his head is so effectively converted to the rock of his twenty-four-hour schedule. His explanation is offered in one word: "Compartments."

The reason the Kingdom Holding Company can function with such a small staff for such a diverse multibillion-dollar operation is purely because the Prince puts everything into compartments. What swirls around in his head is released into specific channels.

The Royal finger wags emphatically: "It's all about compartmentalizing. I have people who are specialists in a particular area, and I make sure I delegate the right tasks to the right people. There's little or no crossover—each one knows what he or she has to do, and they just get on with it. Each compartment of my life runs itself. I just have to manage it."

Before the automatic pilot is engaged, though, the Prince pays very close attention to the details, in order to get the system in place and bring people up to speed. Unlike other top businessmen who have layers and layers of advisers, the Prince has just a few people involved, and he makes most of the decisions himself. In fact, he often advises his advisers because he accumulates a massive knowledge bank and is completely up-to-date on current affairs due to the huge volume of research and reading he does.

Amjed Shacker heads the "public relations compartment" and is one of those who frequently gets articles dropped on his desk from the Prince's office, marked up in green ink in Alwaleed's handwriting, suggesting that he follow up on the items high-lighted. He says it is hard to figure out how the Prince can get through so much information daily. Alwaleed has his eye on everything, says Amjed, and is also prone to closely watching new recruits and overseeing everything they do: "Micromanagement is prevalent in areas where employees have not been on the job for a long time and do not understand the Prince very well. The Prince micromanages these areas up until these people have gained his trust to the full extent, and that depends on the individual. If the individual fails to gain the trust, it means the individual has failed to fulfill the task he or she was hired to accomplish."

MANAGING COMPARTMENTS

The compartments at Kingdom Holding Company deal with the major, day-to-day investment and business work of the Prince, along with his scheduling, traveling, public relations and media and communications. Run for years from a very unassuming, small, marble two-story building in the center of Riyadh, the company only moved to plush new offices in April of 2004.

Located on the sixty-sixth floor of the massive, monolithic Kingdom Tower, which is majority-owned by the Prince, the staff now looks out onto the most exclusive, elevated views of the city.

Despite the up-market new setting for the company, and a noticeable increase in office space, there is still a relatively small, core staff, says Amjed, because the increased comfort was not a signal for decreased efficiency: "We did a head count, because every year we get a form to fill out to find out which company is ranked where in Saudi Arabia. Incidentally, we've been ranked the top company three years in a row in Saudi Arabia. We had trouble trying to figure out what is the exact number of people working at Kingdom Holding Company because would that figure also include the tea-boys? Would that also include the aviation department, the maintenance department? Where do you stop, because these people supply a service not only for the office but also the palace? So, initially, the number was also really small but then we started adding people because nobody would have believed this number, and we came up to forty-nine. But I can tell you that the people who are close to the Prince are about a dozen, through whom the Prince contacts other people and gets data and information that he wants. He believes in outsourcing, and he believes in keeping a very small number of people around him because that close net would, first of all, help him to compartmentalize. It would also help him to give everybody a chance to understand him, because if you keep a small number of close people around you, you don't have to explain to yourself to a large number of people."

Amjed says that each of the compartments contains a very small team, even though there are quite a few compartments in total: "We have administration, we have domestic investments, international investments, we have hotels, human resources, government relations, accounting, secretarial, interior design, IT department, telecommunications, travel and public relations."

Saleh Al Ghoul has been with the Prince since 1995, prior to the business converting from being the Kingdom Establishment to the Kingdom Holding Company. It was undergoing a lot of reorganization with the help of consultants such as Arthur Andersen, and it was expanding from being an even smaller operation than it is now. The consultants helped to set new strategies for how the company should be run and which positions it should be looking to fill. Al Ghoul got the "Accounting Compartment" as the chief financial officer. From day one, he says, the Prince was focused on efficiency and running a tight operation all-round: "You would imagine that because he has all this money, he would be relaxed and not pay much attention to all the details, but believe me, we run our operation as if we have very little money (laughs). So, it's tight, no waste—no room for error or waste. We have, thank God, a very wealthy organization in terms of assets and in terms of revenues, but everything is very well controlled, and there is always fine-tuning of the way we run the business. So, you think you reach 100 percent, and then you find there is still room to fine-tune and reach greater efficiency of the operation."

Alwaleed describes his philosophy as, "Work smart, then work hard."

He says he doesn't like the expression "Work smart, not hard," explaining that he still wants hard work, but it should be approached in a smart way first: "We are very aggressive—very aggressive—and I like to stretch my people to their limits. I'll take it to the brink, but not beyond. I will always be lean and mean but not to the extent where it will backfire. If someone tells me we are in need of help, we will find the help."

The public relations compartment, for example, is a team of only four, which is kept rather busy dealing with the frequent media interest that Alwaleed's wide range of business and activities generate. In fact, after the straight-talking Royal started making quasi-political statements on the situation in the Saudi Kingdom, from around November 2003, the workload for this compartment cranked up a couple of notches.

Amjed stays close to Alwaleed as his public relations adviser. It's a full-time job that requires him to be with the Prince on most of his overseas trips. Holding fort back in Riyadh are the communications team, Hani, Abdulrahman, and Abed. Once approved by Amjed and the big boss, they put out press releases based around the Prince's activities, such as his donation of more than a million dollars to Sudan, to help victims of a severe passenger airline jet crash in June 2003, or his frequent meetings in his office with visiting international dignitaries.

In Saudi Arabia and other areas of the Middle East, Prince Alwaleed makes regular headlines and appearances in newspapers and magazines, relating to everything from his charitable work to his business dealings, to his occasional politically slanted comments.

So far, there's no official "political compartment," as the Prince insists that he's still primarily focused on his role as a businessman.

Khaled Almaeena, the editor in chief of the *Arab News*, has met the Prince from time to time and has an overall positive impression of the way he has grown: "I think he is a person who is very driven. He's made his mark in the local economy and the international economy. He wants to succeed—he has succeeded—and I think he's always moving the goalposts. He's viewed here by many as somebody who is also playing a pivotal role in society, the development of societal expectations, by donating—not just throwing money around—but he seems to be involved in quite a few things."

OPEN FOR BUSINESS

Alwaleed's business strategy has certainly been maturing over the years, having come through the general stress of the dot-com era largely unhurt, early in the new millennium. He has been very open about his investments and insistent on transparency in his dealings, unlike many others in the Middle East who still employ numbered Swiss bank accounts to conservatively manage their assets in secret.

His staff at Kingdom describes his business strategy nowadays as being a combination of three approaches. First, he keeps the number of investments limited, but looks for big stakes in what he describes as "situations where the sheer weight of his capital will bring about a change in people's perception of a company's real value."

Second, he is increasingly keen on global businesses, looking for industries or brands that have already crossed international barriers, such as hotels, the media, and banking. He feels that in the global economy, brands have added value, and he attaches a lot of importance to that value.

Finally, he looks for what he considers to be "value-added partners," who will bring more to the business than simply cash. For example, his deal with Kwek Leng Beng, to jointly buy The Plaza Hotel, in New York, was based on Alwaleed's assessment of Kwek's hotel company, CDL, as a high-quality hotel operator. In the end, Alwaleed might have been inclined to upgrade the property, which Kwek was not, but the sale in August 2004, at $675 million, proved incredibly profitable for both.

Alwaleed's private banker, Mike Jensen, describes the Prince's strategy as more macro nowadays, saying that he has put aside the micromanagement style he originally used with his ventures like the United Saudi Commercial Bank: "I think he's given an accurate description of himself when he says he likes to see himself as in a helicopter over a forest of trees, so he can see the whole forest, and when he can see a problem, he goes right down and gets involved in the nitty-gritty. Then, as soon as he understands the problem and sees the potential solution—and gets the right people involved with the solution—he goes back up and views the overall situation from the helicopter again. He's become quite good at that. He's giving more authority to others. Is it as much authority in his own local holding company as maybe some of his people would like? No. He's still walking in that direction, but I believe he's much more chairman and CEO in his actions than he was a few years ago. He's really doing that helicopter approach."

The Prince believes that being in the helicopter, up in the sky, with a spotlight looking for those in trouble on the ground, allows him to stay on the outside of major companies—not actually live in the forest of trees. This way, he feels that he can have influence without getting trapped. Alwaleed says that as a major shareholder on the outside, if the board members make a mistake, he can hammer them. But if he takes a position on the board of the company, he has to—as he sees it—"hammer myself."

In one interview, when asked about how much of a stake in a company he likes to acquire, he stressed that he prefers a minority shareholding because majority means control, which means possession, which means management. The Prince reiterates that he likes to buy into good management, not have to undertake the task himself, as he is a financial investor covering many sectors around the world. In the same way, as he steps back into the macro picture, he likes to leave managers to get on with the job: "When I buy a company, I buy the brains—the management, the expertise, the know-how, the track record, the experience and the name—and I always like the best."

Jensen adds the observation that Alwaleed has become a lot more patient in waiting in between investments in order to find extraordinary opportunities and is still looking for good companies that will be around for a long time, giving him a minimum seven- to ten-year investment window. He still works as a top-down investor, starting by studying a country's market, then the industries within that market, and then a few companies within that industry. When he sees the right sort of opportunity according to his stringent criteria, he is ready to move quickly. When the price target he has set is achieved, he is willing to buy big.

His winners with Citibank, Apple, News Corp., Four Seasons and Fairmont Hotels, and Canary Wharf, for example, were in that category, while what might have been hasty judgment during the dot-com boom cost him heavily when it went bust. He will listen closely to his advisers, but ultimately he makes the final decision based on his ever-growing and updated knowledge base, and his intuition. In this way, he follows his own edict, when he advises his investment team to "trust, but verify."

Although the Prince does some short-term trading, Jensen explains that it is not a significant amount: "He does indeed have a trading portfolio, which he does separately out of Riyadh, but that's a tiny aspect of his (overall) portfolio. The vast majority is based on a long-term strategy, and it's one of the most sophisticated strategies I have ever come across, by any businessman, anywhere I've worked in the last thirty-five years."

The Prince, for his part, admits that he is doing more short-term trades now, but his major strategy remains focused on the long term. His cash liquidity, however, means that he can take advantage of any opportunity easily. By trading when there are no clear, extraordinary long-term openings around, he can still make the most of short-term and medium-term opportunities, which he does not want to miss. He sums up his long-term approach in a clear and simple way: "I never believe the cow has been milked completely."

In addition, Alwaleed doesn't like doing business with debt and borrows only short term to fund opportunities.

A lot of proposals do come his way, many of them opportunistic. According to one of his staff, he can get up to two hundred fifty business ideas sent to him per day, but Alwaleed never makes a move without proper research: "Whenever I spot something, I study it very thoroughly, I evaluate it. I have all my people with me and I like to get their feedback, and sometimes be swift. Sometimes we have to start quickly because the opportunities may not be there for long, but sometimes we take our time and evaluate it and go for it. But I have very good people and I am very proud of that. For me to tell you that I do this whole thing alone is not true."

All too often, top businessmen are surrounded by "yes men," who will not challenge the boss. Alwaleed definitely encounters those, but says he values people who are willing to step forth with honest opinions: "I look at criticism very favorably, because it is important to look at criticism, at least if it comes from people who are close to you. I like to hear them. Sometimes on my board of directors members say, 'Prince, we are with you.' I say, 'Please let me hear those who are against,' to get the other side of the story. I am a person who likes to get the other side of the story. I like to create debates, discussions, arguments. It's very important, very healthy, to create that."

Easier said than done, and his staff admit that the Prince genuinely likes to be challenged, but those who do step out onto that tightrope have to be ready to defend their position, because he does not tolerate fools lightly, and certainly won't waste time indulging them.

GO WEST, YOUNG MAN

Alwaleed has also faced the interesting challenge of fitting in— being accepted as part of the Western scene—as he started focusing on international investments. The way he operated his business style in Saudi Arabia in the 1980s had to be adapted to the very different environment of Western business, particularly the high-powered big guns of America.

Bailing out Citibank helped his reputation on Wall Street, but he still had to go face-to-face with internationally recognized corporate heads.

Michael Eisner, who has ruled Disney with something of an iron fist for two decades, encountered no serious issues with him, even though Eisner's first conversation over a satellite phone had the Disney boss wondering why on earth he would call someone sitting in the middle of the desert "Your Royal Highness" during a business deal: "I think he seems a nice guy, well educated. I have only met him in person in France and the United States, so I see his Western business attire and his Western thinking, and his American education comes through, and he seems like a type A aggressive American capitalist to me."

A cynic might suggest that only a "type A aggressive American capitalist" himself would offer such an assessment as a compliment, but, either way, to win over a tough judge like Eisner is something of an achievement: "I think he's smart. If you're a global investor and you have patience, and a company's been around for a long time, and is a piece of people's brains, their fiber, their genetics, you're safe investing in that kind of institution. He started investing at a time when some of these big brands were depressed, and he was fairly certain that a depressed quality brand would become strong again, and the weakness would disappear, either through new management or a new economy."

Another businessman known for his shrewd deals is Rupert Murdoch, the chairman of News Corporation, who marvels at Alwaleed's ability to work so effectively in both the Middle East and the United States: "He's a true mixture. He bridges the two cultures very well. He is clearly very shrewd, very analytical, and at the same time prepared to gamble and to go against the prevailing thoughts about markets, and I think he's done very well doing it. He dived in at a time when people thought it was crazy and invested in the Internet, and the main stocks that he bought at that time are doing brilliantly, and so he's very original in his thinking."

On the face of it, the Prince's tactics for grabbing big names when they are down is opportunistic and leaves him open to the criticism that he is exploiting them when they are at their weakest. That is an accusation Jensen is more than happy to address: "Citibank didn't see it as exploitation. They saw it as, not a godsend, but as a real critical factor in them continuing to be successful in their business. The same would hold true, I think you'll find, with Rupert Murdoch of News Corp., who has been very happy with the Prince as an investor, and we can go into Canary Wharf—it was a critical factor in (Paul) Reichmann's success, the fact that the Prince came back in—and you see where Canary Wharf is today compared with when the Prince made his investment."

The Prince is a little more blunt: "Look, we lifted every guy off his knees: Reed, Reichmann, Sharp, even Berlusconi," referring to the chairmen of Citicorp, Canary Wharf, Four Seasons, and Mediaset, respectively.

Another of the team looking after Alwaleed's business interests is a young and dynamic Lebanese man, P.J. Shoucair, who was recruited in the "international investment compartment." He had moved to Saudi Arabia in 1997 to work for a consulting firm and ended up handling the Kingdom Holding Company as his major client. Seeing how energetic and motivated he was, it was not long before P.J. was poached and found himself given the responsibility of being the special adviser on international investment to the Prince: "He (Alwaleed) is strategic. He's able to see how one investment can lead to another. He's long term, he's friendly . . . these things add value. A lot of people are doing deals when they don't trust each other, but he has basically the ability to win people's trust, and they know he's friendly to management. He's not trying to arbitrage a position either way, and he's got patient money. His money is sometimes expensive, because we are demanding on our terms, but people know that once they have us behind them, that we are not going to second-guess them every day."

That trust is exemplified by the fact that the key businessmen with whom he deals make a point of keeping him informed of major issues and events.

When former Treasury secretary Robert Rubin was due to join Citigroup, the company's vice-chairman, Paul Collins, gave Alwaleed a courtesy call at his desert camp outside Riyadh, saying that the news was about to be announced on CNBC shortly. The Prince, who is even connected to satellite television among the sand dunes and camels, tuned in and, sure enough, a few minutes later it was on the news.

Collins says he enjoyed dealing with the Prince and found he could relate to the way does business: "He thinks like an entrepreneur. He thinks like a very disciplined businessman, you know, 'How do I make this better? How does it get better?'"

P.J. estimates that about 75 percent of the Prince's investment portfolio is international and sits overseas, but he points out that more big deals have been appearing in Saudi Arabia and the Middle East region since the early part of the new millennium. He says that exactly how the Prince gets involved with these deals in the first place can vary: "Sometimes we get the leads from investment banks, sometimes from private equity houses, sometimes it is something he has read—a hot story in the press that we somehow inject into and pursue. It's different. Each case is different."

But the process of getting Alwaleed involved starts with the challenge of getting him interested in the first place, notes P.J.: "There is nothing typical about an investment deal, but you always have to start with trying to see if this is something that gets the Prince's attention, if this is interesting for him—and then you have to basically cut to the chase. You have to do a lot of homework, quickly trying to size up the opportunities and risk, and be able to get back to him in a concise way, saying this is what we've been able to find out, strategically it makes sense or doesn't make sense, can add value to your portfolio in this way, or can't; and kind of get his blessing there. Then basically go out and build a team of advisers who start doing the detailed work, all the way taking him through it. He's very detail-orientated, and he's very macro at the same time."

Those who walk by P.J.'s office at the Kingdom Holding Company often find him looking distracted or preoccupied, as the number of deals he has going at the same time start to pile up. P.J. explains that his responsibility covers everything from looking for ideas, dealing with investment banks and lawyers, monitoring the existing portfolio, doing some derivatives options trading, and working on project development. It is, he says, the amount of work normally given to a team of four or five people. It is made that much harder by virtue of the fact that Saudi Arabia is opening up and privatizing more, which has the Prince carefully monitoring certain key industries and segments of the economy.

That change in the Saudi Kingdom also keeps the Prince's executive director of domestic investments on his toes.

Talal Al Maiman joined Alwaleed just a year before P.J., in 1996, through rather unusual circumstances. He had written a paper on the need for a high-level education facility in Saudi Arabia,

and not knowing who to send it to, passed it on to the office of Alwaleed, having heard of some of his philanthropic work. Talal had
been working for the government, in the Saudi Arabian Monetary
Agency, the central bank of the country, having graduated with a
degree in Electrical Engineering from university in the United
States. He was on a visit to the U.S. Federal Reserve in America, a
year later, when he got a call saying the Prince wanted to see him.
Talal explained that he could not make it until he returned from
his trip, and he only turned up at Kingdom once he had finally
landed back in Saudi Arabia. The Prince had a good feeling about
Talal after talking with him for a while, and so as he got up to go,
Alwaleed said he would take a chance on him and offer him a
job—and then gave him two minutes to make up his mind.

Jumping at the chance, he was thrown in the deep end, with
the 400 million Saudi riyal ($107 millon dollar) Kingdom City
project.

Talal admits that his work is tough, but says it comes down to
mentally adjusting to the task: "The most important thing you
have to remember working for Prince Alwaleed Bin Talal is that
it's not a job—it's a way of life. It is not about a particular job description. Either you live it, or you don't last. One thing that the
Prince would never allow is a failure of any of his businesses, so he
expects his people to understand that bottom line."

The demands are high on the staff because the Prince has
made it clear to them that success is paramount. According to P.J.,
the Prince has a natural ability in selecting a deal and then sealing
it: "He is still very driven, in fact even more driven, and has a very
keen knack for negotiations. He smells a deal, and he knows what
buttons to push, and what not to push, and how to extract value.
In negotiations he can be disarmingly charming and win you over,
so that's his real strength—he smells a deal and has a real instinct
for it."

But, above all, P.J. adds, Alwaleed knows how to be a tough negotiator: "He plays a poker hand, you do not know if he really
wants to continue the deal or if he has lost interest. He even has

his own people sometimes confused as to what is happening, but it's a style that works, let's put it that way."

DEALMAKER

Once the deal is done, he sticks by his word, according to many of those who have been in the negotiating seat opposite him. Alwaleed believes that if he has taken all that trouble to identify a good company, and good management, then he should be looking to enhance it, not make life difficult by meddling: "I have a very good relationship with all the chairmen and CEOs of all the companies I invest in, because my strategy and my objective is not to be against any of these companies but to be with them. My idea is that if you are against the company, why invest in it to begin with? You don't invest in a company and then curse them the next day in the newspapers and magazines. If you don't like these companies, then just divest and go somewhere else. I don't invest in a company and then go and hammer it the next day in the media. No, I become an ally of that company."

Even though the Prince made his name in Saudi Arabia in the late 1980s with his unprecedented hostile takeover of a bank, followed by other moves also perceived as hostile in business terms, his approach mellowed somewhat over the next fifteen years or so. As it is, hostile deals did not seem like the best tactic, particularly in the case of international opportunities involving big names, with far bigger sums of money at stake. Alwaleed says that he goes in simply as an investor, making the most of the opening available, and aims to work with those already entrenched in running the company—again, looking at how the relationship might grow in the long term, where he believes most of the success is realized: "When I invest in a company, I invest in it because I believe in it. I believe in the management and the track record. If I don't believe in it I, why should I want it? I'll invest in another company. I believe hostile takeovers are very costly. You have to spend a lot of money."

During his travels throughout the year, the Prince tries to meet up at least once or twice with the key business leaders of the various companies in which he is heavily invested around the world. He says the meetings are arranged partly as a courtesy, to let them know, or remind them, of his goals as a significant shareholder, then partly to build the bonds with them at a more personal level, and finally, to get some sense of what they themselves are about, and what direction they envisage for the company. It is effectively continuing with Alwaleed's affinity for gaining financial intelligence, although the Prince has to be very careful not to cross any line that might constitute an irregularity such as insider trading, or jeopardize his stance as an outside influence: "They know I won't interfere whatsoever in the way they manage their companies. I meet with them as a friend, and to boost their standing in the company and outside, and I'll do anything to serve the company whether it is nationally in Saudi Arabia, regionally, or even internationally."

This is a viewpoint that is certainly substantiated when talking to some of the key businessmen who deal with Alwaleed, such as Disney's Michael Eisner: "He seems to be supportive of good management. He is critical of people who irresponsibly criticize us, but he certainly is willing to have a conversation with me if he thinks he has an idea that would be helpful—and his ideas are helpful. He's impatient, which makes me feel very comfortable because I am impatient. In that way he seems very Western. It feels like he doesn't sleep a lot, and he's certainly easy to get hold of wherever he is in the world. He's not reticent to accept the phone call."

Alwaleed's pragmatic business approach is supported by the Four Seasons boss, Isadore Sharp: "He asks where he could be helpful, to be consulted. He's kept informed, and I am sure if things were happening in a manner that he is not comfortable with, he would make a decision on what to do, but he doesn't involve himself with dictating to management; he trusts management to make the decisions for the company's best interests."

The Prince's potential for interfering is even more significant for Citigroup's boss, Sandy Weill, who is essentially overseeing about half of Alwaleed's multibillion-dollar fortune: "I don't think he tries to influence the board decisions of the company at all. I think he'll talk about things, we'll know where he really stands on something, and he expects you to tell him where you stand on that thing, but I have found him to be flexible and not be dogmatic about positions and really supportive of management. He's not trying to run the institution, but he's trying to be not just a shareholder but a helpful shareholder."

Talal says that this approach is mirrored in the way Alwaleed deals with his own business partners. He makes sure that there is a clear line of communication: "He takes every time, every moment, to go through the thinking process with them, share with them the ideas, even though they have entrusted him with the management of those investments."

Ironically, he adds, being a Royal might even work against the Prince nowadays. Many people approaching him for business partnership make wrong assumptions, such as believing that he has a pile of money but limited understanding of business skills. It usually comes as something of a shock to them when they have to go face-to-face with him over a proposal, only to find that he has meticulously researched it and spent time considering every possible angle in the deal.

Having said that, the Royal status does still open doors, not just at home in Saudi Arabia, but with top businessmen overseas, too. After all, the Saudi Royal family has always collectively had a reputation of being very wealthy investors.

BRICKS AND MORTAR

One area in which Alwaleed has worked extensively as a partner with other businessmen is the hotel industry. In playing the dual role of property owner and major investor in the management company, he has guaranteed himself separate streams of revenue.

The Kingdom Hotel Investment Group (KHI), headed by Sarmad Zok, was set up specifically so that Alwaleed could create a better balance between the real estate he started acquiring in the Middle East and Africa, and the management groups of Four Seasons, Fairmont, and Movenpick. The idea is that KHI could eventually be spun off and floated as a separate company.

Another young executive has worked with Sarmad for a number of years on the "hotel compartment." Ramsey Mankarious was only twenty-seven years old when he became the executive vice-president of development for Kingdom Holding's hotel affairs back in 1996. The Prince specifically targets young people for high positions because he feels they are not only driven, but have the energy to match. Ramsey confirmed that in interviews in the past: "You are so motivated and feel high because he has so much energy. He gives you some of that energy in a meeting and you still feel it the next day. He's very ambitious, aggressive, and enthusiastic. He is very happening."

Sarmad and Ramsey both joke that working with the Prince is "like handling a hot poker," but they vindicate him by pointing out that he has a great sense of humor. The relationship building was strong. Even though Ramsey left the Prince's employment in the summer of 2004 to set up his own consultancy, he still works closely with KHI.

Alwaleed admitted that in recent years he has concentrated on his hotel investments to a disproportionate degree, but he feels the value of this sector is high and has been serving him well. By 2004, Sarmad was charged with an aggressive push to expand the hotel sector in the Middle East and to some degree in Africa, but denies that the Prince is hunting and chasing opportunities too hard: "I wouldn't say he's considered a predator because he is not hostile; he structures transactions around problems because problems provide opportunities. In real estate—the hotels—this is a long-term capital-intensive business, and the Prince is very good at understanding value and building around a structure that will enhance that value, so he's considered as a savvy real estate and hotel investor."

Again, as the Prince grows both as a property investor, and a hotel management group investor, the question of conflict of interest is raised during negotiations, and Sarmad has to explain how the Prince addresses it: "We come across this perceived conflict of interest as we are structuring transactions that we are about to execute. It's actually the opposite; it's not really a conflict of interests because the Prince has two hats: he is an owner in the management company and he is an owner in the real estate, but if you look at his portfolio, most of the value—or let's say the investment that had been made—is at the real estate level. It doesn't mean that he disregards the management interests because of the real estate. He acts as an owner when it comes to owning the real estate, and he acts as a manager when it comes to growth strategy and expansion. We have some leverage as a result, and he can enhance and protect the interests of the partnerships as a result of that, so it's not really a conflict of interest."

Jensen reinforces the balanced approach taken, but notes where issues do arise: "While they both want the success for the individual hotel, the question is, for example, how much are you going to spend on repairs? Are you going to maximize the money you earn for the management company, or maximize the money for the hotel company? His Highness prefers to have small catalytic investments in the hotels with his major investment being in the hotel management, just for that reason."

Plus, even though the Prince is aggressive in this sector, his hotel team says he does not make gut or emotional decisions when it comes to hotel properties, and that he walks away from more deals than he makes.

Alwaleed says: "We don't go where the ego is; we go where the profit is and the viability is."

According to the media, that was not quite the case when the Prince bought the George V Hotel in 1996. He definitely was

looking to have a high-profile property: "Three factors came together; you have the George V name, you have the Paris factor,
and most importantly you have the Four Seasons management
factor also. All these three factors combined created the (world's)
best hotel, within two years of its completion. So clearly to me, it
is very crucial and important to have this hotel. As for the cost, I
have been more than vindicated, because now the value of this hotel is more than double what we paid for it and if you use this from
an IRR (internal rate of return) point of view, we have 25 percent
IRR so far."

As mentioned earlier, the George V Hotel purchase did put
him at odds with the Four Seasons chairman, Isadore Sharp, but
the Canadian hotelier denies that it was the source of friction between the two men, more a case of brief divergence in goals: "No,
not friction, but he would like to become the biggest, my interest
is to become the best, so in that regard, he deals in a few extra investments than I would, but he places no pressure in any way to alter the course of the company, other than more things that we can
do together. So he's made himself available to help the company
grow but would always rely on our judgment of how it should
grow."

In an interview in 1999, the Four Seasons vice-chairman,
Roger Garland, echoed Sarmad Zok's description of Alwaleed's
approach to the hotel sector as a "catalyst." Garland said that the
Prince's money attracts other money to any deal that is being negotiated, and added: "When we go into negotiations carrying his
(Alwaleed's) card in our pocket, the other side knows we can deliver the capital."

One interesting consequence of the Prince's involvement in
two major, high-end hotel management groups is that he has been
able to play mediator when difficulties have arisen. Bill Fatt of
Fairmont was impressed with his ability to look at the bigger picture on at least one occasion: "There was a minor dispute between
Four Seasons and Fairmont and what I noticed about the Prince—
who has a much larger dollar investment in Four Seasons than he

does in Fairmont—is that he wanted to understand the issues from both sides, and he was absolutely clear in saying that he had no interest in trying to side with one group or the other. He just wanted to understand the issues, and he hoped that each of us would be working to the conclusion that would advantage our shareholders the most. That was a very disciplined approach, where he was conscious of his potential for conflict, and I think he handled it very well."

As the Prince's bank account has grown in size, he has been able to handle the hotel sector with a continued long-term approach—"patient money" as P.J. had put it. With his own money behind a deal, he does not suffer the plague of those who use public money—mainly, someone constantly looking over their shoulder, making demands for large and rapid returns. It also allows him to approach deals with much more flexibility, in terms of choosing how he commits his money, whether it is as a direct long-term investor, or a strategic partner, for example. Above all, his staff says, he is a good problem solver. He will find effective solutions and does not restrict himself from getting involved in a deal because there seem to be problems at the outset.

The consequence is that the Prince found himself to be in a very strong position in the hotel sector going into the first few years of the new century. His people can use the success he has had, and the reputation he has built, to more easily secure backing or attract strategic partners. As the Prince's North America and Europe hotel consultant, Chuck Henry, puts it, he has created enough value in his hotel portfolio to allow his people not to have to write many checks. Others line up to sign on the bottom line.

In this respect, the Prince generally finds reliable partners, and he further values them if they have expertise in areas where he has little exposure or experience. He prefers to buy in, or team up with, existing expertise because he believes it is established and saves him the trouble of having to start from scratch in carving out market share.

Bill Fatt of Fairmont Hotels says the Prince does his best to be an investor who adds value: "He's a person who certainly wants to understand the direction and the strategy we're following. He's quite happy, and likes to discuss strategy, and challenge various aspects of it so that his understanding of it is confirmed. As a shareholder I have found him to be delightful. He doesn't look at the value of his interests on a day-to-day basis, at least as far as I am aware. What he does is he looks at the strategy of the company, and he says, how can I, or how can my company, Kingdom, help this company—this investment that I've got? I can help that company to get better. I find that refreshing, because he has the talents, the vision and the skills to advance our strategy and is not simply a shareholder who is there for a short period of time and looking to get out on fairly short notice."

Of all of the Prince's divisions, the team dealing with hotels definitely is one of the busiest, but also probably is the team that is most appreciative of his drive. Simon Turner, who works alongside Chuck Henry, describes it as "quite exhilarating" to be in a job that demands so much, adding: "He (Alwaleed) hates wasting time or resources and is very disciplined in reacting to things quickly and efficiently. It forces us, quite willingly, to work very much in that fashion."

The hotel teams describe the Prince as tenacious, committed, and enthusiastic. He certainly keeps them busy.

BIG, BOLD BRANDS

The first sign of a call coming in was a blue light flickering on, followed rapidly by the warbling of a ring tone.

Raouf Aboud grabbed the phone from its clip on his belt and flipped open the clamshell, answering "Allo?" in a hybrid Arab-French accent, common to the Francophone Algerians and Arabs.

Close examination of the logo on the mobile he held to his head revealed the name, Motorola.

As head of the "communications compartment," Raouf is more than familiar with the latest mobile phones. As someone who works closely with Prince Alwaleed, Raouf is also more than familiar with the Prince's loyalty to the brands in which he invests. For that reason, Raouf was hardly surprised to find Alwaleed asking him to order a couple of hundred Motorola StarTac phones when they were first released. With the Prince's large share in the chip, electronics, and mobile phone manufacturer, there was no doubt that his people were going to have to use Motorola from now on. What had caught Raouf by surprise was that Alwaleed wanted to buy so many phones. It was, in fact, so he could give them out to his family and friends. The Prince was keen for not only the staff at Kingdom to be using his brands, but as many family and friends as possible, too.

Watching Alwaleed going through his daily activities, certain brands keep reappearing. Sitting next to his dinner plate (or more likely, intruding into Princess Reem's table space) is a can of Diet Pepsi. Perched to one side on his large black, lacquered office desk sits a white Apple laptop, although the Prince still prefers to work with pen and paper most of the time. As he pulls away from his office to head home for lunch, Alwaleed is behind the wheel of a large, black Hyundai limousine. He swapped his fleet of top-of-the-range Mercedes S600 V12 limousines for cars made by the Korean company, along with a selection of Fords—both companies in which he had put money.

Behind the Prince, at almost any of his locations—home, office, yacht, even his private jet—sits a small tree of flags bearing the logos of the brands holding money from Alwaleed. He is particularly proud of them, and even arranged for the video screens in the Boeing 767 to scroll through the logos at times when the air map display is not switched on.

When the expansive barbecue deck on the Kingdom yacht is being prepared for the Prince to either sit and relax, hold a meeting, or even have lunch or dinner, the tree of brand flags is brought over and perched prominently. In fact, until the autumn of 2003, one of the flags visibly stood out because it was not a proper, printed square a few inches in size, like all the others. It was simply a piece of paper onto which the letters "DKNY" were scribbled with pen, and it was then wedged in precariously between the others, including Compaq, News Corp., Time Warner, Citigroup, and so on.

When asked about the makeshift flag, Alwaleed pauses, gives it another good look, and then says, "That was Reem." His daughter, having instigated his interest in the Donna Karan New York fashion and accessories group in 1997, had insisted on having it represented on the brands tree once the Prince put $20 million into the company. He parted with the brand a couple of years later, once it became part of the Louis Vuitton Moët Hennessy group, LVMH, which is famous for alcoholic products such as Moët and Chandon champagne, and Hennessy cognac.

It was a flag that had cost him a loss of $7 million to add to his collection. Although he no longer owned shares in the company, it was probably overlooked in the brands tree on the yacht because Alwaleed was nostalgic for the way his then young teenage daughter had wanted to put her mark on his company.

One or two articles in the media have commented on the Prince's fascination with Western brands, saying that often that fascination has backfired.

Despite the odd blip, the Prince remains optimistic when it comes to brands and their value: "I believe in brand names, and I believe in number one. For example, when I looked at the George V, I saw it as a big opportunity, like I saw in Citigroup. Frankly speaking, George V, when I bought it, was rated three star; really it was on the verge of collapse, so I bought it, shut it down for two years, renovated it, everything, back office, front office, completely gutted—plumbing, sewage, everything. We opened up in two years and guess what? For an unprecendented four consecutive years, the George V, managed by the Four Seasons in Paris, was chosen as the number one hotel in the world and guess what? Its restaurant received a three-star Michelin rating—the first time for a hotel restaurant so soon after opening."

By the time the CEO of Fairmont Hotels and Resorts, Bill Fatt, had met the Prince, he had been primed to expect an intelligent and driven person: "Once I met him in person, compared to his public image at the time, he was quite different. He is a very down-to-earth kind of person. He's clearly very intelligent—that comes across in the first few words of meeting him—but his perspective is what fascinates me. He has a long-term perspective, sometimes contrarian, and what I certainly appreciate, coming from my business background, is the value he places on brands. That is critical to me and is also I think a central investment theme as far as the Prince is concerned."

Alwaleed's goal is for all of his businesses to achieve number one position, and he takes pride in the way so many of them have already managed it. In one year alone, there were ten world-class awards to those companies: "Number one is of utter importance. It's crucial to me. Crucial! And the fact that my investment in Citigroup is in the number one bank in the whole world, I'm proud of that, and the fact that we invested in the number one hotel company in the world, the Four Seasons, I'm proud of that. SAMBA, the bank I established, by merging it with USCB—number one. I like to be number one. Everybody likes to be number one."

In this respect, the Prince has certainly clocked up more number ones than most people.

Apart from the George V's remarkable consistency in being voted the world's number one hotel, the Fairmont's New York Plaza was voted number one hotel in North America, News Corp. is normally regarded as the number one global media group, and on the home front, SAMBA is clearly the number one bank in the region, while the Kingdom Tower received the accolade of being the best new skyscraper in 2002, by skyscraper.com.

Alwaleed's international investment adviser, P.J., adds a cautionary note to anyone having a blind interest in big brand names, but he says they are useful in grabbing Alwaleed's attention when it comes to prospective deals: "It helps, but you know brands these days are expensive so it's a double-edged sword."

Nevertheless, Alwaleed is leveraging the success of his brand investments, and even created a television advertising campaign for Kingdom Holding Company for the first time in 2004. The basic message states that Kingdom has been successfully investing in number one brands, and will continue to do so, and is building bridges from east to west through world-class investments.

P.J. explains that Kingdom Holding Company holds only Saudi domestic investments, while international investments are held by the Prince and his trusts.

As Kingdom is not a public company, it is surprising that the Prince would want to engage in a global commercial campaign, but he admits that his strategy is to increase Western awareness of what is a major, global business player based in the Middle East. Alwaleed says it shows that a Saudi company can do business according to Western standards and succeed quite exceptionally: "We would like to put it more on the radar screen internationally, so people can understand what Kingdom Holding is all about."

The Prince's public relations chief, Amjed Shacker, expands on the idea: "Kingdom in Saudi Arabia is a brand name, and in certain parts of the Middle East it is, too, but what has become a bigger brand is the name 'Alwaleed.' It's interesting, because in Saudi Arabia descendants of the Royal family and descendants of the late King Abdul Aziz are addressed as Your Royal Highness. When people refer to Prince Alwaleed they don't call him His Royal Highness, they just say 'Alwaleed' because he has become a brand name."

THE MELODY OF MONEY

Cannes was the setting for an intense series of meetings beginning in August 2003. Actually, the location was about half a mile off the coast of Cannes, to be more accurate.

Huddled together in a sumptuously furnished cabin of the 5-KR yacht, the Prince and four key players from the Arabian music business were planning to turn their industry upside down. They were all key players in their own right, respected for their achievements in areas such as music production, artist management, marketing, and distribution, but their eyes were on the one man.

His relaxed vacation dress code, pastel shorts, light cotton shirt, and deck shoes did nothing to hide his intense manner as he set the agenda.

"I want the beef! Not the sauce, or the mushrooms. I want the beef!"

Then a short pause, "Actually, I don't eat beef . . . I want the fish!"

The Prince was emphasizing that he wanted his team to make sure they got the best deal in the negotiations to establish a new channel.

Alwaleed was aiming to better leverage the Rotana music production company, which he now owned 100 percent. In 2003, he had swung a deal with Sheikh Saleh Kamel, his partner in Arab Radio Television, ART, swapping most of his holding in the network for a 49 percent share in the Lebanese satellite channel, LBC, and an opportunity to convert ART's music channel into a more dynamic player, combining it with his music production company, Rotana Audiovisual.

The people the Prince had gathered on his yacht were summoned to develop a plan that would unite all his music industry assets: "We discussed this production company (Rotana) and we are a dominant force in the singing arena of the Arab world. We thought we should translate this into viewership—translate this into TV stations."

One of those sweating it out at the intense meetings was Michel El Murr, a soft-spoken thinker who had clashed on and off with the Lebanese government over his local Murr Television, MTV, channel: "We were brainstorming, in fact, because it was the first time we met a lot of the heads of the different departments, a lot of different countries. You know Rotana is not only a TV company but is a production company; it's a distribution company, a record company. So we were all of us there, in order to establish this strategy of Rotana, and we were brainstorming, because what I like about the Prince is that while doing business with him, I learned that he listens a lot before taking any decision."

As much as he was listening, Alwaleed had a very clear idea of where he wanted to take his concept: "There was a gap, there was an opening. Whenever I see an opening, I like to fill it. This whole thing began by me owning a music production company. We have more than one hundred artists, and we have almost 80 percent of the market in Arab singers. We thought that we would add a TV channel that has control of all those artists and do video clips and do some concerts and parties that involve these Arab singers. Within the first four months we established the Rotana One channel, and then we had Rotana Two."

Sure enough, on October 8, 2003, Rotana One, with its mixture of music videos, clips from concerts, and entertainment shows was making its mark with Arab music fans. According to the Prince, by February of 2004, it was rated as number two in popularity among those fans, who have around a hundred channels from which to choose: "We are integrating audio with video, we are integrating the audiovisual parts of Rotana, and this was really very successful. It hasn't made us billions yet, but what we have is millions of dollars. We put in small amounts of money and that now has already increased in value by more than four times."

Alwaleed puts that success not down to being tough in the approach to the market, but more to the values that were set from the start: "I don't think we were very aggressive; I think people came to us because we have a good reputation. We don't show controversial video clips, we have taboos on those controversial video clips that go beyond the limits. For example, we don't have naked people, we don't accept that, so we try to, to obey our religion and our culture and that's very important. Families can let their children watch us without being with them. So that's a great plus."

Michel concurs, but differentiates the channel from the others in a couple of other ways: "Let's say we are different since we are only Arabic. We are very committed to the Arabic music, whereas the others have a mix of Western and Oriental music. Secondly, we are on (distribution) platforms that others aren't on, and thirdly, we have program with very famous artists. It has been outstanding, as a matter of fact; the companies that do research and studies were really amazed at how successful we were."

Michel quotes ratings of 23 percent of viewership in a matter of months, and attributes much of the success to Alwaleed's overall approach to the project: "The Prince selected the right people for it, plus he was involved directly in each and every small detail and you know how energetic he is, and how dedicated he is when doing something. He's very picky, and he follows every small detail, and I think this is what made the success."

In steering away from the controversial material, Michel said that Rotana made sure it did not lose any appeal to young Arabs by actively involving them in various ways: "We bring a lot of interactivity in our TV station, a lot of youth on air. It's a pan-Arab station where you have Egyptian anchors, Emiratis from the Gulf region, Lebanese, working altogether and interacting. Plus the interactivity through SMS, MMS, and all this is what makes it very dynamic looking."

The SMS (Short Messaging Service) and MMS (Multimedia Messaging Service) were a unique feature that Alwaleed added when he launched a second Rotana channel, known as Rotana Clip, just two months later. This channel concentrated less on show formats and largely on video clips from around the Middle East.

It was an instant hit with viewers, who they found they could use their mobile phones to send texts that would appear on television. Within weeks, there were up to forty thousand messages being sent to Rotana every day.

Pursuing his belief that the Arab music world has a number of gaps and opportunities, the Prince sees Rotana growing into a bouquet containing a number of channels serving specific needs: "If you look at Rotana One, it's a bit more formal, it's for the twenty- to fifty-year-olds. If you look at Rotana Two, it's for the teenagers, seventeen to mid-twenties, and they love to have SMS, they love to have their letters appear, they like to interact, for such things to be there, and we provide all that for them."

Not hanging around, Alwaleed launched his third channel, Rotana Classic, playing golden oldies from the Arab music scene, on October 8, 2004—the first anniversary of Rotana One: "This is our niche. Rotana Three offers the classical music, the old ones, songs that are ten, twenty, thirty years old. So, with the three different channels, we are trying to cover all the tastes, whether it's for fifteen-year-olds or sixty-five-year-olds."

Michel El Murr says that the Prince seems to know what he is doing, even though most people might not have associated him with a business project such as a music channel: "He used to have a lot of experience with ART before that, and while talking in Cannes, I think we were all amazed that when we were speaking, we were in tune with him, on the same wavelength. This is what made Rotana successful, that most of us were convinced of what we were doing and we were sharing the same vision."

Other players in the Arabic music industry watched in surprise as the presence and impact of Rotana grew with remarkable speed. Michel fully understands why there was so much progress, considering the effort put in by Alwaleed: "The energy that he has . . . I mean, it's like spending eighteen or twenty hours a day, working all the time without breathing! Everything is planned, every step of the way, nothing is done randomly. I don't know where he finds all this energy, it's really amazing, and he is a man of principle. This is very important. We lack these things in the Arab world, accuracy and honesty, and he is very honest and accurate in whatever he does."

But accuracy and honesty did not stop him going after the big names aggressively.

Alwaleed was proactively seeking to recruit the top artists he did not already have under the Rotana label, and this led to some speculation that he was aiming to secure a monopoly on the market. He has never denied wanting as many of the top names in his camp as possible, and with the launch and growth of Rotana, it became harder and harder to name many singers and performers not already signed up. The Prince says his approach is misunderstood: "I don't say I have a monopoly, but I have a majority. I don't believe in monopolies, frankly speaking. I think they are just not healthy, because if you have a monopoly you become lax. You become lenient, and I like competition, and sometimes when I see companies competing with me I like it, because it not only keeps me on my toes, it keeps my people on their toes. Definitely, I like it to be number one, but I don't mind competition at all. Clearly, the fact that I have a very strong foothold in music may be a big barrier to others to enter (the market), because I will defend what is mine very, very aggressively."

Just to consolidate the strength of his position, Alwaleed announced at the end of 2004 that there would be more Rotana channels on the way in 2005—two showing movies, and one with an Islamic focus.

Michel El Murr can understand why Alwaleed is so willing to fight for his corner, after spending so much time shuttling between Cannes, Paris, Riyadh, and Beirut, setting up the channel—now channels—in just a matter of months. The Rotana boss notes that the negotiations he and the others had with Alwaleed on his yacht clearly demonstrated how tricky it can be to maneuver the Prince in a deal: "Not easy at all. (Laughs.) It's very hard to negotiate with him, but at least he has a certain logic and, well, he always goes for something after convincing you it's right. He's not a dictator, so he always convinces you about what he does, and usually he's right about it."

FINANCIAL FOCUS

The analogy of Prince Alwaleed in a helicopter with a spotlight looking down onto the forest below for opportunities has probably become more and more applicable as the Prince continues to mature as an international businessman and becomes more cautious with his accumulated wealth. The helicopter does not land as much as it used to and waits until it spots major problems on the ground before moving in. That does not mean that there are not more and more people on the ground trying to wave down the Kingdom helicopter circling overhead.

Disney was in that very position by 2003, hoping the Prince would land on their territory once more. Equally, a number of others see the Royal investor as a potential savior when they get into trouble and need bailing out. Alwaleed has no issue with carrying that image: "I don't think it creates problems; I think it creates opportunities. I think you rarely find a week where you don't have five or six deals being negotiated with me, nationally, regionally, or internationally. Clearly we look at deals that serve us, serve our communities, or serve the nations that we are involved with—and serve the project itself—so we are very selective; we wait for the right opportunity to come by to get involved in such projects."

Alwaleed's executive director of finance and administration, Saleh Al Ghoul, has watched the Prince from an an accounting perspective and has no worries that the Prince might become a target for opportunists: "I think he has this instinct that he can tell, before you even talk, what you are going to say. So he is awake, he is always alert, and all his senses are ready to judge. He is an excellent judge of character, and I think this is one of his major strengths."

One of those he seemed to have judged accurately, way back in 1996, was his executive director of domestic investments, Talal Al Maiman, who has worked closely with Alwaleed since accepting a job offer on the spot: "In my opinion, the Prince has changed to being more prudent. He always takes the other angle today, versus the past. He likes to hear more of people today than he used to, in my opinion. He listens, and might not show you that he's paying attention, but you bet your life while he's watching TV and hearing three others, he's hearing you, too. One thing, I think, is that he has changed in personality. I think he is becoming a tougher man, knowing the tougher environment. He's no nonsense, I mean, and if you just look him in the face and tell him, 'Your Highness, one, two, three'—he can see and read into your eyes if you are trying to fabricate the subject, and he bases the way he answers, prior to knowing the subject, on the way you present it. If you are coming with a different face, different worry, different look, different statement, sometimes that would be the basis of his refusal or approval, but I honestly believe the Prince is a little bit far away from his group (staff). He needs to get closer, in my opinion."

Talal expands his last point by explaining that part of that perception comes from the changes at the Kingdom Holding Company in recent years. In the past, he says, particularly with a smaller team, the Prince was able to spend more time with every individual. As the company grew and became more institutionalized—and the Prince focused on a broader range of businesses across the globe—the time that Alwaleed had for each individual diminished and it became harder for him to find time to directly communicate with people. He began to delegate more. Having said that, Alwaleed did start to play a more active part in recruiting diverse people into his company, especially when he pushed for a greater role for women at the Kingdom Holding Company.

But that worry about his having more distance from people is almost an echo of the sentiments of Alwaleed's cousin and childhood friend, Riad Assaad, who worries that the Prince is becoming more institutional in his approach to people, that emotional connection is being sacrificed.

In making his assessment that the Prince needs to get closer to his staff, Talal looks a little somber, and he remembers one story concerning his boss that touched him personally about four years after he joined the company: "My son had an accident and he was actually in a short coma at the time when I saw him. I did not come to work and he (Alwaleed) called me and said, 'Talal'—as I remember it, it's not a direct quote—'Talal, don't worry. I am sure he'll be well, and if you need me, my money, my plane, it's ready to take him anywhere in the world,' and that was a moment in my own life that would never let me think about the (financial) package or the treatment (at work). When it comes to the bottom line, he's there for his employees, and I think that affected my personality a lot, and my tolerance, if I may say so."

SENDING THE RIGHT MESSAGE

At the international level, Alwaleed is still going from strength to strength.

The world's top businessmen, particularly those in the United States who might normally be a little suspicious of a Saudi, have now let him into their circle. People like Disney's Michael Eisner: "No conversation is without interest; he (Alwaleed) is quick, he's sharp, he's excitable, he's charismatic. People in his country talk about him, so he's well known not just as an investor but as a personality. I don't know if he's the norm or if he's eccentric in his own environment, but he's interesting and fun to be with."

And, of course, Citigroup's Sandy Weill: "I just try to relate to him in my time frame and not necessarily in his time frame, because he used to walk through the hotel and the kitchen in the middle of the night when I was sleeping, but I've never had a problem relating to him. I think he is a fun person to be with, I think he has an incredible mind, he's always thinking, and he's very interesting to talk to and talk ideas with, to get another perspective on the world."

They still see him mostly as a tough businessman, though, and the Four Seasons boss, Issy Sharp, is aware of the wit it takes to negotiate with Alwaleed: "There's an expression that I would use that sort of describes him; he knows what he wants, he asks for it, and then to the degree he makes sure he gets what he needs. So he's got a certain objective, which is fine because he makes it right out front. You know exactly what to expect, and he's a decision maker, he's not a procrastinator. He gets into the detail enough for him to make the decision, and once he does that he moves forward so, the word *tough* I am not sure is correct, but he's a diligent businessman."

Still, the Prince can come up with some surprising trump cards when he wants to, in order to show a smarter and more sensitive side.

When Fairmont Hotel's Bill Fatt went to see him in Riyadh, the Prince insisted on personally driving him from the office to his palatial home for lunch. Even though Alwaleed would regularly get behind the wheel of one of his cars, Alwaleed's staff were surprised to see the Prince drive a foreign visitor around personally. Fatt remembers it well: "We arrived at his palace and were introduced to his family and others at the house. What I was told by him afterward was the fact that he drove me to his palace was an extremely important event for him, and the message that he was trying to get to his people was that Kingdom was there to serve Fairmont, that Fairmont was a very important and strategic investment for him. The fact that the Prince would drive me to his house for lunch was a symbol of how Kingdom resources should be used to help Fairmont as it moves forward and develops the brand, and I thought that was an interesting way to relay messages to his people."

Alwaleed surprised former U.S. president Jimmy Carter, too: "When I started mentioning some of the places we (the Carter Center team) had been, I was really surprised at how wide ranging his interests were, and when I talked to him about some of the corporations in which we had been involved, I found out that to my amazement that he owned either all of them or half of them! When we visited some of the finest hotels in the world, as a guest of the hotel, quite often I discovered to my surprise that he owned the hotel or had a major investment. So I was really impressed with his modesty because he never puts forward 'I own this or I control that, I am a major partner in that'—he always lets it come out from other sources. So I kind of kid him about trying to hide his lantern under a bushel, and not letting people know the great potential that he has, and also, of course, my main relationship with him is one of gratitude for joining us in embarking on some of these common (charitable) commitments."

DEFINING SUCCESS

"Do I want to be the richest man in the world?"

Repeating the question Alwaleed adjusts his posture from leaning back and relaxing to propped forward and engaging: "See, I can either look ahead to the three or four people in front of me in the world, and ask why I am not in the front, or I can look over my shoulder and see the six billion or so behind me. I choose to look behind and say 'Thank God' I am this far ahead."

The answer is not entirely convincing coming from a man who has proved himself capable of achieving incredible leaps and bounds in a relatively short amount of time. It is even less convincing considering he is obviously not one to sit back and revel in his achievements in a complacent manner. Alwaleed is also a man who, in his own words, is clearly after success, saying: "Success! I just love it and I adore it."

Plus, he is a man who admits that he never switches off and believes that sleep is wasted time, when the mind is stagnant.

Alwaleed is too close to the very top to stop now: "There are many ways to measure success. Clearly, from a business point of view, the results of your companies—that's one indicator. Number two is the amount of feedback you get from the people around you. The third is the amount of feedback you get from the international community. Number four is feedback you get from the media. So there are many meters, many indicators, to gauge the amount of success that each person has achieved in his life. Plus, most importantly, number five is the personal satisfaction that the person gets. A person knows if he is doing a good job or not. A person knows that, and knows when he makes mistakes and he needs to correct them. I'm a guy who makes mistakes and I admit them to myself and sometimes to others, and I correct them, and I move on."

In the world of business, the Prince has been able to ride his mistakes very comfortably. He may lose hundreds of millions in a day, but equally, he is quite capable of making that amount in the same period of time.

One of his staff quoted in the media once said of Alwaleed: "There isn't a major transaction on Earth he doesn't see in some way, shape, or form. So his knowledge of industries and situations is extraordinary. For one man to have that much exposure is unique."

As the Prince points out, success from a business perspective can be measured to some degree by the company results. The situation might be a little trickier as he gets more and more embroiled in the political scene. Mistakes there are not measured as much by financial gain or loss, as they are by the more sensitive barometer of people's trust and support.

That is a career path he has yet to define. In the meantime, he has won over the staff at the Kingdom Holding Company to a large degree. They confess to the stress of their daily pressure, but they often laugh off the difficulties in the work environment caused by the Prince's hectic schedule and demanding nature. His finance chief, Saleh Al Ghoul, says he is willing to pay the price of a high-pressured job for being with a unique boss: "He has matured; he gained a lot of knowledge, I would say, but in terms of energy I think he's as energetic as I knew him sixteen years ago. He is a workaholic—I don't know if it is a weakness or not, but it definitely takes a lot of the energy of the people around him. Since I joined, I am now diabetic and have a high blood pressure (laughs), but what I enjoy most about it is that it is not boring at all.

You come in the morning or evening, there is always action. (Laughs.)"

Talal Al Maiman agrees: "It is a way of life. You have to take pressure, but pressure sometimes is a pleasure, provided that it's controlled and bound by logic and a fair evaluation at the end. You know, life without a challenge is no life, in my opinion."

So the people around Alwaleed continue to move to the pulsing beat of the heavy rock tune he plays out for them day by day. Heavy rock is an acquired taste to which not everyone can adjust. At Kingdom, it soon becomes clear who can rock, and who cannot. Those who can—and agree to—enjoy, and sometimes endure, the hectic pace and the action, knowing that the Prince makes hard and fast decisions for each of his compartments.

What they do not get to hear is the complex jazz melody inside his head, playing its variations and off-beats, making a myriad of decisions moment by moment.

But then, jazz is an acquired taste, too.

CHAPTER 11

Arabs and Americans

I always tell Americans that the Muslim is not your enemy, but they just don't want to believe it because they would like to be swayed by a group of people who do not have America's interests at heart.

—KHALED ALMAEENA, EDITOR IN CHIEF,
THE ARAB NEWS

Thanks to the media, certain words have become almost impossible to separate.

Muslim terrorist. . . . Arab extremist . . . Islamic fundamentalist.

Prejudice has existed across the world ever since humankind was able to utter coherent curses, but in an age of so-called civilization, it is surprising that more is not done to address the hatred such automatic stereotyping creates.

While political correctness has eradicated the use of certain racist phrases and expressions in the United States of America, particularly pertaining to the African American and Hispanic communities, and even negative connotations against women, the disabled, and minority groups, there is little to guard against the perpetuation of the stereotypes applied to Muslims and particularly Arab nations.

The media drops those expressions liberally into most stories about the Middle East. In essence, it is simply poor and lazy journalism. Consequently, Arabs in general, and Saudis in particular, have a very negative reputation in the Western public eye.

In his 2004 documentary film, *Fahrenheit 9/11*, Michael Moore devoted a substantial amount of time criticizing Saudi Arabians. Moore is an excellent filmmaker, but it seems a little disingenuous to talk about "the Saudis" as if every one of them supports Osama Bin Laden or has covert financial interests in the United States. To his credit, Moore is openly honest about his political agenda— mostly anti–George W. Bush—which gained him large audiences and repeated applause among many Arab cinemagoers. Unfortunately, in that groundbreaking documentary about the foibles of U.S. politics, others got dragged into the finger-pointing, perhaps unfairly.

So where do Arabs and Muslims stand as far as typical Western perceptions?

Perhaps one of the best people to cast some light on the situation is a man, in the past, who has been a resident of the White House and a frequent traveler to the Middle East, overseeing peace initiatives. He is an advocate for a change in the stagnant situation that is brewing bitterness in the hearts and minds of so many young people in the Arab world and, at the same time, perpetuating stereotypes among the average American. Jimmy Carter is the consummate peacemaker: "Unfortunately, there is a great lack of knowledge, a great degree of ignorance, I would say, among many Westerners concerning the Arab world, and people who are Arabs or are Muslims and who are different from us, in geography and ethnic background, and also in religion, and this is a tragedy. I have felt frustrated in this case, by the way. Sometimes I tried, while I was in office, to bring some rationality and some justice and peace to the Palestinian people, but quite often because of distortions in the news media and even among top public official statements there's a denigration of Palestinians and even of all Arabs as if they were more guilty of terrorism or crime or violence than other people in the world, and this is completely false."

Whether you believe him or not, it poses a problem for Arabs trying to interact with the West as equals. The prevailing stereotypes and prejudices place barriers that are easy to reinforce, and hard to overcome. For Prince Alwaleed, the added factor of being a Saudi—and a Saudi Royal at that—only adds to the problem. His country has traditionally been considered a closed-off kingdom, enforcing strict rules and harsh penalties, including beheading as a capital punishment. Little has been done over the past three decades to change that perception.

The image of Saudis was already troubled by the oil boom of the 1970s and 1980s, when large numbers carted their wealth, literally by the stuffed briefcase, to Europe's most chic stores in search of designer validation. That picture of oil-wealth-driven excess continued for years after, as even many in the next generation of young and wealthy Saudis painted European resorts red in a fairly debauched style.

Alwaleed is aware of it. Relaxing in resorts such as Cannes and St. Tropez, he would witness what was going on around him: "This is typical of what all young people do in the West or in the East. Unfortunately, the stereotyping of the Saudis is from the things they do in the West when they go out—and they are not obviously liked—and then they still do it when they are a bit older, so they have no excuse at all. Obviously we are fighting an uphill battle to try to change this stereotype, and I think from my own point of view, I have been successful in trying to give a better image of Muslims, of Arabs, and more specifically of Saudis more generally in the West."

He is referring to his more conservative presence when he travels. No alcohol, no smoking, no nightclubs or bars, no excessive behavior permitted by his entourage, and a low-key professional approach to his dealings with Westerners he encounters. In this, he is very strict.

But, even if the Prince was managing to present a different picture of how a wealthy Arab might behave, through his business dealings in the 1990s, his effort, along with that of others, took quite a severe knock on September 11, 2001.

Fifteen of the nineteen hijackers involved in the terrorist attacks on the United States were Saudi nationals, a fact that was readily repeated in the American media well after the ruins of Ground Zero stopped smoking.

From Alwaleed's perspective, it was not so much the American government who made a big deal of it, and he tried to make that clear in interviews soon after the attacks: "I think the U.S. administration is saying 'Okay, you have fifteen terrorists and they are Saudis but we will not generalize against all Saudis. (However,) the media has been pushed very intensively and aggressively by the rightist Jewish lobby, which is really trying to capitalize on this to ruin the friendship between Saudi Arabia and the United States. Although the relationship between the United States and Saudi Arabia is excellent, it is not as good as it was before. There is a wound, and this wound is pretty deep."

Watching this, a little disturbed, is President Carter, who is confronted with the undoing of much of his years of hard work as a mediator for peace in the region: "Well, I think it's been one of the major sources for the worldwide threat now of terrorism, which has not always been the case. It's a recent development really. I would say justice and return to sovereignty and the end of violence in Iraq, plus the Palestinian-Israeli confrontation, and a few others of that kind, need to be resolved with the full involvement of the entire international community—at least the leading nations of the world. I believe that this is something that the U.S. government is reluctantly coming to realize—that we cannot do it alone, that we have to bring in others, even including those that we may not have always been compatible with like France, and Germany and Russia as major powers, to join in the common effort to bring peace there."

The effort to heal the wound of 9/11 came from many quarters. Even though the West generally berated the Arab world collectively for not being vocal enough in condemning the attacks of 9/11, there were voices in the region calling for calm.

Jordan's Queen Rania, the beautiful, youthful wife of King Abdullah, is considered something of a role model for many young people not only in her own country but also in the wider community. Just a few weeks after the attacks in 2001, in November, she was interviewed by CNBC's star presenter, Maria Bartiromo, on the show *Market Week*. The Queen remained diplomatic in her message: "I think it's been a really . . . a reality shock for all of us. We've all had to look into ourselves, to go through a process of self-assessment and soul-searching, so to speak. In the United States, people are looking at the foreign policy to see what can be done to ensure justice around the world. In our part of the world, we're also looking inward and seeing what can we do to make sure that we have a healthy environment for our youth to grow up in, transparency, democracy, equal opportunities. And those were—are—the things we need to look at to preempt any circumstances that could cause terrorism to arise."

For the Prince, there was also the concern, post-9/11, that he was now walking a fine line between the Arab world and the United States. On the one hand, he had tried to make a gesture of friendship with his $10 million donation to New York's mayor, Rudy Giuliani, only to have it publicly rejected after his press release calling for a rethinking of U.S. foreign policy in the Middle East. On the other hand, his credibility went up among the skeptics back home, who had originally thought he was selling out to the United States by rushing over offering a fat check. His comments alluding to the Palestinian situation and terrorism showed his critics in the Arab world that he had not forgotten matters close to the region's heart.

Still, it became something of a juggling act for a man who splits his financial interests between two very different regions. In a joint interview for a number of Arab publications in November 2003, the Prince categorically stated his concerns. He said that there was still a warm relationship at the highest levels between the United States and Saudi leadership. He had witnessed it personally when he attended a meeting between President George W. Bush and the Kingdom's Crown Prince Abdullah, at his Four Seasons hotel in the Egyptian resort of Sharm al-Sheikh. However, though Alwaleed did not believe that Osama Bin Laden or Al Qaeda would be allowed to damage that relationship between the two countries at the top, it might be a different matter at the level of everyday people: "American public opinion, Congress, and the media will always remember that Saudis were involved in what happened on September 11, and we did not help matters by our claim that Saudis were incapable of mounting such operations, and therefore Israel must have been the real culprit."

It was too easy and disingenuous of the Arab world to automatically point the finger at the Israelis, he explained, adding: "We have to accept that fact that fifteen Saudi terrorists committed a horrible terrorist act against America, and we have to recognize that this act will not easily fade from their collective memory, or their history books."

When asked why he has such a fascination with the United States, Alwaleed states: "Simply because it is the most important country in the world. Furthermore, our relationship with America has been a strategic one, ever since the meeting between King Abdulaziz and President Roosevelt in the Bitter Lakes in 1945. If the Americans have certain requests that we cannot satisfy, then we need to open a dialogue with them. We should not let them listen only to our adversaries."

So how was he to continue as a respected and valued international investor—the biggest foreign investor in the United States—while at the same time building his reputation on the home front?

First, Alwaleed made it publicly clear that he was a long-term investor in the United States.

Investments in America, following 9/11 and George W. Bush's "war against terrorism," were taking a severe hit—particularly for someone like the Prince, being the country's biggest foreign investor—but he confirmed he was was there to stay.

However, the Prince did express concern when President Bush declared those "who aren't with us are against us," believing this would only fuel the argument for extremists and cynics that America was a dictator, and therefore an enemy.

The pressure was now on the Arab world to address its political and social issues. Alwaleed could feel the desert heat of Riyadh start to get just that little bit warmer.

To some extent, Saudi Arabia was vindicated in the whole business of its relationship with Osama Bin Laden, when his supporters started attacking the Saudi capital with a series of deadly bombings—many of them suicide bombings. One in May 2003, directed at a foreign residential compound, took thirty-four lives, including Westerners, Saudis, and other Arab nationals. It showed that targets in the Kingdom were now being selected irrespective of the obvious potential to hit civilians. Alwaleed came out straight after that attack, saying: "It's time to face reality head-on. There's no need to procrastinate, no room for error. We have to acknowledge this problem. We have to acknowledge we have a disease called terrorism. There's no doubt about that anymore."

Alwaleed took offense to the idea that Saudi Arabia was funding and supporting Bin Laden and Al Qaeda, pointing to the fact that the extremist group attacked not only American and Western targets, but also Saudi ones, stating that the downfall of the ruling family in the Kingdom was one of its goals: "If this is not a wake-up call for us, we will never wake up! Extremism has to be extracted from its roots now—not tomorrow."

Second, in his bid to show his neutral position sitting on the East-West fence, the Prince made it clear that he has nothing against Jews. He had always been very open about doing high-level deals with heads of key companies, even though they were Jewish. Much of the Arab world is guilty of blind prejudice, particularly in equating every person of Jewish faith with being a rabid supporter of Israel's policies toward the Palestinians.

The first time he was confronted face-to-face with the prospect that it might be an issue is when he was meeting the head of the Four Seasons Hotel Group, Isadore Sharp, for the first

time. As Sharp settled down to discussions aboard the Prince's
yacht moored off Cannes, in the late summer of 1994, he told Alwaleed straight out that he was apprehensive about the meeting: "I
made it clear that I am Jewish and that I have significant ties to Israel. If that's a problem, we shouldn't even get started."

Alwaleed understood Sharp's concern due to the reputation
Arab businessmen had of staying away from dealing with Jews—
irrespective of any real connection to Israel. The Prince made it
clear that it would be of no concern whatsoever. In fact, when
questioned by one Arab journalist about the fact he had a relationship with Sharp. Alwaleed came quickly to his defense: "Issy Sharp
does not support the present Israeli policy. Yes, he is Jewish, but he
strongly supports the need to find a solution to the Palestinian-
Israeli crisis on the basis of two states living peacefully side by
side. He accepts giving the Palestinians their rights. He has no relationship with the Sharon government. He is a moderate Jew, and
we should build bridges with those."

Alwaleed was asked a similar question when dealing with Canary Wharf's Paul Reichmann, again onboard the Prince's yacht
off Cannes. On this occasion, one of Reichmann's assistants asked
Alwaleed during a quiet, private moment, whether or not the Jewish beliefs the Canadian business tycoon held so deeply would ever
get in the way of their business dealings. Alwaleed always relates
the anecdote with a laugh, saying that he told the assistant that
Reichmann was an Orthodox Jew and he was an Orthodox Muslim,
so they were both effectively Orthodox. What was the problem?

The comment coming from Reichmann after their deal making was: "He is traditional and religious, yet modern."

And in defending that relationship with Reichmann, Alwaleed
told the Arab media: "He is a religious Jew, but he is not involved
in politics at all."

Sandy Weill, another prominent Jew, heads Citigroup and has a
close relationship with Alwaleed. Weill and his wife even went out
to the Prince's weekend desert camp near Riyadh to experience

Bedouin culture at its roots: "He (Alwaleed) has always done business with whoever he thought it appropriate to do business with, who would have the right kind of ethics and morality, no matter what the religion. But I have never found that to be a problem. I am Jewish but I have not had any issues. It's a great excuse but I think that disappears with education."

Weill's desert trip was notable because just a few years earlier, soon after Alwaleed signed the Euro Disney deal with Michael Eisner, the Disney boss's Jewish background was raised in the media. Eisner was upset to read in articles that, due to his religion, he would not be allowed to visit the Saudi Kingdom. It is reported that he sent a fax to Alwaleed, expressing his anger at this information. Dismissing his concerns, the Prince assured Eisner that he had an open invitation to Saudi Arabia.

Alwaleed has tried to explain what seems to be a perceived split personality in his friendship with Jewish businessmen on one hand, and his clear support for the Palestinian cause on the other: "I do not have any problem with Jews. My problem is with the Zionism that seeks to destroy the Palestinian existence in Palestine."

The Prince goes further to state that it is unfair to see someone willing to work with both sides as a "split personality," when he is effectively trying to be a bridge between the two business communities.

The editor in chief of the *Arab Times* is, like Alwaleed, something of a progressive, pro-reform Saudi, who sees no issue with the Prince dealing with Jews: "The Prophet Mohammed was married to a Jewish lady, so it doesn't make a difference. I mean, our relationship with them is on a one-on-one basis. There are Jewish journalists writing for Arab papers, there are Jewish people who marched in Palestine, who marched in London, and who marched in Rome in protest against Israeli policies, but, yes, there are some (Arabs) who get upset about this, that we are dealing with them (Jews)."

Interestingly, Almaeena says that since George W. Bush came

to power, there's been possibly more backlash from Arabs against their own people for doing business with Americans, than for dealing with Jews: "(They ask) 'Why are you dealing with the Americans when these Americans are against our aspirations,' and this happened when the attacks in the occupied West Bank took place, and America's support was given by Mr. Bush calling (Israeli Prime Minister) Sharon a 'man of peace.' That was not taken very well, and many American products and brands suffered because there were people who boycotted the whole establishment that offered anything, from fast foods to drinks, to cars. (There was) appreciable loss of American business."

A CLASH OF CIVILIZATIONS

All this confrontation between the United States and the Arab world is often portrayed as a conflict between Christians and Muslims.

Most people outside the Middle East are totally unaware of the number of Arab Christians living in the region. There are many Palestinians, Lebanese, Syrians, and Jordanians, for example, who are not Muslims, but share the same concerns as their countrymen. The Palestinian issue is usually mistakenly portrayed as a religious fight by Muslims, whereas it is more simply a fight for United Nations–sanctioned territorial rights by the displaced Palestinian people—irrespective of religious belief. Many of the prominent voices among the Palestinians are, in fact, Christian, such as the charismatic Palestinian National Council member Dr. Hanan Ashrawi. She, in fact, resigned from her post in the cabinet, in frustration at the lack of reforms among her own people.

The fact that there is actually this diverse religious demographic in the Middle East gives fuel to the critics of the "clash of civilizations" theory promulgated by author Samuel Huntington in an article the Summer 1993 *Foreign Affairs*.

Huntington states, among other things:

> *It is my hypothesis that the fundamental source of conflict in this new world will not be primarily ideological or primarily economic. The great divisions among humankind and the dominating source of conflict will be cultural. Nation states will remain the most powerful actors in world affairs, but the principal conflicts of global politics will occur between nations and groups of different civilizations. The clash of civilizations will dominate global politics. The fault lines between civilizations will be the battle lines of the future.*

One of the critics is the outspoken Almaeena, who is not a proponent of Huntington's theory and feels that depicting the Palestinian-Israeli conflict as a fight between Islam and the West is only aggravating the situation. He worries that there will be damage to the youth on all sides and believes that for a pro-American Arab like himself, it is getting very hard to be a voice of reason to young skeptics: "When people like me tell them America is a great country, a believer in democracy, they come and say, 'Well, what do you mean democracy and human rights?' Three and a half million people in Palestine have been deprived, their people are being killed, and all America does is talk about suicide bombers and stuff—and every day Palestinians are being killed. When you talk about democracy, why do you deprive people of democracy?'"

Almaeena watched the change in attitude in the Middle East once George W. Bush moved on Saddam Hussein's regime. He feels that it had already gone downhill from September 11 for the Saudis, but did not stop there: "Saudi-American relations are deteriorating right now. I think they will further deteriorate because America is not in the mood to listen. Unfortunately, that group in America, sort of, thinks it can walk roughshod over people without taking into consideration people's aspirations and hopes. I always tell Americans that the Muslim is not your enemy, but they just don't want to believe it because they would like to be swayed by a group of people who do not have America's interests at heart. The Americans have been natural allies of the Muslims, in the cold war, in Baghdad, and all. Suddenly to brand one billion people as enemies of certain group—I think that's very unfair. So I don't see relations between Saudi Arabia and America improving for quite some time. It's difficult. In the last two, three years they have ingrained into the minds of the people that we are the enemy."

NEWS VIEWS

Global newsman Rupert Murdoch sees the problem more with the Arab world than U.S. policy: "I think it is a very dangerous situation at the moment, particularly with the different terrorist organizations that come from a younger generation, who've been trained to hate the West—or the infidels as they call them—and America is seen as the most prominent and the most prosperous. It's the most obvious target—though, I think for the most part, these people really want to change the Middle East itself and stop any modernizing forces there, and take them it back to sixteenth-century theocratic rule. So there are a lot of tensions and cross tensions, and clearly the terrorists—if I may call them that broadly—who I am sure are in a minority in these countries, are divided themselves between those who want to first overthrow regimes in their own country such as Saudi Arabia, and those who want to make spectacular damage to the West, through attacks here and in Europe."

Murdoch's News Corporation media empire includes the right-wing U.S. news network FOX. Although it is widely accepted to have conservative views and has certainly been a growing hit with the more right-wing so-called middle-America viewers, Murdoch denies that it is biased in any way, and he says he has certainly not had such concerns expressed to him by one of his major investors, Prince Alwaleed: "We think we are fair, we publish both sides. It's

very hard to get prominent Muslims to come forward and give different opinions to the anti-American position, but we certainly
cover it, and he (Alwaleed) follows it, and I've never had any comments on our coverage from him. He's a very intelligent man. He
knows what is going on in the world very well, and he takes a pretty
deep concern in it, not just from his own financial interest. He is
not just a very senior member of Saudi Arabia, but one who is very
concerned about the issues that affect his country."

It is interesting to examine how the media has influenced Arab-
U.S. relations. There was naturally a lot of interest in the coverage
from the invasion of Kuwait and U.S. first offensive against Saddam
Hussein in 1991, to the second, more decisive battle a dozen years
later.

During that first conflict, most Arab viewers depended on the
American Cable News Network (CNN), based in Atlanta, Georgia, for their coverage of events. It was round the clock and pretty
candid, and viewed by the Arab world as largely free of political
influence.

By the time U.S. troops were heading to Iraq for the second,
larger-scale incursion, the Arab media picture had changed completely. For a start, there was Aljazeera, the dominant Arabic-
language news channel that gave hard-hitting coverage from a
much more regional perspective. In fact, if there was any com-
plaint against the network, headquartered in Doha, Qatar, it was
that it was too emotional and graphic in its coverage, much in the
way that FOX TV was criticized for being the polar opposite and
blindly supportive of the U.S. administration.

Quick on the heels of Aljazeera in Iraq came Al-Arabiya, a very
young spin-off from the Middle East Broadcasting Corporation
(MBC), with its studios in the Dubai Media City, centered in the
United Arab Emirates, plus, a surprise contender, Abu Dhabi TV,
which managed to surprise all with its extensive penetration and
coverage from the heart of the conflict.

Beyond these key players, there was a slew of other national
channels in various Middle Eastern countries, giving their public a

very different picture from the satellite channels of the West, who for their part, struggled with accusations of bias and propaganda.

Respected Palestinian writer Rami Khouri, who is Christian— contrary to the general misconception in the West that all Palestinians are Muslims—stated his view simply in his article in the *Daily Star* in November 2003: "We have deep and serious problems in two arenas: Middle Eastern mindsets and U.S. foreign policy."

Defending Arab sovereignty in the face of American troops in Iraq, he added: "The U.S. is not mandated to define our political cultures; the U.S. has supported autocracy for decades, so its sudden embrace of Middle Eastern democracy seems slightly suspect."

Another well-known Palestinian commentator, Marwan Bishara, illustrates how the Arab world sees the connection between the United States and Israel, and how it is a negative perception. In an article he wrote in June of 2003, entitled "The Israelization of American Policy," examining the U.S. troop presence in Iraq, he stated:

> *Two pictures in the* International Herald Tribune *on the same day, June 16, spoke volumes. One showed an Israeli soldier in Hebron pointing his automatic rifle at civilians with their hands in the air, and another of an American soldier doing exactly the same thing in Falluja, Iraq. If there were no captions, you couldn't tell one photograph from the other.*

Bishara also posed an interesting question in the same article:

> *Neither Israel nor America is bothering to ask why the Palestinians and Muslims of the Middle East are carrying out suicide attacks, something not previously seen in Islam or Palestine for the last 14 centuries. Have Israeli military occupation and American military domination transformed the Middle East killing fields into fertile ground for hatred and conflict that has taken on a religious fervor?*

Bishara is also a Christian Palestinian.

The writings of both of these commentators, among others, serve as clues as to why there is a growing gap between the people of the United States and the people of many of the Middle Eastern countries.

That is not to say there are no optimists. Prince Khaled, the son of Alwaleed, is American educated, but he feels a solid link to his Saudi roots. He believes that there are many like him who can see a middle path between the East and West: "I'm very optimistic about my generation, in Saudi Arabia specifically. There are very open-minded people that I have come to know. Saudi Arabia has got a beautiful future ahead of it. It's rocky right now, but there's a lot of faith to be put in some really dedicated and well-informed, well-spoken young men of my generation."

Even if individuals like Khaled's father attempt to keep the dialogue open at the top level, there is a grassroots divide that seems to be widening.

Former Australian prime minister Bob Hawke is a vocal advocate for peace in the Middle East, demanding strong steps to be taken on both sides. He, too, fails to cater to the idea of a major conflict between Islam and the West: "I had an argument with Samuel Huntington about it. I think it's simplistic. I don't think there is a clash of civilizations now, but what there is, within the Islamic world, there is a clash between those fundamentally decent people who want to see a modern Islam in terms of its approach to economics and its approach to basic spiritual core. Against that, there are these fanatics who are saying the only true faith involves destroying the satans of the West, who have just blasphemed."

Another former world leader involved in promoting conflict resolution and dialogue is the former president of the Philippines, Fidel Ramos. He also feels that there is no chance of two civilizations simply colliding: "I'm optimistic that a greater understanding is going to develop, because there is quite a big overlap between these two civilizations. First of all, with regards to ethics, the Islamic people are just as moral and ethical as Christians are. Secondly, economic recovery will lead to the sharing of benefits of the developed world more equitably. The long-term solution is to remove the resentments that have been happening over the last five hundred years."

There is a school of thought that blames the growth of terrorism on exactly the issue touched upon by Ramos. Poverty, according to many analysts, is one of the major root causes of religious extremism and sows the seeds for an army of disillusioned and disgruntled people. Ramos says he believes the masterminds of terrorism to be the bright, intelligent, middle- and upper-middle-class young people who have an agenda to promote, and that it is in conditions of poverty and inequality that they are easily able to recruit the poorest to do their bidding in the name of religion, even to the extent of becoming suicide bombers.

The former president of the United States and Nobel Peace Laureate Jimmy Carter has made a name for himself as a peacemaker and a world-class negotiator. He and his team from the Carter Center, based out of Atlanta, in the U.S. state of Georgia, travel the globe dealing with a range of issues from poverty to political instability. He sees the divide between nations as something that occurs at three distinctive levels—between rich and poor, between religions, and between the East and West: "The rich and poor is not particularly between the East and West, but is between, I would say, the wealthier nations in the Middle East, which have oil for instance, and the West and Europe and the United States, and maybe including Japan. I would say the northern rich nations compared to the southern poverty-stricken nations . . . but ethnically and religiously, obviously it is between the Middle East and the Western world."

But some basic misunderstandings play a big part in this division, according to Almaeena: "There are a lot of people who do not know in America that Muslims believe in Jesus Christ. It's not possible for somebody to write a book, like Mr. Rushdie wrote, about Jesus Christ, because we believe in the arrival of Jesus Christ, we believe he will come back and lead and fight, so where is the difference? Those who are against peace are trying to digress us from our Judo-Christian roots. If you read the Koran and if you read the Bible, all the stories of the prophets are 95 percent similar, but we dress differently, or we talk in a different language, or someone wears the turban. As far as the principles are concerned—right and wrong—good will be rewarded, evil will be punished in the hereafter. Muslims and Christians and Jews believe in that."

A MIDDLE GROUND

Prince Alwaleed makes one thing clear when he advocates reform in his country, and that is that modernization does not necessarily mean blindly copying America in every way: "I am for change in our society but yet I am for keeping the Islamic roots here. I am asking to keep our Islamic heritage here; I don't want to change that. It just so happens that some of the points that I am asking for do coincide with what the West and United States are asking for, and it just so happens that many people in Saudi Arabia are asking for them also."

Alwaleed's mother, Princess Mona, is known for her independent views and thoughts, which might be expected from the daughter of the late Riad El Solh, independent Lebanon's first prime minister. Still, she does express concern for what she considers to be her son's blatant support for the United States: "He says good things about America, that's why I worry (about a backlash from Arabs). If he doesn't say good things about America, they (Americans) will not hate him just because he is willing to help the Palestinians (with charitable donations)."

Princess Mona's concern centers on the prevailing anti-American attitude in the Middle East, particularly following the U.S. attack on Iraq, which effectively toppled the sovereign regime of Saddam Hussein. She is worried that her son, being so closely associated with the United States, might also suffer the same antagonistic feelings that Arabs project on Americans.

The Princess has firsthand experience of the consequences of speaking out. Remember, her ex-husband, Alwaleed's father, Prince Talal, was one of the most outspoken reformers in the 1960s in Saudi Arabia, and as a consequence, faced exile and isolation from the ruling family for a few years, until he reconciled with the King. Princess Mona does, however, recognize the way her son has tried to position himself very much as a man of the people in Saudi Arabia and the region, and something of an East-West bridge. With him taking that approach, she feels she can be more comfortable with his public stance on Western matters: "He (Alwaleed) does a lot for charity, which helps him to get some support (in the region). (For this reason) I am proud that Talal and Alwaleed speak out for reform."

CHAPTER 12

Bridging East and West

Unfortunately, there is a great lack of knowledge, a great degree of ignorance, I would say, among many Westerners concerning the Arab world, and people who are Arabs or are Muslims . . . and this is a tragedy.

—JIMMY CARTER, FORMER PRESIDENT OF THE UNITED STATES OF AMERICA

It was an easy mistake.

Most corporate business leaders from the United States rarely get to see the real world, even the small fraction of that community which travels across the globe extensively. It's a uniform, cosseted environment of business-class flights, five-star hotels, and meetings with other top-level people in a conference room that could be anywhere.

Consistency marks the domain of the elite American businessman. No surprises, please.

The real world and its many issues and conflicts only enter through the limited surface area of a television screen. True grassroots experience is rare.

So, at the end of 1999, when Disney bosses decided to create an exhibit at their theme park in the U.S. state of Florida, showing Jerusalem as the capital of Israel, little did they know what they were unleashing.

Israel had annexed east Jerusalem, ever since it captured it in the 1967 war with its neighbors, and was claiming the whole city as its natural capital.

The Palestinians made the conflict over Jerusalem one of their central issues in peace talks, arguing that the eastern part of the city should be the capital of their future state.

When Disney's intentions were discovered, the corridors of the United Nations were filled with Arab diplomats storming up and down, demanding a widespread boycott of the giant American entertainment company.

The Arab League nations were in an uproar.

Disney executives were quickly pressed into crisis management mode, explaining that the EPCOT Millennium celebrations, featuring a Millennium Village would not, as reported, show Jerusalem as Israel's political capital. But despite their backtracking, they faced skepticism. Some countries in the Middle East were threatening not to deal with the American company in any way, anymore.

Not the best way for Mickey Mouse to bring in the new millennium.

Eventually, Disney's boss, Michael Eisner, was asked to call on Prince Alwaleed Bin Talal for help. When the media was directed to the Royal investor, the Prince defended the company, explaining that he would be consulting Eisner closely on a solution, and stressing that Eisner had assured him that Disney was in entertainment, not politics.

"An Arab boycott of Disney will hurt the Arabs more than it will hurt Disney. It will backfire on them," he stressed, calling it a "Mickey Mouse decision."

It would also have been disastrous for the Prince, who has held on to his large investment in the Euro Disney theme park since 1994 in the hope that its fortunes will one day rise.

Eisner was certainly glad for the Prince's help in calming the situation down and finally resolving the issue: "My problem is that I don't have a lot of experience with the Arab world. . . . I know there were fundamental issues, and he (Alwaleed) was very helpful and Prince Bandar (Saudi's ambassador to the United States) was very helpful and explained to me how close—genetically how close—we all are, but also culturally how close we all are together. I just felt very comfortable getting advice. You know I got advice from Henry Kissinger, I got advice from Prince Bandar, I got advice from the Prince."

Alwaleed proved to have the ideal balanced approach to the problem because he had already dealt with Arab-Israeli sensitivities in working with so many top Jewish businessmen, including the Four Seasons Hotel founder, Isadore Sharp: "He shows that we're the same, we have the same interests really in terms of what our main desires are in life and business, despite, of course, I being Jewish and he being an Arab. I said when you work with people, it's a way to building bridges of peace because the only way to get people to come together is to confront people and let them see who you are, so I think that is what he has been able to do worldwide."

Whether he chose it or not, Prince Alwaleed's status as one of the most powerful businessmen in the world was making him something of a cultural bridge.

ACROSS THE DIVIDE

Television is a very powerful medium.

Before it really became a force at a global level, from around the late 1980s, the majority of people in most countries had limited real-time experience of what was going on in different regions. BBC World Service Radio, with its hundreds of millions of listeners was about the nearest thing to an international news resource, but it still did not have the same impact that raw, often harrowing, video footage did, once it was available on satellite.

America's Cable News Network (CNN) pioneered the way, with its coverage of events, such as China's Tiananmen Square uprising in 1989, and then secured its dominance through unprecedented coverage of the Iraqi invasion of Kuwait in 1990, and the subsequent U.S.-led action to expel Saddam Hussain's forces a few months later in1991.

Since then the airwaves—or more accurately, "satellite waves"—have become almost clogged with new and highly influential networks. Most significantly, there has been the arrival of networks specifically serving a particular region or audience base.

Arab-language Aljazeera News, launched in 1996, out of the small Gulf state of Qatar, was one of those that radically challenged the Western-centric mind-set of the existing global players. Its managing director, Wadah Khanfar, believes that not only did his channel offer a different view from American and British ones, but it also gave the Arab world a chance to examine itself a little more critically: "For decades, we were not able to see ourselves except through the Western media. When Aljazeera came and started reporting, they started to see themselves and the world through Arab eyes."

The BBC's highly respected veteran of world affairs, John Simpson, is quite candid in his views on the subject: "That notion that people in a particular region should be obliged to see themselves through the image that is created by a completely foreign culture of them is something which is unacceptable. If we play the same old patronizing, colonial terms, then it's possible that nobody's going to watch us. Why would they bother?"

Khanfar points out that his channel, and other new players like Al-Arabiya, do not toe the traditional deferential and noncontroversial lines favored by most Arab media: "We started the issue of speaking about a lot of taboos in the Arab world, speaking about the political issues, speaking about the social and even cultural problems, speaking about the Palestinian issue. We were the first television station to host an Israeli spokesperson to speak to the Arab world—in their own language."

Aljazeera managed to upset everyone . . . but then, as the phrase commonly goes among journalists, "If we're upsetting everybody, we must be doing something right!"

The U.S. administration constantly condemned Aljazeera's candid coverage of its military action in Afghanistan and then Iraq following the terrorism of 9/11.

On the home front, many Arab countries have kept a distance from Aljazeera commercially, due to its candid regional coverage, although it remains a popular news source.

Interestingly, this is precisely the issue Prince Alwaleed Bin Talal faces as he tries to bridge the Middle East and West. He has to tactfully explain the American position to people in his region, and defend at least some aspects of the Western cultural values and lifestyle: "We can't just be anti-West for the sake of being anti-West. Unfortunately, in the Arab world you have some people that are just anti-West because of some things that are bad over there, but there are many good things in the West that you have to adopt, and I don't feel sorry in advocating that and making this public."

Simultaneously, the Prince has to persuade the people and leadership of the United States that the Arab and Muslim stereotype is not only unfair, but extremely dangerous, as it only fuels the resentment on both sides.

In this he gets support from former U.S. president Jimmy Carter: "The fact is there is an inherent belief in many (Western) people that the Palestinians are inherently violent people, or the Israelis are inherently violent people, is completely wrong, but that's the kind of thing that a few leaders on both sides need to continue striving to achieve, and I think that Prince Alwaleed has been one of those who has persisted in trying to call for peace and recognition for the nation of Israel's people among all Arab countries, on the one hand, but Israeli withdrawal from the occupied territories and justice for and peace for the Palestinians so I feel I share that with him in a very deep and penetrating way."

Alwaleed is adamant, however, that the Arab world must do more for itself. The image of many Arab rulers—Saddam Hussein being one of them, and for the past couple of decades, Libya's

Muammar Gaddafi being another—has not sat well in the Western world.

By the end of 2003, Gaddafi had changed his approach to his
protagonists in the West, opting for engagement rather than confrontation. Two big moves on his part were, first, in August, when
Libya accepted responsibility for the explosion of the Pan Am
passenger jet above the town of Lockerbie, Scotland, and second,
when Gaddafi decided, in December, to renounce weapons of
mass destruction and permit United Nations weapons inspections
on his soil.

He was largely redeemed and welcomed back into international circles. The Prince has been open about his relationship
with the long-standing leader and has pursued business ventures
in the north African country. Despite the risk of criticism in the
West, Alwaleed did not intend on abandoning the relationship, as
his public relations director, Amjed Shacker, explains: "The Prince
is an Arab and Gadaffi is an Arab. You cannot separate the Arabs
from each other. Gadaffi might have had some issues with the
West, but as far as the Prince is concerned, that's Gadaffi's business, not ours. Having said that, the Prince has always looked at
himself as being a bridge between East and West. Just because the
Prince has excellent relations with the West does not mean he
cannot have excellent relations with Gadaffi. They are not mutually exclusive. Besides we don't have any dealings with Gadaffi that
would make anyone suspicious. We are very open. The Libyans
came onboard to invest with us in hotels, and in an agricultural
project in Egypt. These are not shady projects, these are existing
projects on the ground—nothing to worry about—and we are
transparent about them."

Alwaleed says that as Gaddafi contemplated the lengthy isolation he had faced from the West due to sanctions, he decided to
try to address the issue by asking the Prince for help to build
bridges across the divide: "I think that came at a time when there
were secret discussions to compensate the families of the Lockerbie (Pan Am plane bombing in 1989) incident. At the time, they

wanted to help them tame that tarnished image in the West. They eventually fared well on their own, but if we can help, why not."

In recent years, the Prince has been more vocal on the subject of Arabs doing more for themselves. Speaking in a rare public appearance at the Dubai Strategy Forum in October of 2002, Alwaleed said: "The Arab private sector needs to be a strong participant in launching a dialogue that reaches the U.S. public and projects the real image of Arabs, of Islam, and of Saudi Arabia, which was damaged by the events of 9/11. Improving our image might contribute to reducing the platform on which radicals rely to justify their actions."

BACK TO SCHOOL

In an effort to formally reduce the widespread ill-feelings toward the United States, Alwaleed has tried to promote better understanding by funding a number of American Studies programs in the Arab world. At the start of 2003, he donated $10 million to the American University in Cairo (AUC), a highly recognized institution that was established in 1919 and caters to around forty-five hundred students. The money was used to fund the Center for American Studies and Research at the Humanities and Social Sciences Building on the new AUC campus. The university moved to a residential suburb east of Cairo, to ease the students away from the difficulties of studying in the capital's extremely crowded city center. Those attending the center at the new building would get a better understanding of American society and politics.

In thanking the Prince for his efforts, the American ambassador to Egypt, David Welch, commented: "It's hard sometimes for us each to understand each other and there are some very serious misperceptions that exist on both sides. And despite, or maybe even because of, the speed of information and the spread of technology, those gaps have persisted and some might even argue those gaps have grown."

The ambassador added that he agreed with the Prince's words, when he had said that many Arabs mistakenly believe that they already know the United States, and that "Familiarity with the trappings of American culture has . . . created an illusion of knowledge. The relationship between the Arab world and the U.S. is far too important, for both parties, to allow this state of affairs to exist."

Following the endowment, AUC started to consider initiatives to include exchange programs between students and lecturers, as well as deeper community and grassroots involvement for better understanding, which the Prince believes is crucial: "Clearly, you can't just keep everything at the upper level, because then you'd just be skimming everything and missing the real roots of both societies. You have to begin somewhere and I am beginning with the world of academia, and with the world of politics, and I cannot do it alone; I need people from both societies, I need business entities from both sides to assist me in having this gap bridged."

Around the same time that he donated $10 million to create a center at AUC, Alwaleed also funded a similar program at American University in Beirut (AUB), for $5 million.

The university had managed to establish limited courses on subjects including American foreign policy, and more on American history and literature, but by then was still lacking studies in race, religion, or even economics in the United States.

Naturally, it is an uphill task to persuade much of the youth of the Middle East that they should learn more about the United States. Questioned by the media in Beirut, the more cynical students came out with comments suggesting that they knew all they needed to by simply witnessing U.S. foreign policy, and by watching American media. One even suggested that Lebanese young people are already American in their culture, and that within five years, they will be more American than the Americans themselves.

But Alwaleed remained persistent in his efforts to bridge the gap and has his supporters in Lebanon, such as the editor in chief

of the *An Nahar* paper, Gebran Tueni: "I think that he can understand the mentality of the West and the East and he can help a lot,
in you know, creating a sort of bridge between the new Arab
world, the new Gulf and Europeans and American countries, and
we hope that he'll play this role, especially now, after what happened 11th of September."

In a lengthy interview conducted at his desert camp outside
Riyadh in November 2003, and published in a number of Arab
newspapers, the outspoken Prince said that the fact that Saudi terrorists were involved in the September 11 attacks made it that
much more difficult for him in his aspirations of building bridges
between Saudi Arabia and the United States: "We have to admit
that a deep wound was inflicted on the relationship between the
two countries. This wound will not heal in a matter of two or
three years. Nevertheless, we should do our utmost to restore the
good relationship that our two peoples have traditionally enjoyed,
and not allow Bin Laden to boast that he has succeeded in destroying it."

News Corp. chairman, Rupert Murdoch, recognizes the difficulty Alwaleed has in trying to be a bridge between the East and
West: "I think he does a lot that we don't hear of. He is clearly
very understanding of America and pro–America, but first and
foremost pro-Saudi Arabia. But you know, this country still has a
very close and friendly relationship with Saudi Arabia, and he'd
like to see that preserved."

In fact, up until his donations to AUC and AUB, and more recently the Maxwell School of Citizenship and Public Affairs at
Syracuse University, Alwaleed's efforts had been more targeted to
educating the West on Islam and the Arab world. He had donated
$500,000 to the Council on American Islamic Relations in the
United States, one of the biggest groups in the country advocating
on behalf of Muslims. The Council targeted the money to place
books on Islam in libraries across the United States.

In the summer of 2003, Exeter University, located in the west
of England, received $1.2 million for an Arab and Islamic studies

program, providing scholarships that would help European students to study Islam and the Middle East through travel in the region and direct field experience, in order to help break stereotypes and barriers, particularly as so many people fear going to the Middle East since 9/11.

Journalist Khaled Almaeena says there is an onus on the nations of the region to handle tensions with the United States more delicately: "The Arab world has to react in a positive way. I mean the Arab world has reacted by hiring PR firms and slick operators who have taken us for a ride and milked us out of millions of dollars. I think we should have more exchanges, and people should go and meet, and have a dialogue, you know, across America, with NGOs, with organizations, with churches, with synagogues. That's the way to do it. It has to be a massive campaign, and also at the same time, we should open up and let people come and see that we have nothing to hide. Yes, we make mistakes. Mistakes have been made in this country and elsewhere in the Arab world. We lack many things, but we are normal human beings like them. But we shouldn't be apologists and try to tell, them, you know, we are good, because in many ways, this society here, has a lot to offer to the United States and vice versa, and I'm not talking about getting technology from them. Americans have many good things, work ethics, good management, and from us they can learn some good values, too."

Alwaleed's efforts on the educational front have received a positive endorsement from Jimmy Carter: "I know already that Prince Alwaleed has taken perhaps a unique leadership role in this respect, in Exeter and in Lebanon and in Cairo, and he's now contemplating, I understand, developing a similar faculty in maybe one or two universities in the United States, which could be a major step forward."

Alwaleed would not be the first Saudi to donate money to Arab studies in America. King Fahd gave $20 million to the University of Arkansas in 1993, to set up a Middle East Studies Center, and other princes from the Kingdom donated sums to the University of California and Harvard, also to establish Arab Studies programs.

Almaeena says the Prince can be very different in his approach, depending largely on the kind of role he plays personally: "What he does, what contribution he adds to presenting the right image—not propaganda. The way he conducts himself, both domestically and internationally . . . I think it would be important for him to be perceived in the West as a serious person, rather than as somebody who has money, and who's just going around (donating)."

Alwaleed said he was looking not to simply give money, but to be more active in bridging the cultural gap. Professors at AUC and AUB both support his effort in changing what they believe is the widely held misconception that the United States is one big "Jewish conspiracy."

BUSINESS BRIDGES

The Prince is carefully watching how his efforts through academic institutions pan out, and he wants the next step to be a high-level multinational body focused on ideas and concepts, and how to implement them: "We are going to have a think tank that will add value, that will add to what I am doing already in the world of academia. I am going to have a think tank that has Saudis, Arabs, and Americans, and other people from the West, to try to create a better dialogue between both societies."

Another idea that Alwaleed touted when he met with Jimmy Carter in January 2004 was to stage a major multireligious, multicultural conference bringing together a combination of leaders with ordinary people, for an honest discussion. The idea appealed to Carter, even though he had his reservations: "That would be very difficult to organize, bringing in the leaders of the three great religions, to have a very frank and perhaps even antagonistic and brutal discussion. To bring some of the subterranean questions out in the open to be tabled and studied openly, I think, would be a great step forward."

While the Prince's efforts continue to grow in this area of intellectual and academic dialogue, his position as an extremely influential global businessman is playing more and more of a role in bridging divides. Sometimes it is direct, as in the case of the Disney intervention, but also indirect, by virtue of the fact that he invests in multinational businesses.

An advertising campaign for Alwaleed's Kingdom Holding Company, released early in 2004, has the bridge-building concept at the core of it. It shows the various international brands that the Prince has under his corporate umbrella, and how not only are many of them recognized as number one in their field, but how they are being wholeheartedly supported by a company that has its headquarters and origins in the Kingdom of Saudi Arabia—an unlikely hub for such a concept, according to many Western people.

The images in the advertisements transition through the leading brands in which Alwaleed has a stake: Citigroup, Movenpick, Time Warner, News Corp., Apple, Disney, The Four Seasons . . . it is a long list, ending with the message that the Kingdom Holding Company is bridging the world through business.

One perspective of how that might work comes from the CEO of the Kingdom Hotel Investment Group, Sarmad Zok: "Hotels have a great impact, you know; they generate employment, they generate cottage industries around them. The chef has to go and buy tomatoes from the local market so there's a multiplier effect generating from hotels. The brands are international, Western brands, and they are managing hotels in Middle Eastern and Eastern territories, so, yes, it is a great bridge between East and West, and it is for that reason that hotels are viewed as part of this globalization—they are very global in nature, so, yes, it is a substantial bridge."

Alwaleed is fairly honest about the coincidence, but appreciates it: "Clearly you bridge the gap, for sure. You do it implicitly, but that was not my main purpose. Obviously, you don't buy a hotel just to bridge the gap between West and East, but if it happens implicitly, I'll work on that."

Riad Assaad has known Alwaleed since they were little boys together in Beirut. He knew him as a driven and hyperactive youngster, and he witnessed the difficulties the Prince faced in reconciling the very different lifestyles he led in Lebanon with his mother and that which he experienced when he stayed with his father in Riyadh. The gap between the Middle East and the West is even more polar and, as Riad points out, in constant flux: "I think Waleed is trying to play on two levels, two dimensions, two platforms. The problem with this is they're dynamic, they're moving. You cannot continue juggling on these two things, and I think with his ability, he has succeeded on maintaining a decent balance between these platforms. But things are getting worse in the Middle East. Things are showing more of a violent outcome. Between present and past, between sons and fathers, between what is supposed to be and what we want to be, between basic values. This is coming to a clash. Part of this clash is Al Qaeda, part of this clash is Iraq, part of this clash is fundamentalism. Waleed is on these scenes, so I think he's tense and he's going to be under more tension."

Being mostly centered in Lebanon, and not being involved with Western infrastructure like his cousin, it is natural that Riad sees a darker picture, and something closer to a "clash of Civilizations," but that is not enough to deter Alwaleed from pursuing his agenda of bridging the gap between his culture and the West. So far, it has been well received in the academic world, and he looks set to expand on that approach.

If nothing else, his constant partnering and networking with truly global brands will keep Alwaleed comfortably straddling the broad fence separating the two sides of the political and cultural divide.

In his speech to the Dubai Strategy Forum in 2002, the Prince concluded by giving a Muslim view on diversity, saying that Islam's holy book, the Koran, advocates human beings getting to know each other and communicating.

In other words . . . networking.

CHAPTER 13

A Call to Prayer

I did not pray for three months, but all of a sudden I decided that I was so scared that I woke up in the night and I decided to pray all the ninety days . . . all in one go, and thereafter I have not missed one prayer.

— PRINCE ALWALEED BIN TALAL

The elevator stops at the sixty-sixth floor of the 300-meter (984-foot) building, leading out to an entire floor reserved exclusively for the offices of the Kingdom Holding Company.

Through the reception, smoked glass walls along the corridor mark the inner boundary of the company's offices, hugging the elliptical shape of the tower.

Walking around, the visitor comes across a door marked simply "Mosque."

What it does not say is, "The Highest Mosque in the World," a title that it happens to hold.

When Alwaleed built this prayer facility, he had not actually intended to claim that title, but simply by putting his office so high up in the Kingdom Tower, the mosque in it was equally elevated.

Philosophically, one might say it is a chance to pray that much nearer to God, but in actual fact, the Prince goes one better.

On his Boeing 767, his two television monitors usually cycle between the logos of his investment brands and occasionally the air map familiar to most travelers, but when it is time for prayer, the screen displays the "Kibla"—the direction of Mecca, so those who want to pray will know which way to face.

A Muslim is required to pray five times a day, facing Islam's holiest site, the Kaaba, in the center of the Great Mosque in Mecca, Saudi Arabia. Most hotels in the Middle East, and many non-Arab Muslim countries, will have a discreet marker in their rooms to indicate the direction for prayer. Many Arab national airlines display the Kibla, too, around prayer times, which are linked to certain times of the day between sunrise and sunset.

While flying, Alwaleed will grab the neatly folded prayer mat placed near his centrally located chair in the front lounge, head back a few steps into the conference/dining room behind the lounge, spread the small rug out, and discreetly pray according to the direction indicated on the screen. It takes just a few minutes before he is back in the chair, and continuing to read or do business.

In the desert, while spending his weekend at his tent camp, the Prince heeds all prayer times, usually having his religious adviser, Sheikh Ali, lead the group in prayer. Carpets are laid out in a large rectangular format on the sand, in order to accommodate the dozens of staff who join the Prince and Sheikh Ali as they go through the ritual. It is held in a quiet and orderly fashion and punctuates the regular routine activities of running the desert camp. If the Prince can organize it so efficiently in between the sand dunes, it is not surprising that he has a comfortable facility at his office at the top of the Kingdom Tower. The ritual is the same, only the view is different.

THE PRIORITY OF PRAYER

Alwaleed says he never misses a prayer.

"I'm a very religious person, and religion gives me a lot of strength. Religion keeps me on the ground."

At home or on the road, in any corner of the world, it is built into his schedule. In fact, during overseas trips, when his travel staff, Robert and Hani, hand out the itinerary for the day, they include a sheet indicating the various prayer times.

Many of the team under Alwaleed are Christian Lebanese, showing by example that the Muslim-Christian axis in the Middle East is generally a very comfortable one. Those who want to go and pray are perfectly free to do so at their own discretion. It is a very "live and let live" environment with no interreligious rivalry or tensions, and no pressure on anyone to have to be particularly religious. Alwaleed says he believes that religion is between the individual and God.

Having said that, for those brought up in Saudi Arabia, religion is a totally integral part of life, so it is not surprising that when Alwaleed went through a phase of not praying, he started to get anxious: "One time, when I was in Lebanon, I didn't pray. I don't know why. At that time I was in my late teens. I did not pray for three months, but all of a sudden I decided that I was so scared that I woke up in the night and I decided to pray all the ninety days, five times a day, so obviously I prayed the 450 prayers all in one go, and thereafter I have not missed one prayer."

The Prince says it would have been enough for him to be able to state his repentance and ask God's forgiveness, rather than have to go through the entire number of missed prayers, but he felt driven to do it.

The Prince believes that because of Islam he had solid foundations from an early age: "I was raised that way. I was raised in an Islamic society, whether it was in Lebanon or in Saudi Arabia, so this thing began with me from conception really."

Some of those who work closely with him actually credit his Lebanese upbringing and influence with his high level of tolerance for other people's beliefs. They say that it has kept him away from the far more critical and dogmatic approach for which many Saudis are known.

But Alwaleed says his religious beliefs keep him grounded and help him to handle his life in an orderly fashion, through thick and thin: "Sometimes you think, well, I am above the clouds. However, when you pray, when you are down to earth, when you interact with people, you just know, this makes you remember that after all you are a human being. It just so happens that God has blessed you with so many things."

By all accounts, prayer also played a major part in keeping him focused and sustaining him when his son, Prince Khaled, had his life-threatening jet ski accident at the age of fifteen.

UNDER COVER

Life in Saudi Arabia, for the large part, still conforms to strict interpretation of Islam. Much of the restriction is cultural and passes for religious. That has been the source of much debate in the Islamic world.

In the Saudi Kingdom, women are not allowed to drive and must remain largely covered, showing little other than their face. Many opt to cover everything but their eyes. Some do actually claim they find it liberating not to have to endure the stares of men, which they would if they wore Western clothes.

Either way, Alwaleed has called quite vocally for women to be a more inclusive part of Saudi society, and he is not happy that his daughter cannot get behind the wheel of a car, even though she demonstrates her competency as a driver when traveling overseas.

It is also because of the sensitivity to Saudi society, particularly when it comes to the Royal family, that the Prince generally does not approve of foreign camera interviews or photos involving the women in his life, from his daughter to his mother to his wife, at times he was married. He knows that his uncles from the King down would frown upon public appearances of women who are part of the ruling elite.

On occasions, there are photos of Princess Mona taken for publications in Lebanon, where she spends most of her time, but despite retaining her glamour into her later years, the Prince's mother cannot be shown so readily in Western clothes in Saudi magazines.

It is something the Prince is very aware of, and has to show respect for, in his relationship with his extended family. He also has to conform to the social norms of the society, which show a high degree of respect for Saudi and Muslim values and traditions.

When Alwaleed built the Kingdom Centre in Riyadh, the shopping center was designed specifically with a separate entrance for women, where they could arrive by car and use separate parking, elevators, and shopping areas, exclusively for women.

The shopping center, like many other public places, also includes separate male and female prayer rooms.

It was these values, and respect for his religion, that made the Prince commission two stone plaques with short verses from the holy book, the Koran, carved onto them. He then had the plaques put up inside the lobby of the George V Hotel in Paris. Alwaleed finds it ironic that the world's elite visitors pass under them as they enter the prestigious building, not knowing that they say, which is effectively, "If you thank God, God will give you more," and "All this is from God's blessings."

But in trying to overcome what he feels are social constraints, Alwaleed consults his religious adviser, Sheikh Ali, in order to get what he feels is a clearer understanding of Islam. In this way, he can avoid tangling cultural expectations with the teachings of the Koran. The Prince has, in this way, been able to justify his push for women's right to play a bigger part in society and not have to face restrictions such as not being able to drive—which, he says, has nothing to do with Islam.

Religion guides the Prince not only in prayer, but also in a number of other rituals, obligations, and sometimes just little habits.

Green is the color of Islam and used widely in Saudi Arabia as a result. Alwaleed's aircraft, yacht, helicopter, and a number of service vehicles all display the distinctive green and beige livery of Kingdom's colors.

He almost always writes in green ink, too. Most of the articles and notes he sends around to his various staff appear with his handwriting as a green scrawl across the page.

The Five Pillars of Islam guide the core of a Muslim's life. They are basically:

An unquestioning belief in God

Prayer—five times a day

Fasting—during the month of Ramadan

Zakat—charitable donations

Haj—a once in a lifetime pilgrimage to the holy city of Mecca for those who are physically and financially able

Zakat is obligatory and sets the foundations for charity given by Muslims to support the needy of society. It is worked out on a formula, based on a person's financial income and commitments, and is generally donations totaling about 2.5 percent of a person's savings annually.

Alwaleed has worked out a number of ways to distribute Zakat, some of it centered specifically around religious needs. In addition to this obligation, he has built dozens of mosques throughout the Middle East and has promoted the translation of the Koran into a number of languages, including Albanian, Sindi, and Persian, among others.

The Prince also gives millions of dollars to needy Saudis over the year, when they come to visit him at home or his weekend desert camps. That, like the Prince's prayer, has become a ritual, which he fulfills despite the time and energy it takes.

One time over dinner, a visitor commented on the Prince's rigid rituals, particularly the daily prayers. When Alwaleed was asked if it would be okay if he woke up late one morning and missed his prayers, he smiled, shook his head, and replied, "You can fool people, but you can't fool God!"

CHAPTER 14

Opening Doors to the Needy

It's a machine and he's got a whole group to handle the charities.... He is very sophisticated in how he uses the money.

— MICHAEL JENSEN, PRINCE ALWALEED'S
PRIVATE BANKER

Carpet after carpet covers the floor of the huge tent, which has a totally open front, spanning about a third of the size of a football field.

When the first robed figures start to appear at the entrance, they seem a little startled at the size of the space, but then they spot their benefactor standing at the back of the tent. Hushed, and a little in awe, they are led ceremoniously in his direction in quick formation, receiving a brief hello from him.

Following the personal welcome, they allow themselves to be led in silence to the seating areas facing the Prince on either side of the tent center. The entire process, though handled efficiently by a large number of staff guiding the visitors, is still quite lengthy, taking over an hour.

Once the final handshakes are over, the staff lead the last of long stream of people to the few remaining free spots in the seating area, during which time the Prince settles down on the floor cross-legged against low cushions placed the length of the black canvas wall.

The staff then go around making sure the seated men are briefed on how they will proceed once it is their turn.

While all of this is going on, Alwaleed Bin Talal barely notices. He's too busy simultaneously reading articles and watching a small LCD TV monitor to his right, and occasionally answering the phone, which remains plopped on his lap as he uses a headset cord with an earpiece and microphone.

Before long, there is hush in the packed tent, and a charge of anticipation for the proceedings to begin. It is a small sea of men, many old, but mostly middle-aged, some holding their young sons close to them. They try to be as smartly dressed as possible for this appearance before a member of their Royal family. Their heads are covered by the traditional Saudi red-and-white-checkered gutra, although a few do opt for a simple white one, and they wear flowing thobes, some cream-colored, but some made of a heavier dark material that provides better protection against the chill desert night air. Many wear Western suit or sports jackets over the top to stay warm. A large number come from remote, sparsely inhabited areas of Saudi Arabia, having been specifically invited after their applications to see the Prince were screened and approved. It is a very organized system, which avoids duplication of visits and ensures that everyone who wants to see Alwaleed will eventually get a chance. This is their moment. Sitting hunched and cross-legged on the carpets, no one says a word.

Finally, one of the tall camp staff strides over to the Prince and stands patiently before him, off to one side. He is typical of many of the Bedouins working for the Prince at the desert site. Burly and square shouldered, thick moustache, dark, dark eyes that give away nothing, and a leathery skin beaten into respect by nature. Across his large chest, a bullet belt replete with ammunition is adjusted to fit diagonally, from shoulder to hip, and what appears to be a rather antiquated pistol with a dark wooden handle protrudes from a holster under his left armpit.

After few moments, the Prince looks up over the top of his glasses at the man, and then he glances around the now crowded tent. There are close to two thousand people. When he gives a small nod, the tall Bedouin staff member turns around and walks off toward the entrance, vigorously giving hand signals to his subordinates. They quickly start organizing the large gathered group of men into a line starting about fifteen feet from the Prince. The visitors shuffle into place easily, many of them pulling out sheets of paper from within their robes. The line is formed efficiently as the handlers are more than used to this weekly ritual and can manage it with little noise or trouble.

When given the cue, the first Bedouin takes one step forward, and barely using his sheet of notes, starts a steady stream of chanting phrases in Arabic. The undulating rhythms of his extremely husky voice emphasize the emotion of what he is saying, but he waves the notes toward the sky with one hand, while clutching his other hand to his chest.

As his emotions quickly rise, along with the volume of his delivery, a handler steps in, ushers him forward to promptly hand the paper to the Prince, and them moves him off to one side to resume his seated position in the tent.

The next man goes through a similar ritual. And the next. And the next.

From time to time, the chanting voice is that of a squeaky preadolescent youth, attempting the same emotional tone as the elders; often a father is standing behind, quietly encouraging his son with a hand on the shoulder. Occasionally, there is a round of applause, as a speaker expresses himself in a particularly eloquent way. They are usually expounding the Prince's virtues, wishing him a long life, or reciting poetry they have written featuring him as a generous hero or savior.

For most of the time during the chanting and speeches, the Prince sits glancing at the television or looking at paperwork that a member of staff might step over and hand him. It seems like he is paying no attention to the stream of men stepping up to him one after the other. The only indicator that the Prince actually notices absolutely *everything* going on is when he looks up at one or two of them to question them about something they have just said, or a sentiment they expressed. Alwaleed may be a prince by birth, but he is the king of multitasking.

As the pile of papers in the Prince's hand starts to grow to the point where he has trouble clutching them, he hands them over to a staff member at his side.

The papers are petitions, requesting help from the Prince in a number of ways, ranging from requests for support for education or medical treatment, to particular goods they require, such as a vehicle or equipment, or even covering difficult debts. Each visitor gets only a few moments in front of the Royal, before being led away—although a particularly eloquent speaker is granted a little more time—but even then, the proceedings take anything up to four hours. Due to lack of time, not everyone gets to actually stand in front of the Prince, but every petition is received and looked at personally by him, and by virtue of the fact they've been screened before being invited to the desert camp, they are almost guaranteed to get their request fulfilled, or at least a part of it.

Alwaleed does point out, though, that not everyone is there to make a demand: "Some of them will just come and say hello and give their good wishes. Some of them petition and give their certain requests, and the process is that all these papers are taken, and there is a committee in my palace that goes over all of them. There are certain criteria that have to be met, and each person is granted an amount proportionate to the need that has been designated by our people."

Four Seasons boss Isadore Sharp paid a visit to Alwaleed at his desert camp one weekend and witnessed the Bedouin lineup: "He takes the time to deal with these people individually and I think that's great. He's respectful of his heritage, and he believes he's been blessed, and he's giving back. These are the stories I guess the world doesn't hear about, but you gain an insight into the man when you sit quietly and you are not talking about business."

The crowd is finally ushered out of the tent and sent on its way. It is an almost eerie scene as the mumbling mass of robed figures goes ambling off into the dark night, occasionally silhouetted against the spotlights of Alwaleed's desert camp.

It is quite a spectacle for those who visit the Prince at this or a similar location, to witness the Bedouins petitioning. Sometimes it is in a tent, sometimes out in the open. On most weekends, the number of Bedouins invited is between one and two thousand, while on some of the longer desert trips the Prince takes, particularly his ten-day retreat in early spring, the number can be more than thirty thousand. In a Kingdom with a population of only twenty-two million or so, spread across a very large desert nation, that is a massive attendance, as Alwaleed is quite aware: "Your ego could really grow out of proportion not only by witnessing these humble people coming to see you also, but by being so financially powerful. Sure, money potentially could corrupt if you are not down to earth, and one process for keeping me down to earth is religion. When you pray five times a day, when you pray with your people, when you pray with everybody else, it's really a humbling process, and that brings you down to earth. I never had this feeling of being aloof, of being up beyond people—never . . . and I think religion played a crucial role in that."

His longtime friend from California, Chuck Gulan, believes being charitable is part of Alwaleed's character: "I always considered him a fair person and especially now, more than before. He knows from where all of his fame and fortune came. He realizes that, and he prays to God every day and not many people realize that, and in turn, my feeling is that he helps and is generous not just to many people but to many countries. He is on a good track and a real considerate person, that's the way I believe it."

But, for a man who ranks among the world's richest and most powerful, to be sitting in a tent among the sand dunes every week, listening to an endless stream of adulating desert locals seems such a contrast to the lifestyle of a fast-paced global businessman who jets through a handful of countries in a day. Alwaleed's expression turns serious when he touches on this subject: "The system of our Saudi Kingdom, the Royal system, was established more than two hundred fifty years ago, and it has been through interacting with the people, the subjects of the Royal family. I do it not because it's culture or because it's habit; I do it, also, because I like it."

Keeping up with traditions also keeps Alwaleed close to the people, with his ear to the ground, listening to the rumblings of everyday society. By being heavily networked into the community's mind-set and issues, he is better able to address social and quasi-political problems, and show he is a man of the people.

His wealth allows him to be relatively generous during the weekly Bedouin petitions, where he may part with more than a million dollars: "I target all those that should be targeted, the needy people, the one who has a loan, the one who needs to go to hospital, the one who wants to get married, the one who has debts, the one who needs to have a house; it's a wide variety of people that we contribute to."

It is not surprising they come in the thousands to see him; in Saudi Arabia, Alwaleed has developed a reputation as a man who gives a lot to charity.

ISSUES OF WEALTH

When questioned about his extremely large bank account, the Prince expresses no guilt, and he feels that by religious law and by man's law, he is entitled to accumulate wealth without any weight on his conscience: "I think it becomes a burden if a person becomes obsessed about just increasing his wealth without looking at the society that he is living in, without looking at the poor people around him. If a man becomes obsessed just about increasing his wealth without looking at other aspects of his life, it becomes a factor that is negative, but in my case I think this will never happen because I am a practicing Muslim. I abide by what my religion says, by contributing a certain amount of my wealth to my society and to poor people."

His overall wealth may be around $20 billion, but he hints at an income of around $500 million per year to cover living expenses, running costs and so on, plus, a lot of it gets reinvested. He says his charity bill comes to around $100 million dollars annually: "I have no guilt at all, because the money I got was earned the hard way. It was not inherited, it was not given to me, so I don't have guilt at all from that point of view. As for the idea of giving just for the sake of giving, no, I give it on a very systematic manner. Some of the contributions I give are confidential and not announced, but some of them are announced."

His people make careful note of where the money is going and to whom. Through computerized records, they are able to target the needy or charitable causes in a structured manner. His two full-time Islamic scholars, led by his religious adviser, Sheikh Ali Al Nishwan, oversee a staff of half a dozen people as they hand out donations ranging between $500 and $3,000 to more than a hundred thousand Saudis a year. The small, single-story stand-alone building that houses his "charity compartment" is bustling, filled with people rushing around with bits of paper from computer to computer. Outside, from early morning, a line of people forms on the dusty street, stretching the length of the building, and overspilling onto the footpaths and streets surrounding it. Saudis in need know to whom to turn for help.

The Prince is looking to give his daughter, Princess Reem, the key to the charity division of his company. It is an area he would like her to take over, manage, and improve in efficiency. Until now, she candidly admits that it might not be the area in her father's company of most interest to her.

As the Kingdom Holding Company has moved out of the old building and located at the top of the Kingdom Tower, Alwaleed converted the original two-story marble structure into the headquarters of his charity work, where it can expand from its current small location.

Mike Jensen, his private banker, gets to see the account books, and how the system works: "One of the most impressive experiences I've had with His Highness is that he is as dedicated on the charity side as he is on the business side. It's a machine and he's got a whole group to handle the charities, and whether it's the five or six hundred people who come to his home every day, or whether it's in the desert, he's giving money to people who need it for jeeps or for camels or whatever. Whether it's fellow members of the Royal family who have come on hard times, or whether it's Ethiopia, where he's handing them food, or whether it's flood victims or that sort of stuff, he is very sophisticated in how he uses the money, and how he keeps track of all of this. For example, in Saudi Arabia he doesn't give to a nuclear family twice in the same year, so he spreads his money around as much as possible. I am very impressed with his charity side, as it is as sophisticated as his business side."

The bulk of the donations that the Prince makes remain in his own Kingdom, where he feels there is still a large number of people heavily in need. Much of it is practical, such as a project to build one thousand homes per year for ten years for the needy, and his announcement in April of 2001 that he was going to set up a one billion Saudi riyal ($267 million) fund that would support Islamic charitable and social causes mostly in the Saudi Kingdom.

Those watching the Prince closely, particularly for signs of political ambitions, believe that his grassroots charitable work is a way to build popularity on a large scale in his country, and perhaps even to give himself protection from Islamic extremists, who are drawn mostly from the poor in society and are generally against the Saudi ruling elite.

A large part of his philanthropy involves building dozens of mosques in his home country, where he has focused on putting up places of worship in rural areas. He hit the headlines when he announced in December 2001 that he was going to fund construction of fifty mosques in Saudi Arabia, where he had already built thirty-nine, but he has also backed some big regional projects, such as $4 million to the Grand Mosque project in Carthage, Tunisia, and $2 million for a mosque in Lebanon.

The Prince feels the need to support the Muslim community internationally, not just in the Arab region. When the former Yugoslavia fragmented in a bloody civil war at the start of the 1990s, Bosnian Muslims were often in the weakest position. In 1995, as Bosnian Muslims were trying to restructure, he gave $8 million in support.

Perhaps most significantly, Alwaleed also wins a lot of praise across the Arab world for his support of the Palestinian people. The coffee shops around the region are full of groups in heated discussion, berating Arab governments for not doing enough to help the difficult Palestinian situation. Alwaleed's efforts are widely noted, from his donation of a Boeing 727 jet to the Palestinian Authority for its new airport, to the highly visible $27 million pledge he made during a telethon, to help rebuild infrastructure in areas destroyed by Israeli military action and to supply clothing and vehicles. He has also given $6 million to Palestinians left out of work due to the intifada uprising, and $1 million to the Arab League fund aimed at repairing Islam's image in the West after the September 11 attacks.

Beyond that, his name often makes the news following natural and man-made disasters in the region, when he quickly steps in with funds to help. He has helped in such cases in Lebanon, Morocco, and Algeria; an example is when a train fire in Cairo claimed 373 lives. The Prince donated $2,200 to each family affected—a figure substantially higher than the Egyptian government was offering. Another was when a dam burst in Syria, killing twenty-two people and leaving thousands homeless in the village of Zeyzon. Alwaleed offered to rebuild the village.

Syria offered to name the new village after him.

THE SAUDI SON OF LEBANON

Saudi Arabia may be the main beneficiary of Prince Alwaleed's charitable contributions, but he pays a lot of attention to his second home, Lebanon.

In a country devastated by civil war, the level of poverty is significant, as is the ruined infrastructure, particularly in places like Beirut. A drive around the capital reveals a large number of buildings still wrecked by mortar fire, riddled with bullet holes and often with entire walls missing. Many still have people living in them.

Part of the city center has been renovated beautifully, drawing Lebanon's elite and middle class to its cafés and restaurants, but there are still large parts of Beirut's sprawling suburbs that need attention.

Alwaleed has mentioned in the past that he would like to play a major part in rebuilding the country—comments that media often linked to political undertones. This is fueled somewhat by the fact he has a number of investments there, particularly in the hotel sector, where he has been creating landmark venues such as the Movenpick Resort on the seafront in the trendy Raouche District, and he naturally has an interest in the Four Seasons Hotel. Alwaleed also has investments through other avenues, including companies like Lebanon Invest, a large financial institution, and significant tracts of real estate, as well as two television stations and two newspapers.

When Israel bombed the country's electricity infrastructure in 1996, he was quick to help, putting his hand in his pocket for $12 million, and he undertook to build six medical centers at his own cost. Another million dollars benefited twenty-two charitable organizations of various political persuasion, and he spent about $350,000 in getting the Lebanese basketball team to Indianapolis in the United States.

His charitable work in Lebanon has taken a more focused approach in recent years through the establishment of the Alwaleed Bin Talal Humanitarian Foundation, run by his mother's sister Leila El Solh. Awaleed had been receiving a large number of requests for charity from people and groups in Lebanon and had been dealing with them as best he could through his Saudi-based team. In the end, he decided to set up an organization in Lebanon itself and handed all the charity requests to his aunt Leila, whom he asked to head the foundation: "It helps developing Lebanon, developing all the areas in Lebanon, and without any discrimination, between the Christians, Muslims, in any area—in education, in medicine, but especially in medicine, for the time being."

Leila says that the country has a particularly large number of poor people who are unable to afford access to a doctor or hospital treatment; hence, the focus on the medical sector right now. Alwaleed's Foundation is also careful not to simply throw money at the problem. Each case, each group receiving assistance, is carefully vetted, pretty much in the same way that Alwaleed monitors his Saudi-based charity work. Help is often provided by the Foundation in the form of supplies and materials, rather than just cash.

One of the first organizations to benefit was a local hospital, St. Jude's—a branch of St. Jude's Hospital in Tennessee in the United States—which was taking in children with leukemia but had little or no money to provide the care required. The Foundation stepped in with much needed help. Leila says the next couple of projects will include care for the handicapped and a kidney dialysis center.

The head of the *An Nahar* newspaper, Gebran Tueni, describes the work of Alwaleed's Foundation in Lebanon as different from others: "He understood the Lebanese mentality. He is not giving money just like that. He is really trying to help organizations in Lebanon, who are trying also to help people who need money, who need to go to school, who need to build hospitals and things like that. It is very serious and is different from what we are used to seeing in the Arab world and the Gulf countries. It is organized. The team around Al-Waleed is also very well organized."

Leila lived close to Alwaleed during his childhood years in Beirut. Although she is his aunt, she is not that much older than him and was one of those who watched the young prince growing up: "He used to take his allowance from his mother, the weekly allowance, and he went to the suburbs—we were living next to the camp of Palestinians (refugees). In the suburbs there were many little Palestinian and Lebanese (kids) and he went there and shared his money with them, to help them."

Even as a youngster, those around him would benefit from his generosity, although it was often his mother having to reach in her pocket to fund his charity in those days: "He was calling his mother all the time and telling her, 'bring a delivery.' She said, 'Yes, for you, for your friends?' He said, 'No, for the whole school, for the whole school!' Every two, three days it was the same demand, the same request. Grilled chicken, always it was grilled chicken he liked. She said, 'We are not in Saudi Arabia here, we are in Lebanon.' He said, 'No, no, no, I will eat, and they will eat with me. I cannot eat alone.'"

GLOBAL DONOR

Prince Alwaleed realizes the political value of his donations on the Saudi home front and regionally across the Middle East, but as his international presence grows, his philanthropy is also extending further across the globe.

His head of media relations, Amjed Shacker, has traveled with him extensively, and witnessed how his interest in the situation in Africa developed from around 2003. Amjed noted that apart from seeing business opportunities that would benefit his own company, as well as the countries he was targeting, the Prince did not want to be seen by those countries as simply a man with a big bank account.

"He did identify the need for aid in certain areas," says Amjed, "and he acted upon it immediately and took out his checkbook and wrote out nice hefty checks . . . (but) one of the things that the Prince was keen on is that he wouldn't throw his money away. He told them that he wanted the money to be earmarked for sustainable projects such as education or health programs, to inoculate people against diseases—and these were ongoing projects . . . these were requests that came from either presidents, or in one incident, the First Lady of Senegal, so these were very legitimate requests by the state and we knew exactly where the money was going."

In the eight months between April 2003 and January 2004, Al-waleed's donations to sub-Saharan Africa totaled $7.35 million, with money targeted to causes such as building rural wells, supporting women and educating children in Niger, constructing schools and providing mineral water to children in Senegal, dentistry for children in Burkino Faso, medicines in Mali, and HIV/AIDS research in Ghana.

Two million dollars of that money were specifically targeted to airlifting 105 tons of food to Ethiopia in April 2003.

Jimmy Carter was particularly glad to see the Prince develop an interest in helping Africa, as that part of the world has been a major focus for the work of the former U.S. president: "Well, he and I have had extensive conversations. The first one was when we were in Riyadh, but he's been to the Carter Center, and he's thoroughly familiar with our work, and he's been kind enough to share with us his special projects or investments in the developed countries, industrialized countries, as well as the undeveloped part of the world."

The Prince donated $1 million to the Carter Center, but the relationship between Alwaleed and Carter grew into a warm one largely through the Prince's effort to support specific projects and goals of the elder statesman: "There are some very poor countries like Mali for instance . . . more than 90 percent of the people in Mali live on less than two dollars a day and 60 percent of them live on less than a dollar per day—which is almost inconceivable to someone living in Plains, Georgia, or in Saudi Arabia, and to reverse that trend, and to give those people hope and self-respect is a major challenge, along with eradicating disease. Prince Alwaleed has also been involved in that kind of effort, for which we are very grateful."

CHARITY BEGINS AT HOME

Back at home in Riyadh, charitable work makes its way into Al-waleed's life every single day, in the form of people sitting waiting outside his palatial home.

As he pulls up toward the drive, dozens of people are milling around near the gate. There is almost always some hopeful outside the property, night and day. Whenever they spot the large Hyundai limousine, which they recognize to be the type that the Prince uses, they start waving frantically, approaching the car and wailing their demands. They are mostly elderly women completely covered in traditional abayas, the black flowing robes that hide the entire body, head, and face. They know that there is a good chance that he will heed them.

Every day, as the Prince returns home from the office around five o'clock for his usual late lunch, he tells his staff to invite in a half a dozen or so of the women. They are brought through the security gate to the luxurious living environment, then seated comfortably and fed well. They tend to huddle close to one another, being a little nervous in the alien surroundings, particularly as most of the Prince's staff are in Western clothes, including the women. Once the meal is over, they get a brief word with the Prince, their requests are dealt with, and they are sent on their way.

One time, a woman pleaded with the Prince to provide her with a pickup truck. He let her continue the dramatic delivery of her request, done mostly at the top of her voice, before he laughed and asked in Arabic who the pickup truck was for. She repeated that she desperately needed it, at which point he laughed again, and asked how come . . . she would not be allowed to drive it— that in Saudi Arabia, women were not allowed behind the wheel of a car, let alone a pickup truck.

She fell silent for a moment, contemplating, while the Prince glanced around at some of the smiling faces in the entourage near the dining area. Then she burst out that, of course, it would be her *son* driving the pickup truck, not her.

The Prince burst out laughing once more and told her that she could have her pickup truck, and then he moved on to his seating area, as his staff led the ecstatic woman out, looking back over her shoulder, shouting at the top of her voice that she wished God grant him a long life.

As he sat down, he observed to one of the people near him that no matter what law existed in the city, in the desert the Bedouins had their own laws, and quite often women would quite happily drive even pickup trucks.

DOOR TO DOOR

It is not only at his house or in the desert that Alwaleed gets to meet the ordinary people of Saudi Arabia. He prides himself in having a close connection with what is going on in the country, and he makes a point of visiting people in poor neighborhoods every Ramadan, during the fasting month. He heads out at around 11 P.M. or so, to give out charity in the form of cash.

Each envelope contains 5,000 Saudi riyals ($1,370)—which is about a year's rent for some of the residents in the slum apartments of these impoverished neighborhoods. Managing eight hundred to a thousand visits over the month, he would give out anything between $1.2 million and $1.5 million in this way.

Traditionally the Saudi government had taken the approach of publicly ignoring the existence of any such poor areas, but as the country started to slowly embrace reform in the new millennium, Crown Prince Abdullah—Prince Alwaleed's uncle, and de facto head of the Kingdom—admitted that Saudi Arabia does actually have poor people. The authorities had finally come to accept that for their nation to progress, certain realities had to be faced.

Alwaleed already knew of these realities from his trips to run-down areas on his charity runs. He would do them about four or five times every Ramadan, usually on a Sunday night. The majority of people stay up late during the fasting month because most of the eating is done at night, along with any socializing. Daytime is largely quiet in the Kingdom, as it is in many Islamic countries when the majority of the population observes the fast.

Another Sunday night during Ramadan came around, and Alwaleed's small convoy of customized minibuses and oversized sports utility vehicles set off from the palace gates. One of the Prince's aides sported a pouch containing around two hundred hundred envelopes for the trip—a total of more than a quarter of a million dollars.

It was close to 11:30 P.M. by the time the string of large black vehicles pulled up in the quiet, run-down neighborhood. The temperature had been dropping, so despite the fact that most people were still up, few were inclined to leave the shelter of their homes, even if they were living in basic, run-down stone shacks.

The few stragglers on the streets stared in surprise, and a certain amount of fear, as the occupants of the vehicles clambered out quickly and efficiently. From the first—a large SUV—Prince Alwaleed emerged, quickly accompanied by one of his security men. Within a moment, a number of bodyguards from the other vehicles had flanked the Prince and his entourage. He waved three of four of his staff toward the rubble and litter-strewn doorways. They spread out and started banging on the doors—most of which were metal, gatelike structures.

There was a response from the first place, and a signal was sent to Alwaleed, who sped toward the hovel. As soon as he got to the entrance, he started edging his way through the door, ignoring the startled look of the occupant, a thin, elderly man. Initially frightened that this was some kind of government raid, the wide-eyed face soon started showing a cautious hope that someone was actually here to do something positive for him. The Prince started asking questions as he stepped past the man.

"Who's the head of the household?" he snapped in his usual energetic way, not waiting for an answer, and started pacing through the rooms of the property.

"Look at the condition these people live in," he remarked to his entourage, waving his hands around the makeshift kitchen area, which had two bare brick walls, and large breeze blocks stacked up as makeshift stands on which rested a small, twin-gas-burner portable stove. The area was littered with cooking utensils, discarded containers, and tatty storage boxes or compartments.

"It's disgusting. People shouldn't have to live this way."

He pulled out one of the envelopes he clutched in his right hand and waved it at the curious family that had started to gather in the room. A stout, burka-clad woman stepped forward and positioned herself in front of the quiet old man, identifying herself as the head of the house, raising absolutely no protest from him. The Prince started to thrust the envelope at her, although she seemed to almost grab it midair and then clutched it to her chest. The Prince spun around on his heel and started walking toward the door, which prompted her to follow him and serenade his exit by chanting his praises and wishing him a long life with God's protection.

Once outside, it was only a few yards' stroll to the next place his people had identified. The front door was already open by the time the Prince reached it, and he stepped straight in, unhindered. It was physically similar to the first. A shabby corridor serving as a hallway, leading into equally dank rooms strewn with either temporary bedding or cushions on which people could sit or lounge. A distinct lack of furniture gave most of these dwellings a feeling of being occupied by squatters rather than a family of six or seven people.

As the Prince zigzagged his way along the narrow, dusty track between the buildings, the average standard of living of these people became very evident. Most were families with a handful of kids—anything up to eight. The occupants would wave official documents declaring the number of their offspring, in the hope that evidence of a large family might serve to boost the amount the unexpected benefactor would plant in their hand.

Some homes were definitely better maintained than others.

"Look how some people are poor, but they still have the dignity to try to keep their place clean and organized," Alwaleed commented, stepping into one place that had colorful walls, and bits of carpet strategically laid down to cover the stone floor. "Other people don't seem to care."

It was true. Every now and then, the group would walk into a house that was littered with discarded food and wrappings and clutter that was obviously collected off the streets. One family had piled up an odd assortment of old shoes, sandals, and slippers in a dusty box placed near a corner by the front door. Inside other rooms were bits from old electrical appliances, and knickknacks that only served to consume the limited space the battered old building had to offer.

Another property was surprisingly orderly, and comparatively affluent, with an aging but functional television, sideboard cabinets, and a tatty but clean couch and cushions against the various walls. The owner, a tall, African-looking man, explained that he was from Nigeria.

The Prince hesitated, explaining that he normally targets only Saudi nationals for these particular donations, saying that if he didn't keep it focused, he'd be opening up Pandora's box in terms of expectations.

This man would not normally have qualified, but the Prince, seemingly impressed with how he was trying to make his home so orderly in the middle of a slum, handed over an envelope.

He got a large, bright toothy grin from the dark face.

As he left the Nigerian's home, the Prince mumbled to one of his entourage: "Once I enter a man's home, I can't simply walk out, saying 'Nothing for you. Bye, bye!' I have to give him something. I normally prefer my team to identify the houses of poor Saudis, so that I only enter their houses."

Within a short while word was getting around the houses that a stranger was knocking on doors and giving money to the occupants. The buzz started to generate a lot more activity in the neighborhood, and people started appearing at their doors before the Prince's group had even approached.

In the street, one frantic woman, recognizing this late-night stranger as Alwaleed, started following him, shouting his praises at the top of her voice. A group rapidly collected, many of them women completely covered by burkas. At first the Prince managed to pass a few envelopes to some of them, but that only encouraged more to come, and in the barely lit road, it was almost impossible to see whether or not the same woman was coming around more than once. Plus, the crowd was starting to worry Alwaleed's security people now. It was not so much that someone would want to harm him, but the press of the mob was getting heavy and it was getting physically difficult for the group to move around.

The Prince picked up the pace and, with strategic shielding from the bodyguards, managed to visit a couple of dozen more houses, before having to abandon the hope of entering any more places. He started talking to people as they lined up on their doorsteps and handed over money where he thought appropriate.

One or two women managed to barge past the security, and almost floating over to Alwaleed like black ghosts in the dim light, they wailed at full volume for money. Slightly stuck with no direction to escape, Alwaleed handed over money to them, but instead of leaving, they continued wailing for more, by which time the security and other staff stepped in and told them off, saying they should be ashamed asking for more when there were so many other needy people in the area. That did not deter them, and as the Prince managed to continue walking, they glided alongside, separated only by the large Bedouins protecting him.

Finally, with only a few envelopes left, but a seriously large mob making passage almost impossible through the narrow streets of the slum, Alwaleed decided to call it a night.

Handing over the remaining cash to one of his staff, he told him to make sure that it was distributed discreetly to people who had not received anything yet.

Then he tried to make his way back to the vehicles, inadvertently taking a wrong turn and ending up in a dark street with building rubble all around. The crowd started to gather as he stood still trying to get his bearings. Just then, one of the large black cars appeared close behind, having tracked the group. Squeezing through the noisy men and women shouting to get his attention, Alwaleed managed to get inside the SUV.

With the door shut, the sound of the mob was muted, although he could see through the smoked glass that faces were trying to peer in from all around.

A couple of the security guards managed to clear the way for the car to drive out toward the main road and back to the palace.

For once, the Prince looked a little drained from the experience.

One of the staff quietly commented in good humor, "Your Highness, there are easier ways to spend money."

CHAPTER 15

Billionaire Lifestyle with an Eye for a Bargain

I think that for Waleed, twenty-four hours a day is not enough.

— GEBRAN TUENI, EDITOR-IN-CHIEF,
AN NAHAR NEWSPAPER

The distinct color scheme made it clear that this Boeing 767 belonged to the Kingdom Holding Company. Strikingly large, as far as private jets go, the beige-colored jet with dark green trim was ready and waiting at the side of the runway at the private airport terminal, used mostly by the Saudi Royal family. It's a facility designed to create minimum hassle for VIP travelers such as kings and princes. Cars carrying the VIPs drive straight through the security barrier after a quick and painless clearance procedure. It is helped by the fact that an advance party carrying the passports has already taken care of the immigration paperwork and any customs formalities.

Passenger hell does not exist here. There is no traffic, no scramble for parking, no difficult check-in, no baggage issues, no standing in line to get through uptight security, or hanging around in a crowded lounge or terminal. Just drive and board.

The Prince arrived in a large, black Hyundai limousine, followed by a convoy of other vehicles carrying the entourage. They all pulled up in a line beside the massive jet, which is actually one of the biggest private aircraft owned by any individual. The cars were so close, the passengers could almost step out of the vehicles' doors and onto the steps up to the aircraft. At the bottom, the staircase was flanked by the Prince's personal pilot and head of the "aviation compartment," Captain Duncan Gillespie, and one of his crew. Those taking the trouble to look up would see the words *Khaled & Reem* near the nose of the plane, named after Alwaleed's children.

At the top of the stairs, just inside the entrance, the smartly dressed, beautiful cabin crew of nine efficient, smiling young women was waiting lined up on the plush carpets.

This Boeing 767 was obviously a little different from most.

This was Alwaleed's plane.

His mark was on every little detail, from the color schemes, layout of the rooms, type of leather on the chairs, and choice of silk rugs on the floor, to the style and cut of the aircrew's uniforms, the kind of food served, and the sweets and snacks placed in the small golden trays dotted around the cabins.

Inside the front lounge section, four sofas—two on either side—led up to a central, thronelike "captain's" chair, placed in the middle of the cabin, facing forward. Glass screens behind it separated that lounge area from the large dining table that also served as a spot for business conferences. Off to the right side from there, a corridor led to fully fitted bedrooms and sitting rooms. Beyond those were washrooms and minioffices on the right and a large comfortable seating area for most of the entourage on the left. Unlike many of the world's elite, who have regular economy seats at the back of the plane for their staff, Alwaleed opted for comfortable armchair seating that can rotate 180 degrees, allowing the staff to face each other to chat, or even play cards or board games on strategically located foldout tables. At the back of the jet, the crew had a fully functioning galley and storage areas for bags and coats. It was made clear to all the staff that the Prince likes his aircraft tidy, and no bags must be placed on seats, or jackets randomly draped across them.

Not all is right, though. Luxurious though it sounds, this plane is actually no longer big enough for the Prince's needs.

Alwaleed will always have a lean staff, but the growth of his business empire has compelled him to recruit additional people. With the increase in travel that his children are doing as young adults, there is a need for expansion. Knowing that he pushes his people to the limit already, Alwaleed finally committed to hiring more staff.

The trouble is, it is hard to find people who can, first and foremost, keep up with the crazy schedule, and second—though equally important—fit in with the extended family that surrounds the Prince.

The solution? A bigger plane.

Alwaleed now has a jumbo jet, which is effectively *the* biggest privately owned aircraft in the world. Once it is refurbished, it is likely to also be the most expensive Boeing 747 to reach thirty-seven thousand feet.

Flying in such comfort is enough to spoil anyone. Everything is spotless, just as the Prince demands it should be. Food is of the highest standard, with any special items the Prince might desire brought in from the nearest Four Seasons Hotel. There is no need to choose between the standard "aisle or window" seat, when there is the option of "sofa."

Even the elite who regularly travel by private jet cannot help commenting on the comfort Alwaleed has created inside his personal aircraft. Imagine their reaction once they get in a plane with nearly three times the space.

It is hard to doubt that the 747 will become something of a flying palace.

FLOATING PALACE

Then there is the yacht, the 5-KR (taking its initials from Khaled and Reem).

At 83 meters (283 feet) long, it's almost a third of the length of the *Titanic*.

It was too getting too expensive for American celebrity billionaire and property magnate Donald Trump to hold on to at that
time, so he sold it to the Prince, who always keeps his eyes open
for such a steal. At $19 million dollars, he got his hands on a prime
vessel valued by insurers at around $100 million. He had been due
to build a yacht for himself, but when he was offered a great deal,
he could not resist.

Even billionaires like a bargain.

In the Kingdom company colors, it stands out on the water
against the regular array of standard white boats, particularly with
the beige and green helicopter perched on the top deck. The captain explains there is an year-round crew of about thirty-four, but
once the full operation is under way, there are thirty-eight, including the helicopter pilot. It takes nearly a month to convert the vessel from winter position to cruising mode, due to the preparations
needed, including maintenance checks, and getting fuel and supplies on board before departing. It consumes about 1,000 liters (a
little over 250 gallons) per day, can reach a top speed of sixteen
knots, and even cruises comfortably at fifteen knots at which it can
cover around five thousand miles, taking it across the Atlantic
Ocean and back.

Total operating cost is reported to be between $5 million and
$6 million per year.

For a while, the yacht had been the possession of the Sultan of
Brunei, once considered the world's richest man, and before
Trump, it had been owned by the controversial billionaire arms
dealer Adnan Kashoggi.

As one of the yacht's long-serving crew put it, "It has certainly
changed since those days of partying, when the Jacuzzi was usually
filled with Cristal champagne and bathing beauties!"

Under Alwaleed, it is quite clearly a family boat, and the crew
has a lot less cleaning up to do after parties.

Every year in late summer, the 5-KR leaves its berth in the
south of France, and moves to a position just half a mile off the
coast of Cannes, usually lined up in the most central position

available, opposite the famous Carlton Hotel. The Prince and his family, and occasionally close friends passing through, stay onboard the large vessel, while most of the entourage and staff stay at the Carlton.

The Bedouins ignore the stares of the fancy guests who gawp at these desert folk wandering around one of France's elite hotels. The fact is, they are here because their Prince is on vacation, and they are part of the extended family. In reality, the Bedouins are bemused by the strange Western habit of sitting around just to be seen, are baffled by the discomfort of wearing relatively tight and constraining Western suits, and frankly would be far more comfortable in a thobe, back in the natural surrounding of the desert—or at least at home in Riyadh. Unlike those posing in the cafés, the Bedouins have no interest in designer labels and brand names, although while walking through the Carlton, one of the elderly men in the entourage spotted someone sitting in a trendy leather jacket with the Camel logo on it, featuring a cartoon camel wearing sunglasses and smoking a cigarette. He nudged eighty-year-old Aghsain, who scrunched up his face to focus on the design and then, realizing what it was, burst out laughing with his husky loud cackle and large, toothless grin. Not quite the camels he was used to seeing back home, it seems.

Some of those traveling to Cannes nowadays complain that it has lost its charm, and that most of the summer visitors now are only there to show off. Alwaleed says that for him, there's a large nostalgic attachment to the place: "I have been coming to Cannes for more than thirty years. The whole thing began with my father when he began coming more than thirty years ago, and I continue to. I like this area because it's central. From here you can go to many other areas, like Italy . . . or you can go to Corsica. You can go to Spain within twelve hours on my boat, it is centrally located in the Mediterranean, so that is the reason for me to come here."

After daily meetings on the yacht, the Prince spends part of his daytime on the shore, having lunch in the local restaurants, which the "travel compartment," Robert and Hani, will organize and commandeer. Afternoon and evening exercise is usually a rapid walk along the promenade, covering anything up to four miles.

One sunny day in August 2003, the Prince decided he wanted to vary the exercise and take everyone for a cycle ride. He had brought a personal trainer, Luna Eid Masri, over from Riyadh to see if he might benefit from a more structured training regime. Looking professional, dressed in a Lycra training outfit, she hurriedly wired him up with a heart monitor, as twenty-two sturdy mountain bikes were lined up against the wall for the trip. Before she could explain to him what he would need to do to maximize the cardiovascular impact of the ride, he had picked up one of the bikes and shot off, pedaling furiously. Everyone else, including the bodyguards were caught by surprise, and scrambled to catch up. Luna, stumped by what had just happened, ran back to grab a bike, hoping to make some adjustments to the saddle height before setting off, too. When she saw even the less fit guys already on bikes, zooming past, she just had to hop on and go.

For around fourteen miles, up and down Cannes's beach road, Alwaleed sped almost nonstop, only occasionally glancing behind to see if people were keeping up. The slow, ambling traffic did not have a clue what was going on. Drivers, aware this was definitely not the Tour de France, peered through their windscreens at the sight of a visibly determined man propeling a mountain bike at high speed, with two burly men staying close behind, followed by a straggling stream of other bikes ridden by a rather unusual mix of people.

Much of the Prince's activities and meetings are recorded as video and photographs for his archives. Whether Alwaleed is with presidents, prime ministers, businessmen, or pop stars, the "Audiovisual Compartment" is there to capture it. Cameraman Alphonse Dagher, another one of the twenty-something, trim Lebanese crew at Kingdom Holding Company, positions himself strategically, armed with the latest video gear, to get good footage of the Prince. His assistant, Ahmed Al Malki, tries to capture another angle on a second camera, or deals with lighting or sound, if those are problematic. Usually close by is stills photographer, Mohamed Al Jandal, a couple of 35 mm and digital cameras dangling around his neck as he snaps away with a professional long lens.

The blur of the Prince whizzing by proved to be more challenging than usual. All three were used to Alwaleed's frenetic pace, but this was something else. Worried that he might miss getting a good shot of his boss on a rare bike ride, Alphonse worked up quite a sweat, running to and fro, in the hope of finding a good vantage point. If the traffic was bewildered by the cycling entourage, they were totally baffled to find a young man squatting on the road beside the parked cars, peering patiently through a video camera viewfinder, holding a low-angle shot, waiting for the pedaling Prince to pass.

An hour and a half later, Alwaleed was dismounting outside the Carlton Hotel, where he had begun the ride. With a big smile, the glow of a workout but no signs of being breathless, the Prince looked at the few people around him and said, "Good exercise, huh?"

Luna pulled up a few moments later, Lycra damp from perspiration. She dismounted and walked over to the Prince, who was ripping off the heart monitor from under his short-sleeve casual shirt. He handed it to her distractedly, spun around, and walked into the Carlton followed by the bodyguards.

Luna looked at the discarded monitor in her hand, straps dangling, and watched the back of Alwaleed pass through the hotel doors. She shook her head and mumbled, "Well, at least he's fit."

Alwaleed had enjoyed the bike ride, but did not like having to weave through the town's heavy traffic, which constantly threatened his enthusiastic pace. He decided to stick with the walking and other sports for the rest of the vacation.

Between the beach and the yacht, there is quite a lot of choice for the Prince: "I am very obsessed about being healthy, being athletic, doing exercise every day. You can never be too obsessed about having good health. I don't like jet skiing because it's a very passive exercise, but I do waterskiing, I swim, I walk, I jog, volleyball, tennis, and basketball . . . everything."

Considering his mother had kept him away from water as a child for fear he would drown, he ended up becoming a proficient swimmer. In fact, Alwaleed is known to dive into the 150-feet-deep water around his yacht, and swim for an hour or ninety minutes, despite the choppy waves created by the wake of passing powerboats and other vessels. His bodyguards join him, along with some of his staff, whom he encourages to exercise too. Nearby, a small dinghy bobs up and down, waiting, in case any of the swimmers get into trouble.

Part of the drive to exercise so vigorously comes from those days when he was a very overweight youth: "Actually I was very fat before. At the end of the 1970s when I went to the United States, I was really pretty chubby. I decided I had to change that. I became very disciplined, very structured. I had to do some drastic things with my life, and I began dieting and to lose some weight."

In fact, he has reached a stage now where he has cut out meat and only eats vegetables and sometimes fish. Every calorie is counted, and the Prince has a mental chart that lets him quote the calorie value of almost anything around. He indulges his sweet tooth only carefully, with artificially sweetened apple pie (minus the crust, of course), and sometimes takes a mouthful of sugar-free and fat-free ice cream.

Alwaleed has something of a craving for macaroons made from egg white and Splenda, the calorie-free sugar-derivative sweetener. Staff at his regular haunts, particularly the George V Hotel, have dozens of these ready daily, as the Prince likes to have them sitting nearby during his various meetings in his exclusive back lobby area. The visitors readily tuck into the pile of colored discs and find themselves reaching repeatedly for more of them, as the Prince explains that they are only ten calories each. That draws some dubious looks from his guests, but they continue to steadily reduce the pile on the plate. Alwaleed goes more often for the cappucinno-flavored ones—decaffeinated, of course.

One little discovery made him happy recently. Manufacturers have started making one-carb ketchup. As he is particularly fond of ketchup, but keeps an eye on his carbohydrate intake, the Prince has taken to having one of his people bring this to him at mealtimes.

As much as he encourages his staff to stay healthy, he does not deny them the opportunity to eat what they want, so his dinner table is usually decorated with a large variety of mouthwatering desserts. Almost as if to test his own willpower, he picks them up and passes them around himself, to make sure those who want some can indulge.

Constant activity keeps him fit, though, and a brisk stroll is what the Prince actually enjoys the most, because it is a time during which he can still conduct business by phone. In the cluster of people closely following him is his telecoms expert, Rauof, who has mobile phones at the ready. When the Prince feels inspired to follow up on a deal or idea, he can be on the line with the right people within moments. He says he has never had to compromise either his vacation or work, because he is so totally connected: "It's continuous, because if I am here, my office is here and everyone is here with me, so there's no need to cut my vacation short to do business because everyone comes to me here—or I can travel to make a deal and then come back—that's okay."

Mobile phones and walkie-talkies also connect ship to shore, and when people need to move to and from the 5-KR or the Carlton Hotel, there is a fleet of tenders on hand. These powerboats, costing around $120,000 each, were modified to the Prince's specifications and can comfortably accommodate a dozen people. In the words of one of the crew, "These are the Ferrari of powerboats."

The Prince's floating palace also caters perfectly to his family's interest in sports activities, housing a number of smaller speedboats, dinghies, jet skis, and even a parasail—complete in Kingdom colors with the logo branded across it. When any of the Royal party takes to the sky, connected to the speedboat by one hundred fifty feet of cable, the Prince jokes, "Kingdom is flying high."

At night, when the Prince returns from the café scene in Cannes, usually around 2 A.M., he likes to sit out on the sprawling rear deck with his huge projection TV tuned to his Rotana music channel—although, being the restless person he is, his well-worn remote control unit takes him frequently between the Rotana channels, CNBC, the BBC, and CNN. He pauses less frequently at ART since he swapped out most of his shares in Arab Radio Television in 2003.

From his deck, the lights of the shore glimmer close by, and the peaceful environment on the water allows him the time to concentrate on his reading. Rauof has the latest editions of key international and Arab newspapers waiting for him, and Alwaleed devours publications such as *Newsweek*, *Time*, *Fortune*, and *Forbes* within hours of them hitting his coffee table.

Unlike his nocturnal sessions on shore, he is unable to go for a long walk around dawn, so he packs himself off relatively early to his plush bedroom cabin, around 4 A.M., to read alone, and eventually sleep—or so it is rumored.

As he bids goodnight to his guests and staff, the tenders prepare to return people to shore. They may be the Ferrari of powerboats, but at 4 A.M., they're obliged to purr along slowly and quietly past the dark cabins of the other boats around.

In the same way that his Boeing 767 is starting to bulge with staff and guests, the Prince is starting to outgrow the yacht and has another one under construction, or at least at the design stage. This one will comfortably accommodate two helicopters—one of them landing on a protruding platform that retracts back into the hull, enclosing the chopper in a hangar within the boat.

The team designing the vessel found themselves challenged to give the Prince his desired three-story-high glass walls up the side of the top decks, in order to create a light-filled atrium. This glass would have to be able to flex with the vessel as it traveled through water. Even more challenging for the designers was having to deal with a client who had read up on so much information that he could ask specific, probing questions, about anything from technical specs to deck layout.

The Prince pays attention because he invites a lot of people to his vessel, and he expects them to be in comfortable and efficient surroundings. He wants to impress, particularly as visitors regularly come to the 5-KR, for either social or business meetings.

One summer, the trail of celebrities and dignitaries getting on and off the tenders included Citigroup's chairman and outgoing CEO Sandy Weill, who had brought the incoming CEO, Chuck Prince, to meet the bank's biggest investor over a nocturnal lunch on the yacht. As they boarded to a warm handshake from Alwaleed, he commented, "Oh no! Now there are two Princes at Citigroup."

Weill remembers the particularly relaxed and jovial mood of the Prince while he was on his vacation: "When I went with Chuck (Prince) to Cannes and introduced them, he (Alwaleed) said he thinks there is only room for one Prince in this company, so maybe Chuck should change his name to King. (Laughs.)"

U2 singer Bono made a brief visit, and the vacation was punctuated by meetings with a string of famous Arab singers, whom the Prince was wooing to his then soon-to-launch Rotana music channel. The Rotana deal was almost entirely formulated on the boat that same summer in 2003.

And, remember, it was on the water that the Four Seasons' Issy Sharp and Canary Wharf's Paul Reichmann did their deal making with the Royal investor.

Even though it is only a total of three weeks or so every year that Alwaleed gets to use his luxurious floating home-cum-office, he considers it a very special time for him and his family, and those working onboard have to make sure absolutely nothing goes wrong during the period that "Number One" is onboard.

As the Royal party departs for Paris, for the final stage of the summer vacation, the crew of the 5-KR line up on the dock to bid the Prince farewell. He makes a point giving a large tip to each of the staff and shakes every person's hand, with his son, Prince Khaled, following behind doing the same. Then Alwaleed and the entourage are off in a large coach to the airport, where the Boeing 767 awaits.

The crew head back up the steps to the berthed vessel, where their work will continue for the next eleven months, maintaining and servicing the yacht and its accessories.

At least they won't have to clean the Jacuzzis.

PLANE SAILING

To a large degree, the summer vacation of 2003 was similar to others Alwaleed had had in the past—a couple of weeks in Cannes, and then decamping to the George V Hotel in Paris for another week or ten days. This year, however, there was a little shopping to be done between the two venues.

At 8:45 P.M., the Boeing 767 landed at Le Bourget Airport, just outside Paris, with hardly a bump, as would be expected from Alwaleed's highly experienced pilots. However, this evening their job was not just to get the Prince from Nice Airport to the French capital in comfort. They were actually helping with the shopping.

It had already turned totally dark by the time the big jet taxied to a halt, and the steps were positioned to allow the Prince to disembark. In black slacks, and a partially unbuttoned black shirt, with sleeves rolled up halfway toward the elbow, ready to do business, he strode down the steps toward a row of aircraft hangars. Powerful floodlights had been wheeled into the area in front, and they were running off a number of noisy portable generators. In their direct glare stood six sleek, small jets, lined up for inspection. They included a couple of Falcons and a couple of Hawker Siddleys.

Wasting no time, Alwaleed started walking toward the first one, Captain Duncan Gillespie catching up and staying close to him.

Two men were waiting at the jet, which had all its interior lights switched on, and the small door open, steps unfolded to the tarmac. The men bowed a little too deeply and awkwardly, not quite knowing how to handle protocol for a wealthy businessman they had learned was also a prince. Alwaleed, nodding, walked straight past them, up the steps, and into the small cabin. The men tried to follow him, and Gillespie struggled to get close to the potential buyer but was held back somewhat due to the restrictions of the tightly spaced, narrow cabin.

Alwaleed explained that he was looking for a plane that would seat around ten people and be low cost to operate, because it would serve a number of divisions of the Kingdom Holding Company. Primarily, he would use it for Rotana music work, and would have the markings on the jet depicting it as such, but it could also be used by other parts of the company, such as the hotel division, when they needed to make short regional hops from country to country. Of the six aircraft, he said, he had to choose the most suitable: "The idea is to buy a plane—not necessarily the cheapest. It should be cheap, but with best utilization and minimum cost of utilization—best value."

Nothing was going to stop him looking for a bargain. He wanted to ensure he got the jet with the most efficient running cost per hour, as each of the company divisions using it would have to formally hire it out from Kingdom headquarters and account for the costs.

Glancing around the first jet briefly, and asking one or two questions, the Prince then hopped out and waltzed over to the next one, again climbing straight onboard.

The representative for the company hoping to sell this aircraft managed to squeeze in next to the Prince, as he tried out one of the seats. The rep explained that his company chartered airplanes and had three—but only the business to support two, which is why it was on the market. The Prince asked a couple of cursory questions and again hopped out.

He quickly headed to the third aircraft, making the same sort of snappy inspection, commenting on the use of storage space and seating arrangement. Within three minutes or so, he was out on the tarmac again.

Before going over to the next plane sitting under the floodlights, Alwaleed pulled Gillespie to one side and had a quiet word with him about one of the sellers: "This guy will go down a lot, I think. Speak to both of them and get them down below four ($4 million). Tell them we pay tomorrow morning."

It was one of his pressure tactics—dangling the prospect of a signed contract by morning in front of the guy who needed to get rid of his aircraft—a guy who knew Alwaleed was a man who would be good for a check of $4 million or $5 million without blinking.

Thirty minutes was all Alwaleed had scheduled for his aircraft shopping trip at Le Bourget Airport, and thirty minutes was all it took for him to inspect all six jets, from the moment he stepped off his 767 until he got on the large coach to head for the hotel.

It seemed like a remarkably impetuous and fast event for deciding on a multi-million-dollar jet, but Alwaleed says that was not the case: "It's done very quickly and decisions are made very swiftly. The captain knows exactly what I want. He's been working on it right now for a month or two, and he knows what I want. The result of his research is all on display right now. He searched the whole world from Hong Kong to Singapore to America, even South Africa, and this is the conclusion. That's it. You have to decide quickly. You can't just procrastinate and delay things."

In true Alwaleed style, he had everything meticulously planned prior to execution. The research was done, the opportunities examined, and now it was a case of getting the right price. That sounded ironically like his investment strategy.

He was asked, as he walked toward the coach, whether or not he would actually have another jet by morning. The Prince paused, turned around with a smile on his face, held up his forefinger, and said, "Tonight!"

SPOTTING THE SMALL THINGS

An eye for detail is one of Alwaleed's strongest characteristics. Whether it is on his private airplane, on his yacht, or in his home, he notices everything. It does not matter how big the space is or how much stuff is around him, he will spot the smallest thing out of place.

Conducting a tour of his home, one of his household staff describes how they quietly test the Prince by moving ornaments and ashtrays out of place even an inch or two. Walking around the house, Alwaleed almost subconsciously heads to those items and adjusts them. He is prone to positioning ornaments and items in patterns—always symmetrical—and has a keen eye for spotting if there is no symmetry, or if a pattern is disrupted. In fact, he is obsessed with symmetry. He does not have to remember where specific things are in his house; he can merely spot when things in his line of sight are not in order the way he would intend. The staff cannot catch him out. He notices every time. They find it hard to explain, in the same way they cannot believe how he manages to be so involved in every detail that went into designing the property.

Keep in mind, his house is referred to by his staff as the "palace," which perhaps better fits the description. It is more than 460,000 square feet of living space, divided into about 317 rooms, which house more than 500 television sets and 400 phones and are reached by one of a dozen elevators.

Once a car enters through the security gate, it passes a row of tall palm trees lining the long driveway, which has a waterfall feature against a sloping rock face. The building itself is a modern, angular, block structure with a marble sheen for the most part, and tall windows. The oversized front doors open to an entrance hall rising almost eighty feet, facing two sweeping staircases that curve up from either side and meet at the top.

Around two hundred staff armed with walkie-talkies and mobile phones patrol the corridors, grounds, and service areas. They maintain the huge property, with its indoor and outdoor swimming pools, a minicinema seating forty-five people in leather-bound armchairs, and a hundred-thousand-square-foot sports complex that would put most professional fitness clubs to shame. That complex has every conceivable piece of training equipment, an Olympic-sized swimming pool, tennis courts (indoor and out) and a bowling alley. There is also a large landscaped garden enclosure with seating areas that can accommodate dozens of people for dinner. Their food comes from a central kitchen spanning around thirty thousand square feet, staffed by professional chefs who have been hired from around the world. They can cater dinner for up to one thousand people at any one time. They would, in such an instance, probably look for backup from another twenty or so kitchens located elsewhere in the palace.

The weather in Riyadh is too hot to sit out during the summer months, particularly in July and August, but for most of the year, it is the kind of place where the dry, comfortably warm temperatures encourage a life outdoors. For this reason, Alwaleed spends most of his time dining in the fresh air. He could, otherwise, turn to any of fifteen dining rooms within the palace.

Whether inside or out, the Prince likes to have a television set nearby, to monitor international news and current affairs, as well as to keep an eye on his own Rotana music channels. Those programs he wants to see, but has been unable to, are recorded for him at a central audiovisual control room with dozens of VHS machines banked along the wall, tuned to his favorite channels from around the globe. Each bedroom—ten master ones included—have up to four televisions, as do his private offices in the house.

There is a distinct absence of staff milling around inside the property, only the people Alwaleed directly needs around him. Anything they cannot attend to immediately can be backed up by others who are only a walkie-talkie away.

The executive assistant to the Prince, Dina Abdulaziz Jokhdar, is also his palace manager and says that he runs his household with military precision: "He's very strict about discipline. Everything is disciplined. He's tough if you are not following the rules. If you are not doing your job right, he's very tough, but, on the other side, he's human. He's very soft."

She also says that, because of his experience, the Prince is not like many of the other Royals, or rich elite, particularly in the way he manages his staff: "He is different. He's different with the way he lives, he's different with the way he treats (people). He is unique."

She adds that it is really important for Alwaleed to give women a greater role not only in his business environment, but at his home, too. In the autumn of 2004, after working her way through the system, Dina became the first woman to run his extensive palace and its staff.

The Prince believes the trick is hiring the right people to suit his temperament in the first place: "I am very disciplined and structured. I like things to be overorganized. I think it is in me, and unfortunately, sometimes I get tired from seeing things that are not right. I like to correct them, but I think I have staff around me, whether it is in my business community or in my house, or in my planes or boat—they all understand my mentality and I really have very good staff that supports me. They have all that's going on in my mind implemented on the ground, so it is really a very structured life."

Most of the support household staff are tucked into the various service areas around and below the ground floor of the house. It is a maze underneath, interconnecting the entire building and leading into the garage. The cars parked there change from time to time. Dozens of them are neatly lined up, including customized Hummers and vans, which allow the Prince to have satellite-based television and communications while on the road, as well as a fleet of Hyundai limousines bought in support of his investment in the Korean carmaker. A handful of sports and novelty cars rotate through the site, including, at one time, the original Batmobile from the Tim Burton movie, bought as a surprise for Alwaleed's son, though only kept briefly.

As the time comes for Khaled to move out of his father's house, he does not have to go too far. Next door is the old palace, left untouched for the young prince to make into a home for his own wife and family. Apart from taking over his father's old home, Khaled has to live up to great expectations in business: "There's a lot of pressure on me, for sure, there's no doubt about it. I mean I have huge shoes to fill—huge! From the business point of view, from the humane point of view, from a role model like him. It's a huge responsibility and it's a huge burden, but, again that was the hand I was dealt with, and I am ready for it."

LAST RESORT

Cruising out of the center of Riyadh, Khaled saw a long stretch of open road before him. There was not a car in sight. He gave a lopsided, conspiratorial smile as he said, "I hope you don't mind speed."

The large Mercedes CL 600 reacted instantly to his foot as it floored the accelerator, and the speedometer dial climbed without flinching to 260 kilometers per hour (162 mph).

The Prince did not blink as a big smile spread across his face. This was not a standard-issue Mercedes Benz. But then, this was not a standard-issue Saudi youth.

The car stuck to the road like a limpet through a couple of mild bends, and then suddenly, Khaled took his foot off the accelerator and, as the engine slowed with a low moan, he steered the sleek vehicle up an exit ramp to a roundabout. Directly to the left was the entrance to the Kingdom Resort, set in an open, sparsely populated area outside the city. He was arriving here around 5 P.M. to have lunch with his father, who had decided not to eat at the

palace because the evening was particularly nice for open-air dining. Khaled was in a relaxed mood: "I can talk to my father about
everything, and I am proud to say that. It has only happened
within the last four years. Before, I really didn't know how to act;
I really didn't know how to approach my father. He was a father
figure, yet he was very strict, and I was afraid of that."

Now Khaled spends his time switching between two distinct
modes—that of employer and employee, and that of father and
son. He feels that by keeping them separated, he is able to balance
his interaction with him: "I'm with him 24-7 and I have a teacher,
I have a mentor, and, by the way, it's free. So if he's in a business
meeting, I'm always there. I'm always listening or taking notes;
what's going on, how is he acting? How is he not acting? Why did
he back down? Why did he not back down? Yes, I've learned a lot,
and I'm learning a lot."

Khaled parked near the front gate of the resort and was greeted
by one of the staff in a small beige and green vehicle, much like a
golf cart, but in the design of a miniature 1930s vintage car, with the
Kingdom logo on it. The Prince hopped in, and the buggy took off
with the typical whine of an electric car. It wound its way down a
curving path, past a nine-hole golf course, to a wide, open-plan seating area that overlooked what appeared to be a mini Grand Canyon.

Alwaleed was already there, being attended to by staff, and going through his daily prelunch ritual of catching up on information and glancing at the omnipresent television set off to one side.

There was a clear blue sky, and apart from a section of public
road visible in the distance, it could have been an oasis in the middle of nowhere. In fact, the Prince did build an oasis as part of the
resort. The path wound down steeply into the small valley, passing
a riding area and stables, a miniature zoo with a variety of animals
milling about, and a large aviary set into the hillside. At the bottom
of the valley, row upon row of tall palm trees stood majestically
beside a small lake. A small green island, close to the center, provided a connecting point for two stone bridges traversing the lake,
and a fountain sprayed water up high from the middle of the lake.

With about ten properties dotted around the resort, some of them substantially large, it seemed like an expensive project to have undertaken, but true to form, Alwaleed had found another bargain: "Actually this was land that was forgotten, and no one really utilized it, so I just took it and I developed it. I bought it for almost nothing, and I just developed it with a minimal amount of money and got this gorgeous result. This is now valued at more than ten times what I bought it for and what I spent on it."

It was complete desert when he acquired it, and he did his best to keep it natural looking. The miniature canyon was merely cleaned up, subtly wired for lighting with a waterfall, and a path carved into the side of it so Alwaleed could take long walks.

One of the properties was built to look like a natural cave formation in Lebanon, which is popular with tourists, and a place Alwaleed's father was always keen to visit.

Another was like an American ranch, complete with midwestern floor tiles and trimmings. A massive tent sat near the entrance so that the Prince could receive a large number of visitors at once, and there was a recreational building near the oasis, complete with a pool going from inside the building to the outside.

At the top of the canyon, the prime structure was the building named "Hilltop," the interior of which was centered around a large swimming pool with a sunken bar area, stepping-stones, miniature wooden bridges, and a spiral staircase leading up to the upper section, which had a glass floor allowing those lounging upstairs to look down on the pool below.

Family pictures featuring Alwaleed and his children dotted the various seating areas and bedrooms, and from every vantage point, a television screen was visible.

Once again, this resort was clearly modeled and supervised by the detailed eye of Alwaleed Bin Talal.

It seemed to be so much for one man and his family, but the Prince points out that he does use the Kingdom Resort extensively, and most of the two dozen seating areas get a look-in at some point during the year.

As night set in, the road running near the resort became more visible as cars turned on their headlights, but traffic was very light, and no noise filtered across the small valley dividing the main area of the resort and the rest of the world.

Just before the stars became clearly visible, the sky turned a very deep purple color, which contrasted beautifully with the silhouettes of the palm trees dotted around near the Prince and his team.

"Look!" one person suddenly commented very loudly. Everyone turned to see where she was pointing.

In the totally cloudless, purple sky, there was just one small, very low, white cloud, catching a bluish haze at its edges. It looked really peculiar floating around like a small cotton bud entirely on its own.

The Prince, who had been talking with someone, turned and glanced up. In complete surprise, with a small laugh, he commented, "Oh! It's lost."

FROM SAND TO SNOW

As 2003 came to an end, the guys in the "travel compartment" were sweating it out once more.

Anyone poking their head through the door of Robert and Hani's office at the Kingdom Holding Company would have had a very hard time getting a coherent answer from either of them. The Prince's big trip to Jackson Hole, Wyoming, in the United States, was only a couple of weeks away. They had no time to think, let alone chat. They had managed to get one more person, Faisal, to join them for this trip, to test his mettle as a prospective addition to the team, but he was still inexperienced, and it was still a massive workload for all of them.

Over the past few years, Alwaleed had been taking his winter vacation at ski resorts, since his children had persuaded him to hit the slopes. The problem was, being in the United States, where he keeps most of his investments, Alwaleed was not going to simply kick back, relax, and enjoy après-ski. For the world's hardest-working billionaire, après-ski means squeezing in some serious work between taking off the ski boots and putting them back on again.

Chuck Gulan, who had traveled over from California to see his old friend, is never surprised by anything Alwaleed does: "If people envision His Highness being a great big playboy because he has a ship, a plane, or three planes, and goes on extravagant vacations, well . . . that's his enjoyment, but then again it's his work life as well. When he goes on these excursions, it's basically all business; he has very little time for play."

Not entirely true.

In Jackson Hole, Alwaleed certainly donned his skis and enthusiastically carved his way through the snow with constant coaching from Bill, his personal ski instructor. Bill, though incredibly fit for his twilight years, wore a permanent smile on his ruddy suntanned face, and he had the kind of patient nature that contrasted Alwaleed dramatically. Bill even seemed to speak in slow motion compared with the rapid gunfire of the Prince's sentences, whose remarkable brain works almost too fast for him to manage it.

Bill would gently tilt from side to side, gliding down the hill, shouting encouragement, while the Prince, with particularly strong legs from all his walking, took on gravity with gusto.

The team skiing with the Prince would respectfully follow in line behind, though in reality, many of them struggled to keep up with the Royal pace.

Alwaleed's children had encouraged him to take up skiing so that they could all take a winter vacation together as a family. Khaled and Reem, being of another generation altogether, would often cross paths with their father on the slopes, but he would usually come across them lying down in the white stuff, with snowboards locked to their feet. Lying in snow seems to be the preferred resting position of snowboarders.

Chuck was actually right to some extent—business does not stop just because Alwaleed is plowing through snow at high speed on the mountainside. Every now and then, Rauof would speed forward, Motorola phone extended in hand, open and ready for the Prince to take or make a call. Fortunately, the telecoms chief is a good skier and can make his way efficiently to the Prince at high speed when called. One day, however, he handed over the phone but lost his balance as the Prince began the conversation. Having nothing else to hang on to, Raouf instinctively grabbed the Prince in an effort to stay upright and inadvertently locked skis with him. The tangled twosome slid down the hill backward for a few seconds before tumbling over completely.

Everyone else looked away, whistling, pretending they had not noticed. Alwaleed, somehow, managed to continue his conversation throughout the whole incident.

Even wiping out, the Prince was doing business.

The Jackson Hole trip was a tense time for Robert and Hani, largely because the Prince had crammed so much into it.

From Riyadh, the group had flown to New York, where more than a dozen meetings a day had been arranged, including Citigroup's chairman, Sandy Weill, and the bank's "other Prince," the incoming CEO, Chuck Prince, along with Dick Parsons of Time Warner; Hank Greenberg, the boss of insurance giant AIG; and a number of others. Bill Fatt, the CEO of the Fairmont Group came down from Toronto to see the Prince in the Big Apple, so that they could discuss what to do with The Plaza Hotel, in which Alwaleed had a 50 percent stake at the time.

To some degree, the highlight of the New York part of the trip was Alwaleed's meeting with former U.S. president Bill Clinton.

Robert and Hani had arranged the security clearance needed to get into the building Clinton used as an office in Harlem, north of Manhattan's central district, and they had arranged transportation in the form of long, black limousines. If these were not going to attract attention in Harlem, nothing was, but as it happens, Alwaleed's own bodyguard, Nasser Al Otaibi, was joined by two local security men—both ex-New York cops—in case anyone was worried about safety.

As the Prince stepped out of the limo, which had parked very close to the building housing Clinton's office, he commented that he was about fifteen minutes early, which was just enough time to take a power walk. It was wintertime, and the drains of New York's streets released a steady stream of mist into the air. People were huddled deeply into their jackets and coats, their breath coming out as white smoke.

Alwaleed, in a midlength black leather jacket with a furry collar, took off down the road, twirling the worry beads he likes to carry most of the time. The bodyguards rushed to flank him, and the entourage dropped in line. He managed a number of city blocks before stopping and pausing to ask no one in particular, "Is it safe to walk in Harlem?"

Fortunately, even if it was not the Champs Élysées, Harlem was certainly not what it used to be twenty years ago—a ghetto of crime, according to all the Hollywood cops and robbers movies. The rehabilitation of the neighborhood starting in the late 1990s had made it something of a trendy, up-and-coming area.

The security was discreet at Clinton's building, but no doubt rather secure. The former president requested that Alwaleed join him with only one adviser, so that they could talk as privately as possible. The Prince and his banker, Mike Jensen, slipped past the security at their invitation and disappeared into the office. Neither gave much detail about the discussions once they emerged an hour later.

The New York stay was certainly packed with meetings, but they had to be scheduled so that Alwaleed would be free to travel to New Haven on January 17. That was the day his daughter, Reem, was graduating from university. Alwaleed had also pulled strings to get his friend Sandy Weill to leave Citigroup behind for a while to speak at the ceremony.

The striking young princess was visibly nervous and excited as the event got going, particularly seeing her father and brother in the audience accompanied by her mother. Princess Dalal had flown in to give her daughter support on her big day.

With both his children successfully through their hardest part of schooling, the Prince was glowing with pride. They would both soon be working with him full-time. He picked Reem up off her feet in a bear hug and carried her around outside the hall.

As he dropped her back down, he joked about the pressure she now faced, saying, "It's just begun!"

Even that day through New Haven was carefully scheduled by Alwaleed. He had arrived by bus from New York, but had his Boeing 767 fly up to the local Hartford Bradley Airport. He had also arranged for the arrival of his new Hawker Siddley—the one bought that late night at Paris's Le Bourget Airport. By now it had been refitted according to his specifications and bearing the Rotana music logo.

Just before loading the staff and entourage onto the Boeing, Alwaleed gave the small plane a thorough inspection, noticing a couple of minor items that most would miss. For example, he spotted that the small Arabic texts from the Koran, discreetly placed on the bulkhead, were on a background that was a tiny shade off from the rest of the finish. The crew assured him it would be fixed by the next time he saw the plane.

Once everyone was onboard the 767, it set off for Idaho Falls. That was the nearest airport to Jackson Hole that could accommodate such a large jet. The one at Jackson Hole itself was tiny. A bus completed the journey to the low-rise Four Seasons Hotel, nestled beside the ski slopes at the resort.

There were only three days of skiing before the restless Prince was off again.

This time, using the small jet to fly directly from Jackson Hole with only a team of eight, Alwaleed was heading east to Atlanta, Georgia, the home of Coca-Cola, Delta Airlines, and CNN, as well as Jimmy Carter's think tank, the Carter Center.

The Prince was paying the former U.S. president a social visit, as well as paying him $1 million dollars to help fund the valuable work done by his organization. The team traveled twelve hours across the country to spend just an hour with Carter, but it was invaluable time in building the friendship and bond between the two men.

Oh, and the Prince did manage to sneak in a quick look at the Four Seasons in Atlanta, where they found him a quiet room for a few minutes so he could pray.

The next four days were spent in Jackson Hole skiing, but not one to miss work for too long, Alwaleed invited the News Corporation chairman and CEO, Rupert Murdoch, over for dinner. More accurately, when Alwaleed mentioned to Murdoch he would like to meet up, the Australian media magnate volunteered to come over to Jackson Hole for the evening in his private jet.

Alwaleed spent a good couple of hours with the hotel staff selecting a menu for the dinner and making sure the seating arrangement was satisfactory. Once again, preparation and planning made it a cozy meeting. As Murdoch left just a few hours after arriving at the hotel, he was personally escorted to the front entrance by the Prince. While waiting for Murdoch's transportation to arrive, the two billionaires stood in the chill air, idly chatting about things that billionaires seem to chat about . . . such as the size of the fuel tanks on their private jets, and what range they can manage in one go.

During those four days, the boss of the Four Seasons Hotel management company, Isadore Sharp, also dropped in with his wife. It gave Alwaleed a chance to not only talk hotel business with the Canadian but also to spend a couple of days skiing with a man who had grown up on North American ski slopes. Sharp marveled at the progress the Prince had made in just a few seasons since starting the sport, but confessed that he himself had curbed his wild ways on the snow as he had gotten older.

NO BEATING AROUND THE BUSH

The next trip was another "Alwaleed special." He was heading west this time, and had a scheduled start at 6 A.M. Soon after seven, the Hawker Siddley had taken off for Burbank, California, home of Mickey Mouse, and his boss, Michael Eisner.

The Prince had been rallying behind the embattled Disney CEO, as he faced troubles with the company's board. Alwaleed wanted to reassure him of continued support, while also turning the screws on the need for more action on the struggling Euro Disney project near Paris, where his large investment had been stagnating for the past ten years.

It was a quick and efficient meeting at the Disney HQ, and by corporate coffee time, around 10:30 A.M., the small jet was on its way to San Jose, to meet Steve Jobs at Apple headquarters.

There was a little time left to spare after that one-hour session with Jobs, as Larry Ellison, of the software giant Oracle, had postponed his meeting with Alwaleed to a later date. So the Prince decided it was an ideal opportunity to drive through Atherton, past his old house and place of study, Menlo College.

For a moment, he looked a little nostalgic as he stood outside the dark wood ranch house on El Camino Real, the main road through the town. Then he shook his head and walked back to the parked limo, mumbling how that period in the late 1970s had been a lonely time for him in the United States.

Just down the road, he told the driver to pull up outside the entrance gate to Menlo College. Stretching his legs for a few moments, he glanced over to the main buildings, but again, was ready to move on quickly. His next meeting was waiting.

The Sun Microsystems campus was very much like many of the dot-com and tech sector sites in California, in that it felt more like a college than a corporation. The company's founder, Scott McNealy, even turned up for the meeting in training shoes and a track suit, looking like he had just been for some serious exercise.

McNealy took the Prince through the advances that the belea-
guered company had made since its stock took a massive hit during the dot-com crash, particularly in 2001. Alwaleed was looking
for a real bargain and decided after the meeting that he needed to
look more closely at this company. He ordered Jensen, who stood
close by during all the day's meetings, to do some further research
on Sun.

By 8 P.M., the Prince was pulling in again to the Four Seasons
Hotel in Jackson Hole. He had been to see some of the biggest
corporate players on the West Coast, in one day—while on his
vacation.

This time there was only two days of skiing before the Hawker
Siddley jet hit the skies once more, again starting early in the
morning. Houston was the destination, and the target was the father of the current American president, and himself, formerly the
forty-first president of the United States, George H.W. Bush.
Lunch had been arranged with the senior Bush, at the Bayou
Club, not far from his office.

The tall, genial Texan greeted the Prince with a big, warm
handshake, and then he had a thought.

"Where's Jim?" he asked his secretary. "Can you tell him to
join us for lunch at the Bayou Club, please?"

Bush invited Alwaleed into his relatively modest office, decorated with a few souvenirs from his time at the White House, but
more visibly with pictures of his wife, Barbara, and his sons.

The two talked in general terms for a few minutes, before the
secretary came to the door and indicated that the transportation
was ready.

Rising up with his arms spread in a hearty gesture, Bush ushered everyone out to the cars, and the fifteen-minute drive to the
lunch venue, set at a peaceful country club.

"Jim" arrived just a few minutes after Bush and the Prince. It
was, of course, close friend and confidant of the former president,
James Baker, himself a former U.S. secretary of state.

After a relaxed lunch, punctuated by some frank and candid

discussion on the sorry state of U.S.-Arab relations, George Bush stood up, thanked the Prince for taking the trouble to come and see him, and held out his hand. Jim Baker, with his usual urbane smile, extended his hand, too, in a warm farewell.

As he left, Alwaleed noted that it was not that long ago these hands he just shook held the future of the world very much in their grasp.

The person he was heading to see that evening also had a substantial grip on the world's future, through the power of his company, Microsoft Corporation. Bill Gates had invited Alwaleed to his house in Seattle for dinner.

As the flight from Houston Intercontinental Airport to Seattle Boeing Airport was just over four hours, the Prince decided to have his more comfortable 767 meet him in Houston so he could use it for that longer journey.

By 6 P.M., the fourth-richest man in the world was in a car, heading to the home of the richest man in the world.

After a very private dinner, the Prince was back at the airport in Seattle, where the 767 had been swapped out for the small Hawker Siddley. The flight to Jackson Hole was only eighty-five minutes, and the small jet could go directly there.

There was now one full day of skiing left, and the Prince was back on the slopes by morning, contemplating what had been a very successful round of meetings in the United States.

When asked what he got out of such encounters—why he would want to be seeing these people in the first place—the Prince explained that talking with the business leaders gave him financial intelligence. Even a general conversation with these people gave him a sense of whether or not they were optimistic or pessimistic about the future. As for the polticial leaders: "Inevitably politics, finance, economics, and business are entwined . . ."

But there is no doubt that having high-level contacts around the world holds Alwaleed in good stead for any political ambitions. The Prince adds that he feels he is in a good position to create a positive impression of the Middle East and his country in particular: "The relationship between Saudi Arabia and the United States is going through a very difficult period nowadays. I, as a private citizen of Saudi Arabia, and as a member of the Royal Family, have a duty and responsibility to try to have contacts with all of these political leaders and business leaders, and the business community, to try to bridge the gap that came because of the events of 9/11."

As the small Hawker sped back to Jackson Hole, Robert and Hani were visibly breathing easier. The tough part was over with absolutely no hitches. The travel division had proved itself once more to be a well-oiled machine. Faisal had been initiated by being flung in the deep end, seeing a nonstop pace that he would never otherwise witness from any other Saudi businessman. Awaleed had even arranged for a midsized charter jet to collect the staff and entourage at Jackson Hole Airport and take them to Denver International Airport, where his spacious Boeing was waiting. From what Faisal could see, this man shuffled aircraft as if they were a deck of cards.

All Robert and Hani cared about was that their boss was pleased.

As he set off the next day, for the final leg of his trip, in Paris, Alwaleed was in a buoyant mood. He had one short stop in the Cayman Islands to meet with some financial folk, but beyond that, he was on the home stretch.

He landed at Cayman in the early hours and had a meeting that was scheduled for around one in the morning. That went fine, but once the accountants and advisers had gone, there seemed to be an unusual delay. He was getting restless hanging around.

When it was obvious the Boeing was not going to take off on time, he called Captain Duncan Gillespie to find out the problem.

It seemed that the man who drove the fueling truck was off his shift and fast asleep at home.

Owen Roberts International Airport is actually an important

destination for many people, as the Cayman Islands serve numerous off-shore businesses and accounts, but that is certainly not reflected in the airport. Some might call it quaint, while others could easily believe that it runs on an elastic band and a prayer.

Alwaleed, being a person obsessed with scheduling, was simply there for business. He looked at Gillespie and used his much-loved phrase: "I want solutions, not problems."

Gillespie, a mild-mannered, slim man standing eye level with the Prince, knew this might get tricky. Alwaleed, on the other hand, was not too worried, because he knew his people would find an answer: "At the end of the day, we have reached a stage where things are almost perfect everywhere. Obviously it cannot be utopia, but I have reached a stage where I am at serenity with what's around me, with what people are doing, with the way things are organized. So I don't worry about it very much."

A few conversations with the skeleton staff manning the airport at that hour secured Gillespie the fuel truck driver's home number. He put in a call and got the sleepy and rather irate local, who told him that his shift had finished hours earlier, and that he was not due back for quite a few hours more. Gillespie tried to explain the urgency of the matter, but got a response of total disinterest.

A short while later, he returned to the Prince and told him that the fuel truck driver would be there within thirty minutes, and the jet would be ready to take off within the hour.

It is amazing how $200 can stir the sleepy.

Content that he had his solution, the Prince gathered some of his staff and said, "While we wait, let's go for a walk."

In these days of heightened security where airports are largely no-go areas, except for heavily screened passengers, it is certainly quite rare for a Saudi man with another dozen or so Arab men to be traipsing around the tarmac of an airport, weaving around past parked planes and disappearing into dark, unlit areas of the airfield. The two or three people working at the airport watched from their small, single-story terminal building, somewhat bemused at the Prince and entourage doing large, fast laps of their tiny facility.

Two hours late, but somewhat refreshed from his exercise, Alwaleed was once again up at thirty-seven thousand feet, looking out over a world where he knew he could make almost anything happen.

CHAPTER 16

The Business of Politics

The fact that I am a member of the Royal family, it goes by definition that politics is in my veins.

— PRINCE ALWALEED BIN TALAL

The controversial effort to donate $10 million to New York's Twin Towers Fund was probably the first sign that Prince Alwaleed was drawn into the international political arena, even though he played it down. He stated his position clearly on that visit to Ground Zero: "I speak, first of all, as a Saudi citizen, then as a businessman, and then as a member of the Saudi Royal family."

Alwaleed was also emphatic about stating that he had informed his uncle, Crown Prince Abdullah, and the Saudi government, about his intent to make the trip to the United States with his large check in hand. According to some commentators, the Saudi system is too closely knit for Alwaleed to play politics on the outside. These people believe that if he says something controversial, it is only with tacit approval of the ruling family.

Leading journalist Khaled Almaeena, of the *Arab News*, disagrees, saying that nowadays, it is possible to be outspoken in the Kingdom, but being a Saudi himself, he does understand the strict protocol Alwaleed faces: "You cannot survive here without showing respect for the system, and you have to abide by the system. It doesn't mean you have to follow it 100 percent, but as far as, in terms of being respectful to elders and taking into consideration what is happening to your family, and sensitivity, I think you can't go out of that perimeter, because these are values that are firmly engrained in our behavior and mind-set."

But, in actual fact, the Prince's position is somewhat different from that of many of his cousins. First, his father is the twenty-first son of the late King Abdulaziz, and therefore too far removed from the line of ascension to the Kingdom's throne to be an immediate contender. Having said that, Alwaleed's paternal grandfather was still the founding figure of the country. Second, his mother's family is arguably the most politically elite Lebanese family around. His maternal grandfather, Riad El Solh, was the first to lead the country as it achieved independence.

Politically, Alwaleed has the pedigree to play in both the arena of Saudi Arabia and Lebanon.

The question is does he *want* to play politics?

If the answer is yes, the next question is—in *which* country?

BEGUILING BEIRUT

"I have absolutely no political ambitions," the Prince declared in a magazine article in April 1999, but by March 2002, the media in the Middle East started to report stories placing Alwaleed as a potential contender for the prime minister's position in Lebanon.

They first surfaced when he visited Beirut as the Arab League summit was taking place that month, and he made comments criticizing the late prime minister, Rafic Hariri, for his economic policies. The well-established and powerful Hariri boasted strong credentials through his close connections with the Saudi ruling family, and an immense wealth accumulated from the construction industry in the kingdom. Hariri, recognized for overseeing much of the rebuilding of Beirut's Solidere city center area, also had widespread support from the Lebanese Sunni community and within international circles, particularly the United States.

The second time Alwaleed went on the attack was only a couple of months later, in July, at the opening of his landmark $140 million Movenpick Hotel on Beirut's trendy seafront. Alwaleed continued the sharp commentary, beginning his speech with the statement that he did not "pretend to be qualified to offer advice to the government of Lebanon."

However, in remarks that clearly suggested economic failure by Hariri and his supporters, Alwaleed went on to state that the Lebanese government needed to outline a five- or ten-year economic plan that would clarify its position on investments as well as its plans for the country's economy. The Prince also called for extensive privatization of the public sector to take place in phases, advising Lebanon's finance minister to heed that advice.

The speech at the Movenpick was described as "a true course of anti-Hariri policy" by the daily *l'Orient Le Jour*, and the leading daily newspaper, *An Nahar*, called it a "policy statement."

Other media commented on what they perceived to be a smug and contented expression on the president's face during the speech, and they noted that Emile Lahoud broke protocol by walking *behind* the Prince at the event. Back in March, President Lahoud had bestowed upon the Prince the Order of the Cedars medal, the highest award in Lebanon, which the president declared was in recognition of Alwaleed's contribution to the Lebanese community.

Hariri's tense relationship with Lahoud was already rather public in the country, and somewhat divisive in political circles, which largely had to align with one camp or the other.

Alwaleed was very much positioned as an ally of Lahoud, who had been looking to extend his position as president past the 2004 date set according to the constitution. The media reported that Syria, a major influence in Lebanese politics, with a physical presence of up to twenty thousand troops in the country, supported the move, even though it would involve bypassing the constitutional framework. Hariri, naturally, was extremely vocal in opposing the idea of extending the president's term, but he and those against the proposal, failed to stop it, and Lahoud was granted a three-year extension by the Lebanese Parliament. Within a few weeks, Rafic Hariri had stepped down from the post of prime minister.

Over the years, the Prince's public position on Lebanese politics created a high level of tension between him and Hariri, fueled further by the nature of Alwaleed's responses to media questions about his own interest in the prime minister post. Alwaleed was prone to using answers such as, "when the time comes," and "we'll cross that bridge when we come to it."

For his part, Hariri dismissed any political threat from Alwaleed, although media connected with the prime minister referred to Alwaleed as simply "the owner of Beirut's Movenpick Hotel." The Prince's office responded with a statement that referred to Hariri as "the owner of Saudi-Oger," the contracting company based out of Saudi Arabia, belonging to Prime Minister Hariri.

Media reports have been somewhat speculative in the country, but they included stories of posters of Prince Alwaleed suddenly appearing in mainly Sunni neighborhoods, declaring, "You are our hope!"

He had already received accolades in the press for his charitable donations, such as $12 million to repair two power plants destroyed by Israel when it conducted air raids on the country in 1999, and in 2004 Alwaleed donated another $10 million to various humanitarian causes in Lebanon.

Still, some of the press reported details from demonstrations staged by supporters of Rafic Hariri, denouncing the Prince and his political ambitions.

Until then, Hariri had managed to fend off any serious political competition, and articles started to question whether the Prince was a serious contender or simply trying to weaken Hariri's strong hold on the country, in order to assist Alwaleed's ally, Lahoud.

The chapter of the Alwaleed-Hariri tensions came to a close on St. Valentine's Day, February 14, 2005, when Rafic Hariri was killed in a devastating car bomb explosion in Beirut. Alwaleed was one of the first to pay a personal visit to Hariri's family to pay condolences. The Prince openly declared that no one deserved this kind of fate.

The assassination of Rafic Hariri triggered massive social and political change in Lebanon, particularly in its relationship with Syria. Under very public Lebanese domestic pressure, as witnessed by large-scale demonstrations in the country's streets, and clear international pressure both behind the scenes and in the global media, Syria began the withdrawal of its troops from Lebanon's soil soon after Hariri's death.

The debate over Alwaleed's role in Lebanese politics became low-key, as the country came to terms with a rapidly changing scene. Still, the Prince's childhood cousin Riad Assaad, who has been heavily involved in politics in the south of the country, has always endorsed the idea of a political role for his childhood friend: "I hope that he gets involved more with politics, because somebody like him will not be corrupted. He has the money and he has the power . . . this region is lacking that. Lacking fundamental development and basic economic growth culture. If he can do that he'll become one of the founders of a new movement in the Arab world. Waleed would be a fantastic politician. The politicians that we've been dealing with in the Arab world are basically corrupt and decadent, to say the least."

Despite his scathing views on the status quo, Riad stressed that money alone will not be enough to give the Prince a solid political base in Lebanon. He would definitely need to build grassroots support.

In 2002, the Lebanese press revealed that the Prince had dual citizenship—both Saudi and Lebanese, although some questioned the validity of him reportedly using Walid El Solh as a name on the Lebanese document, issued in 1994. Either way, a ten-year naturalization period bars any formal involvement in Lebanese politics, so Alwaleed would not have been free to do so until after 2004.

In May of 2002, the Prince invested in media in the country, buying a 10 percent stake in the leading *An Nahar* daily newspaper, run by his childhood friend Gebran Tueni: "He likes to play with fire . . . sometimes he gets bored with normal processes . . . he likes to provoke—in the right way, positively—and he thinks, when you want to create a change you should try to move mountains. We feel that he is very interested in Lebanon, and we are happy that he is interested . . . because he knows that the people of Lebanon want him to provoke; they want things to change."

Tueni says the Prince's stake in his publication was purely to help *An Nahar* through a difficult financial situation and was of no political significance, as shareholders cannot influence its editorial stance, pointing out that Hariri actually had a 35 percent stake and had not been able to sway the newspaper in any way. Plus, within a couple of years, Alwaleed had raised his stake in *An Nahar* to 17 percent, and had bought a 25 percent share of another publication, *Ad-Diyar*, considered the number two paper in Lebanon.

Riad sees Alwaleed's interest in Lebanon as less in the country itself, and more as a vehicle to make a point: "Waleed's size and proportions are far beyond this place. This place is a place to talk . . . this place is accessible, this place has easy connections, this place is open, this place has vibrant press, this place has an open society. So, if you want to launch a product, you can come to Lebanon. I think Waleed is launching—is using Lebanon to launch—a product. It's a new vision. Now, it hasn't focused yet, this new vision, because I think that the vision he is aiming at is not a vision that can be limited with a boundary. The agenda has to be a bit more multidimensional."

The Prince has extensive business interests in the country and is widely recognized for his charity work through the Alwaleed Bin Talal Humanitarian Foundation, and beyond.

It is clear that the Prince's relationship with his second homeland is a strong one, but it remains rather cloudy as to whether or not he has true political aspirations in Lebanon. At this point, he is reluctant to shine any light through those clouds.

TWO KINGDOMS, ONE PRINCE

Alwaleed's position in his main homeland, Saudi Arabia, is perhaps even less clear in some ways. As a prince tracing his lineage to his uncle, the King, he is technically on the ladder to be ruler, but there are many rungs above him. Plus, it is not exactly a single, vertical ladder, but one that branches off in many directions, due to there being princes with the same father but different mothers. The Royal family holds most of the elite government positions in the kingdom, and the issue of succession is generally only debated very discreetly.

Social reform, on the other hand, has become a much more open debate, with Alwaleed being one of its leading proponents: "Our society today is very amenable to change, and the important thing is that our ruling family right now, and the government, is also ready and amenable to change. The question right now is not whether to change or not. The question is that the change should happen at what speed? Some people are advocating more swift and rapid change, and some are asking for more conservative and slow change in the reforms. So that's the question. The question is not whether it's going to happen or not. It's going to happen inevitably."

His family history reflects his natural political disposition, with his father, Prince Talal, having been one of the most vocal pro-reform advocates as far back as the late 1950s and early 1960s. It was precisely that which got him exiled to Egypt for a couple of years.

There was, apparently, an unspoken agreement that Prince Talal would steer clear of any political commentary once he returned to the kingdom around 1963. For thirty-eight years he did keep quiet on that front, focusing instead on making a massive fortune in real estate and becoming a highly visible representative for the United Nations Children's Fund (UNICEF) in the region.

However, in 1998, it seems he broke his silence when he called again for government reforms. Some in the media speculated that his newly found voice was actually for the benefit of Alwaleed's political ambitions. Talal's comments were particularly inflammatory in April of that year, when he brought up the touchy subject of succession—predicting a future power struggle, unless a clear mechanism was put into place to govern the line to the throne.

As it is, Alwaleed's politics are not going unnoticed in the Western world. Former U.S. president Jimmy Carter, for example, is one who pays attention: "He (Alwaleed) believes in democracy, and I've read some of his statements that are quite surprising. He is, in effect, calling for elections or direct elections in Saudi Arabia, and as a top member of the Royal family, I am sure he received some criticism from his brothers and sisters and cousins because of that statement, but it demonstrates his personal commitment to expanding the beneficial aspects of democracy."

It will not hurt Alwaleed to be looked upon favorably as a political candidate by the United States. His reputation as essentially a straightforward businessman who works according to Western standards puts him in a different league, and if the political system in Saudi Arabia does invert for any reason, the top position is likely to be open to anyone with the tacit support of the United States, plus popular support at home, which Alwaleed's charitable work has certainly ensured. He responds a little defensively when pressed on the issue of Western hopes for change in the Kingdom: "Just because some of my thoughts are very similar to what the West is asking for, and specifically the United States, it does not mean that all I want is coinciding with what the United States or the West is wanting in general."

Animated and emphatic in his tone of voice, Alwaleed adds a caveat: "Saudi Arabia Westernized—never! Modernized—definitely!"

The Prince has already been vocal in the Western media, for example, stating in the *New York Times* at the end of 2000 that Saudi Arabia could ease public discontent by introducing elections to the country's 120-member advisory council.

"We have people on the right who are utterly conservative,

who are unbelievably conservative, who are going beyond what Islam is asking for. These people are very vocal, so right now, we need to create the other side of the equation with people who are as vocal as those radicals, to create a balance, so the people in the center, in the middle, can really get their equilibrium and be more open."

In that *New York Times* interview, the Prince also called for an end to the allowance system, which provides thousands of dollars per month to the thousands of members of the Royal family. It was a subject that raised the hackles of many of his relatives, some of whom believed his comments were simply political posturing for the benefit of the West.

Alwaleed had no qualms in defending his position: "Look, I'm an open man. I'm a believer in God. I will speak my mind. I believe in this society, I believe in this system, I believe in the Royal family which I am part of. I will speak my mind, and I will not pay any attention to those extremes to my right or my left."

In this candid approach, he has the support of his father, Prince Talal, who describes Saudi Arabia as "still at the beginning of the road" to reform and urges his son to learn from his own experiences: "I'm saying he should not be leaving the arena—the political arena—as such, but I'm saying, he shouldn't be too pushy or involved in that direction for now. I myself have witnessed very hard criticism, and I was fought because of my views and if I went through that, I wouldn't want my son to go through it, and one should learn lessons from people before him."

Talal accepts the heritage they both share, and he understands the outspoken nature his son has in common with him: "He is the grandchild of the late King Abdulaziz, and there is no harm in him giving his political views, but I would much rather see him focus his efforts on economic issues. There is no particular (political) role for him to be assuming for the time being, and I think he could just keep on doing what he's been doing, and the path ahead of him is open."

But even though Alwaleed has said for years that he had no interest in politics, and would only be focusing on his businesses, he now says he sees logic and synergy in developing a political role for himself: "The fact that I am a member of the Royal family, it goes by definition that politics is in my veins. Right now I think we have a duty to be more outspoken, we have a duty to speak our mind, and thank God, the number of people behind me is very noticeable, so I am going to speak up more . . . to create some momentum for the change."

The generational gap is perhaps a little more evident when soliciting the views of Alwaleed's daughter, Princess Reem, on her father's outspoken political comments: "I really believe inside that he is saying the right thing . . . not a lot of people expect him to say this, or expect anyone to say that . . . but it's just the right thing to do."

Reem also harbors a little concern that her father's controversial comments, calling for a change in Saudi Arabia, may actually pose a threat to him: "I think he'll always be a target, because of those things and because of other things, you know . . . people have jealousy."

The young princess says her father's relaxed attitude toward any potential threat comes largely from his religious disposition—that whatever God has in store for him cannot be stopped and will happen anyway.

Journalist Khaled Almaeena is pragmatic about the Prince getting involved more and more in political matters: "I think politics, economics, and society go together. I mean, you have to talk politics because it has been ingrained in our daily life, whether you live in Saudi Arabia or Britain or America, so I don't think that that is seen as something strange."

A BRAVE NEW WORLD

Saudi Arabia, like many countries in the Middle East, has recognized that tough social changes are essential for the true progress of its people.

In many of the oil-dependent countries, wealth came quickly to the small, local populations, and the social safety net created by their rulers meant easy money for them made on commissions, grants, and other forms of disbursement slanted very much in their favor. In most of these countries, a public sector bulging with far too many employees on high salaries, with no incentive to work, formed the basis of a lazy society. That started to change as progressive policymakers could see its disastrous long-term consequences.

As a result, various countries throughout the Middle East, particularly in the Gulf region, started programs to educate, train, and reform the mentality of their people, and then, place them into jobs.

Most Saudis, for example, would have shied away from any kind of job that involved serving people, like being a shop assistant or a restaurant waiter. Now, the youth of the country are having to accept their destiny. It is based far more on them building useful skills and educational foundations, rather than waiting for a handout. According to Almaeena, too much time has already been wasted getting to this point: "Look at the countries around us right now, look at the Gulf region, look at other countries in the Arab world; they are moving very much way ahead of us, politically, financially, economically, and socially, so right now we have to move. We are changing, by the way, and we are moving, but what I am criticizing right now and what I would like to happen is to have the change move at a faster speed, and that's what we need to do right now."

There are teething problems throughout the region, though, and many international employers are still reluctant to recruit local people on the grounds that they are not up to speed. As a result, the governments of these countries, including Saudi Arabia, have enforced rules requiring the hiring of a minimum proportion of locals. In the case of the Saudi kingdom, Saudization means the country's citizens must be given a certain percentage of the jobs in any company and must be granted employment opportunities.

The Prince, who has a large number of Lebanese efficiently running his Kingdom Holding Company, has pushed to recruit skilled Saudis, and he searches relentlessly to find the right caliber of people to meet his extremely tough job requirements.

Amjed Shacker, who overseas the company's public relations, interviewed a number of people in the bid to find an extra member of staff for his division. He explains that Alwaleed has more or less gently blended the Saudization policy into his company, rather than try to hammer it home as quickly as possible: "The Prince has a policy that he's not going to fire anyone, but anyone who quits a position, who is non-Saudi now, will be replaced by a Saudi national."

Amjed also points out that his boss asked him to seriously consider a woman for the job, if he could find someone suitable.

Promoting women in employment is something the Prince is actively pursuing. By the end of 2004, he had replaced five of the aircrew who left the Boeing 767 with female Saudi flight attendants—having hired the very first one earlier in the year. Alwaleed stresses that he first spoke to the woman's husband and family, to make sure that they were fine with the idea. Sure enough, before long, the largely British crew welcomed her onboard as part of their team.

The Prince then took a huge step at the end of November of that year, when he hired Captain Hanadi Zakariya Hindi to be one of his pilots. The media reported the irony that women in the Saudi Kingdom are not allowed to drive cars—a law Alwaleed disagrees with—and yet Hindi became the first accredited female pilot to fly in Saudi Arabia. The Prince, who had been contributing a grant toward Hindi's aviation studies in Amman, Jordan, said he saw it as a historic move that allowed women to transcend their traditionally limited roles in the Saudi work sector.

The Prince has always looked forward to his daughter coming onboard at the Kingdom Holding Company, as an employee first, and working up through the ranks to manage at least part of the company.

There is an inkling that part of the reason the Prince is keen to reform Saudi society, particularly in promoting rights for women, is so that his own daughter can play a more active part in the community, and not be shackled to old-fashioned sensitivities that prevent her from even driving around by herself.

Alwaleed's push for reform in his homeland has become an increasing priority for him. Apart from women's issues and rights, he continues to highlight issues of poverty in the Saudi Kingdom. He had developed a reputation widely through society for his direct grassroots charity, and projects targeting the very low-income groups through the construction of affordable housing. The impact of his work has been felt at the top levels of the ruling family, where the existence of poverty in Saudi Arabia is finally being officially recognized.

According to some of those in the media, like Khaled Almaeena, the Prince also has the added advantage of generally being recognized more for his business acumen than simply having a privileged Royal status. Almaeena says this allows Alwaleed to be a little more candid in his comments on political matters. Almaeena feels a greater acceptance nowadays to such direct comments on the state of the country: "I'm outspoken, people are outspoken here, and I think society is changing. The past four, five years, Saudi Arabia has gone up ahead. People talk, people focus on issues that were taboo before. So, I think we would like to view him as somebody who is part of the business community rather than be seen as a Prince with special favors . . . so I think he's viewed more as a businessman."

Some of Alwaleed's close staff would agree with that, including the head of his accounting division, Saleh Al Ghoul: "In the Saudi community he has a lot of respect. He is outspoken, especially in political matters; even in the economy he has views that people wish . . . could be implemented."

When reflecting on his position in the world of politics, the Prince now feels that, whether he likes it or not, he is at least tangentially involved in political issues. He says that in effect, he is a political player without an official portfolio. An example he gives of this work includes what he sees as social engineering, such as his hiring of women much more widely, helping to change their position in society. Even his charitable work with Saudi Arabia's poor is focused on social betterment, he says, and hopefully helps to lead official bodies toward greater involvement in such issues.

The Prince adds that he believes he was also instrumental in securing the move toward greater democracy and, despite his non-governmental position, helped to push the country to the first stage of elections. Remember, he had already been vocal in the international press with calls for Saudi Arabia's rulers to introduce elections to their 120-member advisory council.

So where does Alwaleed stand on the prospect of getting more directly involved in politics internationally?

"I have a very good relationship in the West, and very good relationship in the East, not only in my country, but in my region. So I'm going to use that to really bridge both sides as much as I can. This is happening in the midst of me continuing to be a businessman, being involved in economics and finance, et cetera. This is something additional that I'm going to do. So I'm not going to say I'm *not* going to get involved in politics, I'm *not* going to get involved in what's going on between West and East, when I know I can do something; I can't just go and say I am a businessman and that's about it—no!"

But despite some natural synergy between the worlds of business and politics, commentators believe that the Prince might need to adjust his mind-set to enter the latter more actively. He is used to making decisions unhindered and often on the spot. His various advisers have already described how liberating it is to have a large pool of private resources to work with, rather than having to go to banks to ask for money to make deals. The Prince is not used to having people looking over his shoulder, trying to second-guess him.

If anything, the world of politics is a world of uncomfortable compromises, and Alwaleed has found himself on that fine line as he negotiates various political dealings behind the scenes. It doesn't have the freedom of the path a straightforward dealmaker follows, but Prince Alwaleed is essentially already making his way along the wider road of the political highway.

CHAPTER 17

The Desert Prince

*No big investment decision, no professional decision in my life,
no personal decision has been made unless I come to the desert.*

— PRINCE ALWALEED BIN TALAL

The silhouetted figure walks along the edge of the water, cane waving rhythmically, marking out the line of his path.

As he approaches the kneeling camels, they start braying. He ignores them and weaves his way through, heading toward the seating area near the water, on the outskirts of the camp.

Before he has even reached the row of cushions, laid out like three sides of a square, each about thirty feet in length, all the men waiting for him are on their feet. They watch him in silence as he walks over to the middle of the seating area, facing the lake. He drops into a cross-legged posture and picks up the remote control to the small LCD television screen, located directly to his right, and immediately starts pushing the buttons, eyes fixed on the screen. The others around him all settle back down again, still making no sounds.

It's approaching 6:30 A.M., and the sun is just rising up over the distant sandbanks. There is an incredible chill in the December air, which even the large log fire in the middle of the square has a hard time fending off. Most of the men scattered along the cushions to the right and left have wrapped their headdresses almost entirely around their faces, leaving only wrinkled eyes in view. Thick jackets over their winter thobes help somewhat, but in reality, these Bedouins do not notice the cold in the same way as the city folk. They know the desert well and are used to its demands.

This is where Prince Alwaleed Bin Talal feels most comfortable: "At the end of the day, that's where my ancestors and that's where my grandfather and father were raised, so I believe instinctively or intuitively I am going back to my roots and I always feel at home when I go to the desert. To me this is very important when I make strategic decisions. Whether it's professional or business or personal, to me the desert is something very important, especially when I walk alone and meditate."

It is a stark contrast to see this man, one of the world's most wealthy and powerful—and certainly one of the most connected—sitting among simple desert folk on the ground, beside camels, horses, and falcons, surrounded by tents.

This is almost the perfect desert scene from a Hollywood movie, and one that few Arabs themselves get to experience nowadays.

Here Alwaleed does not have to explain himself, dress a certain way for meetings, deal with travel issues, or worry about his schedule.

This is desert time.

"We work hard during the week. We put in at least sixteen hours of work a day during the weekdays, so during the weekend, on Wednesday and Thursday, it's very important for me to come to unwind in the desert."

Remember, unwinding to Alwaleed means simply thinking of a thousand things at once . . . instead of a million.

This desert camp has been set up about a two hours' drive outside Riyadh, at a location spotted by Bedouins working for the Prince. They keep an eye on the land and are in tune with it to such a degree that they can spot areas that might become an oasis or provide a particularly scenic view for a while. The desert is constantly changing, and they can forecast those changes.

The spot chosen for this weekend in December is quite far out from the Saudi capital. Alwaleed often has a camp set up less than an hour away, but this location was special as the Bedouins had noticed more rain than usual and identified a spot where a large lake was forming. Around it, greenery was rapidly springing up in the form of shrubs and patches of rough grass. The Prince had his men bulldoze about twenty miles (thirty-two kilometers) of soft ocher-colored sand into a rough path from the main Riyadh road to the campsite. They had also trailed rope lights around the lake and around the shrubs—even the ones sprouting out of islets in the middle of the lake—creating a warm, yellow glow, and fairy-tale atmosphere. Back some way from the water's edge, the main bulk of the camp includes large camper vans and cabins, housing everything from telecommunications to kitchens and supplies. A number of squat, oversized SUV trucks perch ominously near the entrance, and a number of big tents indicate covered seating areas set up in case the Prince wants shelter from the chill of the winter air.

Alwaleed seems relatively impervious to cold.

The air-conditioning in his office is noticeably chilly, often prompting his staff to wear jackets for long meetings.

Even skiing, the Prince whizzes down the slopes with his head uncovered, while the rest of the team look like modern-day mummies. The icicles may form on his moustache and coiffured head, but he pays no heed. Meanwhile, the staff wonder if their eyes are at risk of being frozen shut if they blink.

Out at the desert camp, the Prince sits equally comfortable with no cover on his head. The Bedouins around him all look the same—each one a set of eyes peering through a heavy head wrap. Even the falcons are hooded; although that is actually to stop them flying off their perches, it probably helps to keep their tiny heads warm.

Many of the Bedouins around the camp carry old rifles slung over their backs or carry old pistols in holsters beside their ribs. Guns still symbolize power to some degree, harking back to the old feudal culture where firepower and strategic alliances determined survival or demise among the sand dunes. The contrast of these old weapons, with the modern mobile phones and satellite linkups at the camp, shows the true diversity of this international man.

In between his meditating, walking, and peaceful thinking, the Prince does multimillion-dollar deals on the other side of the world.

His deal with Euro Disney was finalized from his desert camp, and his biggest investment, Citicorp, was something he conceived, pondered, and then finally decided in the desert, too: "No big investment decision, no professional decision in my life, no personal decision has been made unless I come to the desert. I meditate alone. I think it over and I decide from here."

As the Prince repeatedly explains, not only does he have significant family history with the desert, but the weekend camps with thousands of Saudis visiting him is a tradition going back centuries to where rulers would meet with far-flung Bedouins to hear the community's thoughts, concerns, and hopes.

Alwaleed says that the desert environment creates a different frame of mind in a person: "My thought pattern is very much different here. Although there is still a lot of work here, it's not done with an office setting. It's still done, but in a very serene and relaxed manner."

It is also a place to which the Prince likes to invite his close Western business friends, such as Sandy Weill, the Citigroup boss, who has strong memories of his desert visit: "I recall a lot of things: I recall the falcons, I recall the massive spread of food on a blanket on the floor of the desert, I recall the Bedouins coming in singing songs and making up poems to him, and asking help to buy this or that car, or to make their wife happy or whatever. I remember a lot of that trip. My making a call back to our offices in the United States, where the Prince wanted to sell a big block of stock in our company, and negotiating the commission he would pay on it, and making sure it was done at the best possible price for him—which all ended up happening. The communications are unbelievable."

BRIDGE OVER TROUBLED WATERS

With the whole world at his fingertips even out here in the wilderness, it is unlikely that Alwaleed will ever change his routine.

It is hard to imagine him giving up his special time in the desert, where his frenetic pace clicks down a couple of notches, and he seems visibly recharged after spending time out, away from the city, in such simple surroundings. What he does want to change, however, is the strained relationship between the Middle East and the Western world, in particular the United States of America. Considering recent events, that is going to take every ounce of even his remarkable energy. He has developed some strong relationships in the West with those who can endorse his efforts, including influential players, such as former president Jimmy Carter: "How overwhelmed I was during our first conversation at his superb knowledge of his own country . . . but he knew as much about America as I did in many respects, and I could see that more than anyone I had ever met, he had a way of bridging the two societies, the two environments, and two peoples together, and with a very enlightened and progressive attitude. I think he has a very rare if not unique capability of looking at the best of both American and Westerns on the one hand, and the Arab and Saudi Arabia society on the other, and then trying to find ways constantly as a major goal in his life to bridge the gap between the two, so we were very impressed with him."

Bridge is a key word to the Prince as he steps into what seems to be a new phase in his life. A pretty full and notably profitable half-century is approaching, and with no sign of the pace slowing, it looks like the coming decades will be interesting ones to watch.

He has been described as something of a phenomenon by the media and the people who know him. It is evident that he has achieved so much in relatively little time and with an energy that is unmatched by his peers. Alwaleed himself admits the extent of his drive: "I don't believe I will ever retire. I strive on success. There is no retiring whatsoever."

Even though he is becoming more and more visible through his growing business success, Alwaleed is not an easy man to know. First impressions are complicated as much by *who* he is, *how* he behaves, and *where* he is, as they are by *what* he is doing, *why* he is doing it, and with *whom*. It is like going into a car showroom, examining the wheels of a particular model, and then walking out without seeing the rest of the car, but believing that the whole vehicle was viewed. And the Prince does not make it easy to see the whole vehicle in one go.

The successes are certainly far easier to see than the person.

Apart from hitting the *Forbes* magazine list as the fourth-richest man in the world in 2004, the Prince has methodically built a diverse business and investment portfolio in so many different disciplines, from media, finance, and entertainment to real estate, hospitality, and technology—to name just a few. In fact, his approach to the hotel sector, as someone who seamlessly combines real estate with management, has changed traditional thinking in that industry and prompted others to copy the model.

Efforts to discredit him have hit dead ends, and he has had endorsements at the highest possible level in the East and West that his success is entirely a product of his own hard work.

Alwaleed's business and political connections are almost unrivaled. He is constantly in the company of people who shape the world in one way or another, and through these connections, he is building himself the role of an East-West bridge, especially at a time when the differences and divisions seem so great.

One of the most remarkable aspects of this successful man, however, has to be his mind. It works at a level that certainly is phenomenal, tracking so many different thoughts—in incredible detail—all at once. In this respect, Alwaleed never fails to surprise. His working knowledge comes from a massive database he retains in his head and accesses with lightning speed. This cerebral library is constantly replenished and updated through the Prince's almost obsessive amount of reading of news and current affairs publications.

Still, despite these visible successes, the Prince is not one to sit back and retire. Even though he is in a position to support the most indulgent lifestyle without lifting a finger again, he feels he has far too much left to do in his life. Alwaleed wants to be recognized for making a difference at a global level. Part of that means letting people around the world get a better understanding of who he is, and what his goals are for the long term.

Some serious and quality time spent with him proves that he is far removed from the Western stereotype of Arabs and Muslims, and he has made it something of a mission to show the West that these stereotypes are not only wrong, but extremely dangerous in the long run for both communities. There is no doubt that he will have his detractors as far as his business skills, his political ambitions, and his billion-dollar lifestyle, but in reality, there are very few who are as intricately linked into all three as Alwaleed.

A British comedian once noted that "Money can't buy you friends . . . but it can get you a better class of enemy."

Alwaleed no doubt has his enemies, which will grow in number as he starts to make waves in the world of politics. In the footsteps of his father, Prince Talal, he already has made ripples in both Saudi Arabia and Lebanon.

When assessing a person as successful as Prince Alwaleed Bin Talal, it is all too easy to look for the mistakes and overlook the achievements. The media, in particular, always want to know what the mistakes were—what went wrong?

In the case of Alwaleed, very little. And he is essentially a relatively content person who seems to enjoy life to the fullest.

Maturity and success have served him well. His children are considered incredibly "normal," mature, and exceptionally likable. Even though their parents divorced, Khaled and Reem are remarkably stable and have an excellent relationship with both parents.

The Prince continues at an incredible pace, however, and his goals remain extremely high. He has proved himself able to achieve phenomenal success and expects to build on that without slowing down.

Is that expectation realistic?

Time will tell, but his determination certainly cannot be denied. It goes way back to when he was a boy, playing competitive, aggressive Monopoly with his cousin Riad Assaad, who regards their childhood days together with great affection. Riad watched Alwaleed grow up with a bright fire in his eyes: "He is a winner, and I always remember Waleed wanted to be the richest man in the world, and I think it will never leave him. He's gonna become the richest man in the world, so Bill Gates watch out!"

As his mother, Princess Mona, illustrates through old film footage of her young boy, he was a determined lad from the start. Her old film shows the Prince as a toddler, chasing a baby goat and falling over repeatedly in the process, but persevering until he finally got his hands on it. As an adult, most of the things he has persistently chased have also come into his grasp.

It takes time to get a complete picture of the Prince, and even then the picture doesn't tell the full story.

It cannot.

The story of Alwaleed, businessman, billionaire, prince—politician?—is far from over.

ACKNOWLEDGMENTS

All successful projects are based on teamwork. This book wouldn't have happened without the hard work of some very significant people.

James Wright, you are more than a manager. Your tireless effort and dedication to this project was key to its completion. Thanks for pushing me on. I can still hear the crack of your whip!

Jeff, my brother, it was great to have you with me during this adventure. Your photos bring this book to life and your creativity was instrumental to the look and feel of the final product.

Also, warm wishes to those who were a part of this at various stages. Sasja Scheeptsra and Jessica Piper, you saw it from the inside. Thanks for your help. Amjed Shacker, thanks for your patience with our constant requests for information.

Mike Jensen, my dear friend and nocturnal support as we stayed awake with the Prince into the wee hours—I can't thank you enough.

Also, deep gratitude to the colorful entourage of His Royal Highness for accepting me so warmly. So many stories to tell...so few pages.

APPENDIX

The full press release that created so much controversy when Prince Alwaleed visited Ground Zero in New York, post-9/11.

PRESS RELEASE

For more information, contact:
   Amjed Shacker
   Office: +966-1-488-1111 ext. 1151
   Facsimile: +966-1-481-1227
   Mobile: +966-5-544-2066
   E-mail: aes@kingdom.net

**For Immediate Release
Thursday, October 11, 2001**

Mayor Giuliani and Prince Alwaleed Visit Ground Zero

Prince Alwaleed Donates $10 Million to Twin Towers Fund

"The United States should adopt a more balanced stance towards the Palestinian cause," Prince Alwaleed

HRH Prince Alwaleed Bin Talal Bin AbdulAziz Alsaud, Chairman of Kingdom Holding Company, along with New York Mayor Mr. Rudolf Giuliani visited Ground Zero in New York at 9:00 am Thursday 11 October, one month after the tragic terrorist attack on the World Trade Centre. After the visit, the Prince handed Mayor Giuliani a $10 million check for the Twin Towers Fund.

"We have come here today to offer our condolences to the people of New York, to condemn terrorism, and to donate $10 million to the Twin Towers Fund," Prince Alwaleed said.

Number of Pages 3

PRESS
RELEASE

"However, at times like this one, we must address some of the issues that led to such a criminal attack. I believe the government of the United States of America should reexamine its policies in the Middle East and adopt a more balanced stance towards the Palestinian cause. While the UN passed clear resolutions numbered 242 and 338 calling for the Israeli withdrawal from the West Bank and Gaza Strip decades ago, our Palestinian brethren continue to be slaughtered at the hands of Israelis while the world turns the other cheek," Prince Alwaleed stressed.

The Prince strongly advocates peace and believes in dialogue. "Arabs believe that if the U.S. government wanted, it could play a pivotal role in pushing Israel to sign and fully implement a comprehensive peace treaty. We want bloodshed to stop and we want to start working for a better Middle East."

Prince Alwaleed is the world's most heavily invested individual in the United States, and particularly in New York city. His Highness has stakes in various New York ventures including Citigroup, AOL Time Warner, News Corp., The Plaza Hotel, The Pierre Hotel, and Saks Fifth Avenue.

Prince Alwaleed has a special affinity to New York, both the city and the state. As an investor, he holds stakes in numerous investment ventures in the Big Apple. Additionally, His Highness did his postgraduate studies at Syracuse University, where he also received an Honorary Doctor of Laws degree. "I feel like a New Yorker in Saudi Arabia," commented the Prince.

PRESS RELEASE

Prince Alwaleed is hoping the visit will send a clear message to the world. "I speak for all Muslims, Arabs and Saudis when I say that we represent the absolute antithesis of terror. My mission is to bridge east and west. I also want to reiterate Saudi Arabia's stance in condemning all forms of terrorism."

"Islam is a great religion that is premised on peace. The word Islam is derived from the Arabic verb meaning peace. Incidentally, after the atrocious September 11 attacks, people in the U.S. have been eager to find out more about Islam. This desire to get to the root of this wrongfully accused religion is evidenced by the enormous demand for books on Islam published in my country Saudi Arabia. The bulk of requests for these books comes from the United States of America," added the Prince.

Prince Alwaleed, according to the 2001 Guinness Book of World Records, is the wealthiest businessman outside north America. He has a $20 billion portfolio mainly invested in U.S. equity markets. Forbes ranked the Saudi self-made billionaire the world's sixth wealthiest businessman.

His Highness' north American holdings include stakes in companies like Citigroup ($9.6 billion), News Corp. ADR ($1.1 billion), AOL Time Warner ($0.9 billion), Four Seasons Hotels & Resorts ADR ($0.5 billion), Apple Computer ($0.3 billion), Compaq ($0.3 billion), Motorola ($0.26 billion), Fairmont Hotels ($0.26 billion), Teledesic ($0.2 billion), WorldCom ($120 million), The Plaza Hotel-NY ($120 million), Kodak ($80 million), Pepsi ($70 million), Procter & Gamble ($67 million), Ford Motor Company ($56 million), Walt Disney ($50 million), Planet Hollywood ($40 million), Saks Fifth Avenue ($26 million), eBay.com ($47 million), priceline.com ($20 million), and Amazon.com ($20 million).

Prince Alwaleed's letter to Citibank in Saudi Arabia requesting a loan of about
U.S. $30,000 in January 1978 (translated opposite).

حضرة المكرم / مدير ستي بنك بالرياض   سلمه الله
السلام عليكم ورحمة الله وبركاته :-

نظرا لانني احتاج الى تأثيث مكتبي ومصاريف بدايه لاعمالي التجاريه
آمل الموافقه على منحي قرضا بمبلغ وقدره (١٠٠٠٠٠) فقط مليون ريال لا غــير
وتسديد جميع ما يستحـق على حسابي لديكــم .

تحياتــــا . ....

                                                  loan application
                                                  for SR ...

صوره :- للمحاسبه
صوره :- للملف العام

بسم الله الرحمن الرحيم

Alwaleed Bin Talal Bin Abdulaziz Alsaud

To: Manager
        Citibank, Riyadh
        K.S.A.

Dear Sir,

Due to my desire to furnish my office as well as to meet other expenses to start my business, I, therefore, would like your approval for a loan of SR 1,000,000 (One Million Saudi Riyals Only) which will also enable me to pay-off all outstanding debt that I owe you.

Sincerely,

Cc: Accounting
        General File

Prince Alwaleed authorizes repayments of his Citibank loan. Just over a decade later,
he would own nearly 15 percent of the bank.

الرياض في ٦/٢/١٣٩٨ هـ

١٥/١/١٩٧٨م

المكرم مدير الغيرست ناشونال سبتي بنك   الموقر

الرياض

تحية ومــــــــبـد :ـ

افيضكم بموجب خطابي هذا بخصم القسط الشهري المترتب علـــي
من جراء اعطائي القرض بمبلغ (١٠٠٠,٠٠٠ر) مليون ريال فقط ، من حسابي
الجاري لديكم رقم ١ ـــ ٦٩٩٠ ، وذلك لمدة سنتين من تاريخ ١٣ صفر ١٣٩٨هـ.
وتقبلـــــوا تحياتـــــي ،،،،

الوليد بن طلال بن عبد العزيز آل سعود

بِسْمِ اللَّهِ الرَّحْمَنِ الرَّحِيمِ

Alwaleed Bin Talal Bin Abdulaziz Alsaud

Date: 6 / 2 /1398
        15 / 1/1978

To: **Manager**
       First National Citibank
       Riyadh, K.S.A.

Dear Sir,

I hereby authorize you to deduct the monthly payment on the SR 1,000,000 (One Million
Saudi Riyals Only) loan from my current account no. 6990-1 , for a total period of two
years starting on 13/2/1398 (22/01/1978).

Sincerely,

The Investment Portfolio of HRH Prince Alwaleed Bin Talal

at the time of the Forbes listing in March 2005 placing him as
the fifth-richest person in the world.

Sector	%	Total in Millions
Banking		
Citigroup	3.90%	
Samba Financial Group (SAMBA)	5.00%	
Al-Azizia Commercial Investment	20.00%	
International Financial Advisors (IFA)	5.00%	
Kuwait Invest Holding	5.00%	
Other financial investments	**	
SUBTOTAL		$11,380
Technology		
Apple Computer	*	
Hewlett Packard	1.00%	
Kodak	1.00%	
Motorola	*	
SUBTOTAL		$900
Internet		
Amazon.com	*	
eBay.com	*	
priceline.com	*	
SUBTOTAL		$305
Media & Entertainment		
News Corp. ADR	6.00%	
Time Warner	*	
Disneyland-Paris	17.30%	
Walt Disney	*	
Planet Hollywood + Franchise	20.00%	
Rotana	100.00%	
LBC Satellite	49.00%	
Various Arabic newspapers	**	
Other Media Investments	**	
SUBTOTAL		$3,100
Hotels, Real Estate & Construction		
Four Seasons Hotels & Resorts ADR + Related Real Estate*	22.00%	
Movenpick Hotels & Resorts + Related Real Estate*	33.00%	
Fairmont Hotels and Resorts + Related Real Estate*	4.90%	

George V Hotel	100.00%	
The Plaza New York	10.00%	
Fairmont Savoy	**	
Fairmont Monte Carlo Grand Hotel	**	
Kingdom Hotel Investments (KHI)	46.90%	
Canary Wharf	2.25%	
Saudi Real Estate	100.00%	
Kingdom Holding's Head Quarters	100.00%	
Kingdom Centre	32.50%	
Kingdom City	38.90%	
Ballast Nedam (construction)	3.00%	
SUBTOTAL		$4,580
Retail & Consumer Products		
Saks Incorporated	2.29%	
Procter & Gamble	*	
Pepsi	*	
SUBTOTAL		$285
Automobiles & Manufacturing		
Ford Motor Company	*	
National Industrialization Company	15.00%	
SUBTOTAL		$300
Agriculture & Food Industry		
Kingdom Agriculture & Develp. Comp (KADCO), EGYPT	100.00%	
Savola Group	10.00%	
SUBTOTAL		$470
Health & Education		
Kingdom Hospital	65.00%	
Kingdom Schools	47.00%	
SUBTOTAL		$160
African Investments		
Cal Merchant Bank, Ecobank, Joina Centre, Sonatel, and United Bank for Africa	**	
Kingdom Zephyr Africa Management Company (KZAM)	50.00%	
SUBTOTAL		$80
Private Assets, Cash & Others		
Palaces, Yacht, Planes, Cash, and Small Investments	100.00%	
SUBTOTAL		$2,100
Grand Total		**$23,660**

* Investment share is less than 1%

** Varying Shareholdings

INDEX